MW00903533

The Complete Instant Pot Cookbook 2020

1000 Effortless Tasty Healthy Instant Pot recipes Help to Save You Time and Money, Live Happier and Longer

By Jenny Lucy

Contents

Preface

Hello friend! Thank you and congratulations on reading this amazing Instant Pot Cookbook *"The Complete Instant Pot Cookbook 2020- 1000 Effortless Tasty Healthy Instant Pot recipes Help to Save You Time and Money, Live Happier and Longer"*

How many times have you ever failed cooking your dinner? Do you want to cook your food in few minutes? **Do you want to be healthier, with fewer illnesses and still be able to have delicious foods?**

How often you don't have the time to prepare a meal? Do you just want to put all the ingredients into an instant pot, wait for the cooking process to end, and have delectable dinner in a few minutes? Keep reading, you will find all the answers in this book!

This book is the ultimate guide of Instant Pot cooking, which will not only let you know all essentials about Instant Pot cooking, but also will show you around 1000 easy Instant Pot recipes. With **1000 recipes**, you certainly have a new meal everyday. The recipes are divided into different parts, which will let you find your dream recipes easily! Such as: **Breakfast recipes, Chicken and Poultry recipes, Beef, Pork and Lamb recipes, Soups and Stews, Fish and Seafood, Appetizers and Side Dishes, Dessert and Snacks, Vegetarian and Vegan Recipes,20- Minute Recipes, 5-Ingredient or Less Recipes, Wicked Recipes, Holiday and Weekend Recipes, Ketogenic Mediterranean Diet recipes, etc.**

This book will open the splendid world of flavorsome foods to you. All the recipes are unique, delicious, easy to make, and with ingredients that are inexpensive. Consider this book not just your average cookbook but as your ally. This book is created for daily use; it contains a multitude of healthy and wonderful recipes you can enjoy each day.

Start living a healthier, happier, and fulfilling life with this cookbook. If you're ready to launch this life-changing experience, head on to the next page!

\

Part 1: The Beginners' Guide of Instant Pot Cooking

The Instant Pot is a revolutionary kitchen appliance that is changing the way we prepare foods. Much better than traditional pressure cooking, this machine can prepare your meals much faster with an extra dose of flavor.

In this chapter, it will serve as an all-inclusive guide to the Instant Pot, we will answer questions which includes:

- What is the Instant Pot?
- How does the Instant Pot work?
- Why you should use the Instant Pot?
- What do the settings and buttons do?
- What kind of tips and tricks can I use for the Instant Pot?
- How to choose a good Instant Pot?
- Dos and Don'ts of using Instant Pot

Let's get down to business!

What is the Instant Pot and How Does It Work?

Anyone who has used an Instant Pot before knows what a true life changer the appliance is. This revolutionary multi-cooker is a true delight to have in all kitchens as it serves various functions. It posses all the qualities of a pressure cooker, slow cooker, steamer, rice cooker, sauté/browning pan, yogurt maker and warmer. Some Instant Pot models can also become a cake maker, egg maker, and sterilizer.

The Instant Pot can make your life in the kitchen a whole lot easier as it can clear up the counter space and money. The appliance also includes preset buttons and a timer that can help you whip up any meal you have in mind. A list of foods you can cook using your Instant Pot includes all sorts of meat, fish, stews, soups, porridge and a whole lot more.

To make it all better your Instant Pot can help enhance the flavor of your meals and prepare them a whole lot faster. As a matter of fact, the Instant Pot can prepare healthy and delicious meals 70% faster than most traditional cooking methods.

The science behind this is that hot steam is trap in an airtight chamber that cooks food quicker and safer than most kitchen appliances. Super-hot steam circulates around your food ensuring even cooking and nutrient-dense foods. Your Instant Pot is also built with safety features that make it impossible to remove the lid until all the pressure has been released. It is also built with automatic temperature control, which maintains a safe temperature range inside your pot.

Top Benefits of Using the Instant Pot

Purchasing your first Instant Pot comes with a wide variety of benefits. After just a week of using your Instant Pot, you will notice some huge changes happening in your life. Some of the top benefits that come with your Instant Pot includes:

1. The Instant Pot is highly multifunctional. Not only is your Instant pot a pressure cooker but it can sear your meats, brown vegetables, steam fish, and make beautifully delicious cakes. It can also be used to make some yogurt as well.
2. The Instant Pot cooks meals fast. Way fast. Normally it can take hours to cook ribs, briskets and a whole chicken. But using your handy dandy Instant Pot, it can take a mere 30 minutes or less! So, no need to waste any more of your precious time cooking dinner – instead you have more time for yourself!
3. It's safe to use. As we talked about earlier, the Instant Pot comes with safety features which ensure easy cooking. You don't need to ever worry about your Instant Pot blowing up, catching on fire or hurting anyone due to the sensors, automatic lid lock, and temperature control.
4. It's convenient to use. Sometimes all you need is to dump your ingredients into the pot, close the lid and press a few buttons and voila! It also includes a number of pre-programmable buttons which can make things less complicated.
5. Easy and simple. What's not to love about that? The only thing you need to clean is the inner pot after you are done eating! Not to mention that the other parts are safe to use inside a dishwasher.
6. It can help you save time and help the environment. Using your Instant Pot compared to your stove will result in faster cooking time and less power usage.
7. The Instant Pot can make your foods much healthier. When you boil your foods or use your microwave, it dilutes the flavor and lowers its nutritional value. Opting for your Instant Pot will help your vegetables and foods retain most of its precious needed vitamins and nutrients.

All About Your Instant Pot Settings and Buttons

Here I provided a fully comprehensive guide to all those settings and buttons on your Instant Pot. If you ever have a hard time understanding your Instant Pot, take a look at this section and you will be all set.

- SOUP: This button cooks for 30 minutes at high pressure
- MEAT/STEW: This button cooks for 20 minutes at high pressure
- BEAN/CHILI: This button cooks for 30 minutes at high pressure
- POULTRY: This button cooks for 12 minutes at high pressure.
- RICE: This button cooks for 12 minutes at low pressure.
- PORRIDGE/MULTIGRAIN: This button cooks for 20 minutes at high pressure.
- SLOW COOK: This button can turn your Instant Pot into a slow cooker and the time range can be adjusted up to 24 hours.
- SAUTÉ: This button can turn your Instant Pot into a browning pan. Use this button to sear meats and brown onions.
- STEAM: This button is a normal high-pressure mode. The time can be adjusted.
- PRESSURE: This button adjusts your Instant Pot to low and high pressure.
- MANUAL: This is your go-to button for most of your meals.
- ADJUST: This button is used to adjust the cooking temperature.
- TIMER: This button can be used to delay cooking and adjust the time.
- KEEP WARM/CANCEL: This button turns off your Instant Pot. If you have food inside, it will warm your food.

Incredible Tips and Tricks for Your Instant Pot

Psst! Want to know some secrets of your Instant Pot? Here I've compiled some of my favorite tips and tricks that can make things a lot easier and faster.

1. You don't need to defrost your vegetables and meats! Yes, you heard that right. You can skip the thawing step and throw foods directly from your freezer into the Instant Pot to begin cooking. However, with this in mind, you will need to add some extra time when cooking with frozen ingredients.
2. Use the natural release method whenever you are cooking with liquid. When cooking soups, stews or anything with lots of liquids always uses a natural release method. This is because the pressure will be gradually released rather than all at once.
3. Always make sure there is ½ to 1 cup of liquid. Pressure cooking utilizes steam and you need some sort of liquid to create that steam. Some sorts of liquid you can use include water, chicken broth, vegetable broth, juice from vegetables, etc.
4. Don't force the lid open. Your Instant Pot comes with many safety features, but if you use sheer strength to remove the lid – that's a sure recipe for disaster. Before you remove the lid, you need to make sure the pressure is fully released; or else, the hot steam will hit your hand, arm, or even face.
5. Use the sauté function to brown meats. To enhance the flavor of your meals, I recommend sautéing several of your ingredients before pressure cooking. For example, use the sauté function to brown your chicken, beef, and pork before pressure cooking.
6. Use the sauté function for other uses as well. Did you know you can use the sauté mode to help reduce the liquid volume inside your pot? Or that you can help build up pressure quicker so you can have your dinner minutes before?
7. Use dairy carefully in your Instant Pot. It's universal to know that milk can curdle very fast and cheese can get watery. If you want your soups to become cheesy or creamy, then stir in the ingredients after the cooking is done, not before.

How to Choose a Good Instant Pot

There are various versions of the Instant Pot available in the market. Nevertheless, which is the best one for you? From the most popular 6-quart version to larger and more advanced varieties. Here are af few to consider when choosing an Instant Pot:

IP-DUO60.
This is the most popular model of the Instant Pot. This 7-in-1 multifunctional countertop appliance combines a pressure cooker, slow cooker, rice cooker, yogurt maker, steamer, warmer, and sauté/browning functionality.

IP-DUO Plus60.
The Plus 60 is an upgrade to the regular IP-DUO60. It includes more settings, such as the *Cake, Egg,* and *Sterilize* buttons. The alarm clock on this Instant Pot is a blue LCD screen. The Instant Pot's inner bowl also has more comprehensive max/min fill lines.

IP-DUO50.
This Instant Pot holds 5-quarts.

IP-DUO80.
This Instant Pot has a capacity of 8-quarts. It is pricier than the others are, but the extra space might be useful.

IP-LUX60 V3.
This Instant Pot has cake and egg cook settings in the control panel. However, this Instant Pot does not have the Beans/Chili, Poultry, or Yogurt setting, nor an option to cook on low pressure. It also arrives without some of the accessories seen on other models.

IP-Smart Bluetooth.
This Instant Pot is a 6-quart with all the basic functions, and can connect via Bluetooth to your phone; so you can program and monitor cooking from anywhere using the Instant Pot Smart Cooker app.

Choosing a good Instant Pot should not be complicated. It is also best to purchase a new appliance rather than a used one, as they may have broken buttons and complications.

Dos and Don'ts of Instant Pot

If you just started using an Instant Pot, it will be helpful to find out what you should and not do when using the Instant Pot. Here are some valuable tips for cooking with an Instant Pot:

Don't add ingredients to the Instant Pot without the Inner Pot.
It would be a pain if you were to pour ingredients into your Instant Pot without the Inner Pot. Believe me; this happens a lot. That causes damage and is time-consuming to clean.

Don't press the timer button to set the cooking time.
People often mistake the 'timer' button for setting the cook time, and then wonder why the Instant Pot isn't working. Be sure the 'timer' button is not lit before you leave.

Don't overfill your instant pot.
New users frequently fill their Instant Pot with too much food and liquid, which risks clogging the venting knob. To make certain you never overfill, establish that you never pass the max line indicated on the inner pot.

Don't use quick-release for foamy foods or when your Instant Pot is overfilled.
Many new users are confused when it comes to Quick Pressure Release and Natural Pressure Release. If you use Quick-Release when cooking foamy foods, such as grains, beans, or applesauce, it could splatter everywhere. To prevent this from happening, use natural release or release the pressure gradually.

Pay attention to cooking times.
While cooking times for a recipe is a great indicator of the amount of time it takes for your food to cook, the actual cooking time can vary. It is due to the different ingredients and the situations. For example, various meats will take dissimilar times to soften up. To make sure the foods are cooked thouroughly, do not rush through the recipe and mind the end result. Test a small piece from the recipe to asssure that it is done before removing it completely from your Instant Pot.

Read all the instructions carefully.
When you purchase your Instant Pot, read all the instructions carefully to prevent any damages, mishaps, and to be sure that nobody gets hurt.

Inspect your Instant Pot warily.
It is important you keep your instant pot extremely clean so it remains a reliable appliance and in working condition. If parts on your pressure cooker begin to wear out, replace them with original parts, or you risk permanently damaging the appliance.

Clean your Instant Pot.
As previously mentioned, always clean and take care of your Instant Pot to ensure it is in optimal condition. After cooking with your Instant Pot, remove the inner pot and wash it with warm soapy water. Then, use a clean dishrag to wipe the outer parts of the pressure cooker.

Instant Pot Cooking Timetable for the Ketogenic Diet

I've compiled the definitive cooking times for ketogenic-friendly foods for your Instant Pot below. Use the timetable as a reference to make cooking a whole lot easier. Many factors can affect the time it takes to cook your food such as the temperature, type of meat, thickness of the ingredient, the ingredient brand, quantity, instructions, and liquid volume may take more or less time to finish the recipe.

Below you will find the general cooking times for the following categories of food:

- Vegetables
- Meat (Including poultry, beef, pork, and lamb)
- Fruit
- Seafood and Fish

Meat – Cooking Time Guidelines

- 1 pound of beef stew meat, 20 minutes
- 1 pound of beef meatballs, 5 minutes
- 1 pound of dressed beef, 20 to 25 minutes
- 1 pound of beef pot roast, steak or brisket, 20 minutes
- Beef ribs, 20 to 25 minutes
- Beef shanks, 25 to 30 minutes
- Oxtails, 40 to 50 minutes
- Chicken breasts, 6 to 8 minutes
- 1 pound of whole chicken, 8 minutes
- Chicken bones for stock, 12 to 15 minutes
- 1 pound of whole duck, 10 minutes
- Ham sliced, 9 to 12 minutes

- Lamb cubes, 10 to 15 minutes
- Lamb leg, 15 minutes
- Pheasant, 8 minutes
- Pork loin roast, 20 minutes
- Pork butt roast, 15 minutes
- Pork ribs, 15 to 20 minutes
- Turkey breast, 7 to 9 minutes
- Whole turkey breast, 20 to 25 minutes
- Turkey drumsticks, 15 to 20 minutes
- Veal chops, 5 to 8 minutes
- Veal roast, 12 minutes
- Whole quail, 8 minutes

Seafood and Fish – Cooking Time Guidelines

- Whole crab, 2 to 3 minutes
- Whole fish, 4 to 5 minutes
- Fish fillet, 2 to 3 minutes
- Fish steak, 3 to 4 minutes

- Lobster, 2 to 3 minutes
- Mussels, 1 to 2 minutes
- Seafood soup or stock, 7 to 8 minutes
- Shrimp and prawns, 1 to 3 minutes

Vegetables – Cooking Time Guidelines (for fresh ingredients ONLY)

- Whole artichokes, 9 to 11 minutes
- Artichoke hearts, 4 to 5 minutes
- Small beetroots, 11 to 13 minutes
- Large beetroots, 20 to 25 minutes
- Broccoli florets, 1 to 2 minutes
- Broccoli stalks, 3 to 4 minutes
- Whole brussel sprouts, 2 to 3 minutes
- Red, purple, or green cabbage, 2 to 3 minutes
- Wedged cabbage, 3 to 4 minutes
- Sliced or shredded carrots, 2 to 3 minutes
- Whole carrots, 6 to 8 minutes
- Cauliflower florets, 2 to 3 minutes
- Celery chunks, 2 to 3 minutes
- Collard greens, 4 to 5 minutes
- Corn kernels, 1 to 2 minutes
- Corn on the cob, 3 to 4 minutes
- Eggplant slices, 2 to 3 minutes

- Endive, 2 to 3 minutes
- Escarole, 3 to 4 minutes
- Escarole, 3 to 4 minutes
- Green beans, 2 to 3 minutes
- Leeks, 2 to 3 minutes
- Mixed vegetables, 3 to 5 minutes
- Okra, 2 to 3 minutes
- Sliced onions, 2 to 3 minutes
- Parsnips, 3 to 4 minutes
- Peas, 2 to 3 minutes
- Cubed potatoes, 2 to 3 minutes
- Pumpkin pieces, 2 to 3 minutes
- Spinach, 2 to 3 minutes
- Sliced acorn squash, 3 to 4 minutes
- Butternut squash, 2 to 3 minutes
- Cubed sweet potatoes, 2 to 3 minutes
- Sliced or chunked sweet peppers, 2 to 3 minutes

Fruits – Cooking Time Guideline (for fresh ingredients ONLY)

- Apple slices, 1 to 2 minutes
- Whole apples, 3 to 4 minutes
- Peaches, 2 to 3 minutes

- Whole pears, 3 to 4 minutes
- Plums, 2 to 3 minutes

Now that we got through all this valuable information, we can finally indulge in the 500 best ketogenic instant pot recipes. I truly hope you enjoy all these delicious recipes.

Part 2: Breakfast Recipes

Breakfast Chili
Time: 20 minutes   Servings: 4

Ingredients:

- 12 breakfast sausage patties, thawed and chopped
- 1 (15-ounce) can of diced tomatoes
- 2 medium garlic cloves, peeled and minced
- 1 large onion, finely chopped
- ¼ cup of water

- 2 tablespoons of olive oil
- 1 tablespoon of ground cumin
- 1 teaspoon of chili powder
- 1 teaspoon of fine sea salt
- 1 teaspoon of freshly cracked black pepper

Optional Topping Ingredients:

- Shredded cheddar cheese
- Scallions, chopped
- Fresh cilantro, chopped

- Sour cream
- Avocado wedges

Instructions:

- Press the "Sauté" function on your Instant Pot and add the olive oil, onion, and garlic. Cook until translucent, stirring occasionally.
- Add the breakfast sausage and cook until brown and almost cooked through, stirring occasionally.
- Add the remaining chili ingredients to your Instant Pot and stir until well combined.
- Lock the lid and cook at high pressure for 10 minutes.
- When the timer beeps, naturally release the pressure and remove the lid. Adjust the seasoning if necessary. Serve and enjoy!

Pork Sausage and Kale Egg Muffins
Time: 15 minutes   Servings: 4

Ingredients:

- 6 large organic eggs, beaten
- ¼ cup of heavy whipping cream
- ¼ cup of shredded cheddar cheese
- 1/2 pound of ground pork sausage
- 1 teaspoon of avocado oil

- ½ cup of kale, stemmed and roughly chopped
- ½ teaspoon of fine sea salt
- ½ teaspoon of freshly cracked black pepper
- 1 cup of water

Instructions:

- Press the "Sauté" function on your Instant Pot and add the ground pork sausage. Cook until brown.
- Add the kale and sauté until wilted, stirring occasionally. Turn off "Sauté" function and remove the contents.
- Grease 4 silicone muffin cups or ramekins with nonstick cooking spray.
- In a large bowl, add the cooked sausage, kale, and the remaining ingredients except for the water. Stir until well combined.
- Divide and pour the egg mixture into the muffin cups and ramekins.
- Add 1 cup of water and a trivet to your Instant Pot. Place the muffin cups on top of the trivet.
- Lock the lid and cook at high pressure for 5 minutes.
- When the cooking is done, naturally release the pressure for 10 minutes, then quick release the remaining pressure. Carefully remove the lid. Serve and enjoy!

Spicy Egg Muffin with Chorizo and Bell Peppers
Time: 20 minutes   Servings: 6

Ingredients:

- 8 large organic eggs
- ½ pound of chorizo
- 1 small onion, finely chopped
- 2 medium garlic cloves, minced
- 2 tablespoons of olive oil

- 1 medium red bell pepper, chopped
- 1 red chili pepper, finely chopped
- 1 teaspoon of fine sea salt
- 1 teaspoon of freshly cracked black pepper

Instructions:

- Press the "Sauté" function on your Instant Pot and add the olive oil.
- Once hot, add the onions and garlic cloves. Cook until lightly browned, stirring occasionally.
- Add the chorizo and cook until brown, stirring frequently.
- Add the chopped bell pepper and red chili pepper. Sauté for another minute. Turn off the "Sauté" function.
- Transfer the contents to a large bowl along with the remaining ingredients. Stir until well combined.
- Divide and pour the egg mixture into silicone egg molds or greased ramekins.
- Add 1 cup of water and a trivet inside your Instant Pot. Place the egg muffins on top and lock the lid.
- Cook at high pressure for 8 minutes. Once done, quick release or naturally release the pressure and carefully remove the lid. Check if the eggs are cooked through. Serve and enjoy!

Jalapeno Popper Egg Cups
Time: 10 minutes   Servings: 4

Ingredients:

- ½ cup of shredded cheddar cheese
- 4-ounces of cream cheese, softened and cubed
- 4 medium jalapenos, seeds removed and finely chopped
- 12 medium bacon strips, chopped

- 8 organic large eggs
- 1 teaspoon of garlic powder
- 1 teaspoon of onion powder
- 1 teaspoon of fine sea salt
- 1 teaspoon of freshly cracked black pepper

Instructions:

- Grease 4 ramekins with nonstick cooking spray.
- Press the "Sauté" function on your Instant Pot and add the chopped bacon. Cook until brown and crispy. Turn off "Sauté" function and transfer the bacon to a plate lined with paper towels.
- In a large bowl, add all the ingredients including the bacon. Stir until well combined.
- Divide and add the egg mixture into the four ramekins.
- Add 1 cup of water and a trivet to your Instant Pot. Place the ramekins on top of the trivet.
- Lock the lid and cook at high pressure for 5 minutes. When the cooking is done, naturally release the pressure for 10 minutes, then quick release the remaining pressure. Carefully remove the lid.
- Serve and enjoy!

Breakfast Tarts with Ham, Kale and Cauliflower Rice
Time: 20 minutes   Servings: 6

Ingredients:

- 1 ½ cups of cauliflower rice
- 6 large eggs, beaten
- 1 ½ cups of kale, stemmed and roughly chopped

- 1 ½ cups of cooked ham, cut into cubes
- 1 teaspoon of fine sea salt
- 1 teaspoon of freshly cracked black pepper

Instructions:

- Grease 6 ramekins or oven-safe containers with nonstick cooking spray.
- In a large bowl, add all the ingredients and stir until well combined.
- Divide and add the egg mixture between the 6 ramekins and lightly cover with aluminum foil.
- Add 2 cups of water and a trivet inside your Instant Pot. Place the ramekins on top of the trivet and lock the lid.
- Cook at high pressure for 8 minutes. When the timer beeps, quick release the pressure and remove the lid. Serve and enjoy!

Southwestern Crustless Breakfast Tarts
Time: 20 minutes   Servings: 4

Ingredients:

- 6 large organic eggs
- ¼ cup of heavy whipping cream
- 1 large red bell pepper, seeds removed and finely chopped
- 1 (4-ounce) can of diced green chiles
- ½ cup of shredded cheddar cheese

- 2 medium garlic cloves, peeled and minced
- 2 green onions, thinly sliced
- 1 teaspoon of ground cumin
- 1 teaspoon of fine sea salt
- 1 teaspoon of freshly cracked black pepper
- 1 tablespoon of olive oil

Instructions:

- Grease 4 ramekins with nonstick cooking spray.
- Press the "Sauté" function on your Instant Pot and add the olive oil. Once hot, add the chopped red pepper, onions and garlic. Sauté for 2 to 4 minutes or until softened. Turn off "Sauté" function.
- Transfer the contents to a large bowl. Add the remaining ingredients and stir until well combined.
- Divide and add the mixture amongst the four ramekins.
- Add 1 cup of water and a trivet inside your Instant Pot. Place the ramekins on top of the trivet and lock the lid.
- Cook at high pressure for 8 minutes. When the timer beeps, quick release the pressure and carefully remove the lid. Serve and enjoy!

Asparagus and Shiitake Mushroom Egg Casserole
Time: 35 minutes   Servings: 6

Ingredients:

- 6 large organic eggs
- 1 tablespoon of extra-virgin olive oil
- 2 medium garlic cloves, minced
- ½ cup of shiitake mushrooms, finely sliced
- ½ cup of asparagus, quartered and chopped

- 1 teaspoon of fine sea salt
- 1 teaspoon of freshly cracked black pepper
- 2 tablespoons of unsweetened almond milk
- 3 tablespoons of cheddar cheese, finely grated

Instructions:

- Press the "Sauté" function on your Instant Pot and add the extra-virgin olive oil.
- Once hot, add the garlic, mushrooms, and asparagus. Sauté for 2 minutes, stirring occasionally. Turn off "Sauté" function and transfer the contents to a large bowl.
- Add the remaining ingredients and stir until well combined.
- Grease an oven-proof dish suitable for your Instant Pot with nonstick cooking spray.
- Add 1 cup of water and a trivet to your Instant Pot. Place the dish on top of the trivet and cover with aluminum foil.
- Lock the lid and cook at high pressure for 20 minutes.
- When the cooking is done, quick release the pressure and carefully remove the lid.
- Serve and enjoy!

Turkey Sausage and Pepper Casserole
Time: 35 minutes   Servings: 6

Ingredients:

- 12 large organic eggs
- 1 pound of ground turkey
- 1 medium yellow or white onion, finely chopped

- 1 medium red bell pepper, finely chopped
- 1 teaspoon of fine sea salt
- 1 teaspoon of freshly cracked black pepper

Instructions:

- Press the "Sauté" function on your Instant Pot and add the ground turkey, onions and garlic. Cook until the ground turkey has browned. Turn off the "Sauté" function and remove the contents.
- In a large bowl, add all the ingredients and stir until well combined. Remove and set aside.
- Grease an oven-safe dish that fits inside your Instant Pot with nonstick cooking spray and add the egg mixture.
- Add 1 cup of water and a trivet to your Instant Pot. Place the dish on top of the trivet and cover with aluminum foil.
- Lock the lid and cook at high pressure for 20 minutes. When the cooking is done, naturally release the pressure for 10 minutes and then quick release the remaining pressure. Carefully remove the lid. Serve and enjoy!

Bacon Cheddar Egg Casserole
Time: 35 minutes   Servings: 6

Ingredients:

- 6 large organic eggs
- ½ medium red bell pepper, deseeded and chopped
- 2 handfuls of fresh baby spinach
- ½ cup of bacon, cooked and crumbled

- 1 cup of shredded cheddar cheese
- ½ cup of half and half
- ½ teaspoon of fine sea salt
- ¼ teaspoon of freshly cracked black pepper

Instructions:

- In a large bowl, add all the ingredients and stir until well combined. Remove and set aside.
- Grease an oven-safe dish that fits inside your Instant Pot with nonstick cooking spray and add the egg mixture.
- Add 1 cup of water and a trivet to your Instant Pot. Place the dish on top of the trivet and cover with aluminum foil.
- Lock the lid and cook at high pressure for 20 minutes. When the cooking is done, naturally release the pressure for 10 minutes and then quick release the remaining pressure. Carefully remove the lid. Serve and enjoy!

Ham and Cheddar Cheese Breakfast Casserole
Time: 20 minutes   Servings: 8

Ingredients:

- 4 cups of cauliflower florets
- 2 tablespoons of extra-virgin olive oil or other cooking fat
- 12 large organic eggs
- ½ cup of heavy cream
- 2 cups of cooked ham, cut into cubes
- 1 cup of shredded mozzarella cheese
- 1 cup of shredded cheddar cheese
- 1 cup of scallions, chopped
- 1 teaspoon of fine sea salt
- 1 teaspoon of freshly cracked black pepper
- 2 cups of water

Instructions:

- Grease a large oven-proof dish that can fit inside your Instant Pot. A round metal bowl will work very well.
- In a large bowl, add all the ingredients except for the water and stir until well combined.
- Transfer the egg mixture to the greased dish and cover with aluminum foil.
- Add 2 cups of water and a trivet to your Instant Pot. Place the dish on top and lock the lid. Cook at high pressure for 15 minutes.
- When the cooking is done, quick release the pressure and remove the lid. Check if the casserole is cooked through. Serve and enjoy!

Pulled Pork Breakfast Hash
Time: 15 minutes   Servings: 2

Ingredients:

- 2 tablespoons of olive oil
- 1 turnip, finely chopped
- 2 tablespoons of red onion, finely chopped
- ½ cup of cooked pulled pork
- 2 large organic eggs
- 1 cup of kale, stemmed and roughly chopped
- 4 brussel sprouts, halved
- 1 teaspoon of smoked paprika
- 1 teaspoon of fine sea salt
- 1 teaspoon of freshly cracked black pepper

Instructions:

- Press the "Sauté" function on your Instant Pot and add the olive oil, turnips and onions. Cook until the vegetables have softened, stirring occasionally.
- Add the seasoning and remaining vegetables. Sauté for another 2 minutes, stirring occasionally.
- Add the pulled pork and cook for another 2 minutes.
- Remove all the contents and transfer to an oven-proof dish that fits inside your Instant Pot.
- Create two separate divots into the dish and crack the eggs. Cover with aluminum foil.
- Add 2 cups of water and a trivet to your Instant Pot. Lock the lid and cook at high pressure for 3 minutes.
- When the cooking is done, naturally release the pressure and remove the lid. Check if the eggs are set. Serve and enjoy!

Morning Meatloaf
Time: 30 minutes   Servings: 6

Ingredients:

- 1 ½ pound of breakfast sausage
- 6 large organic eggs
- 2 tablespoons of unsweetened non-dairy milk
- 1 small onion, finely chopped
- 2 medium garlic cloves, peeled and minced
- 4-ounces of cream cheese, softened and cubed
- 1 cup of shredded cheddar cheese
- 2 tablespoons of scallions, chopped

- 1 cup of water

Instructions:

- In a large bowl, add all the ingredients except for the water. Stir until well combined.
- Form the sausage mixture into a meatloaf and wrap with a sheet of aluminum foil. Ensure that the meatloaf fits inside your Instant Pot. If not, remove parts of the mixture and reserve for future use.
- Once you wrap the meatloaf into a packet, add 1 cup of water and a trivet to your Instant Pot. Place the meatloaf on top of the trivet.
- Lock the lid and cook at high pressure for 25 minutes. When the cooking is done, quick release or naturally release the pressure. Carefully remove the lid.
- Unwrap the meatloaf and check if the meatloaf is done. Serve and enjoy!

Keto Oatmeal
Time: 5 minutes   Servings: 2

Ingredients:

- 1 cup of unsweetened coconut milk or unsweetened almond milk
- 1 tablespoon of coconut butter or ghee
- 1 tablespoon of whole flax seeds
- 1 tablespoon of chia seeds
- 1 tablespoon of sunflower seeds
- 1/8 teaspoons of fine sea salt
- Blueberries (for garnish)

Instructions:

- Add all the ingredients to your Instant Pot and mix well.
- Lock the lid and cook at high pressure for 3 minutes.
- When the cooking is done, quick release the pressure and remove the lid.
- Transfer to a bowl and top with blueberries. Serve and enjoy!

Cinnamon and Pecan Porridge
Time: 20 minutes   Servings: 2

Ingredients:

- 1 cup of unsweetened coconut milk or unsweetened almond milk
- ¼ cup of almond butter
- 1 tablespoon of coconut oil, melted
- 2 tablespoons of whole chia seeds
- 2 tablespoons of hemp seeds
- ¼ cup of pecans, chopped
- ¼ cups of walnuts, chopped
- ¼ cups of unsweetened and toasted coconut
- 1 teaspoon of cinnamon

Instructions:

- Add all the ingredients to your Instant Pot and mix well.
- Lock the lid and cook at high pressure for 9 minutes.
- When the cooking is done, naturally release the pressure and remove the lid. Serve and enjoy!

Auntie's Awesome Keto Oatmeal
Time: 10 minutes   Servings: 4

Ingredients:

- 1 cup of unsweetened coconut flakes
- 2 tablespoons of butter or coconut oil
- ½ cup of hemp seeds
- 2 tablespoons of coconut flour
- 1 cup of water
- 2/3 cups of coconut cream
- ½ tablespoon of ground cinnamon
- 1 teaspoon of pure vanilla extract
- 1 tablespoon of pure pumpkin pureed
- 1 teaspoon of finely grated ginger
- A small pinch of fine sea salt

Instructions:

- Add all the ingredients to your Instant Pot and give a good stir.
- Lock the lid and cook at high pressure for 3 minutes. When the cooking is done, allow for a full natural release. Carefully remove the lid.

- Stir the oatmeal again and allow to cool. Serve and enjoy!

Pumpkin Spice Breakfast Porridge
Time: 20 minutes   Servings: 1

Ingredients:

- 2 tablespoons of almond flour
- 1 tablespoon of flax meal
- ¾ cups of unsweetened coconut milk or unsweetened almond milk
- 1 teaspoon of pumpkin pie spice
- 1 large organic egg
- 1/8 teaspoon of fine sea salt

Topping Ingredients:

- 2 drops of pure vanilla extract
- 2 tablespoons of canned pumpkin
- 1 tablespoon of granulated stevia
- 1 tablespoon of heavy cream
- 1 tablespoon of coconut butter
- ¼ cup of mixed berries

Instructions:

- Add all the porridge ingredients to your Instant Pot and stir until well combined.
- Lock the lid and cook at high pressure for 3 minutes.
- When the cooking is done, naturally release the pressure for 10 minutes. Quick release the remaining pressure and remove the lid.
- Top the porridge with your desired toppings. Serve and enjoy!

Anti-Inflammatory Keto Porridge
Time: 15 minutes   Servings: 2

Ingredients:

- 2 tablespoons of hemp seeds
- ¼ cup of walnuts, chopped
- ¼ cup of pecans, chopped
- ¼ cup of unsweetened coconut flakes
- 2 tablespoons of whole chia seeds
- ¾ cups of unsweetened almond milk
- ¼ cup of unsweetened coconut milk
- ¼ cup of almond butter
- 1 tablespoon of coconut oil, melted
- ½ teaspoon of cinnamon
- 1 teaspoon of freshly grated turmeric root
- 2 tablespoons of granulated erythritol

Instructions:

- Press the "Sauté" function on your Instant Pot and add the hemp seeds, chopped walnuts, chopped pecans and unsweetened coconut flakes. Sauté for 1 minute, stirring frequently to avoid burning.
- Add the remaining ingredients to your Instant Pot and stir until well combined.
- Lock the lid and cook at high pressure for 15 minutes.
- When the cooking is done, naturally release or quick release the pressure. Carefully remove the lid and allow to cool as needed. Serve and enjoy!

Blueberry Coconut Porridge
Time: 10 minutes   Servings: 2

Ingredients:

- 1 cup of unsweetened almond milk
- ¼ cup of ground flaxseed
- ¼ cup of coconut flour
- 1 teaspoon of cinnamon
- 1 teaspoon of pure vanilla extract

Topping Ingredients:

- 2 tablespoons of coconut butter or ghee
- Fresh blueberries
- 2-ounces of grated coconut
- 2 tablespoons of toasted pumpkin seeds

Instructions:

- Add all the ingredients to your Instant Pot and stir until well combined.
- Lock the lid and cook at high pressure for 15 minutes. When the cooking is done, quick release or naturally release the pressure. Carefully remove the lid.

- Spoon the porridge into serving bowls and top with coconut butter, blueberries, grated coconut and toasted pumpkin seeds.

Herbed Baked Eggs
Time: 12 minutes　　　　Servings: 4

Ingredients:

- 12 large organic eggs
- 1 cup of heavy cream
- 2 teaspoons of coconut oil or extra-virgin olive oil
- 2 tablespoons of parmesan cheese, freshly grated
- 2 tablespoons of fresh parsley, finely chopped

- 2 tablespoons of fresh rosemary, finely chopped
- 2 tablespoons of fresh thyme, finely chopped
- 4 medium garlic cloves, peeled and minced
- 1 teaspoon of fine sea salt
- 1 teaspoon of freshly cracked black pepper
- 1 cup of water

Instructions:

- Grease 4 ramekins with the coconut oil.
- In a large bowl, add all the ingredients except for the water and stir until well combined.
- Divide and pour the egg mixture into the four ramekins and wrap with aluminum foil.
- Add 1 cup of water and a trivet to your Instant Pot. Place the four ramekins on top of the trivet.
- Lock the lid and cook at high pressure for 7 minutes. When the cooking is done, quick release the pressure and remove the lid. Check if the eggs are cooked through. Serve and enjoy!

Italian Breakfast Egg
Time: 13 minutes　　　　Servings: 4

Ingredients:

- 2 cups of cooked chicken breasts
- 12 organic large eggs
- 3 tablespoons of mustard
- 2 teaspoons of minced garlic
- 1 tablespoon of Italian seasoning
- 1 tablespoon of fresh parsley, finely chopped

- ½ cup of heavy whipping cream
- ½ cup of tomato sauce
- 1 ½ cup of broccoli florets or cauliflower florets
- ½ cup of parmesan cheese, finely grated
- 1 cup of shredded cheddar cheese

Instructions:

- In a large bowl, add all the ingredients and stir until well combined.
- Grease 4 individual baking molds or ramekins with nonstick cooking spray.
- Divide and pour the egg mixture into the ramekins and wrap with aluminum foil.
- Add 1 cup of water and a trivet to your Instant Pot. Place the 4 ramekins on top of the trivet.
- Lock the lid and cook at high pressure for 7 minutes. When the cooking is done, quick release the pressure and remove the lid. Check if the eggs are done. Serve and enjoy!

Butternut Squash, Kale and Ground Beef Breakfast Bowls
Time: 25 minutes　　　　Servings: 4

Ingredients:

- 1 pound of ground beef
- 1 medium yellow or white onion, finely chopped
- 4 medium garlic cloves, peeled and minced
- 4 tablespoons of extra-virgin olive oil or coconut oil
- 2 to 4 cups of kale, stemmed and roughly chopped
- ¼ cup of unsweetened coconut milk

- 1 teaspoon of garam masala
- ½ teaspoon of spicy curry
- ¼ teaspoon of ground ginger
- ¼ teaspoon of ground cinnamon
- 1 teaspoon of fine sea salt
- 1 teaspoon of freshly cracked black pepper
- ½ cup of homemade low-sodium chicken broth

Instructions:

- Press the "Sauté" function on your Instant Pot and add all the ingredients except for the ground beef, chicken broth and roughly chopped kale. Cook for 4 to 6 minutes, stirring occasionally.
- Add the ground beef and cook until brown, stirring occasionally.

- Add the chicken broth if needed and stir in the kale. Lock the lid and cook at high pressure for 10 minutes. When the cooking is done, naturally release the pressure and remove the lid.
- Press the "Sauté" function on your Instant Pot and cook until most of the liquid evaporates.
- Serve and enjoy!

Crustless Ham and Asparagus Quiche
Time: 35 minutes

Servings: 6

Ingredients:

- 6 large organic eggs, beaten
- 10-ounces of asparagus spears, trimmed and cut into bite-sized pieces
- ½ pound of cooked ham, cut into cubes
- 1 cup of heavy whipping cream
- 1 cup of finely grated parmesan cheese
- 2 tablespoons of coconut oil, melted
- 2 medium shallots, thinly sliced
- 1 teaspoon of fine sea salt
- 1 teaspoon of freshly cracked black pepper

Instructions:

- Press the 'Sauté' function on your Instant Pot and add the coconut oil. Once melted, add the sliced shallots. Sauté for 1 minute or until translucent, stirring occasionally.
- Add the asparagus pieces and cook for another minute, stirring frequently. Turn off "Sauté" function and set aside.
- Transfer the contents to a large bowl along with the remaining ingredients. Stir until well combined.
- Grease a 7-inch cake pan with nonstick cooking spray and add the egg mixture. Wrap with aluminum foil.
- Add 1 cup of water and a trivet inside your Instant Pot. Place the cake pan on top of the trivet.
- Lock the lid and cook at high pressure for 10 minutes. When the cooking is done, carefully remove the lid and check if the eggs are cooked. Serve and enjoy!

Breakfast Stuffed Avocado Bowl
Time: 20 minutes   Servings: 1

Ingredients:

- 1 avocado, halved and flesh scooped out
- 1 tablespoon of coconut oil or olive oil
- 3 eggs
- 3 bacon slices, chopped
- ½ teaspoon of fine sea salt
- ½ teaspoon of freshly cracked black pepper

Instructions:

- Scoop out most of your avocado flesh. Try to leave ½-inch of avocado for the egg stuffing.
- Press the "Sauté" function on your Instant Pot and add the coconut oil and bacon. Cook until brown and crispy, stirring frequently. Remove and set aside.
- In a bowl, add the eggs, sea salt and freshly cracked black pepper.
- Pour the egg mixture into your avocado. Be careful not to overpour.
- Add 1 cup of water and a trivet to your Instant Pot. Lock the lid and cook at high pressure for 5 minutes.
- When the cooking is done, naturally or quick release the pressure. Carefully remove the lid and check if the eggs are done.
- Top the avocado bowl with cooked bacon. Serve and enjoy!

Breakfast Stuffed Peppers
Time: 15 minutes   Servings: 2

Ingredients:

- 2 bell peppers, tops removed and inner portions removed
- 5 large organic eggs, beaten
- ¼ cup of unsweetened non-dairy milk
- ½ small yellow onion, chopped
- 4 medium slices of bacon, cooked and crumbled
- ½ cup of fresh spinach, roughly chopped
- 1 cup of cheddar cheese, shredded
- 1 teaspoon of fine sea salt
- 1 teaspoon of freshly cracked black pepper

Instructions:

- In a bowl, add all the ingredients except for the bell peppers and half of the cheddar cheese.
- Divide and fill each bell pepper with the egg mixture.
- Add 1 cup of water and a trivet inside your Instant Pot. Place the stuffed bell peppers on top.
- Lock the lid and cook at high pressure for 8 minutes.
- When the cooking is done, naturally release or quick release the pressure. Carefully remove the lid and check if the eggs are done.
- Sprinkle the bell peppers with cheddar cheese and close the lid. Allow the cheese to melt.
- Serve and enjoy!

Roasted Red Pepper Egg Bites
Time: 15 minutes   Servings: 7

Ingredients:

- 4 large eggs, beaten
- ½ cup of cottage cheese
- ½ cup of Monterey jack cheese, shredded
- 1 green onion, finely chopped
- ½ medium roasted red pepper, chopped
- ¼ cup of fresh spinach, chopped
- 1 cup of water

Instructions:

- Add 1 cup of water and a trivet to your Instant Pot.
- In a large bowl, add all the ingredients and beat until well combined.
- Divide the egg mixture between the egg silicon mold and cover with aluminum foil.
- Place the silicone mold on top of the trivet. Lock the lid and press the "Steam" function and steam for 10 minutes.
- When the timer beeps, naturally release the pressure for 10 minutes and remove the lid.
- Remove the egg bites from the silicon mold and allow to cool. Serve and enjoy!

Pepper Jack Cheese Egg Bites with Green Chilis
Time: 15 minutes   Servings: 7

Ingredients:

- 5 large organic eggs
- ½ cup of shredded pepper jack cheese
- ½ cup of cottage cheese
- ½ teaspoon of fine sea salt
- ½ teaspoon of freshly cracked black pepper
- ¼ cup of fresh green chilis, finely chopped

Instructions:

- Add 1 cup of water and a trivet to your Instant Pot.
- In a large bowl, add all the ingredients and beat until well combined.
- Divide the egg mixture between the egg silicon mold and cover with aluminum foil.
- Place the silicone mold on top of the trivet. Lock the lid and press the "Steam" function and steam for 10 minutes.
- When the timer beeps, naturally release the pressure for 10 minutes and remove the lid.
- Remove the egg bites from the silicon mold and allow to cool. Serve and enjoy!

Italian-Style Egg Bites
Time: 15 minutes   Servings: 7

Ingredients:

- 6 large organic eggs, beaten
- ½ cup of cottage cheese
- 1 teaspoon of minced garlic
- ¼ cup of crumbled feta cheese
- ¼ cup of sun-dried tomatoes, finely chopped
- 1 tablespoon of fresh basil, finely chopped
- ½ teaspoon of fine sea salt
- ½ teaspoon of freshly cracked black pepper

Instructions:

- Add 1 cup of water and a trivet to your Instant Pot.
- In a large bowl, add all the ingredients and beat until well combined.

- Divide the egg mixture between the egg silicon mold and cover with aluminum foil.
- Place the silicone mold on top of the trivet. Lock the lid and press the "Steam" function and steam for 10 minutes.
- When the timer beeps, naturally release the pressure for 10 minutes and remove the lid.
- Remove the egg bites from the silicon mold and allow to cool. Serve and enjoy!

Sausage and Swiss Cheese Egg Bites
Time: 15 minutes

Servings: 7

Ingredients:

- 6 large eggs, beaten
- ¼ cup of cooked breakfast sausage, crumbled
- ½ cup of shredded swiss cheese
- ½ cup of cottage cheese

- ¼ cup of shiitake mushrooms, chopped
- 1 tablespoon of fresh green onions, chopped
- ½ teaspoon of fine sea salt
- ½ teaspoon of freshly cracked black pepper

Instructions:

- Add 1 cup of water and a trivet to your Instant Pot.
- In a large bowl, add all the ingredients and beat until well combined.
- Divide the egg mixture between the egg silicon mold and cover with aluminum foil.
- Place the silicone mold on top of the trivet. Lock the lid and press the "Steam" function and steam for 10 minutes.
- When the timer beeps, naturally release the pressure for 10 minutes and remove the lid.
- Remove the egg bites from the silicon mold and allow to cool. Serve and enjoy!

Egg Bites with Gruyere Cheese
Time: 15 minutes   Servings: 7

Ingredients:

- 6 large eggs, beaten
- 4 medium slices of bacon, cooked and crumbled
- ½ cup of gruyere cheese, shredded

- ½ cup of cottage cheese
- ½ teaspoon of fine sea salt
- ½ teaspoon of freshly cracked black pepper

Instructions:

- Add 1 cup of water and a trivet to your Instant Pot.
- In a large bowl, add all the ingredients and beat until well combined.
- Divide the egg mixture between the egg silicon mold and cover with aluminum foil.
- Place the silicone mold on top of the trivet. Lock the lid and press the "Steam" function and steam for 10 minutes.
- When the timer beeps, naturally release the pressure for 10 minutes and remove the lid.
- Remove the egg bites from the silicon mold and allow to cool. Serve and enjoy!

Broccoli Egg Bites
Time: 15 minutes   Servings: 7

Ingredients:

- 6 large organic eggs, beaten
- ½ cup of broccoli, cooked and chopped
- ½ cup of shredded cheddar cheese

- ½ cup of cottage cheese
- ½ teaspoon of fine sea salt
- ½ teaspoon of freshly cracked black pepper

Instructions:

- Add 1 cup of water and a trivet to your Instant Pot.
- In a large bowl, add all the ingredients and beat until well combined.
- Divide the egg mixture between the egg silicon mold and cover with aluminum foil.
- Place the silicone mold on top of the trivet. Lock the lid and press the "Steam" function and steam for 10 minutes.
- When the timer beeps, naturally release the pressure for 10 minutes and remove the lid.

- Remove the egg bites from the silicon mold and allow to cool. Serve and enjoy!

Southwest American Egg Bites
Time: 15 minutes   Servings: 6

Ingredients:

- 6 large organic eggs, beaten
- 1/3 cup of diced tomatoes
- 3 tablespoons of green chilies, finely chopped
- 2 tablespoons of unsweetened milk
- 1 teaspoon of freshly cracked black pepper
- ½ teaspoon of hot pepper sauce
- ½ teaspoon of fine sea salt

Instructions:

- In a large bowl, add all the ingredients and stir until well combined.
- Divide and pour the egg mixture into silicone cups.
- Add 1 cup of water and a trivet to your Instant Pot. Place the silicone cups on top of the trivet.
- Lock the lid and cook at high pressure for 8 minutes.
- When the cooking is done, quick release the pressure and remove the lid. Carefully remove the lid and allow to cool. Serve and enjoy!

Breakfast Egg Muffins
Time: 30 minutes   Servings: 6

Ingredients:

- 8 large organic eggs
- 1 cup of fresh baby spinach, chopped
- ½ cup of tomatoes, finely diced
- 2 scallions, sliced
- 1/3 cup of parmesan cheese, shredded
- ¼ cup of unsweetened almond milk
- ¼ teaspoon of fine sea salt
- 1/8 teaspoon of freshly cracked black pepper

Instructions:

- Grease 6 oven-safe custard cups or ramekins with nonstick cooking spray.
- In a large bowl, add all the ingredients and stir until well combined.
- Divide and add the egg mixture into the custard cups.
- Add 1 cup of water and a trivet to your Instant Pot. Place the custard cops on top of the trivet. Lock the lid and cook at high pressure for 6 minutes.
- When the cooking is done, naturally release the pressure for 5 minutes before quick releasing the remaining pressure. Carefully remove the lid. Serve and enjoy!

Bacon and Egg Breakfast Chili
Time: 25 minutes   Servings: 8

Ingredients:

- 1 pound of breakfast sausage, thawed and roughly chopped
- ½ pound of bacon, chopped
- 6 large organic eggs
- 1 medium white onion, finely chopped
- 2 tablespoons of olive oil
- 1 (28-ounce) can of diced tomatoes with green chiles
- 2-3 cups of homemade low-sodium chicken broth
- 2 teaspoons of smoked paprika or regular paprika
- 2 teaspoons of chili powder
- 2 teaspoons of garlic powder
- 1 teaspoon of onion powder
- 1 teaspoon of fine sea salt
- Avocado slices (for serving)

Instructions:

- Press the "Sauté" function on your Instant Pot and add the bacon. Cook until brown and crispy, stirring occasionally. Transfer the bacon to a plate lined with paper towels.
- Add the breakfast sausage and onions to the bacon grease and cook until the sausage has browned.
- Add the remaining ingredients except for the eggs to your Instant Pot. Lock the lid and cook at high pressure for 10 minutes.
- When the cooking is done, naturally release the pressure and remove the lid.

- Meanwhile, fry or scramble your eggs on a stovetop skillet the way you like. You can skip this step if you only want to use your Instant Pot.
- Once everything is done, scoop the breakfast chili onto serving bowls and top with eggs, bacon and avocado slices. Serve and enjoy!

Lemon Blueberry Muffins
Time: 15 minutes   Servings: 6

Ingredients:

- 2 cups of almond flour
- 1 cup of heavy whipping cream
- 2 large organic eggs, beaten
- ¼ cup of coconut butter or ghee, melted
- 1 tablespoon of granulated erythritol or other keto-friendly sweeteners
- ½ cup of fresh or frozen blueberries
- 1 teaspoon of fresh lemon zest
- 1 teaspoon of lemon extract
- 1/8 teaspoon of fine sea salt

Instructions:

- In a large bowl, add all the ingredients and gently stir until well combined.
- Grease 6 silicone muffin cups with nonstick cooking spray.
- Divide and add the muffin batter into each muffin cup.
- Add 1 cup of water and a trivet inside your Instant Pot. Place the muffin cup on top of the trivet and cover with aluminum foil.
- Lock the lid and cook at high pressure for 8 minutes. When the timer beeps, naturally release the pressure for 10 minutes. Carefully remove the lid.
- Check if the muffins are cooked through using a toothpick. Serve and enjoy!

Zucchini Muffins
Time: 15 minutes   Servings: 6

Ingredients:

- 1 large zucchini, finely grated
- 6 medium bacon slices, chopped
- 4 large organic eggs
- ½ cup of heavy whipping cream
- 1 cup of shredded cheddar cheese
- 1 cup of almond flour
- 4 tablespoons of flax meal
- ½ cup of parmesan cheese, finely grated
- 1 tablespoon of dried Italian herbs
- 2 teaspoons of onion powder
- 1 teaspoon of baking powder
- ½ teaspoon of garlic powder
- ½ teaspoon of fine sea salt
- ½ teaspoon of freshly cracked black pepper

Instructions:

- Grease 6 silicone muffin cups with nonstick cooking spray.
- In a large bowl, add all the ingredients and gently stir until well combined.
- Divide and spoon the batter into each muffin cup.
- Add 2 cups of water and a trivet inside your Instant Pot. Place the muffin cups on top and cover with aluminum foil.
- Lock the lid and cook at high pressure for 10 minutes. When the cooking is done, naturally release the pressure for 10 minutes. Carefully remove the lid and check if the muffins are done. Serve and enjoy!

Italian Sausage Breakfast Cups
Time: 20 minutes   Servings: 4

Ingredients:

- 1 pound of Italian sausage links, cut into bite-sized pieces
- 4 large eggs, beaten
- 1 medium yellow or white onion, finely chopped
- 1 teaspoon of fine sea salt
- 1 teaspoon of freshly cracked black pepper
- ½ cup of mushrooms, finely chopped
- ½ cup of broccoli florets, chopped
- ½ cup of spinach, roughly chopped
- 1 tablespoon of fresh parsley, finely chopped
- 2 tablespoons of olive oil

Instructions:

- Press the "Sauté" function on your Instant Pot and add the olive oil. Once hot, add the onions, mushrooms, and broccoli. Cook until softened, stirring occasionally. Remove and set aside.
- Add the Italian sausage and cook until brown, stirring occasionally. Turn off "Sauté" function on your Instant Pot.
- In a large bowl, add the vegetables, cooked Italian sausage and remaining ingredients. Stir until well combined. Divide the mixture between 6 silicon muffin cups or greased ramekins.
- Add 1 cup of water and a trivet inside your Instant Pot. Place the muffin cups on top and lock the lid. Cook at high pressure for 10 minutes.
- When the cooking is done, naturally release the pressure and carefully remove the lid.
- Serve and enjoy!

Zucchini Bread with Walnuts
Time: 1 hour and 15 minutes   Servings: 16

Ingredients:

- 3 large organic eggs, beaten
- ½ cup of extra-virgin olive oil
- 1 cup of zucchini, finely grated
- ½ cup of walnuts, chopped
- 1 teaspoon of pure vanilla extract
- 2 ½ cups of almond flour
- ½ cup of erythritol or other keto-friendly sweeteners
- ½ teaspoon of fine sea salt
- 1 teaspoon of baking soda or baking powder
- ¼ teaspoon of grated ginger
- 1 teaspoon of cinnamon

Instructions:

- In a large bowl, add all the ingredients and gently stir until well blended together.
- Grease a 7-inch pan that fits inside your Instant Pot with nonstick cooking spray.
- Add the bread batter to the pan and cover with aluminum foil.
- Add 1 cup of water and place a trivet inside your Instant Pot. Place the pan on top of the trivet.
- Lock the lid and cook at high pressure for 55 minutes. When the cooking is done, naturally release the pressure for 10 minutes. Carefully remove the lid. Unfold the aluminum foil and allow to cool. Serve and enjoy!

Breakfast Chicken and Egg
Time: 30 minutes   Servings: 6

Ingredients:

- 1 pound of boneless, skinless chicken breasts
- 6 large organic eggs
- 2 tablespoons of extra-virgin olive oil
- 1 large onion, finely chopped
- 1 cup of water
- ½ cup of cauliflower rice
- 2 tablespoons of fresh parsley, finely chopped
- 1 teaspoon of fine sea salt
- 1 teaspoon of freshly cracked black pepper

Instructions:

- Press the "Sauté" function on your Instant Pot and add the olive oil. Once hot, add the onions and cook until fragrant, stirring occasionally. Remove and set aside.
- Add the chicken and cook for 4 minutes per side or until brown.
- Pour in 1 cup of water and lock the lid. Cook at high pressure for 15 minutes.
- When the cooking is done, naturally release the pressure and remove the lid. Transfer the chicken to a cutting board and shred using two forks.
- In a large bowl, add the shredded chicken, eggs, onions, cauliflower rice, fresh parsley, salt and black pepper. Stir until well combined.
- Grease an oven-proof dish that fits inside your Instant Pot. Add the egg mixture and cover with foil.
- Place a trivet inside your Instant Pot and place the dish on top. Lock the lid and cook at high pressure for another 8 minutes.
- When the cooking is done, naturally release the pressure and remove the lid. Serve!

Eggs en Cocotte
Time: 20 minutes   Servings: 3

Ingredients:

- 3 tablespoons of unsalted butter
- 3 tablespoons of heavy whipping cream
- 3 large organic eggs
- 1 tablespoon of fresh chives, chopped
- ½ teaspoon of fine sea salt
- ½ teaspoon of freshly cracked black pepper
- 1 cup of water

Instructions:

- Grease 3 ramekins with unsalted butter and add 1 tablespoon of heavy whipping cream into each one.
- Crack an egg into each ramekin and sprinkle with fresh chives, salt and black pepper.
- Add 1 cup of water and a trivet inside your Instant Pot. Place the ramekins on top of the trivet and cover with aluminum foil. Lock the lid and cook at low pressure for 2 minutes.
- When the timer beeps, naturally release the pressure and carefully remove the lid. Serve and enjoy!

Breakfast Chocolate Zucchini Muffins

Time: 40 minutes   Servings: Around 24 muffin bites

Ingredients:

- 2 large organic eggs
- ½ cup of coconut oil, melted
- 2 teaspoons of pure vanilla extract
- 1 tablespoon of unsalted butter
- 3 tablespoons of unsweetened cocoa powder
- 1 cup of almond flour
- ½ teaspoon of baking soda or baking powder
- 1 cup of evaporated cane juice
- 1 cup of water
- ½ teaspoon of ground cinnamon
- 1 cup of finely grated zucchini
- 1/3 cup of mini chocolate chips
- A small pinch of fine sea salt

Instructions:

- In a large bowl, add all the ingredients one by one and gently stir until well blended together.
- Fill silicone muffin cups with the batter.
- Add 1 cup of water and a trivet inside your Instant Pot. Layer the muffins on top of the trivet. Cover with aluminum foil.
- Lock the lid and cook at high pressure for 8 minutes. When the cooking is done, naturally release the pressure and remove the lid.
- Remove the muffins and check if done using toothpicks. Serve and enjoy!

Cauliflower Oatmeal

Time: 15 minutes   Servings: 1

Ingredients:

- 1 cup of fine cauliflower rice
- ½ cup of coconut cream
- ½ teaspoon of organic ground cinnamon
- ¼ teaspoon of granulated erythritol
- ½ tablespoon of peanut butter
- A small pinch of fine sea salt

Instructions:

- Add all the ingredients except for the peanut butter and stir until well combined.
- Lock the lid and cook at high pressure for 2 minutes.
- When the cooking is done, naturally release the pressure and remove the lid.
- Transfer to serving bowls and top with peanut butter. Serve and enjoy!

Chocolate Cauliflower Rice Pudding

Time: 16 minutes   Servings: 2

Ingredients:

- 2 cups of fine cauliflower rice
- 1 cup of heavy whipping cream
- 1/3 cup of granulated erythritol or other keto-friendly sweeteners
- 1 to 2 egg whites
- 1 teaspoon of pure vanilla extract
- 3 tablespoons of unsweetened cocoa powder
- A small pinch of fine sea salt

Instructions:

- Add all the ingredients and stir until well combined.

28

- Lock the lid and cook at high pressure for 2 minutes. When the cooking is done, naturally release the pressure and carefully remove the lid. Serve and enjoy!

Mushroom and Cauliflower Risotto
Time: 25 minutes   Servings: 4

Ingredients:

- 1 medium cauliflower head, cut into florets
- 1 pound of shiitake mushrooms, sliced
- 3 medium garlic cloves, peeled and minced
- 2 tablespoons of coconut aminos
- 1 cup of homemade low-sodium chicken stock
- 1 cup of full-fat coconut milk
- 1 tablespoon of coconut oil, melted
- 1 small onion, finely chopped
- 2 tablespoons of almond flour
- ¼ cup of nutritional yeast

Instructions:

- Press the "Sauté" function on your Instant Pot and add the coconut oil.
- Once hot, add the onions, mushrooms and garlic. Sauté for 5 minutes or until softened, stirring occasionally.
- Add the remaining ingredients except for the almond flour. Lock the lid and cook at high pressure for 2 minutes.
- When the cooking is done, naturally release the pressure and remove the lid.
- Sprinkle the almond flour over the risotto and stir to thicken. Serve and enjoy!

Coconut and Lime Cauliflower Rice
Time: 15 minutes   Servings: 4

Ingredients:

- 1 large cauliflower, chopped
- 2 tablespoons of extra-virgin olive oil
- 1 large yellow onion, finely chopped
- 3 medium garlic cloves, peeled and minced
- 1 (15-ounce) can of full-fat coconut milk
- 1 medium lime, zest and juice
- ½ teaspoon of fine sea salt
- ¼ teaspoon of freshly cracked black pepper

Instructions:

- Add the cauliflowers to a food processor and pulse until resembles rice-like consistency.
- Press the "Sauté" function on your Instant Pot and add the olive oil. Once hot, add the onions and garlic. Sauté for 2 to 3 minutes or until fragrant, stirring occasionally.
- Add the remaining ingredients and lock the lid. Cook at high pressure for 3 minutes.
- When the cooking is done, quick release the pressure and remove the lid. Serve and enjoy!

Eggs with Avocados and Feta Cheese
Time: 10 minutes   Servings: 2

Ingredients:

- 4 large organic eggs
- 1 large avocado, peeled and cut into 12 slices
- 2 tablespoons of crumbled feta cheese
- 1 tablespoon of fresh parsley, finely chopped
- ½ teaspoon of fine sea salt
- ½ teaspoon of freshly cracked black pepper

Instructions:

- Grease 2 gratin dishes with nonstick cooking spray..
- Arrange 6 avocado slices into each gratin dish. Crack 2 eggs into each dish. Sprinkle with crumbled feta cheese, fresh parsley, salt and black pepper. Wrap with aluminum foil.
- Add 1 cup of water and a trivet inside your Instant Pot. Place the gratin dish on top of the trivet.
- Lock the lid and cook at high pressure for 4 minutes. When the cooking is done, quick release or naturally release the pressure. Carefully remove the lid and check if the eggs are done. Serve and enjoy!

Giant Keto Pancake
Time: 50 minutes   Servings: 6

Ingredients:

- 2 cups of almond flour or coconut flour
- 2 teaspoons of baking powder
- 2 tablespoons of granulated erythritol or another keto-friendly sweetener
- 2 large organic eggs
- 1 ½ cup of unsweetened almond milk or coconut milk

Instructions:

- In a large bowl, add all the ingredients and stir until well combined.
- Grease a springform pan with nonstick cooking spray and add the pancake batter.
- Add 1 cup of water and a trivet inside your Instant Pot. Place the springform pan on top of the trivet.
- Lock the lid and cook at low pressure for 45 minutes. When the cooking is done, remove the lid and allow the pancake to cool. Serve and enjoy!

Breakfast Burrito Casserole
Time: 25 minutes   Servings: 6

Ingredients:

- 4 large organic eggs
- 1 cup of cheddar cheese, cubed
- ¼ cup of white or yellow onion, finely chopped
- 1 medium jalapeno, finely chopped
- 1 cup of cooked ham, cut into cubes
- ½ teaspoon of fine sea salt
- ½ teaspoon of freshly cracked black pepper
- ½ teaspoon of chili powder
- Lettuce leaves (for serving)
- Salsa (for serving)
- Avocado slices (for serving)

Instructions:

- In a large bowl, add all the ingredients and stir until well combined.
- Grease a springform pan or a round metal bowl with nonstick cooking spray. Add the egg mixture.
- Add 1 cup of water and a trivet inside your Instant Pot. Place the pan on top of the trivet and cover with aluminum foil.
- Lock the lid and cook at high pressure for 12 minutes. When the cooking is done, naturally release the pressure and remove the lid. Remove the pan and spoon the egg mixture onto lettuce leaves. Top with salsa and avocado slices. Serve and enjoy!

Breakfast Ratatouille
Time: 30 minutes   Servings: 6

Ingredients:

- 12 large organic eggs
- ¼ cup of extra-virgin olive oil
- 1 medium yellow onion, finely chopped
- 6 medium garlic cloves, peeled and finely minced
- 1 (28-ounce) can of plum tomatoes, drained
- 1 medium eggplant, chopped
- 1 zucchini, sliced
- 1 medium yellow bell pepper, seeded and chopped
- 1 tablespoon of capers, chopped
- 1 tablespoon of red wine vinegar
- 2 teaspoons of fresh thyme, finely chopped
- 1 teaspoon of fresh oregano, finely chopped
- 3 tablespoons of fresh basil, finely chopped
- 3 tablespoons of fresh parsley, finely chopped

Instructions:

- Press the "Sauté" function on your Instant Pot and add olive oil and onions. Sauté for 4 minutes or until slightly softened, stirring occasionally.
- Add the garlic and herbs. Sauté until fragrant, stirring occasionally.
- Add the tomatoes, eggplant, bell peppers and zucchini. Stir until well combined.
- Lock the lid and cook at high pressure for 5 minutes. When the cooking is done quick release the pressure and remove the lid.
- Stir in the capers and red wine vinegar.
- In a small skillet over medium-high heat, add the vegetables. Make small cavities and crack eggs into the cavity. Cover and allow the eggs to cook through. Serve and enjoy!

Spanish Chorizo and Cauliflower Hash
Time: 20 minutes   Servings: 4

Ingredients:

- 1 pound of cauliflower florets, cut into florets
- 1 tablespoon of extra-virgin olive oil
- 1 medium sweet potato, cut into bite-sized pieces
- 1 pound of chorizo sausage, crumbled
- 1 large onion, finely chopped
- 2 medium garlic cloves, peeled and minced
- 3 tablespoons of fresh rosemary, finely chopped
- 3 tablespoons of fresh basil, finely chopped
- 1 teaspoon of fine sea salt
- 1 teaspoon of freshly cracked black pepper
- ½ cup of homemade low-sodium vegetable stock

Instructions:

- Press the "Sauté" function on your Instant Pot and add the olive oil. Once hot, add the onions and garlic. Sauté for 2 minutes or until softened, stirring occasionally.
- Add the sweet potato pieces, chorizo sausage and cauliflower. Sauté for 3 minutes, stirring occasionally.
- Add the remaining ingredients and stir until well combined.
- Pour in the vegetable stock and lock the lid. Cook at high pressure for 10 minutes. When the cooking is done, naturally release the pressure and remove the lid. Serve and enjoy!

BLT Egg Casserole
Time: 30 minutes   Servings: 4

Ingredients:

- 6 large organic eggs
- 6 medium slices of bacon, chopped
- 1 medium Roma tomato, sliced
- ½ cup of cheddar cheese, shredded
- 2 green onions, thinly sliced
- ½ cup of heavy whipping cream
- ½ cup of fresh spinach
- 1 teaspoon of fine sea salt
- 1 teaspoon of freshly cracked black pepper

Instructions:

- In a large bowl, add all the ingredients and stir until well combined.
- Grease a large springform pan with nonstick cooking spray and add the egg mixture.
- Add 1 cup of water and place a trivet inside your Instant Pot. Place the springform pan on top of the trivet and cover with aluminum foil.
- Lock the lid and cook at high pressure for 13 minutes.
- When the cooking is done, naturally release the pressure for 10 minutes, then quick release the remaining pressure. Remove the lid. Serve and enjoy!

Part 3: Chicken and Poultry Recipes

Supreme Chicken Breasts
Time: 20 minutes   Servings: 4

Ingredients:

- 4 chicken breasts, boneless, skinless
- 2 Tablespoons coconut oil
- 1 teaspoon salt (to taste)
- 1 teaspoon fresh ground black pepper (to taste)
- 2 cups of water

Instructions:

1. Cover trivet with foil.
2. Press Sauté button on Instant Pot. Heat the coconut oil.
3. Season the chicken with salt and pepper. Sauté for 2 minutes per side, until a golden crust forms. Remove chicken breasts and set aside.
4. Press Keep Warm/Cancel setting to end Sauté mode.
5. Pour 2 cups of water in the Instant Pot. Place trivet inside.
6. Place chicken breasts on trivet.
7. Close and seal lid. Press Manual button. Cook at High Pressure for 10 minutes.
8. When done, naturally release pressure. Open the lid with care. Let chicken rest for 5 minutes in Instant Pot. Serve.

Delicious Cheesy Spinach Stuffed Chicken Breasts
Time: 20 minutes   Servings: 2

Ingredients:

- 2 chicken breasts
- 1 red bell pepper, chopped
- 1 cup mozzarella cheese, shredded
- 1 cup parmesan cheese, shredded
- 3 Tablespoons coconut oil
- 2 cups baby spinach
- 1 teaspoon garlic powder
- 1 teaspoon onion powder
- 1 teaspoon salt (to taste)
- 1 teaspoon fresh ground black pepper (to taste)
- 2 cups of water

Instructions:

1. Cover trivet with foil.
2. Press Sauté button on Instant Pot. Heat 2 tablespoons of the coconut oil.
3. Sauté the chicken until golden brown on both sides.
4. Remove the chicken breasts and allow to cool.
5. Press Keep Warm/Cancel button to end Sauté mode.
6. In a large bowl, combine red pepper, parmesan cheese, mozzarella cheese, 1 tablespoon of coconut oil, baby spinach, and seasoning.
7. When chicken is cool, cut down middle, but don't cut all the way through.
8. Stuff with the spinach mixture.
9. Pour 2 cups of water in Instant Pot. Place trivet inside. Place chicken on trivet.
10. Close and seal lid. Press Manual button. Cook at High Pressure for 7 minutes.
11. When done, naturally release pressure. Open the lid with care.
12. Allow chicken to rest 5 minutes. Plate and serve.

Royal Lemon Pepper Chicken
Time: 25 minutes   Servings: 4

Ingredients:

- 4 chicken breasts, skinless, boneless
- 2 Tablespoons coconut oil
- 2 Tablespoons butter, melted
- Zest and juice from 2 lemons
- 2 teaspoons salt (to taste)
- 1 Tablespoon lemon pepper seasoning (to taste)
- 2 Tablespoons fresh parsley, chopped

Instructions:

1. Press Sauté button on Instant Pot. Heat the coconut oil.
2. Sauté the chicken. Cook until golden brown on each side.
3. Press Keep Warm/Cancel setting to end Sauté mode.

4. In a bowl, add melted butter, lemon juice, lemon zest, salt, lemon pepper seasoning, and parsley. Stir well.
5. Coat chicken with seasoning mixture. Return chicken to Instant Pot.
6. Close and seal lid. Press Manual button. Cook at High Pressure for 5 minutes.
7. When done, naturally release pressure. Open the lid with care.
8. Allow chicken to rest for 5 minutes. Serve.

Flaming Buffalo Chicken Strips
Time: 20 minutes   Servings: 2

Ingredients:

- 2 chicken breasts, boneless, skinless
- 1 cup of water
- 1 Tablespoon low-carb barbecue sauce
- 1 Tablespoon cayenne pepper
- 1 Tablespoon dried oregano
- 1 teaspoon garlic powder
- 1 teaspoon ground cumin
- 1 teaspoon chili powder
- 1 Tablespoon coconut oil
- 1 teaspoon salt (to taste)
- 1 teaspoon fresh ground black pepper (to taste)

Instructions:

1. Cover trivet in foil. Press Sauté button on Instant Pot. Heat the coconut oil.
2. Add the chicken. Cook until brown on each side. Remove the chicken breasts and set aside. Press Keep Warm/Cancel setting to end Sauté mode.
3. Flavor the chicken with barbecue sauce, spices, and seasonings.
4. Pour water in Instant Pot. Place trivet in pot. Place chicken on trivet.
5. Close and seal lid. Press Manual button. Cook at High Pressure for 8 minutes.
6. When done, naturally release pressure. Open the lid with care.
7. Allow chicken to rest for 5 minutes. Serve.

Succulent Garlic Paprika Chicken Legs with Green Beans
Time: 20 minutes   Servings: 4

Ingredients:

- 4 chicken drumsticks
- 1 pound green beans, trimmed and chopped
- 1 cup chicken broth
- 1 Tablespoon coconut oil
- 2 Tablespoons onion powder
- 4 Tablespoons fresh herbs, chopped (rosemary, oregano, thyme)
- 1 Tablespoon smoked paprika
- 1 teaspoon salt
- 1 teaspoon fresh ground black pepper

Instructions:

1. In a bowl, combine fresh herbs and seasonings. Stir well.
2. In a large Ziploc bag, add chicken drumsticks and seasoning mixture.
3. Allow to marinate in refrigerator for 6 hours or overnight.
4. When ready to cook. Press Sauté button on Instant Pot. Heat the coconut oil.
5. Add the drumsticks. Cook until a golden crust forms. Press Keep Warm/Cancel setting to end Sauté mode. Add green beans and chicken broth to Instant Pot.
6. Close and seal lid. Press Manual button. Cook at High Pressure for 10 minutes.
7. Quick-release or naturally release pressure when done. Open the lid with care.
8. Allow chicken to rest for 5 minutes before removing. Serve.

Phenomenal Whole Rotisserie Chicken
Time: 30 minutes   Servings: 6

Ingredients:

- 1 whole chicken
- Zest and juice from 1 lemon
- 2 cups chicken broth
- 2 Tablespoons coconut oil
- 2 teaspoons salt
- 2 teaspoons fresh ground black pepper
- 2 teaspoons paprika
- 2 Tablespoons fresh herbs, chopped
- 4 garlic cloves, minced

Instructions:

1. Remove any parts included inside chicken cavity. Rinse and pat dry.
2. In a bowl, combine the seasoning and herbs.
3. Pour coconut oil over the chicken. Rub seasoning mixture into chicken skin.
4. Press Sauté button on Instant Pot. Place chicken in Instant Pot. Sauté all sides for 5 minutes. Press Keep Warm/Cancel setting to stop Sauté mode.
5. Add chicken broth. Close and seal lid. Press Manual switch. Cook at High Pressure for 25 minutes. When done, naturally release pressure. Open the lid with care.
6. Allow to rest for 5 minutes before removing. Serve.

Very Easy Salsa Chicken
Time: 25 minutes   Servings: 4

Ingredients:

- 4 boneless, skinless chicken breasts
- 1 (16-ounce) jar of salsa
- Fine sea salt and freshly cracked black pepper (more or less to taste)

Instructions:

- Season the chicken breast with sea salt and black pepper. Add to your Instant Pot. Pour in the salsa. Lock the lid and cook at high pressure for 15 minutes.
- When the cooking is done, naturally release the pressure for 5 minutes, then quick release the remaining pressure. Carefully remove the lid. Serve and enjoy!

Buffalo Chicken Meatballs
Time: 35 minutes   Servings: 4

Ingredients:

- 2 pounds of ground chicken
- 1 small onion, finely chopped
- 4 medium garlic cloves, peeled and minced
- 2 large organic eggs
- 4 tablespoons of ranch dressing
- 4 tablespoons of almond flour
- 2 tablespoons of fresh parsley, finely chopped
- 2 tablespoons of Worcestershire sauce
- 1 cup of Frank's Buffalo Hot Sauce
- ½ cup of unsalted butter
- ½ cup of water

Instructions:

- In a large bowl, add the ground chicken, onion, garlic, eggs, ranch dressing, parsley, and almond flour. Mix until well combined.
- Preheat your broiler. Form into meatballs and place onto a baking sheet. Broil for 10 minutes or until brown. Remove and set aside.
- Press the "Sauté" function on your Instant Pot and add the butter. Once melted, stir in the hot sauce, Worcestershire sauce and water.
- Stir in the chicken meatballs and lock the lid. Cook at high pressure for 15 minutes. When the cooking is done, naturally release the pressure for 10 minutes, then quick release the remaining pressure. Carefully remove the lid. Serve and enjoy!

Ranch Chicken Wings
Time: 15 minutes   Servings: 4

Ingredients:

- 3 pounds of chicken wings
- 2 tablespoons of liquid smoke
- ½ cup of water
- 1 teaspoon of garlic
- 1 package of ranch seasoning

Instructions:

- Add the garlic, water and liquid smoke.
- Coat the chicken wings with the ranch seasoning and place inside your Instant Pot.
- Lock the lid and cook at high pressure for 10 minutes. When the cooking is done, naturally release the pressure for 5 minutes, then quick release the remaining pressure. Carefully remove the lid. Serve and enjoy!

Salt and Vinegar Chicken Wings
Time: 30 minutes   Servings: 4

Ingredients:

- 2 pounds of chicken wings
- 2 tablespoons of butter, melted
- 2 tablespoons of salt and vinegar seasoning
- Fine sea salt and freshly cracked black pepper (to taste)
- ½ cup of homemade low-sodium chicken broth

Instructions:

- Season the chicken wings with sea salt and freshly cracked black pepper.
- Add the chicken broth and the chicken wings inside your Instant Pot. Lock the lid and cook at high pressure for 10 minutes. When the cooking is done, naturally release the pressure for 10 minutes, then quick release the remaining pressure. Carefully remove the lid.
- Preheat your broiler and transfer the chicken to a baking sheet lined with aluminum foil. Place inside your broiler and broil until golden brown on top.
- Add the chicken wings into a large bowl along with the butter and salt and vinegar seasoning. Toss until well coated. Serve and enjoy!

Lemon Pepper Chicken Wings
Time: 35 minutes   Servings: 6

Ingredients:

- 3 pounds of chicken wings
- 2 tablespoons of avocado oil
- ½ cup of freshly squeezed lemon juice
- ½ cup of homemade low-sodium chicken stock
- 1 tablespoon of freshly cracked black pepper
- 1 teaspoon of fine sea salt
- 1 tablespoon of fresh parsley, finely chopped

Instructions:

- In a large bowl, add the chicken wings and season with sea salt and freshly cracked black pepper. Drizzle with the avocado oil.
- Place inside your Instant Pot along with the chicken stock and lemon juice.
- Lock the lid and cook at high pressure for 10 minutes. When the cooking is done, naturally release the pressure for 10 minutes, then quick release the remaining pressure. Carefully remove the lid. Serve and enjoy!

Tuscan Chicken
Time: 50 minutes   Servings: 6

Ingredients:

- 4 to 6 skinless chicken thighs or chicken breasts
- 2 tablespoons of extra-virgin olive oil
- 2 teaspoons of Italian seasonings
- 1 cup of cremini mushrooms, sliced
- 1 tablespoon of coconut aminos
- 1 cup of homemade low-sodium chicken stock
- 4 medium garlic cloves, minced
- ½ cup of sun-dried tomatoes
- 1 cup of spinach
- ½ cup of heavy whipping cream
- ½ cup of parmesan cheese, freshly grated
- 3 tablespoons of almond flour mixed with 3 tablespoons of water
- Fine sea salt and freshly cracked black pepper (to taste)

Instructions:

- Season the chicken thighs with sea salt and freshly cracked black pepper.
- Press the "Sauté" setting on your Instant Pot and add the olive oil. Once hot, add the chicken thighs and sear for 4 minutes or until brown. Remove and set aside.
- Add the garlic and mushrooms. Sauté for 30 seconds, stirring occasionally.
- Return the chicken and stock inside your Instant Pot. Lock the lid and cook at high pressure for 8 minutes. When the cooking is done, naturally release the pressure for 10 minutes, then quick release the remaining pressure. Carefully remove the lid.
- Remove the chicken and stir in the remaining ingredients. Press the "Sauté" setting on your Instant Pot and allow to heat through or until the liquid thickens. Serve and enjoy!

Chicken Cacciatore
Time: 35 minutes   Servings: 4

Ingredients:

- 4 (6-ounce) bone-in, skin-on chicken thighs
- 2 tablespoons of olive oil
- 3 celery stalks, chopped
- ½ onion, finely chopped
- ½ cup of mushrooms, sliced
- 2 medium garlic cloves, minced

- 1 (14-ounce) can of stewed tomatoes
- 2 teaspoons of herbes de Provence
- ¾ cup of homemade low-sodium chicken stock
- 3 chicken bouillon cubes, crumbled
- 2 tablespoon of tomato paste
- Fine sea salt and freshly cracked black pepper (to taste)

Instructions:

- Press the "Sauté" function on your Instant Pot and add the olive oil. Once hot, add the chicken thighs and sear for 6 minutes per side or until brown. Transfer the chicken to a plate lined with paper towels.
- Add the chopped celery, onions and mushrooms. Sauté for 5 minutes or until softened, stirring occasionally.
- Add the minced garlic and sauté for another minute, stirring frequently.
- Return the chicken along with the stewed tomatoes, tomato paste, herbes de Provence, water and chicken bouillon cubes.
- Lock the lid and cook at high pressure for 11 minutes. When the cooking is done, allow for a full natural release method and carefully remove the lid. Serve and enjoy!

Bang Bang Chicken
Time: 15 minutes   Servings: 4

Ingredients:

- 1 pound of boneless, skinless chicken breasts
- 3 tablespoons of sriracha sauce
- 1 cup of homemade low-sodium chicken stock

- 1 tablespoon of white wine vinegar
- 2 cups of cauliflower rice
- Fine sea salt and freshly cracked black pepper (to taste)

Instructions:

- Add all the ingredients except for the cauliflower rice inside your Instant Pot. Lock the lid and cook at high pressure for 6 minutes. When the cooking is done, allow for a full natural release method and carefully remove the lid. Remove the chicken and set aside.
- Add the cauliflower rice and lock the lid. Cook at high pressure for 1 minute. When the cooking is done, quick release the pressure and carefully remove the lid.
- Meanwhile, shred the chicken using two forks. Return the shredded chicken to the cauliflower rice. Adjust the seasoning if necessary. Serve and enjoy!

Butter Chicken
Time: 25 minutes   Servings: 4

Ingredients:

- 1 pound of boneless, skinless chicken thighs
- 1 (14-ounce) can of diced tomatoes
- 6 garlic cloves, peeled and minced
- 2 teaspoons of ginger, minced
- 1 teaspoon of turmeric
- ½ teaspoon of cayenne pepper
- 1 teaspoon of smoked paprika

- 1 teaspoon of fine sea salt
- 1 teaspoon of garam masala
- 1 teaspoon of ground cumin
- ½ cup of butter, cubed
- ½ cup of heavy cream
- Fine sea salt and freshly cracked black pepper (to taste)

Instructions:

- Add all the ingredients except for the butter and heavy cream inside your Instant Pot. Lock the lid and cook at high pressure for 10 minutes. When the cooking is done, naturally release the pressure for 10 minutes, then quick release the pressure. Carefully remove the lid.
- Remove the chicken and set aside. Use an immersion blender to blend the contents until smooth. Stir in the cubed butter and heavy cream. Stir until well combined.

- Return the chicken to the butter sauce and coat until well combined. Serve and enjoy!

Chicken and Broccoli
Time: 20 minutes   Servings: 4

Ingredients:

- 2 pounds of boneless, skinless chicken breasts, cut into bite-sized pieces
- 2 head of broccoli, cut into florets
- 1 yellow onion, finely chopped
- 1 bunch of scallions, chopped
- 2 tablespoons of extra-virgin olive oil
- 4 garlic cloves, peeled and minced
- 1 cup of homemade low-sodium beef broth
- ¼ cup of coconut aminos
- 1 tablespoon of white wine vinegar
- 2 tablespoons of coconut aminos
- 2 tablespoons of oyster sauce
- 2 tablespoons of almond flour mixed with 2 tablespoons of water
- Fine sea salt and freshly cracked black pepper (to taste)

Instructions:

- Press the "Sauté" setting on your Instant Pot and add the olive oil. Once hot, add the chopped onions and scallions. Sauté until lightly softened, stirring frequently.
- Add the minced garlic and sauté for another minute, stirring occasionally.
- Add the chicken pieces and continue to cook until lightly brown, stirring occasionally.
- Add the remaining ingredients except for the almond flour and lock the lid. Cook at high pressure for 4 minutes. When the cooking is done, quick release the pressure and carefully remove the lid.
- Press the "Sauté" function on your Instant Pot and add the almond flour. Continue to cook until the liquid evaporates, stirring occasionally. Serve and enjoy!

Jalapeno Popper Chicken
Time: 25 minutes   Servings: 12

Ingredients:

- 2 ½ pounds of boneless, skinless chicken breasts
- ½ cup of jarred jalapenos
- 1/3 cup of juice from jarred jalapenos
- 1 (8-ounce) package of cream cheese, softened
- 1 cup of cheddar cheese, shredded
- ¼ cup of finely grated parmesan cheese
- 1 teaspoon of garlic powder
- 1 teaspoon of onion powder
- 1 cup of homemade low-sodium chicken stock
- Fine sea salt and freshly cracked black pepper (more or less to taste)

Instructions:

- In your Instant Pot, add the chicken broth, seasonings and jalapeno juice. Mix well.
- Add the chicken breasts.
- Lock the lid and cook at high pressure for 15 minutes.
- When the cooking is done, naturally release the pressure for 5 minutes, then quick release the remaining pressure. Carefully remove the lid.
- Transfer the chicken to a cutting board and shred using two forks. Set aside.
- Press the "Sauté" setting on your Instant Pot. Simmer for 10 minutes, stirring occasionally.
- Stir in the cream cheese and whisk until smooth.
- Stir in the cheddar cheese and parmesan cheese. Allow to melt. If the sauce is a little bit too thick, stir in some chicken stock.
- Turn off the "Sauté" setting and stir int eh shredded chicken. Serve and enjoy!

Mexican-Style Chicken Stuffed Peppers
Time: 25 minutes   Servings: 4

Ingredients:

- 4 large bell peppers, tops removed and inner portions scooped out
- 1 pound of chicken, cut into bite-sized pieces
- ½ cup of Mexican salsa
- ½ cup of zucchini, chopped
- ½ cup of cauliflower rice
- ½ teaspoon of cumin
- ½ cup of chicken broth
- ½ teaspoon of chili powder
- 1 cup of shredded pepper jack cheese

- 1 cup of water
- Fine sea salt and freshly cracked black pepper (more or less to taste)

Instructions:

- Add all the ingredients except for the bell peppers and cheese inside your Instant Pot.
- Lock the lid and cook at high pressure for 5 minutes.
- When the cooking is done, naturally release the pressure for 5 minutes, then quick release the remaining pressure. Carefully remove the lid.
- Stir the contents inside your Instant Pot and spoon inside your bell peppers.
- Add another 1 cup of water and a trivet inside your Instant Pot.
- Place the bell peppers on top of the trivet and sprinkle with cheese. Lock the lid and cook at high pressure 8 minutes. When the cooking is done, quick release the pressure and remove the lid.
- Serve and enjoy!

General Tso's Chicken
Time: 25 minutes   Servings: 4

Ingredients:

- 2 pounds of boneless, skinless chicken breasts, cut into 1-inch pieces
- 2 tablespoons of olive oil
- ¼ cup of coconut aminos
- 3 tablespoons of white wine vinegar
- 3 tablespoons of granulated erythritol
- 2 medium garlic cloves, minced
- 1 teaspoon of fresh ginger, peeled and grated
- 1 tablespoon of tomato paste
- 2 tablespoons of tomato paste
- ½ teaspoon of fine sea salt
- 1 teaspoon of xanthan gum
- ¼ cup of scallions, chopped (For serving)
- Fine sea salt and freshly cracked black pepper (more or less to taste)

Instructions:

- Press the "Sauté" setting on your Instant Pot and add the olive oil. Once hot, add the chicken and cook until brown, stirring occasionally.
- Add the remaining ingredient except for the xanthan gum.
- Lock the lid and cook at high pressure for 15 minutes.
- When the cooking is done, naturally release the pressure for 5 minutes, then quick release the remaining pressure. Carefully remove the lid.
- Press the "Sauté" setting on your Instant Pot and sprinkle the xanthan gum. Continue to cook until the liquid thickens, stirring occasionally. Serve and enjoy!

Whole Rotisserie Chicken
Time: 50 minutes   Servings: 6

Ingredients:

- 1 (4 to 5 pound) whole chicken
- 2 tablespoons of avocado oil or extra-virgin olive oil
- 1 medium yellow onion, quartered
- 1 lemon, halved
- 1 cup of homemade low-sodium chicken stock
- 1 teaspoon of garlic powder
- 1 teaspoon of smoked paprika
- Fine sea salt and freshly cracked black pepper (to taste)

Instructions:

- Season the whole chicken with garlic powder, smoked paprika, sea salt and freshly cracked black pepper.
- Add the quartered onion and halved lemon inside the chicken cavity.
- Press the "Sauté" setting on your Instant Pot and add the avocado oil. Once hot, add the whole chicken and sear for 4 minutes or until brown.
- Pour in the chicken stock inside your Instant Pot. Lock the lid and cook at high pressure for 25 minutes. When the cooking is done, naturally release the pressure and carefully remove the lid. Serve and enjoy!

Lemon and Thyme Whole Chicken
Time: 50 minutes   Servings: 8

Ingredients:

- 1 (5 to 6 pound) whole chicken
- 2 tablespoons of extra-virgin olive oil
- 8 to 10 garlic cloves
- 4 medium shallots, peeled and quartered
- 1 lemon, quartered
- 2/3 cups of dry white wine
- 1/3 cup of homemade low-sodium chicken stock
- 1 medium onion, quartered
- A bunch of fresh sprigs of thyme
- 2 teaspoons of fine sea salt
- 1 teaspoon of freshly cracked black pepper

Instructions:

- Season the chicken with sea salt and freshly cracked black pepper.
- Add the garlic cloves, onion, shallot, lemon and thyme sprigs inside the cavity inside your chicken.
- Press the "Sauté" setting on your Instant Pot and add the olive oil. Once hot, add the whole chicken and sear for 4 minutes per side or until brown. Add the dry white wine and chicken stock.
- Lock the lid and cook at high pressure for 30 minutes. When the cooking is done, naturally release the pressure and carefully remove the lid. Serve and enjoy!

Peppery Radish and Chicken Stew

Time: 30 minutes   Servings: 4

Ingredients:

- 1 ½ pounds of boneless, skinless chicken breasts
- 5 cups of homemade low-sodium chicken broth
- 1 large onion, finely chopped
- 3 cups of radishes, chopped
- 2 tablespoons of olive oil

Instructions:

- Press the "Sauté" setting on your Instant Pot and add the olive oil. Once hot, add the onions and cook until tender, stirring occasionally. Remove and set aside.
- Add the chicken and sear for 4 minutes per side or until brown.
- Add the onions and radishes to your Instant Pot. Pour in the chicken broth.
- Lock the lid and cook at high pressure for 20 minutes. When the cooking is done, naturally release the pressure for 10 minutes, then quick release the remaining pressure. Carefully remove the lid. Serve and enjoy!

Peruvian Chicken and Green Sauce

Time: 30 minutes   Servings: 6

Chicken Ingredients:

- 2 pounds of chicken legs
- 3 tablespoons of extra-virgin olive oil
- 1 tablespoon of fresh lime juice
- 1 teaspoon of fresh lime zest
- 1 teaspoon of garlic powder
- 1 teaspoon of onion powder
- 2 teaspoons of dried oregano
- 1 tablespoon of smoked paprika or regular paprika
- 1 tablespoon of ground cumin
- 1 teaspoon of fine sea salt
- Fine sea salt and freshly cracked black pepper (to taste)
- 1 cup of homemade low-sodium chicken stock

Green Sauce Ingredients:

- 2 jalapenos, seeded and chopped
- 2 medium garlic cloves, peeled and minced
- 1 cup of fresh cilantro
- 2 tablespoons of extra-virgin olive oil
- 1/3 cup of no-sugar mayonnaise
- 1 tablespoon of white vinegar
- 2 teaspoons of lime juice
- 1 teaspoon of lime zest

Instructions:

- Season the chicken legs with garlic powder, onion powder, dried oregano, paprika, cumin, sea salt and black pepper.
- Press the "Sauté" setting on your Instant Pot and add the olive oil. Once hot and working in batches, add the chicken legs and sear for 2 minutes or until brown.
- Add the chicken stock, lime zest and lime juice inside your Instant Pot. Lock the lid and cook at high pressure for 6 minutes. When the cooking is done, naturally release the pressure and carefully remove the lid.
- Transfer the chicken to a serving platter and set aside.
- Press the "Sauté" setting on your Instant Pot and add all the green sauce to the liquid inside your Instant Pot. Use an immersion blender to blend the contents until smooth. Spoon the sauce over the chicken legs. Serve and enjoy!

Chili Orange Chicken
Time: 35 minutes   Servings: 4

Ingredients:

- 4 chicken thighs
- 3 tablespoons of olive oil
- 1 chili, finely diced
- ½ navel orange, juice and zest

- 2 tablespoons of garlic powder
- ½ cup of homemade low-sodium chicken stock
- Fine sea salt and freshly cracked black pepper (to taste)

Instructions:

- In a bowl, add the chicken thighs, orange juice, orange zest, garlic powder, sea salt and black pepper. Stir until well combined and allow to marinate.
- Press the "Sauté" setting on your Instant Pot and add the olive oil. Once hot, add the chicken thighs and sear for 2 minutes or until brown on both sides. Add the chicken stock and lock the lid. Cook at high pressure for 8 minutes.
- When the cooking is done, naturally release the pressure for 10 minutes, then quick release the remaining pressure. Carefully remove the lid.
- Preheat your broiler and transfer the chicken thighs to a baking sheet. Broil for 5 minutes or until crispy. Serve and enjoy!

Carne Asada Chicken Bowls
Time: 35 minutes   Servings: 4

Ingredients:

- 1 pound of boneless, skinless chicken thighs
- 3 tablespoons of extra-virgin olive oil
- 2 tablespoons of coconut aminos
- 3 tablespoons of freshly squeezed lime juice
- 1 teaspoon of fresh lime zest
- 4 medium garlic cloves, peeled and crushed
- 1 teaspoon of ground cumin

- 1 teaspoon of smoked or sweet paprika
- 1 teaspoon of ground coriander
- 1 teaspoon of cayenne pepper
- 1 cup of homemade low-sodium chicken broth
- 2 avocados (for serving)
- ½ cup of sour cream (for serving)
- Cauliflower rice (for serving)

Instructions:

- Add all the ingredients except for the avocados, cauliflower rice and sour cream inside your Instant Pot.
- Lock the lid and cook at high pressure for 25 minutes. When the cooking is done, naturally release the pressure for 5 minutes, then quick release the remaining pressure.
- Transfer the chicken to a cutting board and shred using two forks. Return to your Instant Pot and stir.
- Spoon some cauliflower rice onto bowls. Top with shredded chicken, liquid, avocados and sour cream.

Garlic Chicken and Radishes
Time: 35 minutes   Servings: 6

Ingredients:

- 6 boneless, skinless chicken breasts
- 4 tablespoons of unsalted butter
- 1 bunch of radishes, trimmed
- 1 cup of homemade low-sodium chicken broth

- 3 medium garlic cloves, minced
- 1 teaspoon of garlic powder
- 3 yellow onions, finely chopped
- Fine sea salt and freshly cracked black pepper (to taste)

Instructions:

- Season the chicken breasts with garlic powder, sea salt and freshly cracked black pepper.
- Press the "Sauté" setting on your Instant Pot and add the butter. Once melted, sear the chicken on both sides or until hot. Remove and set aside.
- Add the sliced onions and cook for 5 minutes, stirring frequently.
- Return the chicken along with the remaining ingredients. Lock the lid and cook at high pressure for 15 minutes. When the cooking is done, naturally release the pressure and remove the lid.Serve and enjoy!

Chicken Carnitas

Time: 30 minutes   Servings: 6

Ingredients:

- 1 pound of boneless, skinless chicken breasts
- ½ cup of homemade low-sodium chicken stock
- ¼ cup of freshly squeezed lime juice
- 4 medium garlic cloves, peeled and minced
- 1 medium onion, chopped
- 2 tablespoons of olive oil

- 1 teaspoon of chili powder
- 1 teaspoon of dried oregano
- 1 tablespoon of cumin
- 1 teaspoon of fine sea salt
- 1 teaspoon of freshly cracked black pepper

Instructions:

- In a small bowl, add the cumin, dried oregano, chili powder, sea salt and freshly cracked black pepper. Mix well.
- Press the "Sauté "setting on your Instant Pot and add the olive oil. Once hot, add the chopped onions and sauté for 3 minutes or until softened, stirring occasionally.
- Add the minced garlic and sauté for another minute.
- Pour in the chicken stock and lime juice. Stir well and add the chicken inside your Instant Pot.
- Lock the lid and cook at high pressure for 8 minutes. When the cooking is done, naturally release the pressure for 10 minutes, then quick release the remaining pressure. Carefully remove the lid.
- Transfer the chicken to a cutting board and shred using two forks. Return the shredded chicken to the liquid and stir until well coated. Serve and enjoy!

Creamy Italian Chicken Breasts

Time: 20 minutes   Servings: 4

Ingredients:

- 4 boneless, skinless chicken breasts
- 1 cup of homemade low-sodium chicken stock
- 1 teaspoon of garlic powder
- 1 teaspoon of Italian seasoning
- 1 teaspoon of freshly cracked black pepper

- 1 teaspoon of fine sea salt
- 1/3 cup of heavy cream
- 1/3 cup of roasted red peppers
- 1 tablespoon of basil pesto
- 1 tablespoon of arrowroot powder mixed with 1 tablespoon of water

Instructions:

- Add the chicken breasts, stock and all the seasonings inside your Instant Pot. Lock the lid and cook at high pressure for 8 minutes. When the cooking is done, naturally release the pressure for 5 minutes, then quick release the remaining pressure. Carefully remove the lid.
- Transfer the chicken to a cutting board and shred using two forks. Set aside.
- Press the "Sauté" setting on your Instant Pot and add the heavy cream, arrowroot powder mixture, roasted red peppers and basil pesto. Cook for 3 to 4 minutes or until thickened, stirring frequently. Return the shredded chicken to the cream. Serve and enjoy!

Chicken Parmesan

Time: 20 minutes   Servings: 4

Ingredients:

- 4 chicken cutlets
- 1 tablespoon of extra-virgin olive oil
- 2 garlic cloves, peeled and minced
- 3 tablespoons of parmesan cheese, grated
- 1 cup of prepared marinara sauce

- ½ teaspoon of fine sea salt
- ½ teaspoon of freshly cracked black pepper
- ½ cup of shredded mozzarella cheese
- Fine sea salt and freshly cracked black pepper (to taste)

Instructions:

- Press the "Sauté" function on your Instant Pot and add the olive oil. Once hot, add the garlic and sauté for 2 minutes or until golden brown.
- Stir in the marinara sauce, parmesan cheese, sea salt and freshly cracked black pepper.
- Place the chicken on top of the sauce. Lock the lid and cook at high pressure for 3 minutes. When the cooking is done, quick release the pressure and carefully remove the lid.
- Sprinkle the shredded mozzarella cheese. Cover the lid and sit for 5 minutes or until the cheese has melted. Serve and enjoy!

Cheesy Buffalo Stuffed Chicken Breasts

Time: 25 minutes   Servings: 4

Ingredients:

- 1 pound of boneless, skinless chicken breasts
- 4-ounces of cream cheese, softened
- 6 bacon slices, cooked and chopped
- ¾ cups of mozzarella cheese, shredded

- 1 cup of buffalo wings sauce
- 2 green onions, sliced
- Fine sea salt and freshly cracked black pepper (more or less to taste)

Instructions:

- In a bowl, add the green onions, bacon, mozzarella and cream cheese. Stir until well combined.
- Butterfly the chicken to make an insert for the stuffing.
- Spoon the mixture into the chicken and secure with toothpicks if necessary.
- Add the buffalo wing sauce along with the chicken inside your Instant Pot.
- Lock the lid and cook at high pressure for 15 minutes.
- When the cooking is done, naturally release the pressure for 5 minutes, then quick release the remaining pressure. Carefully remove the lid. Serve and enjoy!

Cheesy Asparagus Stuffed Chicken Breasts

Time: 25 minutes   Servings: 4

Ingredients:

- 1 pound of boneless, skinless chicken breasts
- Around 12 asparagus spears, ends trimmed
- 4 slices of mozzarella cheese
- 2 tablespoons of olive oil
- ½ teaspoon of garlic powder

- ½ teaspoon of sweet or smoked paprika
- ½ teaspoon of dried oregano
- ½ teaspoon of dried thyme
- Fine sea salt and freshly cracked black pepper (more or less to taste)

Instructions:

- In a small bowl, add the garlic powder, paprika, dried oregano, dried thyme, sea salt and freshly cracked black pepper. Mix well.
- Season the chicken breasts with the seasoning mixture.
- Add 1 cup of water and a trivet inside your Instant Pot.
- Butterfly the chicken to make an insert for the stuffing.
- Divide and stuff the chicken with the asparagus and mozzarella cheese.
- Place the chicken on top. Lock the lid and cook at high pressure for 15 minutes.
- When the cooking is done, naturally release the pressure for 5 minutes, then quick release the remaining pressure. Carefully remove the lid. Serve and enjoy!

Mushroom Stuffed Chicken Breasts

Time: 25 minutes   Servings: 4

Ingredients:

- 1 pound of boneless, skinless chicken breasts
- 1 to 1 ½ cup of mushrooms, finely chopped
- ¼ cup of celery, chopped

- ¼ cup of green onions, chopped
- 2 tablespoons of butter
- Fine sea salt and freshly cracked black pepper (more or less to taste)

Instructions:

- Press the "Sauté" setting on your Instant Pot and add the butter. Once hot, add the mushrooms and cook until brown, stirring occasionally. Transfer the mushrooms to a large bowl along with the celery and green onions. Stir until well combined.
- Add 1 cup of water and a trivet inside your Instant Pot.
- Butterfly the chicken to make an insert for the stuffing.
- Season the chicken with sea salt and black pepper.
- Divide and spoon the mushroom mixture into the chicken.
- Place the chicken on top of the trivet. Lock the lid and cook at high pressure for 15 minutes. When the cooking is done, naturally release the pressure and carefully remove the lid. Serve and enjoy!

Spinach Stuffed Chicken Breasts

Time: 20 minutes   Servings: 4

Ingredients:

- 1 pound of boneless, skinless chicken breasts
- 1 cup of frozen spinach, chopped
- ½ cup of feta cheese, crumbled
- 4-ounces of cream cheese, softened
- 1 medium garlic clove, peeled and crushed
- 1 teaspoon of fine sea salt
- 1 teaspoon of freshly cracked black pepper

Instructions:

- Butterfly the chicken to make an insert for the stuffing.
- In a bowl, add the spinach, feta cheese, cream cheese, crushed garlic, sea salt and freshly cracked black pepper. Stir until well combined.
- Carefully the stuffing into the chicken.
- Add 1 cup of water and a trivet inside your Instant Pot.
- Place the chicken on top. Lock the lid and cook at high pressure for 15 minutes.
- When the cooking is done, naturally release the pressure for 5 minutes, then quick release the remaining pressure. Carefully remove the lid. Serve and enjoy!

Crack Chicken

Time: 25 minutes   Servings: 4

Ingredients:

- 4 boneless, skinless chicken breasts
- 1 (8-ounce) package of cream cheese, softened
- 1 packet of ranch seasoning
- ½ cup of homemade low-sodium chicken stock
- 1 cup of cheddar cheese, shredded
- 6 medium slices of bacon, cooked and chopped
- Fine sea salt and freshly cracked black pepper (to taste)

Instructions:

- Press the "Sauté" setting on your Instant Pot and add all the ingredients except for the cheddar cheese and bacon. Lock the lid and cook at high pressure for 15 minutes. When the cooking is done, quick release the pressure and carefully remove the lid.
- Transfer the chicken to a cutting board and use two forks to shred.
- Press the "Sauté" feature on your Instant Pot and cook until the cheese has completely smoothen, stirring frequently.
- Return the shredded chicken and add the bacon and cheddar cheese. Cover and allow the cheese to melt. Turn off the "Sauté" setting. Serve and enjoy!

Easy Chicken Chili

Time: 30 minutes   Servings: 6

Ingredients:

- 1 pound of ground chicken
- 2 garlic cloves, minced
- ½ medium onion, finely chopped
- 1 (14-ounce) can of diced green chiles
- 1 (14-ounce) can of diced or crushed tomatoes
- 1 (6-ounce) can of tomato paste
- 1 tablespoon of unsweetened cocoa powder
- ½ cup of homemade low-sodium chicken stock
- 3 tablespoons of chili powder
- 2 teaspoons of smoked paprika
- Fine sea salt and freshly cracked black pepper (to taste)

Instructions:

- Press the "Sauté" function on your Instant Pot and add the olive oil. Once hot, add the chopped onions and garlic. Sauté for 30 seconds, stirring frequently.
- Add the ground chicken and cook until brown.
- Add the remaining ingredients and lock the lid. Cook at high pressure for 8 minutes. When the cooking is done, naturally release the pressure and carefully remove the lid.
- Press the "Sauté" setting on your Instant Pot and continue to cook until most of the liquid evaporates. Serve and enjoy!

State Fair Style Turkey Legs
Time: 50 minutes   Servings: 6

Ingredients:

- 6 turkey drumsticks
- 1 tablespoon of fine sea salt
- 1 teaspoon of freshly cracked black pepper
- ½ teaspoon of garlic powder
- ½ cup of water or chicken stock
- ½ cup of coconut aminos

Instructions:

- Season the turkey drumsticks with sea salt, black pepper and garlic powder.
- Add the chicken stock and coconut aminos. Give a good stir.
- Place the drumsticks inside the pot. Lock the lid and cook at high pressure for 20 minutes. When the cooking is done, naturally release the pressure for 15 minutes, then quick release the remaining pressure. Carefully remove the lid. Serve and enjoy!

Turkey Bolognese
Time: 45 minutes   Servings: 6

Ingredients:

- 2 pounds of ground turkey
- 1 (25-ounce) jar of marinara sauce
- 1 teaspoon of dried oregano
- 1 teaspoon of fine sea salt
- 1 large celery stalk, chopped
- 2 carrots, peeled and chopped
- 1 medium, finely chopped
- 3 medium garlic cloves, peeled and minced
- 1 sprig of fresh basil, finely chopped
- 3 tablespoons of extra-virgin olive oil
- 1 pound of zucchini, spiralized (for serving)

Instructions:

- Press the "Sauté" setting on your Instant Pot and add the olive oil. Once hot, add the chopped onions, minced garlic, carrot, celery and sea salt. Saute for 4 to 5 minutes or until softened, stirring occasionally.
- Add the ground turkey and cook for 10 minutes or until brown, stirring occasionally.
- Stir in the marinara sauce, dried oregano, and basil. Lock the lid and cook at high pressure for 20 minutes. When the cooking is done, naturally release the pressure for 10 minutes, then quick release the remaining pressure. Carefully remove the lid.
- Top the sauce on top of the spiralized zucchini. Serve and enjoy!

Turkey Keto Chili
Time: 30 minutes   Servings: 6

Ingredients:

- 1 pound of ground turkey
- 1 tablespoon of coconut oil or other cooking fat
- 1 medium onion, finely chopped
- 2 medium green or red bell peppers, seeds removed and chopped
- 3 medium carrots, peeled and sliced
- 3 celery stalks, chopped
- 3 medium garlic cloves, minced
- 1 (28-ounce) can of crushed tomatoes
- 1 (14.5-ounce) can of diced tomatoes
- ½ cup of homemade low-sodium chicken stock
- 3 to 4 tablespoons of chili powder
- 1 ½ teaspoon of ground cumin
- 1 teaspoon of fine sea salt
- 1 teaspoon of freshly cracked black pepper

Instructions:

- Press the "Sauté" setting on your Instant Pot and add the coconut oil. Once hot, add the ground turkey and continue to cook until brown, stirring occasionally.
- Add the chopped onions, bell peppers, sliced carrots, chopped celery and minced garlic. Sauté for 3 minutes, stirring occasionally.
- Add the diced tomatoes, crushed tomatoes, chicken stock, chili powder, ground cumin, sea salt and freshly cracked black pepper. Stir until well combined.
- Lock the lid and cook at high pressure for 15 minutes. When the cooking is done, quick release the pressure and carefully remove the lid.
- Stir the chili again and adjust the seasoning if necessary. Serve and enjoy!

Ground Turkey Tacos

Time: 12 minutes   Servings: 10

Ingredients:

- 1 ½ pound of ground turkey
- 2 tablespoons of extra-virgin olive oil
- 1 cup of chunky salsa
- 2 tablespoons of taco seasoning

- 1 (4-ounce) can of green chilies, undrained
- Fine sea salt and freshly cracked black pepper (to taste)
- Low-carb tortillas or lettuce leaves (for serving)

Instructions:

- Press the "Sauté" setting on your Instant Pot and add the olive oil. Once hot, add the ground turkey and cook until no longer pink, stirring occasionally.
- Add the chunky salsa, taco seasoning, can of green chilies, sea salt and freshly cracked black pepper.
- Lock the lid and cook at high pressure for 8 minutes. When the cooking is done, quick release the pressure and remove the lid.
- Press the "Sauté" setting on your Instant Pot and continue to cook until most of the liquid evaporates. Top the meat on top of tortillas or lettuce leaves. Serve and enjoy!

Turkey Chili Verde

Time: 43 minutes   Servings: 4

Ingredients:

- 1 ½ pound of ground turkey or shredded cooked turkey
- 1 large head of cauliflower, finely chopped
- 1 (12-ounce) jar of Mexican salsa verde
- ½ cup of homemade low-sodium chicken stock
- 1 (14.5-ounce) cans of diced tomatoes
- 2 tablespoons of extra-virgin olive oil or other cooking fat
- 1 yellow onion, finely chopped

- 2 poblano chilies, finely chopped
- 2 jalapeno peppers, finely chopped
- 2 serrano chilies, finely chopped
- 3 medium garlic cloves, minced
- 1 teaspoon of dried oregano
- 1 teaspoon of ground cumin
- ¼ teaspoon of cayenne pepper
- Fine sea salt and freshly cracked black pepper (to taste)

Instructions:

- Press the "Sauté" setting on your Instant Pot and add the olive oil. Once hot, add the turkey and cook until no longer pink, stirring frequently.
- Add the chopped onions and all the seasonings. Cook for another 5 minutes or until softened, stirring occasionally.
- Stir in the remaining ingredients. Lock the lid and cook at high pressure for 20 minutes.
- When the cooking is done, naturally release the pressure and carefully remove the lid.Serve and enjoy!

Turkey Breast with Gravy

Time: 1 hour   Servings: 8

Ingredients:

- 4 pounds of turkey breast
- 2 tablespoons of extra-virgin olive oil
- 1 tablespoon of smoked paprika
- 1 tablespoon of Italian seasoning

- 1 teaspoon of tarragon
- 2 medium garlic cloves, finely minced
- Fine sea salt and freshly cracked black pepper (to taste)
- ½ cup of homemade low-sodium chicken stock

Gravy Ingredients:

- 2 tablespoons of unsalted butter
- 2 tablespoons of almond flour

- ½ cup of homemade low-sodium chicken broth
- ½ cup of heavy cream

Instructions:

- Drizzle 1 tablespoon of olive oil on the turkey breasts. Add the remaining tablespoon inside your Instant Pot. Season with smoked paprika, Italian seasoning, tarragon, sea salt and freshly cracked black pepper.

- Press the "Sauté" setting on your Instant Pot. Once hot, add the turkey breasts and sear on both sides or until brown. Remove and set aside.
- Add the chicken stock inside your Instant Pot and place a trivet inside. Place the turkey on top. Lock the lid and cook at high pressure for 25 minutes.
- When the cooking is done, allow for a full natural release. Carefully remove the lid.
- Transfer the turkey to a cutting board and make even slices. Cover with a sheet of aluminum foil. Remove the trivet from inside your Instant Pot.
- Discard the liquid from your Instant Pot. Clean if necessary.
- Press the "Sauté" setting on your Instant Pot and add the butter. Once melted, whisk in the almond flour. Whisk in the chicken broth and heavy cream. Cook for 3 minutes or until the gravy has formed and thickened, stirring frequently.
- Spoon the gravy on top of the turkey slices. Serve and enjoy!

Turkey Meatballs
Time: 20 minutes   Servings: 4

Ingredients:

- 1 pound of ground turkey
- 1 large egg
- ¼ teaspoon of garlic powder
- ¼ teaspoon of dried oregano
- ½ teaspoon of fresh or dried thyme
- ½ teaspoon of fine sea salt
- ½ teaspoon of freshly cracked black pepper
- ¼ cup of extra-virgin olive oil

Instructions:

- In a large bowl, add the ground turkey, egg, garlic powder, dried oregano, thyme, sea salt and black pepper. Mix well using your hands. Form the mixture into meatballs.
- Press the "Sauté" setting on your Instant Pot and add the olive oil. Working in batches, add the meatballs and cook for 3 minutes per side or until brown.
- Transfer the meatballs to a plate lined with paper towels and continue to cook until most of the meatballs are done. Serve and enjoy!

Garlic-Herbed Butter Turkey Legs
Time: 50 minutes   Servings: 4

Ingredients:

- 4 turkey drumsticks
- ½ stick of unsalted butter
- 4 medium garlic cloves, minced
- ¼ to ½ cup of fresh herbs, finely chopped (parsley, thyme, rosemary, oregano, etc.)
- 1 teaspoon of fine sea salt
- 1 cup of water

Instructions:

- Add the turkey drumsticks and water inside your Instant Pot. Lock the lid and cook at high pressure for 20 minutes. When the cooking is done, naturally release the pressure and carefully remove the lid. Discard the water and set the turkey legs aside.
- Press the "Sauté" setting on your Instant Pot and add the butter. Once melted, add the minced garlic. Sauté for 1 minute or until fragrant, stirring frequently.
- Add the herbs and sauté for another 10 seconds. Spoon the herb butter on top of the turkey legs. Serve and enjoy!

Chicken Wings with Chili-Lime Butter Sauce
Time: 35 minutes   Servings: 4

Ingredients:

- 3 pounds of chicken wings
- 4 tablespoons of butter
- ½ cup of fresh cilantro, finely chopped
- 2 teaspoons of fresh lime zest
- 2 tablespoons of freshly squeezed lime juice
- 2 teaspoons of chili powder
- ½ teaspoon of cumin
- ½ teaspoon of garlic powder
- ½ cup of homemade low-sodium chicken stock
- Fine sea salt and freshly cracked black pepper (to taste)

Instructions:

- Season the chicken with sea salt and freshly cracked black pepper.
- Add the chicken wings inside your Instant Pot along with the chicken stock. Lock the lid and cook at high pressure for 8 minutes. When the cooking is done, naturally release the pressure for 10 minutes, then quick release the remaining pressure. Carefully remove the lid.
- Preheat your broiler and transfer to a baking sheet lined with aluminum foil. Place inside your broiler and broil for 5 minutes or until golden brown.
- Meanwhile, in a bowl, add the chopped cilantro, lime zest, lime juice, chili powder, cumin, garlic powder, and a pinch of sea salt and freshly cracked black pepper. Mix well.
- In a small saucepan over medium heat, add the butter. Once melted, stir in the lemon mixture and mix well. Spoon the sauce over the winks. Serve and enjoy!

Turkey Taco Skillet
Time: 25 minutes   Servings: 2

Ingredients:

- 1 pound of ground turkey
- 1 tablespoon of olive oil or coconut oil
- 1 red bell pepper, seeds removed and finely chopped
- 1 teaspoon of onion powder
- 1 teaspoon of garlic powder
- 1 teaspoon of dried oregano
- 1 teaspoon of smoked paprika
- 1 teaspoon of ground cumin
- ½ cup of shredded Mexican cheese
- Fine sea salt and freshly cracked black pepper (to taste)

Instructions:

- Press the "Sauté" setting on your Instant Pot and add the oil. Once hot, add the ground turkey and all the seasonings. Sauté until brown.
- Add the bell pepper and continue to cook until softened, stirring occasionally.
- Turn off the "Sauté" setting and sprinkle the cheese and cook until melted. Serve and enjoy!

Turkey Stuffed Bell Peppers
Time: 50 minutes   Servings: 4

Ingredients:

- 4 large bell peppers, tops removed and inner portions scooped out
- 1 pound of ground turkey
- 1 cup of cauliflower rice
- ¾ cups of marinara sauce
- ¼ cup of onions, finely chopped
- 3 tablespoons of fresh parsley, finely chopped
- ¼ cup of parmesan cheese, finely grated
- ¼ cup of mozzarella cheese, shredded
- 2 teaspoons of tomato paste
- ¼ cup of mozzarella cheese
- 1 large egg, beaten
- 2 medium garlic cloves, minced
- 1 cup of water
- Fine sea salt and freshly cracked black pepper (to taste)

Instructions:

- In a large bowl, add the ground turkey, cauliflower rice, ¼ cup of the marinara sauce, chopped onions, parmesan cheese, fresh parsley, sea salt, black pepper, garlic, egg and tomato paste. Mix until well combined
- Divide and stuff the mixture into each bell peppers.
- Add 1 cup of water and a trivet inside your Instant Pot. Place the bell peppers on top and top with the marinara sauce. Lock the lid and cook at high pressure for 15 minutes.
- Sprinkle the mozzarella cheese and cover. Allow the cheese to melt. Serve and enjoy!

Shredded Buffalo Chicken
Time: 15 minutes   Servings: 6

Ingredients:

- 2 pounds of boneless, skinless chicken breasts
- 1 cup of homemade low-sodium chicken stock
- 4 tablespoons of unsalted butter
- ½ bottle of Frank's Red Hot Sauce
- 2 teaspoons of apple cider vinegar
- 2 tablespoons of tabasco sauce

Instructions:

- Add the chicken breasts and chicken stock inside your Instant Pot. Lock the lid and cook at high pressure for 15 minutes. When the cooking is done, quick release the pressure and carefully remove the lid.
- Transfer the chicken to a cutting board and shred using two forks. Set aside.
- Press the "Sauté" setting on your Instant Pot and add the butter, hot sauce, apple cider vinegar and tabasco sauce. Stir until well combined and until the butter has melted.
- Stir the shredded chicken inside your Instant Pot until well coated with the buffalo sauce.

Simple Duck Legs
Time: 2 hours   Servings: 4

Ingredients:

- 4 duck legs, drumsticks or thighs
- 2 tablespoons of extra-virgin olive oil
- 1 tablespoon of fine sea salt
- 4 fresh sprigs of thyme
- 2 bay leaves
- 1 teaspoon of freshly cracked black pepper

Instructions:

- Season the duck legs with sea salt and freshly cracked black pepper
- Press the "Sauté" setting on your Instant Pot and add the extra-virgin olive oil. Once hot, add the duck legs and sear until golden brown on both sides.
- Pour in 1 cup of chicken stock, fresh sprigs of thyme and bay leaves. Lock the lid and cook at high pressure for 40 minutes. When the cooking is done, naturally release the pressure and remove the lid. Serve and enjoy!

Duck Noodle Soup with Bamboo Shoots
Time: 1 hour and 20 minutes   Servings: 8

Ingredients:

- 3 pounds of boneless, duck breasts, cut into large pieces
- 1 large onion, finely chopped
- 2-inch piece of fresh ginger, peeled and minced
- 1 shallot, finely chopped
- 2 bags of dried bamboo shoot, soaked in water for an hour
- ½ green cabbage, finely sliced
- 1 medium onion, finely chopped
- 4 medium garlic cloves, peeled and minced
- ¼ cup of fresh cilantro, chopped
- 2 tablespoons of coconut aminos
- 1 tablespoon of freshly squeezed lime juice
- 4 tablespoons of extra-virgin olive oil
- 7 cups of homemade low-sodium chicken stock

Instructions:

- Press the "Sauté" setting on your Instant Pot and add the olive oil. Once hot, add the chopped onions, shallots, garlic and ginger. Sauté for 4 minutes or until translucent, stirring occasionally. Remove and set aside.
- Add the duck pieces and cook until evenly brown. Return the onion contents and stir in the remaining ingredients.
- Lock the lid and cook at high pressure for 40 minutes. When the cooking is done, allow for a full natural release method. Serve and enjoy!

Duck Beer Chili
Time: 50 minutes   Servings: 8

Ingredients:

- 2 pounds of boneless, duck breasts
- 1 teaspoon of fine sea salt
- 1 cup of white onion, finely chopped
- 5 garlic cloves, peeled and minced
- 1 (28-ounce) can of fire-roasted diced tomatoes
- 1 (6-ounce) can of tomato paste
- 12-ounces of low-carb beer
- 1 tablespoon of Worcestershire sauce
- 2 celery stalks, chopped
- 1 green bell pepper, seeds removed and chopped
- 4 medium bacon strips, roughly chopped
- 2 tablespoons of chili powder
- 2 teaspoons of ground cumin
- 2 teaspoons of dried oregano
- 2 tablespoons of smoked or sweet paprika

Instructions:

- Press the "Sauté" function on your Instant Pot and add the olive oil. Add the duck and sear for 4 minutes or until golden brown. Remove the duck and set aside.
- Add the chopped onions and minced garlic. Sauté for 5 minutes or until softened, stirring occasionally.
- Return the duck to the inner pot along with the remaining ingredients. Lock the lid and cook at high pressure for 30 minutes. When the cooking is done, naturally release the pressure and remove the lid.
- Transfer the duck breasts to a cutting board and shred using two forks. Return to the chili and stir. Adjust the seasoning if necessary. Serve and enjoy!

Duck Ragu

Time: 1 hour   Servings: 2

Ingredients:

- 2 skin-on, bone in duck legs
- 1 pound of zucchini, spiralized
- 2 garlic cloves, crushed
- 2 fresh sprigs of rosemary
- 1 teaspoon of fine sea salt
- 1 celery rib, chopped
- 1 teaspoon of freshly cracked black pepper
- 1 small red onion, finely chopped
- 3 tablespoons of tomato paste
- 3 tablespoons of red wine
- 2 star anise
- 2 tablespoons of extra-virgin olive oil
- 3 cups of homemade low-sodium chicken stock

Instructions:

- Press the "Sauté" setting on your Instant Pot and add the olive oil. Once hot, add the duck legs and brown for 10 minutes. Turn off the "Sauté" setting.
- In a food processor, add the celery, star anise, onions and garlic. Pulse until fine and add inside your Instant Pot.
- Add the remaining ingredients except for the zucchini inside your Instant Pot. Lock the lid and cook at high pressure for 45 minutes. When the cooking is done, naturally release the pressure and carefully remove the lid. Remove and set the duck legs aside.
- Press the "Sauté" setting on your Instant Pot and cook until the liquid reduced. Serve the duck legs with the liquid and zucchini noodles. Serve and enjoy!

Duck Breast with Blackberry Sauce

Time: 50 minutes   Servings: 2

Ingredients:

- 2 bone-in, skin-on duck legs
- ½ cup of dry red wine
- ½ cup of homemade low-sodium veal stock, mushroom stock or chicken stock
- 6 tablespoons of unsalted, butter
- 1 shallot, finely chopped
- ½ cup of shiitake mushrooms, chopped
- ¼ cup of fresh parsley, finely chopped
- 1 teaspoon of fine sea salt
- 1 teaspoon of freshly cracked black pepper
- ¼ cup of blackberries

Instructions:

- Press the "Sauté" setting on your Instant Pot and add 3 tablespoons of butter. Once melted, add the duck legs and sear until brown on both sides. Remove and set aside.
- Add the shallot and mushrooms. Sauté for 4 minutes or until softened, stirring occasionally.
- Return the duck legs and add the dry red wine, stock, salt and black pepper. Lock the lid and cook at high pressure for 30 minutes. When the cooking is done, naturally release the pressure and remove the lid.
- Remove the duck legs and set aside. Press the "Sauté" setting on your Instant Pot and add the fresh parsley, remaining tablespoons of butter and blackberries. Continue to cook until the blackberries have infused with the liquid and thickens. Spoon the sauce over the duck legs. Serve and enjoy!

Whole Duck

Time: 1 hour and 30 minutes   Servings: 10

Ingredients:

- 1 (5 to 6 pound) whole duck
- 1 cup of homemade low-sodium chicken stock
- 1 medium sweet onion, quartered
- 4 tablespoons of extra-virgin olive oil
- 2 fresh sprigs of thyme
- 2 tablespoons of fine sea salt

- 1 tablespoon of smoked or regular paprika
- 1 tablespoon of dried oregano
- 2 tablespoons of garlic powder
- 1 teaspoon of freshly cracked black pepper

Instructions:

- Season the whole duck with the sea salt, paprika, dried oregano, garlic powder and freshly cracked black pepper.
- Place the thyme sprigs and onion inside the cavity of the duck.
- Press the "Sauté" function on your Instant Pot and add the olive oil. Once hot, add the whole duck and sear for 6 minutes on both sides or until golden brown.
- Pour in the 1 cup of chicken stock and lock the lid. Cook at high pressure for 40 minutes. When the cooking is done, naturally release the pressure and remove the lid.
- Preheat your broiler and line a baking sheet with aluminum foil. Place the whole duck on the baking sheet.
- Place the baking sheet inside your broiler and broil for 5 minutes or until the skin is brown and crispy. Serve and enjoy!

Barbecue Duck

Time: 12 hours and 30 minutes   Servings: 12

Ingredients:

- 1 (5 pound) whole duck, quartered
- 4 large carrots, roughly chopped
- 1 pound of butternut squash, cubed
- 1 head of garlic, peeled
- 1 onion, sliced
- 2 tablespoons of paprika
- 2 tablespoons of chili powder
- 1 tablespoon of Worcestershire sauce
- 2 teaspoons of cayenne pepper
- 1 teaspoon of freshly cracked black pepper
- 1 tablespoon of apple cider vinegar
- 3 cups of homemade low-sodium chicken stock
- 2 teaspoons of xanthan gum

Instructions:

- Season the whole duck with the paprika, chili powder, cayenne pepper, sea salt, and black pepper.
- Add the cubed butternut squash, chopped carrots, sliced onions and whole garlic cloves inside your Instant Pot. Place the whole duck on top of the vegetables. Pour in the ½ cup of chicken stock and apple cider vinegar into the inner pot.
- Press the "Sauté" function on your Instant Pot and cook for 50 minutes. When the cooking is done, naturally release the pressure and remove the lid. Transfer the duck to a serving platter and carve using two forks. Strain the liquid from inside your Instant Pot. Press the "Sauté" setting on your Instant Pot and sprinkle with the xanthan gum. Cook until thickens, stirring occasionally.
- Return the duck to the liquid and stir until well combined with the liquid. Serve and enjoy!

Duck Bourguignonne

Time: 2 hours   Servings: 8

Ingredients:

- 2 pounds of boneless, skinless duck breasts, cut into 2-inch pieces
- 1 pound of mushrooms, chopped
- 2 cups of cauliflower florets
- 3 carrots, peeled and cut into bite-sized pieces
- 2 teaspoons of fine sea salt
- 2 teaspoons of freshly cracked black pepper
- 6 medium slices of bacon, roughly chopped
- 3 tablespoons of extra-virgin olive oil
- 1 large red onion, finely chopped
- 4 medium garlic cloves, finely minced
- 3 cups of dry red wine
- 3 cups of homemade low-sodium chicken stock
- 1 (6-ounce) can of tomato paste

Instructions:

- Press the "Sauté" setting on your Instant Pot and add the chopped bacon. Cook until the bacon is brown and crispy, stirring occasionally. Transfer the bacon to a plate lined with paper towels.
- Add the olive oil and duck pieces. Cook until brown, stirring occasionally.
- Add the onions and sauté for another 3 to 4 minutes, stirring occasionally.
- Add the remaining ingredients and lock the lid. Cook at high pressure for 50 minutes. When the cooking is done naturally release the pressure and remove the lid. Serve and enjoy!

White Chicken Chili

Time: 45 minutes   Servings: 4

Ingredients:

- 1 ½ pound of boneless, skinless chicken breasts, cut into large pieces
- 6 cups of homemade low-sodium chicken broth
- 1 (14.5-ounce) can of diced tomatoes
- 2 cups of salsa verde
- 2 teaspoons of ground cumin
- 1 teaspoon of fine sea salt
- ½ teaspoon of freshly cracked black pepper
- 2 tablespoons of extra-virgin olive oil

Instructions:

- Press the "Sauté" function on your Instant Pot and add the olive oil.
- Once hot, add the chicken pieces and cook until lightly brown. Turn off "Sauté" function and add the chicken stock, salsa verde, diced tomatoes, ground cumin, sea salt and freshly cracked black pepper. Stir until well combined.
- Lock the lid and cook at high pressure for 8 minutes. When the cooking is done, quick release the pressure and remove the lid. Adjust the seasoning if necessary. Serve and enjoy!

Part 4: Beef, Pork and Lamb Recipes

Killer Baby Back Ribs
Time: 45 minutes   Servings: 4

Ingredients:

- 1 rack baby back ribs
- 2 Tablespoons soy sauce
- 2 cups beef broth
- 2 Tablespoons granulated Splenda
- 2 Tablespoons coconut oil
- 3 Tablespoons fresh ginger, grated
- 4 garlic cloves, minced
- 1 Tablespoon chili powder

- 1 Tablespoon paprika
- 1 teaspoon ground mustard
- 1 teaspoon low-carb brown sugar
- 1 teaspoon cayenne pepper
- 1 teaspoon onion powder
- 1 teaspoon salt (to taste)
- 1 teaspoon fresh ground black pepper (to taste)

Instructions:

1. In a small bowl, combine ginger, chili powder, paprika, ground mustard, cayenne pepper, onion powder, salt and pepper. Stir well.
2. Add Splenda, brown sugar. Stir well.
3. Rinse the ribs. (You want ribs slightly damp so seasoning will cling.)
4. Rub seasoning mix on both sides of ribs. Place on a flat baking sheet.
5. Pre-heat oven to a broil. Place baking sheet under broiler. Broil 5 minutes per side.
6. Press Sauté mode on Instant Pot. Heat coconut oil. Add garlic and ginger. Cook for 1 minute.
7. Add soy sauce and beef broth. Boil for 15 seconds. Stir well.
8. Press Keep Warm/Cancel setting to end Sauté mode.
9. Slice up the rack of ribs into chunks of 4-5 ribs. Place in Instant Pot.
10. Close and seal lid. Press Manual button. Cook on High Pressure for 35 minutes.
11. When done, release the pressure quickly or naturally. Open the lid with care. Serve.

Juicy Brisket
Time: 50 minutes   Servings: 5

Ingredients:

- 2 pounds of brisket
- 2 Tablespoons coconut oil
- 8-ounces low-carb beer
- 2 Tablespoons soy sauce
- 2 Tablespoons Worcestershire sauce

- 1 Tablespoon dry mustard
- 3 Tablespoons tomato paste
- 2 shallots, thinly sliced
- 1 teaspoon of salt (to taste)
- 1 teaspoon fresh ground black pepper (to taste)

Instructions:

1. In a large Ziploc bag, add all the ingredients. Massage the ingredients.
2. Allow to marinate for 2 hours, up to 12 hours.
3. When ready to cook, transfer all ingredients to Instant Pot.
4. Close and seal lid. Press Manual setting. Cook on High Pressure for 40 minutes.
5. Once done, quick-release or naturally release the pressure. Open the lid with care.
6. Press Sauté mode. Cook until all the liquid evaporates.
7. Remove the brisket. Let it rest for 5 – 15 minutes before slicing. Serve and enjoy!

Contest-Winning Lamb Curry
Time: 40 minutes   Servings: 4

Ingredients:

- 1 pound skinless, boneless lamb
- 1 (8-ounce) can diced tomatoes
- 1 Tablespoon fresh ginger, grated
- 4 garlic cloves, minced
- 1 chili, minced
- ½ cup Greek yogurt

- 1 shallot, chopped
- 1 teaspoon ground cumin
- 1 teaspoon turmeric powder
- ¼ cup fresh cilantro, chopped
- 1 teaspoon salt (to taste)
- 1 teaspoon fresh ground black pepper (to taste)

Instructions:

1. Rinse the lamb, pat dry. Cut into chunks.

2. In a large glass dish, combine all the ingredients. Stir well. Cover with plastic wrap. Place glass dish in refrigerator. Allow to marinate for 2 – 8 hours.
3. When ready to cook, transfer lamb mixture to Instant Pot.
4. Close and seal lid. Press Manual button. Cook on High Pressure for 30 minutes.
5. Release pressure naturally when done. Open the lid with care.
6. Press Sauté button and boil until sauce has thickened. Serve.

Flavorsome Pulled Pork
Time: 45 minutes   Servings: 4

Ingredients:

- 3 pounds boneless pork shoulder
- 2 Tablespoons coconut oil
- 1 teaspoon onion powder
- 1 teaspoon garlic powder
- 1 Tablespoon paprika
- 1 cup beef broth
- 1 teaspoon salt (to taste)
- 1 teaspoon fresh ground black pepper (to taste)

Barbeque Sauce Ingredients:

- 3 Tablespoons low-sugar ketchup
- 4 Tablespoons granulated Splenda
- ¼ cup yellow mustard
- 2 teaspoons hot sauce
- 3 Tablespoons apple cider vinegar

Instructions:

1. In a small bowl, combine onion powder, garlic powder, paprika, salt and pepper. Mix well. Rub seasoning on pork shoulder.
2. Press Sauté mode on Instant Pot. Heat coconut oil. Sear all sides of pork shoulder.
3. In another bowl, combine barbecue sauce ingredients. Stir well.
4. Press Keep Warm/Cancel setting to end Sauté mode.
5. Add the barbecue sauce and beef broth to Instant Pot. Stir well.
6. Close and seal lid. Press Manual button. Cook on high pressure for 35 minutes.
7. Quick-release or naturally release pressure when done. Open the lid with care.
8. Use two forks to pull pork apart.
9. Press Sauté button. Simmer until sauce reduced and clings to pork.
10. Press Keep Warm/Cancel button. Serve.

Super Yummy Pork Chops
Time: 25 minutes   Servings: 4

Ingredients:

- 4 boneless pork chops
- 2 Tablespoons coconut oil
- 2 cups beef broth
- 4 garlic cloves, minced
- 1 teaspoon nutmeg
- 1 teaspoon paprika
- 1 teaspoon onion powder
- 1 teaspoon salt
- 1 teaspoon fresh ground black pepper

Instructions:

1. Season the pork chops with spices listed. Press Sauté button on Instant Pot. Heat the coconut oil. Sear pork chops for 2 minutes per side.
2. Press Keep Warm/Cancel button to end Sauté mode. Pour in beef broth.
3. Close and seal lid. Press Poultry button on control panel. Cook for 15 minutes.
4. Quick-release the pressure when done. Open the lid with care. Serve.

Hearty Lemon & Garlic Pork
Time: 25 minutes   Servings: 4

Ingredients:

- 4 pork chops, boneless
- 2 cups beef broth
- 3 Tablespoons ghee, melted
- 3 Tablespoons coconut oil
- 1 teaspoon salt
- 1 teaspoon fresh ground black pepper
- Zest and juice from 2 lemons
- 6 garlic cloves, minced
- ¼ cup fresh parsley, chopped

Instructions:

1. Season the pork chops with salt and pepper, lemon juice and zest.
2. Press the Sauté button on your Instant Pot. Heat coconut oil.
3. Sauté garlic for 1 minute. Add pork chops. Sear for 2 minutes per side.
4. Press the Keep Warm/Cancel button to end Sauté mode. Add ghee and beef broth to the Instant Pot. Close and seal lid. Press Poultry button. Cook for 15 minutes.
5. Quick-release pressure when done. Open the lid with care. Stir ingredients. Serve.

Tasty Thai Beef
Time: 30 minutes   Servings: 6

Ingredients:

- 1 pound of beef, cut into strips
- 1 green bell pepper, chopped
- 1 red bell pepper, chopped
- Zest and juice from 1 lemon
- 2 cups beef broth
- 2 teaspoons ginger, grated
- 4 garlic cloves, minced
- 2 Tablespoons coconut oil
- 1 Tablespoon coconut amino
- 1 cup roasted pecans
- 1 teaspoon salt
- 1 teaspoon fresh ground black pepper

Instructions:

1. Press Sauté button on Instant Pot. Heat the coconut oil.
2. Sauté garlic and ginger for 1 minute. Add beef strips. Sear 1-2 minutes per side.
3. Add bell peppers. Add salt and pepper.
4. Continue cooking until meat is no longer pink.
5. Add coconut amino, pecans, zest and juice from lemon, beef broth. Stir well.
6. Close and seal lid. Press Manual setting. Cook at High Pressure for 15 minutes.
7. Release pressure naturally when done. Open the lid with care.
8. Let it sit for 5 – 10 minutes. Serve.

Flavorful Beef and Tomato Stuffed Squash
Time: 30 minutes   Servings: 4

Ingredients:

- 1 pound of beef, chopped into chunks
- 1 pound butternut squash, peeled and chopped
- 2 Tablespoons coconut oil
- 2 Tablespoons ghee, melted
- 1 green bell pepper, chopped
- 1 yellow bell pepper, chopped
- 2 (14-ounce) cans diced tomatoes
- 4 garlic cloves, minced
- 1 yellow or red onion, chopped
- 1 Tablespoon fresh thyme, chopped
- 1 Tablespoon fresh rosemary, chopped
- 2 Tablespoons fresh parsley, chopped
- 1 teaspoon cayenne pepper
- 1 teaspoon salt
- 1 teaspoon fresh ground black pepper

Instructions:

1. Press Sauté button on Instant Pot. Heat the coconut oil.
2. Add onion and garlic. Sweat for 2 minutes.
3. Add beef chunks, butternut squash, and bell peppers.
4. Sauté until meat is no longer pink and vegetables have softened.
5. Press Keep Warm/Cancel button to end Sauté mode.
6. Add melted ghee, tomatoes, thyme, rosemary, parsley, cayenne pepper, salt and pepper. Stir well. Close and seal lid. Press Manual button. Cook at High Pressure for 20 minutes.
7. Quick-release the pressure when done.. Open the lid with care. Stir ingredients. Adjust the seasoning if needed. Serve.

Gratifying Meatloaf
Time: 35 minutes   Servings: 4

Ingredients:

- 3 pounds lean ground beef
- 4 garlic cloves, minced
- 1 yellow onion, chopped
- 1 cup mushrooms, chopped

- 3 large eggs
- ½ cup almond flour
- ¼ cup parmesan cheese, grated
- ¼ cup mozzarella cheese, grated
- ¼ cup fresh parsley, chopped

- 2 Tablespoons sugar-free ketchup
- 2 Tablespoons coconut oil
- 2 teaspoons salt
- 2 teaspoons black pepper
- 2 cups of water

Instructions:

1. Cover trivet with aluminum foil.
2. In a large bowl, add and mix all the ingredients (excluding the water) until well combined. Form into a meatloaf. Pour the water in your Instant Pot. Place trivet inside.
3. Place meatloaf on trivet.
4. Close and seal lid. Press Manual button. Cook at High-Pressure for 25 minutes.
5. Release pressure naturally when done.. Open the lid with care.
6. Let the meatloaf rest for 5 minutes before slicing and serve.

Lavender Lamb Chops
Time: 25 minutes   Servings: 2

Ingredients:

- 2 lamb chops, boneless
- 2 Tablespoons ghee, melted
- 1 Tablespoon lavender, chopped
- 2 Tablespoons coconut oil
- 2 Tablespoons fresh rosemary, chopped
- Zest and juice from 1 orange

- Zest and juice from 1 lime
- 1 teaspoon garlic powder
- 1 teaspoon salt
- 1 teaspoon fresh ground black pepper
- 2 cups of water

Instructions:

1. Cover trivet with aluminum foil.
2. Press Sauté button on Instant Pot. Heat the coconut oil.
3. Sear lamb chops for 2 minutes per side. Remove and set aside.
4. Press Keep Warm/Cancel button to end Sauté mode.
5. In a bowl, add and mix the ghee, lavender, rosemary, orange juice, orange zest, lime juice, lime zest, and seasonings.
6. Pour 2 cups of water in Instant Pot. Place trivet inside. Set lamb chops on top.
7. Close and seal lid. Press Manual button. Cook at High Pressure for 15 minutes.
8. Quick-release the pressure when done. Open the lid with care. Serve.

Lovely Ginger Beef and Kale
Time: 35 minutes   Servings: 4

Ingredients:

- 1 pound beef, cut into chunks
- 1 bunch of kale, stemmed and chopped
- ½ pound mushrooms, sliced
- 2 cups beef broth
- 1 red onion, chopped
- 4 garlic cloves, minced

- 2 Tablespoons fresh ginger, grated
- 2 Tablespoons coconut oil
- 1 teaspoon paprika
- 1 teaspoon salt
- 1 teaspoon fresh ground black pepper

Instructions:

1. Press Sauté button on Instant Pot. Heat the coconut oil.
2. Add onions and garlic. Sweat for 1 minute.
3. Add beef chunks. Sauté until meat is no longer pink.
4. Press Keep Warm/Cancel setting to end Sauté mode.
5. Add remaining ingredients. Stir well.
6. Close and seal lid. Press Manual button. Cook at High Pressure for 25 minutes.
7. When the timer beeps, quick-release or naturally release pressure. Open the lid with care. Stir ingredients. Adjust seasoning if necessary. Serve.

Extraordinary Pork Roast
Time: 40 minutes   Servings: 4

Ingredients:

- 2 pounds pork roast
- 1 head cauliflower, chopped into florets
- 1 pound mushrooms, thinly sliced
- 2 Tablespoons coconut oil
- 1 onion, chopped

- 4 garlic cloves, minced
- 2 celery stalks, chopped
- 1 teaspoon salt
- 1 teaspoon fresh ground black pepper
- 2 cups beef broth

Instructions:

1. Press Sauté button on Instant Pot. Heat the coconut oil.
2. Sauté onion and garlic for 1 minute. Season pork roast with salt and pepper. Sear on all sides.
3. Add cauliflower, mushrooms, and celery. Pour in beef broth. Stir.
4. Close and seal lid. Press Manual button. Cook at High Pressure for 30 minutes.
5. Release pressure naturally when done.. Open the lid with care. Stir ingredients.
6. Remove from Instant Pot. Let it sit for 5 – 10 minutes before slicing. Serve.

Remarkable Apple Cider Pork Loin
Time: 40 minutes   Servings: 4

Ingredients:

- 4 pound pork loin
- 2 Tablespoons coconut oil
- 1 onion, sliced
- 4 garlic cloves, minced

- 1 cup apple cider
- 1 teaspoon salt
- 1 teaspoon fresh ground black pepper

Instructions:

1. Press Sauté mode on Instant Pot. Heat the coconut oil.
2. Season pork loin with salt and pepper. Sear all sides.
3. Press Keep Warm/Cancel button to end Sauté mode. Pour in apple cider.
4. Close and seal lid. Press Manual button. Cook at High Pressure 30 minutes.
5. Quick-Release the pressure once done. Open the lid with care.
6. Let the roast rest for 5 – 10 minutes before slicing. Serve.

Awe-Inspiring Lamb Roast
Time: 40 minutes   Servings: 4

Ingredients:

- 5 pound boneless leg of lamb, chopped
- 2 cups beef or vegetable broth
- 2 Tablespoons coconut oil
- 1 broccoli head, chopped into florets
- 1 onion, chopped
- 4 garlic cloves, minced

- 1 Tablespoon balsamic vinegar
- 1 teaspoon salt
- 1 teaspoon fresh ground black pepper
- 1 teaspoon fresh ginger, grated
- 1 teaspoon fresh thyme, chopped
- 1 Tablespoon fresh rosemary, chopped

Instructions:

1. Press Sauté button on Instant Pot. Heat the coconut oil.
2. Add the onion, garlic, ginger, thyme, rosemary. Sweat for 1 minute.
3. Season lamb with salt and pepper. Sear on all sides.
4. Press Keep Warm/Cancel button to end Sauté mode.
5. Add balsamic vinegar and beef broth. Stir well.
6. Close and seal cover. Press Manual switch. Cook at High Pressure for 30 minutes.
7. Quick-Release the pressure when done. Open the lid with care.
8. Let the roast rest for 5 – 10 minutes before slicing. Serve.

Melt-in-Your-Mouth Salisbury Steak
Time: 35 minutes   Servings: 4

Steak Ingredients:

- 2 pounds lean ground beef
- 1 Tablespoon coconut oil

- ½ yellow onion, diced
- 2 garlic cloves, minced

- 1 Tablespoon bread crumbs
- 1 egg
- ¼ cup coconut flour
- ¼ cup beef broth

- 1 Tablespoon Worcestershire sauce
- 1 Tablespoon fresh parsley, chopped
- 1 teaspoon salt
- 1 teaspoon fresh ground black pepper

Gravy Ingredients:

- 2 Tablespoons ghee, melted
- 2 cups mushrooms, sliced
- 1 onion, sliced
- ½ cup beef broth
- ¼ cup sour cream

- 2 Tablespoons fresh parsley, chopped
- 1 Tablespoon tomato paste
- 1 teaspoon Worcestershire sauce
- 1 teaspoon salt
- 1 teaspoon fresh ground black pepper

Instructions:

1. In a large bowl, mix steak ingredients, except coconut oil.
2. Shape into round patties, ¼ inch thick. Set aside.
3. Press Sauté button on Instant Pot. Heat the coconut oil.
4. Cook patties 2 minutes per side, until golden brown.
5. Remove patties. Set aside. Heat the ghee. Add gravy ingredients. Stir well.
6. Press Keep Warm/Cancel button to end Sauté mode. Return patties to Instant Pot.
7. Close and seal cover. Press Manual switch. Cook at High Pressure for 25 minutes.
8. Quick-Release the pressure when done. Open the lid with care. Serve.

Steak Chili

Time: 1 hour and 15 minutes   Servings: 8

Ingredients:

- 3 pounds of beef chuck roast, cut into 1-inch cubes
- 2 tablespoons of extra-virgin olive oil
- 1 large onion, finely chopped
- 3 medium garlic cloves, peeled and crushed
- 2 jalapeno peppers, seeds removed and chopped
- ¼ cup of chili powder

- 2 tablespoons of ground cumin
- 1 tablespoon of dried oregano
- 1 cup of homemade low-sodium beef broth
- 1 (4-ounce) can of chopped green chilies
- 1 (28-ounce) can of diced tomatoes
- 1 teaspoon of fine sea salt
- 1 teaspoon of freshly cracked black pepper

Instructions:

- Press the "Sauté" setting on your Instant Pot and add the olive oil. Once hot and working in batches, add the beef pieces and cook until brown. Transfer to a plate and set aside.
- Add the chopped onions, garlic and jalapeno. Sauté for 5 minutes or until softened, stirring frequently.
- Add the dried oregano, ground cumin, chili powder, sea salt and freshly cracked black pepper. Sauté for 30 seconds to release the aroma, stirring frequently.
- Return the beef pieces to your Instant Pot and add the remaining ingredients. Lock the lid and cook at high pressure for 12 minutes. When the cooking is done, naturally release the pressure and carefully remove the lid. Serve and enjoy!

Salisbury Steak

Time: 35 minutes   Servings: 6

Steak Ingredients:

- 1 ½ pound of ground beef
- 1 large egg yolk
- 3 tablespoons of milk

- ½ teaspoon of fine sea salt
- ½ teaspoon of freshly cracked black pepper
- 2 tablespoons of olive oil

Sauce Ingredients:

- 1 cup of brown or cremini mushrooms, sliced
- 1 small onion, sliced
- 1 ½ cup of homemade low-sodium beef broth
- 1-ounce package of dry brown gravy mix
- 1 tablespoon of tomato paste
- 1 tablespoon of Dijon mustard

- 2 tablespoons of fresh parsley, finely chopped
- 1 tablespoon of Worcestershire sauce
- 2 tablespoons of arrowroot powder mixed with 4 tablespoons of water
- Fine sea salt and freshly cracked black pepper (to taste)

Instructions:

- In a large bowl, add all the steak ingredients (except for the olive oil) and stir until well combined. Form the mixture into 6 beef patties.
- Press the "Sauté" setting on your Instant Pot and add the olive oil. Working in batches, add the beef patties and sear for 3 minutes per side. Remove and set aside.
- Add the sliced mushrooms and onions inside your Instant Pot. Place the beef patties on top of the mushrooms.
- Add the remaining ingredients except for the arrowroot powder. Lock the lid and cook at high pressure for 18 minutes. When the cooking is done, manually release the pressure and carefully remove the lid. Remove the patties.
- Press the "Sauté" setting on your Instant Pot and stir in the arrowroot powder mixture. Continue to cook until the liquid thickens, stirring occasionally. Return the patties to the liquid and spoon the sauce on top. Serve the Salisbury steak with mashed cauliflower.

Keto Beef Stroganoff

Time: 40 minutes   Servings: 4

Ingredients:

- 1 brown onion, finely sliced
- 2 medium garlic cloves, crushed
- 2 medium slices of bacon, roughly chopped
- 1 pound of sirloin steak, thinly sliced into strips
- 1 teaspoon of smoked paprika
- 3 tablespoons of tomato paste
- 2 ½ cups of mushrooms, chopped
- 1 cup of homemade low-sodium beef broth
- ¼ cup of sour cream
- 1 tablespoon of olive oil
- Fine sea salt and freshly cracked black pepper (to taste)
- Zoodles (For serving)

Instructions:

- Select the "Sauté" setting on your Instant Pot and add the olive oil.
- Once hot, add the onion, bacon and garlic. Cook until slightly tender, stirring occasionally.
- Add the beef strips and cook until brown.
- Add the remaining ingredients except for the sour cream. Lock the lid and cook at high pressure for 30 minutes. When the cooking is done, quick release the pressure and carefully remove the lid.
- Gently stir in the sour cream and top the stroganoff on zoodles. Serve and enjoy!

Steak Bacon Cabbage Stew

Time: 50 minutes   Servings: 8

Ingredients:

- ½ pound of bacon strips, roughly chopped
- 3 pounds of sirloin steak, sliced
- 2 large red onions, sliced
- 4 garlic cloves, peeled and minced
- 1 green cabbage, cored and chopped
- 1 fresh sprig of thyme
- 1 (14.5-ounce) can of diced tomatoes
- 1 (6-ounce) can of tomato paste
- 4 cups of homemade low-sodium beef broth
- 2 tablespoons of olive oil
- Fine sea salt and freshly cracked black pepper (to taste)

Instructions:

- Press the "Sauté" setting on your Instant Pot and add the bacon. Cook until brown and crispy. Once done, transfer to a plate lined with paper towels.
- Add the olive oil and sliced red onions and sauté for 4 minutes or until slightly tender.
- Add the sirloin steak and continue to cook for another 2 minutes or so.
- Return the bacon along with the remaining ingredients inside your Instant Pot. Lock the lid and cook at high pressure for 35 minutes. When the cooking is done, naturally release the pressure for 10 minutes, then quick release the remaining pressure. Carefully remove the lid. Serve and enjoy!

Spicy Beef Curry

Time: 40 minutes   Servings: 6

Ingredients:

- 2 ½ pounds of beef chuck roast, cut into bite-sized pieces
- 1 medium white onion, roughly chopped
- 2 tablespoons of curry powder

- 3 medium garlic cloves
- ½-inch piece of fresh ginger, peeled
- 2 cups of whole coconut milk

- 1 teaspoon of fine sea salt
- 2 tablespoons of chili sauce

Instructions:

- In a food processor or blender, add the chopped onions, curry powder, garlic cloves, peeled ginger, and sea salt. Pulse until well combined. Transfer inside your Instant Pot.
- Add the beef pieces along with the coconut milk and chili sauce. Stir until well combined.
- Lock the lid and cook at high pressure for 35 minutes. When the cooking is done, manually release the pressure and carefully remove the lid. Serve and enjoy!

Beef and Chicken Liver Burgers
Time: 25 minutes   Servings: 6

Ingredients:

- 1 ½ pound of ground beef
- ½ pound of chicken livers
- 1 teaspoon of sea salt
- 1 teaspoon of freshly cracked black pepper

- 1 ½ teaspoon of ground coriander
- ½ medium red onion, peeled and finely chopped
- 2 cups of water

Instructions:

- In a food processor, add the chicken livers and onions. Pulse until mushy.
- In a large bowl, dad the ground beef, chicken liver mixture, sea salt, black pepper and ground coriander. Form the beef mixture into 6 patties and wrap tightly with foil.
- Add 2 cups of water and a trivet inside your Instant Pot. Place the patties on top of the trivet. Lock the lid and cook at high pressure for 20 minutes. When the cooking is done, quick release the pressure and carefully remove the lid. Serve and enjoy!

Spicy Jalapeno Burgers
Time: 20 minutes   Servings: 4

Ingredients:

- 2 pounds of ground beef
- 1 jalapeno pepper, finely chopped
- ½ teaspoon of ground cumin
- ½ teaspoon of garlic powder

- ½ teaspoon of crushed red pepper flakes
- ¼ onion, finely chopped
- Fine sea salt and freshly cracked black pepper (to taste)
- 2 cups of water

Instructions:

- In a large bowl, add all the ingredients except for the water. Stir until well combined. Form into 4 patties. Wrap the patties with aluminum foil.
- Add 2 cups of water and a trivet inside your Instant Pot. Place the patties on top.
- Lock the lid and cook at high pressure for 15 minutes. When the cooking is done, quick release the pressure and carefully remove the lid. Serve and enjoy!

Sirloin Beef Roast
Time: 1 hour and 30 minutes   Servings: 8

Ingredients:

- 1 (4 pound) whole beef sirloin roast (make sure it fits inside your Instant Pot)
- 1 large onion, quartered
- 2 celery stalks, roughly chopped
- 2 large carrots, roughly chopped
- 6 whole garlic cloves
- 1 cup of homemade low-sodium beef broth

- ½ cup of red wine
- 1 tablespoon of dried onion flakes
- 2 tablespoons of dried oregano
- 1 tablespoon of coriander seeds
- 1 teaspoon of fine sea salt
- 1 teaspoon of freshly cracked black pepper

Instructions:

- Season the sirloin roast with dried onion flakes, dried oregano, coriander seeds, sea salt and freshly cracked black pepper.
- Add the quartered onions, celery, carrots and garlic cloves inside your Instant Pot.
- Pour in the beef broth and red wine. Place the sirloin roast on top.
- Lock the lid and cook at high pressure for 65 minutes. When the cooking is done, naturally release the pressure and carefully remove the lid. Slice into servings. Serve and enjoy!

Cheddar Burgers

Time: 15 minutes   Servings: 3

Ingredients:

- 1 pound of ground beef
- 2 teaspoons of Worcestershire sauce
- ½ teaspoon of fine sea salt

- 4-ounces of cubed cheddar cheese
- 2 cups of water

Instructions:

- In a large bowl, add the ground beef, Worcestershire sauce, fine sea salt and cubed cheddar cheese. Mix until well combined. Form into 3 patties. Add 2 cups of water and a trivet inside your Instant Pot.
- Wrap the patties into foil and place onto of the trivet. Lock the lid and cook at high pressure for 10 minutes. When the cooking is done, quick release the pressure and carefully remove the lid. Serve and enjoy!

Country Streak

Time: 50 minutes   Servings: 4

Ingredients:

- 1 ½ pounds of beef round steak, cut into 4 pieces
- ¼ cup of almond flour
- 1 tablespoon of olive oil
- ¼ cup of low-sugar ketchup
- 1 teaspoon of Worcestershire sauce
- 3 medium garlic cloves, peeled and minced

- ¼ cup of onions, finely chopped
- ¼ cup of celery, chopped
- 1 cup of homemade low-sodium bone or beef broth
- ½ teaspoon of fine sea salt
- ½ teaspoon of freshly cracked black pepper

Instructions:

- Coat each beef pieces with almond flour.
- Press the "Sauté" setting on your Instant Pot and add the olive oil. Once hot and working in batches, add the steak pieces and sear for 3 minutes per side or until brown.
- Add the remaining ingredients inside your Instant Pot. Lock the lid and cook at high pressure for 30 minutes. When the cooking is done, naturally release the pressure for 10 minutes, then quick release the remaining pressure. Carefully remove the lid. Serve and enjoy!

Philly Cheesesteak

Time: 30 minutes   Servings: 8

Meat Ingredients:

- 2 pounds of sirloin steak, thinly sliced
- 1 large onion, sliced
- 2 cups of homemade low-sodium beef broth

- 2 medium green bell peppers, seeds removed and sliced
- 2 tablespoons of olive oil
- Fine sea salt and freshly cracked black pepper (to taste)

Cheese Sauce Ingredients:

- 4 tablespoons of unsalted butter
- 2 tablespoons of almond flour
- ½ cup of unsweetened almond milk
- 1 teaspoon of fine sea salt

- ½ teaspoon of freshly cracked black pepper
- ½ teaspoon of Dijon mustard
- ¾ cups of cheddar cheese, shredded

Instructions:

- Season the steak slices with sea salt and freshly cracked black pepper.
- Press the "Sauté" setting on your Instant Pot and add the olive oil. Once hot, add the steak, onions and green bell peppers. Sauté for 5 minutes, stirring occasionally.
- Pour in the 2 cups of beef broth. Lock the lid and cook at high pressure for 6 minutes. When the cooking is done, naturally release the pressure for 10 minutes, then quick release the remaining pressure. Carefully remove the lid.
- In a medium saucepan over medium heat, add the butter. Once melted, add the almond flour and cook for 1 minute, stirring frequently. Whisk in the almond milk.
- Add the sea salt, black pepper, Dijon mustard and shredded cheddar cheese. Continue to cook until the cheese has melted. Spoon the cheese on top of the steak slices.

Steak Fajitas
Time: 10 minutes   Servings: 8

Ingredients:

- 1 pound of flank steak, sliced into strips
- 1 tablespoon of taco seasoning
- 1 (16-ounce) bag of frozen onion and peppers slices
- 1 (15-ounce) Can of diced tomatoes with green chiles
- ¼ cup of homemade low-sodium beef broth
- 1 bunch of fresh cilantros, chopped
- 2 medium lime, juice and zest
- Fine sea salt and freshly cracked black pepper (to taste)

Instructions:

- Add all the ingredients except for the lime juice and lime zest inside your Instant Pot. Lock the lid and cook at high pressure for 8 minutes.
- When the cooking is done, naturally release the pressure and carefully remove the lid. Stir in the lime juice and lime zest. Top the fajitas onto cauliflower rice or lettuce leaves. Serve and enjoy!

Swiss Steak
Time: 1 hour   Servings: 8

Ingredients:

- 2 pounds of steak, sliced
- 2 tablespoons of olive oil
- 2 tablespoons of almond flour
- 1 medium yellow or white onion, finely chopped
- 2 medium bell peppers, seeds remove and finely chopped
- 1 cup of homemade low-sodium beef broth
- ½ cup of crushed tomatoes
- 2 teaspoons of garlic powder
- 1 teaspoon of fine sea salt
- 1 teaspoon of freshly cracked black pepper

Instructions:

- Season the steak slices with garlic powder, sea salt and freshly cracked black pepper. Lightly coat the steak slices with the almond flour.
- Press the "Sauté" setting on your Instant Pot and add the olive oil. Once hot and working in batches, add the steak slices and cook until brown. Remove and set aside.
- Add the chopped onions and peppers. Sauté until lightly softened, stirring occasionally.
- Stir in the beef broth and crushed tomatoes. Lock the lid and cook at high pressure for 30 minutes. When the cooking is done, naturally release the pressure for 10 minutes, then quick release the remaining pressure. Carefully remove the lid. Serve and enjoy!

Pepper Steak
Time: 30 minutes   Servings: 4

Ingredients:

- 1 pound of sirloin steaks, sliced into ½-inch strips
- ¼ cup of coconut aminos
- 1 tablespoon of white wine vinegar
- 4 medium garlic cloves, minced
- 2 cups of homemade low-sodium beef broth
- 1 cup of cauliflower rice
- 1 yellow onion, thinly sliced
- 1 green bell pepper, sliced
- 1 red bell pepper, sliced

- 3 green onions, finely chopped
- 2 tablespoons of extra-virgin olive oil

- Fine sea salt and freshly cracked black pepper (to taste)

Instructions:

- Add all the ingredients except for the onions and peppers inside your Instant Pot and lock the lid. Cook at high pressure for 5 minutes. When the cooking is done. Quick release the pressure and carefully remove the lid.
- Add the sliced onions and peppers inside your Instant Pot. Cover with a lid and allow to sit for 10 minutes or until the vegetables have softened, stirring occasionally. Serve and enjoy!

Garlic Butter Beef Steak

Time: 20 minutes   Servings: 2

Ingredients:

- 1 pound of beef sirloin steaks
- ½ cup of red wine
- 4 tablespoons of unsalted butter

- 2 tablespoons of fresh parsley, finely chopped
- 4 medium garlic cloves, peeled and minced
- Fine sea salt and freshly cracked black pepper (to taste)

Instructions:

- Season the beef steaks with sea salt and freshly cracked black pepper.
- Press the "Sauté" setting on your Instant Pot and add the butter. Once melted, add the beef steaks and sear for 2 minutes per side or until brown.
- Pour in the red wine and fresh parsley. Lock the lid and cook at high pressure for 12 minutes. When the cooking is done, naturally release the pressure and carefully remove the lid.
- Top the steak with the butter sauce. Serve and enjoy!

Beef and Broccoli

Time: 30 minutes   Servings: 4

Ingredients:

- 1 ½ pound of boneless beef chuck roast, sliced into thin strips
- 1 pound of broccoli florets
- 3 tablespoons of almond flour mixed with 3 tablespoons of water
- 2 tablespoons of extra-virgin olive oil
- 1 medium onion, finely chopped

- 4 medium garlic cloves, minced
- 1 cup of homemade low-sodium beef broth
- ½ cup of coconut aminos
- 2 tablespoons of sesame oil
- ¼ teaspoon of crushed red pepper flakes
- Fine sea salt and freshly cracked black pepper (to taste)

Instructions:

- Season the beef strips with sea salt and freshly cracked black pepper.
- Press the "Sauté" setting on your Instant Pot and add the olive oil. Once hot, add the beef strips and cook until brown. Transfer the meat to a plate.
- Add the chopped onions and sauté for 2 minutes or until softened, stirring occasionally.
- Add the minced garlic and sauté for 1 minute, stirring occasionally.
- Stir in the beef broth, coconut aminos, sesame oil and red pepper flakes.
- Meanwhile, in a microwavable safe bowl, add the broccoli with a couple of tablespoons of water. Microwave for 3 to 4 minutes or until tender.
- Add the beef inside your Instant Pot and lock the lid. Cook at high pressure for 12 minutes. When done, manually release the pressure and remove the lid.
- Press the "Sauté" setting on your Instant Pot and add the almond flour. Stir until smooth and thickened, stirring occasionally.
- Stir in the steamed broccoli until well coated with the liquid. Serve and enjoy!

Barbacoa Beef

Time: 1 hour and 30 minutes   Servings: 8

Ingredients:

- 3 pounds of beef chuck roast, cut into 2-inch pieces
- 2/3 cups of homemade low-sodium beef broth
- 2 tablespoons of extra-virgin olive oil
- 4 medium garlic cloves
- 2 chipotles in adobo sauce
- 1 small white onion, finely chopped
- 1 (4-ounce) can of chopped green chiles

- ¼ cup of freshly squeezed lime juice
- 2 tablespoons of apple cider vinegar
- 1 tablespoon of ground cumin
- 1 tablespoon of dried oregano
- 2 teaspoons of fine sea salt
- 1 teaspoon of freshly cracked black pepper
- 3 bay leaves

Instructions:

- In a blender or food processor, add the beef broth, garlic, chipotles, onions, green chiles, freshly squeezed lime juice, apple cider vinegar, ground cumin, dried oregano, sea salt and freshly cracked black pepper. Blend until smooth.
- Press the "Sauté' function on your Instant Pot and add the olive oil. Once hot, add the beef pieces and cook for 3 minutes or until brown on all sides.
- Add the bay leaves with the sauce. Lock the lid and cook at high pressure for 60 minutes. When the cooking is done, manually release the pressure and carefully remove the lid. Discard the bay leaves.
- Transfer the beef pieces to a cutting board and shred using two forks.
- Stir in the shredded beef inside your Instant Pot and stir until well coated with the liquid.
- Serve and enjoy!

Spinach and Mushroom Stuffed Beef Heart
Time: 55 minutes   Servings: 6 to 8

Ingredients:

- 1 large beef heart
- 6 slices of bacon, chopped
- 1 medium yellow onion, finely chopped
- ½ cup of mushrooms, chopped
- ½ cup of baby spinach
- 2 medium garlic cloves, minced

- 1 teaspoon of fine sea salt
- 1 teaspoon of freshly cracked black pepper
- ½ teaspoon of cinnamon powder
- ¼ teaspoon of nutmeg, freshly grated
- 1 cup of water

Instructions:

- Press the "Sauté" setting on your Instant Pot and add the bacon. Cook until brown and crispy, stirring occasionally. Transfer the bacon to a plate lined with paper towels.
- Add the chopped onions, minced garlic and mushrooms to the bacon grease. Sauté for 4 to 5 minutes or until fragrant, stirring frequently. Return the bacon along with the sea salt, freshly cracked black pepper, cinnamon powder and finely grated nutmeg.
- Transfer the contents to a bowl and pour in 1 cup of water and add a trivet inside your Instant Pot.
- Lay the beef heart onto a flat surface and spoon the mushroom mixture on top. Spread evenly and roll. Tie with a butcher's twine.
- Place the beef heart on top of the trivet. Lock the lid and cook at high pressure for 40 minutes. When the cooking is done, naturally release the pressure and carefully remove the lid. Serve and enjoy!

Sauté Beef and Zucchini
Time: 15 minutes   Servings: 2

Ingredients:

- ½ pound of beef, sliced into 1 to 2-inch strips
- 1 zucchini, cut into 1 to 2-inch strips
- 3 medium garlic cloves, peeled and minced
- ¼ cup of fresh cilantro, chopped

- 2 tablespoons of coconut aminos
- 2 tablespoons of olive oil
- Fine sea salt and freshly cracked black pepper (to taste)

Instructions:

- Press the "Sauté" setting on your Instant Pot and add the olive oil. Once hot, add the beef strips inside your Instant Pot and sauté for a couple of minutes or until brown, stirring occasionally.
- Add the zucchini strips and continue to sauté until the vegetable has softened, stirring occasionally.
- Stir in the coconut aminos, minced garlic and fresh cilantro. Sauté for another minute, stirring frequently. Serve and enjoy!

Ropa Vieja
Time: 1 hour and 30 minutes　　　　　Servings: 10

Ingredients:

- 1 (3-pound) chuck roast
- 1 onion, sliced
- 4 teaspoons of garlic, minced
- 2 teaspoons of dried oregano
- 2 teaspoons of cumin
- 2 teaspoons of smoked paprika
- 2 teaspoons of fine sea salt

- 1 teaspoon of smoked or regular paprika
- ½ teaspoon of freshly cracked black pepper
- 1 (14.5-ounce) can of diced tomatoes
- 2 bay leaves
- 3 bell peppers, seeds remove and finely chopped
- Green olives, pitted and sliced

Instructions:

- Add all the ingredients except for the bell peppers and green olives inside your Instant Pot. Lock the lid and cook at high pressure for 90 minutes.
- When the cooking is done, naturally release the pressure and carefully remove the lid.
- Transfer the beef to a cutting board and shred using two forks.
- Press the "Sauté" setting on your Instant Pot. Return the shredded beef and add the bell peppers. Cook for 4 to 5 minutes or until the peppers become tender, stirring occasionally.
- Stir in the pitted green olives and adjust the seasoning if necessary. Serve and enjoy!

Ground Beef Stir-Fry
Time: 20 minutes　　　　　Servings: 4

Ingredients:

- 1 pound of ground beef
- 2 green bell peppers, seeds removed and finely chopped
- 3 medium tomatoes, finely chopped
- ½ medium onion, finely chopped
- 2 medium garlic cloves, peeled and minced

- ¼ cup of fresh cilantro, chopped
- 1 teaspoon of hot sauce
- 2 tablespoons of coconut oil
- Fine sea salt and freshly cracked black pepper (to taste)

Instructions:

- Press the "Sauté" setting on your Instant Pot. Once hot, add the ground beef and cook until brown, breaking up the meat with a wooden spoon. Remove and set aside.
- Add the coconut oil. Once hot, add the chopped onions, tomatoes, peppers inside your Instant Pot. Cook for 5 minutes, stirring frequently.
- Return the ground beef to the pot and continue to cook until the vegetables have softened, stir in the hot sauce, cilantro, coconut oil, minced garlic, sea salt and freshly cracked black pepper. Serve and enjoy!

Asian Sesame Beef Salad
Time: 20 minutes　　　　　Servings: 2

Ingredients:

- ½ pound of beef, cut into small cubes
- ¼ cup of coconut aminos
- 1 tablespoon of sesame oil
- 2 tablespoons of olive oil
- 1 cup of chopped iceberg lettuce or spinach
- 2 tablespoons of green onions, finely chopped
- 2 tablespoons of fresh cilantro, chopped

- ¼ cup of zucchini, shredded
- ¼ small carrot, shredded
- 2 tablespoons of almonds, sliced
- 1 tablespoon of toasted sesame seeds
- ¼ cup of homemade low-sodium beef broth
- Fine sea salt and freshly cracked black pepper (to taste)

Instructions:

- In a small bowl, add the beef pieces, toasted sesame oil and coconut aminos. Allow to marinate for 5 minutes.
- Press the "Sauté" setting on your Instant Pot and add the olive oil. Once hot, add the beef pieces and cook until brown, stirring occasionally.
- Lock the lid and cook at high pressure for 15 minutes. When the coking is done, manually release the pressure and carefully remove the lid. Transfer the beef pieces to a large bowl.

64

- Add the remaining ingredients and stir until well combined. Serve and enjoy!

Cantonese Beef with Radishes

Time: 1 hour and 45 minutes   Servings: 6

Ingredients:

- 3 pounds of beef flank steak, cut into 2 ½-inch pieces
- 2 tablespoons of extra-virgin olive oil
- 2 tablespoons of fresh ginger, peeled and grated
- 1/4 cup of coconut aminos
- 5 medium garlic cloves, minced
- 3 bay leaves
- 1 tablespoon of erythritol
- 2 tablespoons of radishes, peeled and cut into 1 ½-inch pieces
- ¼ cup of homemade low-sodium chicken stock
- Fine sea salt and freshly cracked black pepper (to taste)

Instructions:

- Press the "Sauté" setting on your Instant Pot and add the olive oil.
- Once hot, add the ginger and sauté for 2 minute or until fragrant, stirring occasionally.
- Add the remaining ingredients inside your Instant Pot. Lock the lid and cook at high pressure for 35 minutes. When the cooking is done, naturally release the pressure and carefully remove the lid.
- Press the "Sauté" setting on your Instant Pot and continue to cook until the stew has thickened, stirring frequently. Serve and enjoy!

Corned Beef and Cauliflower Hash

Time: 50 minutes   Servings: 2

Ingredients:

- 2 cups of corned beef, chopped
- 2 cups of cauliflower, finely chopped
- ½ cup of onions, chopped
- 1 tablespoon of extra-virgin olive oil
- ½ cup of homemade low-sodium beef broth.
- Fine sea salt and freshly cracked black pepper (to taste)

Instructions:

- Add the corned beef, onions and beef broth inside your Instant Pot. Lock the lid and cook at high pressure for 10 minutes. When the cooking is done, naturally release the pressure and carefully remove the lid.
- Press the "Sauté" setting on your Instant Pot and add the chopped cauliflower, sea salt and freshly cracked black pepper. Continue to cook until most of the liquid evaporates, stirring occasionally. Serve and enjoy!

Mushroom and Beer Pot Roast

Time: 1 hour and 30 minutes   Servings: 6

Ingredients:

- 4 pounds of beef pot roast, cut into 1-inch pieces
- 2 tablespoons of extra-virgin olive oil
- 1 medium white onion, finely chopped
- 2 celery stalks, chopped
- 3 medium garlic cloves, minced
- 1 tablespoon of Worcestershire sauce
- 1 bottle of low-carb beer
- 1 package of onion soup mix
- 1 (10.75-ounce) can of cream of mushroom soup
- 1 (10-ounce) can of mushrooms, undrained
- Fine sea salt and freshly cracked black pepper (to taste)

Instructions:

- Press the "Sauté" setting on your Instant Pot and add the extra-virgin olive oil. Once hot, add the beef pieces and cook for 4 minutes or until brown, stirring occasionally.
- Add the chopped onions, minced garlic, and celery. Sauté until lightly tender, stirring occasionally.
- Add the remaining ingredients inside your Instant Pot and lock the lid. Cook at high pressure for 60 minutes. When the cooking is done, naturally release the pressure and carefully remove the lid. Serve and enjoy!

Taco Meat

Time: 20 minutes   Servings: 6

Ingredients:

- 2 pounds of ground beef
- 1 large onion, finely chopped
- 4 medium garlic cloves, peeled and minced
- 3 medium bell peppers, seeds removed and diced

- 2 packets of taco seasoning
- 1 cup of water
- Fine sea salt and freshly cracked black pepper (to taste)

Instructions:

- Press the "Sauté" setting on your Instant Pot and add the ground beef. Cook until brown, breaking up the meat with a wooden spoon. Discard the liquid when done.
- Add the chopped onions, minced garlic and diced bell peppers. Cook for another minute, stirring occasionally.
- Add the water and taco seasoning. Lock the lid and cook at high pressure for 5 minutes. When the cooking is done, quick release the pressure and carefully remove the lid. Serve and enjoy!

Korean Ground Beef
Time: 25 minutes   Servings: 6

Ingredients:

- 1 tablespoon of extra-virgin olive oil
- 1 ½ pound of ground beef
- 2 teaspoons of garlic powder
- 1 teaspoon of ground ginger
- 1 teaspoon of dried minced onions

- ½ cup of homemade low-sodium beef broth
- ¼ cup of coconut aminos
- 1 teaspoon of sriracha sauce
- Fine sea salt and freshly cracked black pepper (to taste)

Instructions:

- Press the "Sauté" setting on your Instant Pot and add the olive oil. Once hot, add the ground beef and cook until brown, breaking apart the meat with a wooden spoon.
- Add the remaining ingredients and lock the lid. Cook at high pressure for 7 minutes. When the cooking is done, naturally release the pressure for 5 minutes, then quick release the remaining pressure. Carefully remove the lid.
- Press the "Sauté" setting on your Instant Pot and continue to cook until most of the liquid reduces. Serve and enjoy!

Easy Leg of Lamb
Time: 40 minutes   Servings: 10

Ingredients:

- 4 pounds of boneless leg of lamb
- 2 tablespoons of extra-virgin olive oil
- 2 cups of homemade low-sodium beef broth

- 4 garlic cloves, peeled and crushed
- 2 tablespoons of fresh rosemary, chopped
- Fine sea salt and freshly cracked black pepper (to taste)

Instructions:

- Season the leg of lamb with sea salt and freshly cracked black pepper.
- Press the "Sauté" setting on your Instant Pot and add the olive oil. Once hot, add the leg of lamb and sear for 4 minutes or until brown on all sides.
- Add the beef broth, crushed garlic and fresh rosemary. Lock the lid and cook at high pressure for 35 minutes. When the cooking is done, naturally release the pressure and carefully remove the lid.
- Preheat your broiler and transfer the lamb to a baking sheet lined with aluminum foil.
- Broil for 2 minutes or until brown on top. Slice and enjoy!

Lamb Korma
Time: 1 hour and 10 minutes   Servings: 4

Ingredients:

- 1 ½ pound of lamb stew meat
- 2 tablespoons of coconut oil melted
- 2 large shallots, finely chopped

- 1 cup of mushrooms, finely chopped
- 6 tablespoons of korma paste
- 1 (14.5-ounce) can of full-fat coconut milk

- 1 cup of baby spinach
- 1 whole lime juice, juice
- 3 tablespoons of unsweetened Greek yogurt
- Fine sea salt and freshly cracked black pepper (to taste)

Instructions:

- Press the "Sauté" setting on your Instant Pot and add the coconut oil. Once hot, add the shallots and sauté until softened, stirring frequently.
- Add the lamb stew meat and cook for 4 to 5 minutes or until lightly browned, stirring occasionally.
- Add the remaining ingredients except for the spinach and lock the lid. Cook at high pressure for 25 minutes. When the cooking is done, naturally release the pressure and carefully remove the lid.
- Stir in the spinach and cover with a lid. Sit until the spinach has wilted. Serve and enjoy!

Lamb and Spinach Curry (Lamb Saagwala)
Time: 50 minutes   Servings: 4

Ingredients:

- 3 pounds of boneless lamb shoulder, cut into 1-inch pieces
- 4 tablespoons of coconut oil, melted
- 6 cups of spinach
- 1 large onion, finely chopped
- 3 garlic cloves, peeled and minced
- 1 teaspoon of cumin powder
- 2 teaspoons of coriander powder
- ¼ cup of heavy cream
- ½ teaspoon of garam masala
- 2 tomatoes, finely diced
- ½ teaspoon of turmeric
- 1 tablespoon of coriander seeds
- Fine sea salt and freshly cracked black pepper (to taste)

Instructions:

- Press the "Sauté" setting on your Instant Pot and add the coconut oil. Once hot, add the lamb pieces and cook until lightly brown, stirring occasionally.
- Transfer the lamb pieces to a plate and set aside. Add the chopped onion and minced garlic. Sauté for 4 to 6 minutes or until softened, stirring frequently.
- Add the diced tomatoes, turmeric, coriander seeds, coriander powder, cumin powder, sea salt and freshly cracked black pepper. Sauté for 2 minutes, stirring frequently. Turn off the "Sauté" setting on your Instant Pot.
- In a blender or a food processor, add the onion-tomato mixture, 1 cup of water, and spinach.
- Add the lamb pieces inside your Instant Pot along with the spinach mixture. Lock the lid and cook at high pressure for 20 minutes. When the cooking is done, naturally release the pressure and carefully remove the lid. Serve and enjoy!

Pork Carnitas
Time: 1 hour and 20 minutes   Servings: 4

Ingredients:

- 2 ½ pounds of boneless pork shoulder, cut into 4 large pieces
- 6 medium garlic cloves, minced
- 2 teaspoons of ground cumin
- 1 teaspoon of smoked paprika
- 3 chipotle peppers in adobo sauce, minced
- 1 teaspoon of dried oregano
- 2 bay leaves
- 1 cup of homemade low-sodium chicken broth
- Fine sea salt and freshly cracked black pepper (to taste)
- 2 tablespoons of olive oil

Instructions:

- Season the pork shoulder with sea salt, black pepper, ground cumin, dried oregano, and smoked paprika.
- Press the "Sauté" setting on your Instant Pot and add the olive oil.
- Once hot, add the pork pieces and sear for 4 minutes per side or until brown.
- Add the remaining ingredients inside your Instant Pot. Lock the lid and cook at high pressure for 80 minutes. When the cooking is done, quick release the pressure and remove the lid.
- Carefully shred the pork using two forks and continue to stir until well coated with the liquid.
- Remove the bay leave and adjust the seasoning if necessary. Serve and enjoy!

Coconut Pork
Time: 40 minutes   Servings: 8

Ingredients:

- 2 ½ pounds of boneless pork shoulder, cut into large chunks
- 2 tablespoons of coconut oil
- ½ medium yellow onion, finely chopped
- 3 tablespoons of turmeric, freshly grated
- 2 tablespoons of ginger, freshly grated
- 3 medium garlic cloves, peeled and crushed
- ½ teaspoon of cardamom
- 1 cup of diced tomatoes
- 1 (15-ounce) can of coconut milk
- Fine sea salt and freshly cracked black pepper (to taste)

Instructions:

- Press the "Sauté" setting on your Instant Pot and add the coconut oil.
- Once hot, add the chopped onions and sauté for 5 minutes or until softened, stirring occasionally.
- Add the minced garlic, grated ginger, grated turmeric, cinnamon, sea salt, cardamom, and black pepper. Sauté for another 1 minute or until fragrant, stirring occasionally.
- Stir in the crushed tomatoes and coconut milk.
- Add the pork and lock the lid. Cook at high pressure for 30 minutes. When the cooking is done, naturally release the pressure and carefully remove the lid.
- Transfer the pork pieces to a cutting board and shred using two forks.
- Press the "Sauté" setting on your Instant Pot and continue to cook until the liquid inside your Instant Pot thickens, stirring frequently.
- Return the pulled pork to the sauce and stir until well coated. Serve and enjoy!

Buffalo Pulled Pork with Bacons
Time: 1 hour   Servings: 10

Ingredients:

- 1 (2-pound) of pork shoulder
- 6 bacon slices, finely chopped
- 1 ½ cup of Frank's hot sauce
- 4 tablespoons of unsalted butter
- 2 tablespoons of olive oil
- 1 cup of homemade low-sodium beef broth
- Fine sea salt and freshly cracked black pepper (to taste)

Instructions:

- Season the pork shoulder with sea salt and freshly cracked black pepper.
- Press the "Sauté" setting on your Instant Pot and add the olive oil. Once hot, add the pork shoulder and sear for 4 minutes per side or until brown.
- Pour in the beef broth and lock the lid. Cook at high pressure for 35 minutes. When the cooking is done, naturally release the pressure and carefully remove the lid.
- Transfer the pork shoulder to a cutting board and shred using two forks. Discard the liquid from your Instant Pot.
- Press the "Sauté" setting on your Instant Pot and add the chopped bacon. Cook until brown and crispy. Transfer the bacon to a plate lined with paper towels and set aside. Discard the bacon grease.
- Add the unsalted butter. Once melted, stir in the hot sauce. Return the pork shoulder along with the bacon. Gently stir until well coated with the sauce. Serve and enjoy!

Pork Chops with Mushroom Sauce
Time: 1 hour and 10 minutes   Servings: 4

Pork Chop Ingredients:

- 4 large pork loin chops
- 2 tablespoons of olive oil
- 1 large shallot, finely chopped
- ½ cup of Marsala wine
- 1 ½ cup of homemade low-sodium beef broth
- Fine sea salt and freshly cracked black pepper (to taste)

Mushroom Sauce Ingredients:

- ¾ pounds of mushrooms, sliced
- ½ cup of heavy cream
- 3 to 4 tablespoons of Dijon mustard
- 1 tablespoon of unsalted butter
- 1 tablespoon of extra-virgin olive oil
- ½ cup of homemade low-sodium beef broth

Instructions:

- Season the pork chops with sea salt and freshly cracked black pepper.

- Press the "Sauté" setting on your Instant Pot and add the pork chops. Sear for 3 minutes on both sides or until brown. Remove and set aside.
- Add the chopped shallots inside your Instant Pot and sauté for 2 minutes or until softened, stirring occasionally.
- Add the Marsala wine and 1 ½ cup of beef broth. Lock the lid and cook at high pressure for 35 minutes.
- When the cooking is done, naturally release the pressure and carefully remove the lid.
- In a saucepan over medium-high heat, add the butter, olive oil and sliced mushrooms. Sauté until softened, stirring occasionally.
- Stir in the heavy cream, Dijon mustard and beef broth. Continue to boil until most of the liquid evaporates. Spoon the mushroom sauce over the pork chops. Serve and enjoy!

Pork Chops with Creamy Wine Sauce
Time: 30 minutes   Servings: 4

Pork Chops Ingredients:

- 4 boneless pork chops
- 1 teaspoon of garlic powder
- ½ teaspoon of fine sea salt
- ½ teaspoon of freshly cracked black pepper
- 1 teaspoon of dried oregano and Italian seasoning

Wine Sauce Ingredients:

- 2 tablespoons of extra-virgin olive oil
- 3 medium garlic cloves, minced
- ½ medium onion, finely chopped
- 1 cup of white mushrooms, sliced
- 1 cup of dry white wine
- 1 cup of homemade low-sodium chicken stock
- ½ cup of heavy cream
- Fine sea salt and freshly cracked black pepper (to taste)
- 3 tablespoons of unsalted butter, melted
- 3 tablespoons of almond flour

Instructions:

- Season the pork chops with sea salt, garlic powder, black pepper and dried oregano and set aside.
- Press the "Sauté" setting on your Instant Pot and add the olive oil. Once hot, add the chopped onions, minced garlic and sliced mushrooms. Cook until translucent, stirring occasionally.
- Deglaze using the dry white wine. Scrape up the bits from the bottom.
- Stir in the chicken stock, ½ cup heavy cream, sea salt and black pepper.
- Place the pork chops onto the pot. Lock the lid and cook at high pressure for 8 minutes.
- When the cooking is done, naturally release the pressure for 10 minutes, then quick release the remaining pressure and carefully remove the lid.
- In a saucepan over medium heat, add the butter. Once melted, whisk in the almond flour.
- Whisk in the heavy cream and allow to thicken.
- Spoon the gravy on top of the pork chops. Serve and enjoy!

Chile Verde Pork Stew
Time: 50 minutes   Servings: 8

Ingredients:

- 2 pounds of pork loin, cut into bite-sized pieces
- 2 teaspoons of ground cumin
- 2 teaspoons of garlic powder
- 1 teaspoon of ground chile powder
- 1 small onion, finely chopped
- 2 medium garlic cloves
- 1 (28-ounce) can of whole Hatch green chilies, undrained
- 3 tablespoons of extra-virgin olive oil
- 2 cups of homemade low-sodium beef broth
- 2 tablespoons of olive oil
- Fine sea salt and freshly cracked black pepper (to taste)

Instructions:

- Press the "Sauté" setting on your Instant Pot and add the olive oil. Once hot, add the pork pieces and cook until brown. Transfer the pork pieces to a plate lined with paper towels.
- Add the ground cumin, garlic powder, ground chile powder, sea salt and freshly cracked black pepper. Cook for 1 to 2 minutes or until fragrant, stirring occasionally.
- In a food processor, add the green chiles, chopped onion and garlic cloves. Pulse until paste.
- Add the paste to your Instant Pot along with the beef broth and can of Hatch green chilies.
- Lock the lid and cook at high pressure for 30 minutes. When the cooking is done, naturally release the pressure and carefully remove the lid. Serve and enjoy!

Easy Pork Tenderloin with Garlic Herb Rub

Time: 20 minutes   Servings: 4

Ingredients:

- 1 pound of pork tenderloin, cut in half
- 1 teaspoon of garlic powder
- 1 teaspoon of dried parsley
- ½ teaspoon of fine sea salt
- ½ teaspoon of onion powder
- ¼ teaspoon of freshly cracked black pepper
- 1 cup of homemade low-sodium chicken stock
- 1 tablespoon of balsamic vinegar

Instructions:

- In a bowl, add the garlic powder, dried parsley, fine sea salt, onion powder and black pepper. Mix well.
- Rub the seasoning mixture over the pork tenderloins.
- Add the chicken stock and the balsamic vinegar inside your Instant Pot. Place a trivet inside.
- Place the pork on top of the lid. Cook at high pressure for 10 minutes. When the cooking is done, naturally release the pressure for 10 minutes, then quick release the remaining pressure. Carefully remove the lid. Serve and enjoy!

Garlic Zesty Pulled Pork

Time: 1 hour   Servings: 6

Ingredients:

- 1 (3 pound) pork shoulder
- 1 tablespoon of fine sea salt
- 1 teaspoon of freshly cracked black pepper
- 1 teaspoon of ground cumin
- 1 teaspoon of dried oregano
- 2 to 3 limes, juice and zest
- 8 medium garlic cloves, minced
- ¼ cup of homemade low-sodium beef broth

Instructions:

- In a bowl, add the lime juice, lime zest, minced garlic, dried oregano and ground cumin. Mix well and set aside.
- Rub the lime mixture over the pork shoulder. Season with sea salt and freshly cracked black pepper.
- Add the pork shoulder inside your Instant Pot along with the beef broth.
- Lock the lid and cook at high pressure for 35 minutes. When the cooking is done, naturally release the pressure and carefully remove the lid.
- When the cooking is done, transfer the pork shoulder to a cutting board and shred using two forks.
- Gently return the shredded pork to your Instant Pot and stir until well combined. Serve and enjoy!

Pulled Pork Afelia

Time: 1 hour and 25 minutes   Servings: 8

Ingredients:

- 1 (3 pound) pork shoulder
- 2 red onions, sliced
- 1 whole garlic, minced
- 1 cup of red wine
- ½ cup of extra-virgin olive oil
- 2 tablespoons of crushed coriander seeds
- 2 teaspoons of dried thyme
- 1 tablespoon of fine sea salt
- 1 teaspoon of freshly cracked black pepper
- 2 teaspoons of ground cinnamon

Instructions:

- In a large bowl, add the sliced red onions, minced garlic, olive oil, red wine, crushed coriander seeds, dried thyme, sea salt, black pepper and ground cinnamon. Mix well.
- Add the pork shoulder and wrap with plastic wrap. Marinate for 6 hours or overnight.
- Add the pork shoulder and the marinade inside your Instant Pot. Lock the lid and cook at high pressure for 40 minutes. When the cooking is done, naturally release the pressure and remove the lid.
- Transfer the pork shoulder to a cutting board and shred using two forks.

Roast Pork

Time: 45 minutes   Servings: 8

Ingredients:

- 1 (2-pound) pork loin roast
- 2 tablespoons of unsalted butter
- ½ medium onion, finely chopped
- 4 medium garlic cloves, minced
- 2 medium carrots, finely chopped
- 2 celery stalks, chopped
- ½ cup of homemade low-sodium beef broth
- 2 tablespoons of Worcestershire sauce
- 1 teaspoon of yellow mustard
- 2 teaspoons of dried rosemary, dried basil or dried oregano
- 1 tablespoon of arrowroot powder mixed with 2 tablespoons of water
- Fine sea salt and freshly cracked black pepper (to taste)

Instructions:

- Season the pork roast with sea salt and black pepper.
- Press the "Sauté" setting on your Instant Pot and add the butter. Once melted, add the pork roast and sear for 2 to 4 minutes per side or until golden brown.
- Add the chopped onions and minced garlic. Sauté for 2 minutes or until softened, stirring occasionally.
- Add the remaining ingredients inside your Instant Pot except for the arrowroot powder. Lock the lid and cook at high pressure for 30 minutes.
- When the cooking is done, manually release the pressure and carefully remove the lid.
- Remove the pork roast and set aside.
- Press the "Sauté" setting on your Instant Pot and add the arrowroot powder. Continue to cook until thickens, stirring occasionally. Serve and enjoy!

BBQ Ribs
Time: 50 minutes   Servings: 8

Ingredients:

- 2 (2 pounds) of baby back rack ribs
- 2 cups of homemade low-sodium chicken stock
- ½ cup of apple cider vinegar
- 2 teaspoons of fine sea salt
- 2 teaspoons of chili powder
- 2 teaspoons of ground mustard
- 2 teaspoons of smoked paprika
- 1 teaspoon of dried thyme
- 1 teaspoon of dried oregano
- 1 teaspoon of garlic powder
- 1 teaspoon of ground cumin
- ½ teaspoon of cayenne pepper
- 2 cups of sugar-free barbecue sauce

Instructions:

- In a small bowl, add all the seasonings and mix well.
- Rub the ribs with the seasoning on both sides.
- Add the chicken stock and apple cider vinegar inside your Instant Pot. Place a trivet inside.
- Add the ribs on top of the trivet and wrap into a circle in order for it to fit.
- Lock the lid and cook at high pressure for 25 minutes.
- When the cooking is done, manually release the pressure and carefully remove the lid.
- Preheat your broiler and transfer the ribs to a baking sheet lined with aluminum foil.
- Brush the barbecue sauce over the ribs and broil for 4 to 5 minutes or until brown.Serve and enjoy!

Keto BBQ Pulled Pork
Time: 1 hour   Servings: 4

Ingredients:

- 1 (2-pound) pork shoulder, cut into large chunks
- 1 cup of water or homemade low-sodium beef broth
- 1/3 cup of white wine vinegar
- 3 tablespoons of olive oil, divided
- 1 tablespoon of smoked paprika
- 3 teaspoons of dried oregano
- 2 teaspoons of garlic powder
- 1 teaspoon of ground cumin
- 1 teaspoon of chipotle powder
- ½ teaspoon of cayenne pepper
- 1 to 3 tablespoons of erythritol
- 1 teaspoon of fine sea salt
- 1 teaspoon of freshly cracked black pepper
- 3 teaspoons of arrowroot powder

Instructions:

- In a bowl, add the following ingredients: white wine vinegar, 1 tablespoon of olive oil, smoked paprika, dried oregano, garlic powder, ground cumin, chipotle powder, cayenne powder, and water (or beef broth). Mix well and set aside.

- Season the pork shoulder with sea salt and freshly cracked black pepper.
- Press the "Sauté" setting on your Instant Pot and add the remaining 2 tablespoons of olive oil.
- Once hot, add the pork pieces and sear for 3 to 5 minutes per side or until brown. Turn off the "Sauté" setting.
- Pour in the sauce mixture and lock the lid. Cook at high pressure for 30 minutes. When the cooking is done, naturally release the pressure and carefully remove the lid.
- Transfer the meat to a cutting board and shred using two forks.
- Press the "Sauté" setting on your Instant Pot and mix in the arrowroot powder. Continue to cook until thickens, stirring frequently. Gently stir in the shredded pork inside your Instant Pot. Serve and enjoy!

Basque Lamb Stew

Time: 1 hour and 30 minutes　　　　　Servings: 6

Ingredients:

- 3 pounds of boneless lamb shoulder, cut into 2-inch pieces
- 6 medium garlic cloves, peeled and crushed
- 1 sprig of fresh rosemary
- ½ cup of dry white wine
- 1 cup of red wine
- 2 tablespoons of extra-virgin olive oil
- 1 large onion, peeled and chopped
- 1 (10-ounce) can of roasted red peppers,
- 1 large tomato, peeled and diced
- 2 tablespoons of fresh parsley, finely chopped
- 1 bay leaf
- 1 cup of homemade low-sodium chicken stock
- 2 teaspoons of sweet paprika
- Fine sea salt and freshly cracked black pepper (to taste)

Instructions:

- In a large bowl, add the lamb pieces, rosemary and white wine. Mix well using your hands and cover with plastic wrap. Allow to marinate for a few hours.
- Drain the meat from the white wine and pat dry using a paper towel.
- Press the "Sauté" setting on your Instant Pot and add the olive oil. Once hot, add the lamb pieces and brown on all sides. Remove and set aside.
- Add the onions and garlic. Sauté for 5 minutes or until softened, stirring frequently.
- Return the lamb pieces along with the remaining ingredients. Lock the lid and cook at high pressure for 20 minutes. When the cooking is done, naturally release the pressure for 15 minutes, then quick release the remaining pressure. Carefully remove the lid. Serve and enjoy!

Tandoori Lamb Meatloaf

Time: 50 minutes　　　　　Servings: 4

Meatloaf Ingredients:

- 1 pound of ground lamb
- 1 medium white onion, finely chopped
- 5 garlic cloves, minced
- 1 (6-ounce) tablespoons of tomato paste
- 1 serrano pepper, finely chopped
- 2 large eggs, beaten
- 2 teaspoons of paprika
- 1 teaspoon of coriander powder
- 1 teaspoon of turmeric
- Fine sea salt and freshly cracked black pepper (to taste)

Topping Ingredients:

1 (6-ounce) can of tomato paste　　　　　¼ cup of homemade low-sodium beef broth

Instructions:

- In a large bowl, add the meatloaf ingredients and stir until well combined. Form the lamb mixture into a meatloaf and place onto a large sheet of aluminum foil and wrap, ensure the edges are wrap.
- Pour 1 cup of water and a trivet inside your Instant Pot. Place the meatloaf on top. Lock the lid and cook at high pressure for 25 minutes. When the cooking is done, naturally release the pressure and carefully remove the lid.
- Preheat the broiler and transfer the meatloaf to a baking sheet lined with aluminum foil. Place the meatloaf on the baking sheet.
- Meanwhile, in a saucepan over medium heat, add the tomato paste and beef broth. Cook until well heated together. Spoon the tomato topping on top of the meatloaf and place inside your broiler. Broil for 5 minutes. Serve and enjoy!

Lamb and Herbed Koftas

Time: 40 minutes   Servings: 8

Ingredients:

- 1 pound of ground lamb
- 1 red onion, finely grated
- 2 garlic cloves, finely grated
- 2 tablespoons of fresh mint, finely chopped
- 3 tablespoons of fresh parsley, finely chopped
- 1 cup of water
- Fine sea salt and freshly cracked black pepper (to taste)
- 8 medium-sized wooden skewers

Instructions:

- In a large bowl, add the ground lamb, grated onion, grated garlic, fresh mint, fresh parsley, salt and black pepper. Mix until well combined.
- Add the lamb mixture to the skewers. Firmly squeeze to make sure the meat doesn't fall from the skewers.
- Add 1 cup of water and a trivet inside your Instant Pot. Place the skewers on top of the trivet.
- Lock the lid and cook at high pressure for 25 minutes. When the cooking is done, naturally release the pressure and remove the lid. Serve and enjoy!

Easy Lamb Sliders

Time: 25 minutes   Servings: 4

Ingredients:

- 1 pound of minced lamb
- ½ medium onion, finely chopped
- 2 garlic cloves, peeled and minced
- 1 tablespoon of dried dill
- Fine sea salt and freshly cracked black pepper (to taste)
- 1 cup of water

Instructions:

- In a large bowl, add the minced lamb, chopped onions, minced garlic, dried dill, sea salt and freshly cracked black pepper. Stir until well combined.
- Form the lamb mixture into 4 patties. Place the lamb patties onto aluminum foil and wrap with aluminum foil.
- Add 1 ½ cup of water and a trivet inside your Instant Pot. Place the lamb patties on top of the trivet.
- Lock the lid and cook at high pressure for 10 minutes. When the cooking is done, naturally release the pressure and carefully remove the lid. Serve and enjoy!

Lamb Curry with Kale

Time: 1 hour and 10 minutes   Servings: 6

Ingredients:

- 1 ½ pound of lamb stew meat
- 1 pound of spinach
- 6 garlic cloves, peeled and minced
- 2 tablespoons of ginger, peeled and minced
- 1 red onion, peeled and sliced
- 1 teaspoon of garam masala powder
- 2 teaspoons of cumin powder
- ½ teaspoon of chili powder
- 1 teaspoon of turmeric
- 2 teaspoons of ground coriander
- 2 teaspoons of ground cardamom
- Fine sea salt and freshly cracked black pepper (to taste)

Instructions:

- Add all the ingredients inside your Instant Pot and stir until well combined.
- Lock the lid and cook at high pressure for 35 minutes. When the cooking is done, naturally release the pressure and carefully remove the lid. Serve and enjoy!

Lamb Chops with Cauliflower Cream

Time: 35 minutes   Servings: 6

Lamb Ingredients:

- 3 pounds of lamb chops
- 4 sprigs of rosemary
- 2 tablespoons of extra-virgin olive oil
- 2 tablespoons of butter

- 1 tablespoon of tomato paste
- 1 cup of homemade low-sodium beef broth

- 1 shallot, finely chopped
- Fine sea salt and freshly cracked black pepper (to taste)

Creamed Cauliflower Ingredients:

- 1 head of cauliflower, cut into bite-sized florets
- 1 celery stalk, quartered
- 3 garlic cloves, peeled and crushed
- 2 cups of homemade low-sodium beef broth

- 1 tablespoon of water
- ½ cup of non-dairy milk
- 1 tablespoon of heavy cream

Instructions:

- Press the "Sauté" function on your Instant Pot and add the 2 tablespoons of extra-virgin olive oil and butter. Once hot, add the lamb chops and sear on both sides or until brown. Remove and set aside.
- Add the tomato paste and chopped shallots. Sauté for 2 minutes or until browned, stirring frequently.
- Deglaze your Instant Pot with the beef broth. Return the lamb chops to the pot. Lock the lid and cook at high pressure for 5 minutes. When the cooking is done, quick release the pressure and carefully remove the lid. Set the lamb chops aside and discard the liquid inside your Instant Pot.
- Add all the creamed cauliflower ingredients except for the non-dairy milk and heavy cream inside your Instant Pot. Lock the lid and cook at high pressure for 5 minutes. When the cooking is done, naturally release the pressure and remove the lid.
- Press the "Sauté" setting and stir in the non-dairy milk and heavy cream. Continue to cook until thickens, stirring frequently. Spoon the cauliflower cream on top of the lamb chops.Serve and enjoy!

Italian Lemon and Rosemary Lamb Chops
Time: 15 minutes   Servings: 4

Ingredients:

- 4 lamb chops loin
- 4 tablespoons of unsalted butter, softened
- 4 medium garlic cloves, minced
- 4 fresh sprigs of rosemary
- 2 medium lemons, juiced and zest

- 1 bay leaf
- 1 cup of homemade low-sodium beef broth
- 1 tablespoon of dried oregano
- Fine sea salt and freshly cracked black pepper (to taste)

Instructions:

- Press the "Sauté" setting on your Instant Pot and season the lamb chops with sea salt, freshly cracked black pepper and dried oregano.
- Press the "Sauté" setting on your Instant Pot and add the unsalted butter. Once hot, add the lamb chops and sear for 4 minutes on both sides or until brown.
- Pour in the beef broth, bay leaf, lemon juice, lemon zest, sprigs of rosemary and garlic. Lock the lid and cook at high pressure for 5 minutes. When the cooking is done, naturally release the pressure and carefully remove the lid. Serve and enjoy!

Lamb Rogan Josh
Time: 35 minutes   Servings: 4

Ingredients:

- 2 pounds of boneless lamb shoulder, cut into bite-sized pieces
- 2 medium red or white onions, finely chopped
- 4 tablespoons of ghee
- 4 medium garlic cloves, peeled and minced
- 1-inch piece of fresh ginger, peeled and minced
- 1 bay leaf
- 4 teaspoons of paprika

- 3 teaspoons of coriander powder
- 1 teaspoon of turmeric
- 1 teaspoon of garam masala
- 1 (15-ounce) can of tomato sauce
- 1 cup of plain Greek yogurt
- Fine sea salt and freshly cracked black pepper (to taste)

Instructions:

- Press the "Sauté' setting on your Instant Pot and add the ghee. Once hot, add the chopped onions and lamb pieces. Cook for 6 minutes or until brown, stirring frequently.
- Add the minced garlic, minced ginger, bay leaf and all the seasonings. Sauté for 1 minute, stirring frequently.
- Add the tomato sauce and gently stir in the Greek yogurt. Lock the lid and cook at high pressure for 20 minutes. When the cooking is done, naturally release the pressure and carefully remove the lid.

- Press the "Sauté" setting on your Instant Pot and continue to cook until most of the liquid evaporates, stirring occasionally. Turn off the "Sauté" function. Serve and enjoy!

Creamy Lamb Korma
Time: 45 minutes   Servings: 4

Ingredients:

- 1 pound of lamb steak, cut into 1-inch pieces
- 1 tablespoon of extra-virgin olive oil
- 1 medium onion, finely chopped
- 1-inch piece of ginger, peeled and minced
- 6 medium garlic cloves, peeled and minced
- 2 tablespoons of tomato paste
- ½ cup of coconut milk or plain yogurt

- ¾ cups of water
- 3 teaspoons of garam masala
- ½ teaspoon of turmeric powder
- 1 teaspoon of smoked or regular paprika
- ½ teaspoon of cardamom powder
- Fine sea salt and freshly cracked black pepper (to taste)

Instructions:

- Press the "Sauté" setting on your Instant Pot and add the olive oil. Once hot, add the chopped onions, minced garlic and minced ginger. Sauté for 1 minutes, stirring frequently.
- Add the tomato paste along with ¼ cup of water. Give a good stir.
- Stir in all the seasonings and give another good stir.
- Stir in the coconut milk, the remainder of the water and lamb pieces. Lock the lid and cook at high pressure for 15 minutes. When the cooking is done, naturally release the pressure and remove the lid. Serve and enjoy!

Greek-Style Roasted Lamb Shoulder
Time: 1 hour and 30 minutes   Servings: 6

Ingredients:

- 2 pounds of lamb shoulder
- 4 garlic cloves, peeled and sliced
- 4 fresh sprigs of thyme
- 1 cup of homemade low-sodium beef broth

- Fine sea salt and freshly cracked black pepper (to taste)
- 2 tablespoons of pomegranate seeds (for serving)
- 3 lemon wedges (for serving)

Instructions:

- Unroll the lamb shoulder and season with sea salt and freshly cracked black pepper. Add the fresh thyme sprigs and sliced garlic.
- Roll the lamb shoulder and secure with a butcher's string. Make sure it is tightly sealed.
- Add 1 cup of beef broth inside your Instant Pot and place the lamb shoulder inside.
- Lock the lid and cook at high pressure for 40 minutes. When the cooking is done, naturally release the pressure for 10 minutes, then quick release the remaining pressure. Carefully remove the lid.
- Remove the butcher's string and unroll the lamb shoulder. Slice into servings and transfer to serving plates. Top with pomegranate seeds and serve with lemon wedges. Serve and enjoy!

Lamb Chops in Mint Cream Sauce
Time: 50 minutes   Servings: 4

Ingredients:

- 4 lamb chops
- 2 tablespoons of extra-virgin olive oil
- 1 cup of homemade low-sodium beef broth
- 2 tablespoons of fresh dill, chopped

- ¼ cup of fresh mint, chopped
- 1 tablespoon of freshly squeezed lemon juice
- 2 tablespoons of heavy whipping cream
- Fine sea salt and freshly cracked black pepper (to taste)

Instructions:

- Season the lamb ribs with sea salt and freshly cracked black pepper.
- Press the "Sauté" setting on your Instant Pot and add the olive oil. Once hot, add the lamb ribs and sear for 3 minutes or until brown.

- Pour in the beef broth. Lock the lid and cook at high pressure for 30 minutes. When the cooking is done, naturally release the pressure for 10 minutes, then quick release the remaining pressure. Carefully remove the lid.
- In a blender, add the fresh dill, mint, lemon juice, heavy whipping cream. Blend until smooth.
- Transfer the lamb chops to serving plates and top with the mint cream sauce.

Asian-Style Lamb Ribs
Time: 20 minutes   Servings: 4

Ingredients:

- 3 pounds of lamb ribs
- 2 cups of homemade low-sodium beef broth
- ½ cup of coconut aminos
- 2 tablespoons of white wine vinegar

- 2 teaspoons of garlic powder
- 2 teaspoons of fine ginger powder
- 1 teaspoon of Chinese Five Spices
- 1 teaspoon of smoked paprika or regular paprika

Instructions:

- In a small bowl, add the garlic powder, ginger powder, Chinese five spices and paprika. Mix well.
- Rub the seasoning mixture over the lamb ribs.
- Add the lamb ribs along with the beef broth inside your Instant Pot. Lock the lid and cook at high pressure for 10 minutes. When the cooking is done, quick release the pressure and carefully remove the lid.
- Meanwhile, in a small saucepan over medium heat, add the coconut aminos and vinegar. Allow to get heated through.
- Press the "Sauté" setting on your Instant Pot and pour in the heated sauce over the lamb ribs. Continue to cook until the ribs are brown and tender. Serve and enjoy!

Lamb Chops with Basil-Dijon Butter Sauce
Time: 25 minutes   Servings: 4

Ingredients:

- 4 lamb chops
- 2 tablespoons of olive oil
- ½ cup of homemade low-sodium beef broth
- ¼ cup of fresh basil, chopped

- 6 medium garlic cloves, minced
- ¼ cup of Dijon mustard
- ¼ cup of unsalted butter, softened
- Fine sea salt and freshly cracked black pepper (to taste)

Instructions:

- Season the lamb chops with sea salt and freshly cracked black pepper.
- Press the "Sauté" setting on your Instant Pot and add the olive oil. Once hot, add the lamb chops and sear for 4 minutes per side or until brown. Pour in the beef broth. Lock the lid and cook at high pressure for 6 minutes.
- When the cooking is done, naturally release the pressure and carefully remove the lid. Carefully remove the lamb chops and discard the beef broth.
- Press the "Sauté" setting on your Instant Pot and add the butter. Once melted, add the garlic cloves and sauté for 1 minute or until fragrant, stirring frequently.
- Add the chopped fresh basil and Dijon mustard, stirring occasionally. Add a pinch of sea salt and black pepper.
- Place the lamb chops onto serving plates and spoon the butter sauce on top. Serve and enjoy!

Lamb Chops with Pesto Sauce
Time: 30 minutes   Servings: 4

Ingredients:

- 4 lamb chops
- 2 tablespoons of unsalted butter
- 4 cups of basil leaves
- ½ cup of pine nuts or walnuts

- ½ cup of extra-virgin olive oil
- 1 lemon, juice
- Fine sea salt and freshly cracked black pepper (to taste)

Instructions:

- Season the lamb chops with sea salt and freshly cracked black pepper.
- In a blender, add the basil leaves, pine nuts, extra virgin olive oil, and lemon juice. Blend until smooth.

- Press the "Sauté" setting on your Instant Pot and add the butter. Once hot, add the lamb chops and sear for 4 minutes or until brown on both sides.
- Pour in ½ cup of beef broth. Lock the lid and cook at high pressure for 5 minutes. When the cooking is done, naturally release the pressure for 10 minutes, then quick release the remaining pressure. Carefully remove the lid.
- Place the lamb chops onto serving plates and top with the pesto sauce. Serve and enjoy!

Lamb Curry
Time: 50 minutes   Servings: 6

Ingredients:

- 1 ½ pound of lamb stew meat, cut into 1-inch pieces
- 4 garlic cloves, minced
- 1 medium onion, finely chopped
- 3 medium carrots, sliced
- 1 medium zucchini, chopped
- 1-inch piece of fresh ginger, peeled and grated
- ½ cup of unsweetened coconut milk
- ½ lime, juice
- 2 tablespoons of coconut oil
- 1 (14.5-ounce) can of diced tomatoes
- 2 tablespoons of garam masala
- 1 teaspoon of turmeric or curry powder
- Fine sea salt and freshly cracked black pepper (to taste)

Instructions:

- In a large Ziploc bag or a large bowl, add the lamb meat, garlic, ginger, coconut milk, lime juice, sea salt and freshly cracked black pepper. Mix until well combined and allow to marinate overnight.
- When done, add the meat along with the marinade, can of diced tomatoes, coconut oil, garam masala, chopped onions, and sliced carrots. Lock the lid and cook at high pressure for 20 minutes.
- When the cooking is done, allow for a full natural release method before carefully removing the lid.
- Press the "Sauté" setting on your Instant Pot and gently stir in the chopped zucchini. Allow to simmer for a couple of minutes or until the liquid thickens and the zucchini is tender, stirring frequently. Serve and enjoy!

Chinese Lamb Stew
Time: 2 hours   Servings: 4

Ingredients:

- 1 ½ pound of lamb stew meat
- 3 tablespoons of fresh ginger, peeled and sliced
- 8 medium garlic cloves, peeled and crushed
- 4 stalks of green onions, chopped
- 1 small shallot, finely chopped
- 1 cup of shiitake mushrooms, chopped
- 2 tablespoons of olive oil
- ¼ cup of Shaoxing wine
- 3 tablespoons of chu hou paste
- 2 tablespoons of coconut aminos
- 1 cup of homemade low-sodium beef broth
- Fine sea salt and freshly cracked black pepper (to taste)

Instructions:

- Press the "Sauté" Setting on your Instant Pot and add the olive oil. Once hot, add the lamb meat and cook until brown, stirring occasionally.
- Add the minced garlic, ginger, shallots and green onions. Sauté for 2 minutes or until fragrant, stirring frequently.
- Add the mushrooms and sauté for another 4 minutes, stirring frequently.
- Add the remaining ingredients inside your Instant Pot. Lock the lid and cook at high pressure for 50 minutes. When the cooking is done, allow for a full natural release before carefully removing the lid. Serve and enjoy!

Braised Lamb with Cauliflower and Spinach
Time: 50 minutes   Servings: 4

Ingredients:

- 4 bone-in lamb shoulder chops
- 1 large cauliflower head, cut into florets
- 1 large bunch of spinach
- 2 tablespoons of extra-virgin olive oil
- 1 small onion, finely chopped
- 3 medium garlic cloves, peeled and crushed
- ¼ cup of red wine
- 2 cups of homemade low-sodium beef broth

- 4 fresh sprigs of rosemary
- 2 tablespoons of freshly squeezed lemon juice

- Fine sea salt and freshly cracked black pepper (to taste)

Instructions:

- Press the "Sauté" Setting on your Instant Pot and add the olive oil. Once hot, add the lamb chops and sear for 2 minutes on both sides or until golden brown. Transfer to a plate and set aside.
- Add the chopped onions and minced garlic to the inner pot. Sauté for 2 minutes or until fragrant, stirring frequently.
- Deglaze your Instant Pot with the red wine and cook for 2 minutes.
- Return the lamb chops to your Instant Pot along with the beef broth and rosemary. Lock the lid and cook at high pressure for 20 minutes. When the cooking is done, quick release the pressure and carefully remove the lid.
- Transfer the lamb chops to a large bowl and remove the rosemary stems. Press the "Sauté" setting on your Instant Pot and cook until the liquid reduces.
- Meanwhile, shred the lamb and stir to the liquid along with the cauliflower, spinach, lemon juice, sea salt and freshly cracked black pepper.
- Cover and sit for 10 minutes or until the cauliflower is tender and the spinach has wilted.
- Serve and enjoy!

Irish Lamb Stew
Time: 1 hour and 30 minutes   Servings: 6

Ingredients:

- 1 pound of lamb stew meat
- 4 bacon slices, roughly chopped
- 4 cups of homemade low-sodium beef broth
- 2 bay leaves
- 1 sprig of fresh rosemary

- 1 sprig of fresh thyme
- 1 white onion, finely chopped
- 1 cup of button mushrooms, sliced
- 2 tablespoons of almond flour
- Fine sea salt and freshly cracked black pepper (to taste)

Instructions:

- Press the "Sauté" setting on your Instant Pot and add the bacon. Cook for 5 minutes or until brown and crispy, stirring frequently. Transfer the bacon to a plate lined with paper towels.
- Season the lamb with sea salt and freshly cracked black pepper. Sprinkle with 2 tablespoons of almond flour.
- Place the lamb stew meat to the inner pot and cook until brown.
- Deglaze your Instant Pot with the beef broth and stir in the rosemary, thyme and bay leaves.
- Lock the lid and cook at high pressure for 30 minutes. When the cooking is done, quick release the pressure and remove the lid.
- Stir in the chopped onions, mushrooms and return the bacon. Lock the lid and cook at high pressure for 10 minutes. When done, naturally release the pressure for 10 minutes, then quick release the remaining pressure. Carefully remove the lid.
- Adjust the stew seasoning if necessary and give a good stir. Serve and enjoy!

Part 5: Soups and Stews Recipes

Classy Creamy Mushroom Stew
Time: 40 minutes　　　　Servings: 6

Ingredients:

- 1 pound cremini mushrooms, sliced
- 1 celery stalk, chopped
- 2 Tablespoons green onions, chopped
- 2 garlic cloves, minced
- 2 cups beef stock
- ½ cup heavy cream
- 5 ounces cream cheese, softened

- 1 Tablespoon unsalted butter, melted
- 1 Tablespoon lemon juice
- 1 teaspoon fresh or dried thyme
- 2 Tablespoons fresh sage, chopped
- 1 bay leaf
- 1 teaspoon salt
- 1 teaspoon fresh ground black pepper

Instructions:

1. Rinse the mushrooms, pat dry. Press Sauté button on Instant Pot. Melt the butter.
2. Add green onions, garlic. Cook for 1 minute.
3. Add mushrooms, celery, and garlic. Sauté until vegetables are softened.
4. Press Keep Warm/Cancel setting to stop Sauté mode. Add remaining ingredients. Stir well.
5. Close and seal lid. Select Meat/Stew button. Set cooking time to 20 minutes.
6. Once done, Instant Pot will switch to Keep Warm mode.
7. Remain on Keep Warm for 10 minutes.
8. When done, use Quick-Release setting; turn valve from sealing to venting to release pressure quickly. Open the lid with care. Stir ingredients.
9. Serve. Garnish with green onion, grated parmesan cheese.

Divine Cabbage Beef Soup
Time: 40 minutes　　　　Servings: 6

Ingredients:

- 1 pound lean ground beef
- 1 head green cabbage, chopped
- 1 head red cabbage, chopped
- 1 celery stalk, chopped
- 1 can (28-ounce) diced tomatoes

- 3 cups water
- 1 teaspoon salt
- 1 teaspoon fresh ground black pepper
- 1 Tablespoon fresh parsley, chopped

Instructions:

1. Press Sauté button on Instant Pot. Add ground beef. Sauté until no longer pink; drain.
2. Press Keep Warm/Cancel setting to stop Sauté mode.
3. Return ground beef to Instant Pot. Add cabbage, celery, diced tomatoes, water, parsley, salt, and pepper. Stir well.
4. Close and seal lid. Press Meat/Stew. Cook on High Pressure for 20 minutes.
5. Once done, Instant Pot will switch to Keep Warm mode.
6. Remain in Keep Warm mode for 10 minutes.
7. When done, use Quick-Release. Open the lid with care. Stir ingredients.
8. Serve. Garnish with fresh parsley.

Creamy Garlic Chicken Noodle Soup
Time: 40 minutes　　　　Servings: 4

Ingredients:

- 1 pound chicken breasts, boneless, skinless
- 1 pound squash noodle spirals (or any keto-friendly alternative)
- 1 celery stalk, chopped
- 1 cup carrots, chopped

- 2 green onions, chopped
- 6 cups chicken broth
- 2 Tablespoons coconut oil
- 1 teaspoon salt (to taste)
- 1 teaspoon fresh ground black pepper)

Instructions:

1. Rinse the chicken, pat dry.

2. Press the Sauté button on your Instant Pot. Heat the coconut oil.
3. Add chicken breasts. Sauté until brown on both sides and cooked through.
4. Remove chicken and shred with a fork.
5. Add celery, carrots, and green onion to Instant Pot. Sauté for 3 minutes.
6. Press Keep Warm/Cancel setting to stop Sauté mode.
7. Return shredded chicken and remaining ingredients to Instant Pot. Stir well.
8. Close and seal lid. Press Soup button. Cook for 30 minutes.
9. When done, set to quick pressure release to vent steam. Open the lid with care. Stir.
10. Spoon into serving bowls. Garnish with fresh green onions.

Amazing Spinach, Kale, and Artichoke Soup
Time: 25 minutes   Servings: 4

Ingredients:

- 1 bunch of kale, stemmed and chopped
- 4 cups spinach
- 1-ounce jar artichoke hearts, drained and chopped
- 4 cups low-sodium chicken broth
- ¼ cup cheddar cheese, shredded
- ¼ cup mozzarella cheese, shredded
- 1 Tablespoon butter, melted
- 1 Tablespoon Italian seasoning
- 2 teaspoons fresh parsley, chopped
- 1 teaspoon salt
- 1 teaspoon fresh ground black pepper

Instructions:

1. Place all ingredients in Instant Pot. Stir well.
2. Close and seal lid. Press Manual setting. Cook for 15 minutes.
3. When done, use Quick-Release setting. Open the lid with care. Stir ingredients. Serve.

Exquisite Chicken Avocado Soup
Time: 40 minutes   Servings: 4

Ingredients:

- 4 chicken breasts, boneless, skinless
- 1 tablespoon coconut oil
- 4 avocados, peeled and chopped
- 4 cups chicken broth
- Zest and juice from 1 lime
- 1 Tablespoon fresh cilantro, chopped
- 1 teaspoon salt
- 1 teaspoon fresh ground black pepper
- 2 tomatoes, chopped
- 2 garlic cloves, minced

Instructions:

1. Rinse the chicken, pat dry. Cut into strips. Press Sauté button on Instant Pot. Melt the coconut oil. Add chicken strips. Sauté until chicken no longer pink. Add garlic and tomatoes. Stir well.
2. Press Keep Warm/Cancel setting to stop Sauté mode.
3. Add chopped avocados, chicken broth, lime juice, lime zest, cilantro, salt, and black pepper. Stir well.
4. Close and seal lid. Press Meat/Stew button on Instant Pot. Cook for 20 minutes.
5. Once done, Instant Pot will switch to Keep Warm mode.
6. Remain in Keep Warm mode for 10 minutes.
7. When done, use Quick-Release. Open the lid with care. Stir ingredients. Serve.

Deluxe Cauliflower Stew
Time: 40 minutes   Servings: 4

Ingredients:

- 4 slices of bacon, cooked and crumbled
- 1 teaspoon coconut oil
- 1 head cauliflower, chopped into florets
- ¼ cup coconut flour
- 4 cups chicken broth
- 2 celery stalks, chopped
- 1 shallot, chopped
- 2 garlic cloves, minced
- 1 teaspoon salt
- 1 teaspoon fresh ground black pepper
- 1 Tablespoon fresh parsley, chopped

Instructions:

1. In a skillet or your Instant Pot, cook the bacon. Drain on paper towel. Set aside.
2. Press Sauté button on Instant Pot. Heat coconut oil.
3. Add cauliflower, celery, shallots, and garlic cloves. Sauté until vegetables soften.
4. Press Keep Warm/Cancel setting to stop Sauté mode.
5. Add coconut flour to ingredients. Stir well. Add chicken broth. Stir well.
6. Close and seal lid. Press Soup button. Cook 30 minutes.
7. When done, set to quick pressure release. Open the lid with care. Stir ingredients.
8. Serve. Garnish with fresh parsley.

Elegant Cauliflower and Cheddar Soup
Time: 50 minutes   Servings: 4

Ingredients:

- 2 Tablespoons butter
- 1 head cauliflower, chopped into florets
- 4 cups vegetable broth
- 1 red onion, diced
- 2 garlic cloves, minced

- ½ cup heavy cream
- ½ cup cheddar cheese, grated
- 1 teaspoon salt
- 1 teaspoon fresh ground black pepper

Instructions:

1. Press Sauté button on Instant Pot. Melt the butter.
2. Add red onion, garlic. Sweat for 1 minute.
3. Add cauliflower. Sauté until cauliflower softens.
4. Press Keep Warm/Cancel setting to stop Sauté mode.
5. Add remaining ingredients. Mix well.
6. Close and seal lid. Press Soup button. Cook on high pressure for 30 minutes.
7. When done, Instant Pot will switch to Keep Warm mode.
8. Remain in Keep Warm mode for 10 minutes.
9. When done, use Quick-Release setting. Open the lid with care. Stir ingredients. Serve.

Savory Beef and Squash Stew
Time: 50 minutes   Servings: 4

Ingredients:

- 1 pound lean ground beef
- 2 pounds butternut squash, peeled, chopped into chunks
- 1 (6-ounce) can sliced mushrooms
- 2 Tablespoons butter
- 4 cups beef broth

- 1 red onion, diced
- 2 garlic cloves, minced
- 1 teaspoon fresh rosemary, chopped
- 2 teaspoons paprika
- 1 teaspoon salt (to taste)
- 1 teaspoon fresh ground black pepper (to taste)

Instructions:

1. Press Sauté button on Instant Pot. Melt the butter. Sauté the onions, garlic for 1 minute.
2. Add ground beef, butternut squash, and mushrooms.
3. Sauté until the ground beef is no longer pink and vegetables soften.
4. Press Keep Warm/Cancel setting to stop Sauté mode.
5. Add beef stock, rosemary, paprika, salt, and black pepper. Mix well.
6. Close and seal lid. Press Soup button. Cook on high pressure for 30 minutes.
7. After 30 minutes, Instant Pot will switch to Keep Warm. Remain in Keep Warm 10 minutes.
8. When done, use Quick-Release. Open the lid with care. Stir ingredients. Serve.

Smoky Bacon Chili
Time: 40 minutes   Servings: 4

Ingredients:

- 8 slices bacon, cooked and crumbled
- 2 pounds lean ground beef
- 1 can (6-ounce) tomato paste

- 1 can (14-ounce) diced tomatoes
- 1 yellow onion, chopped
- 2 garlic cloves, minced

- 1 yellow bell pepper, chopped
- 1 red bell pepper, chopped
- 1 green bell pepper, chopped
- 2 Tablespoons fresh cilantro, chopped
- 1 Tablespoon smoked paprika
- 1 Tablespoon chili powder
- 2 teaspoons cumin
- 1 teaspoon salt (to taste)
- 1 teaspoon fresh ground black pepper (to taste)

Instructions:

1. Press Sauté button on Instant Pot. Add ground beef.
2. Cook until brown. Drain, and set aside.
3. Drizzle 1 teaspoon coconut oil along bottom of Instant Pot. Add yellow onion, garlic cloves. Cook 1 minute. Add the bell peppers. Sauté until tender to a fork.
4. Press Keep Warm/Cancel setting to stop Sauté mode.
5. Return ground beef, remaining ingredients, seasoning to Instant Pot. Stir well.
6. Close and seal lid. Press Bean/Chili button. Cook for 30 minutes.
7. Once done, naturally release or quick-release pressure. Open the lid with care. Stir ingredients. (Add more seasoning if desired.) Serve.

Weeknight Clam Chowder
Time: 45 minutes   Servings: 4

Ingredients:

- 3 (10-ounce) cans fancy whole baby clams
- 1 pound bacon strips, cooked and crumbled
- 1 Tablespoon butter
- 2 cups chicken broth
- 2 cups heavy cream
- 4 garlic cloves, minced
- 1 red onion, chopped
- 8 ounce package cream cheese
- ¼ cup mozzarella cheese, shredded
- 1 teaspoon ground thyme
- 2 teaspoons salt (to taste)
- 1 teaspoon fresh ground black pepper (to taste)

Instructions:

1. Press Sauté button on Instant Pot. Melt the butter. Add red onion and garlic. Cook/sweat 1 minute. Press Keep Warm/Cancel setting to stop Sauté mode.
2. Add remaining ingredients. Stir well.
3. Close and seal lid. Press Manual setting. Cook on high pressure 30 minutes.
4. Once done, Instant Pot will switch to Keep Warm mode.
5. Remain in Keep Warm mode 5 minutes.
6. Naturally release or quick-release the pressure. Open the lid with care. Stir. Serve.

Enriching Lamb Stew
Time: 45 minutes   Servings: 4

Ingredients:

- 2 pounds lamb shoulder
- 1 Tablespoon butter
- 1 red onion, chopped
- 4 garlic cloves, minced
- 2 tomatoes, diced
- 3 cups vegetable broth
- 1 (14-ounce) can coconut milk
- 1 teaspoon ginger, grated
- 1 Tablespoon fresh cilantro, chopped
- 1 teaspoon salt
- 1 teaspoon fresh ground black pepper

Instructions:

1. Wash the lamb, pat dry. Cut into chunks. Press Sauté button on Instant Pot. Melt the butter.
2. Add red onion, garlic to Instant Pot. Cook/sweat for 1 minute.
3. Add lamb shoulder. Sear (brown) on all sides.
4. Press Keep Warm/Cancel button to stop Sauté mode.
5. Add tomatoes, vegetable stock, coconut milk, ginger, cilantro, salt and pepper. Stir well.
6. Close and seal lid. Press Meat/Stew button. Cook for 35 minutes.
7. Quick-release the pressure when done. Open the lid with care. Stir ingredients.
8. Serve. Garnish with fresh cilantro.

Almost-Famous Chicken Chili
Time: 40 minutes   Servings: 4

Ingredients:

- 1 pound ground chicken
- 1 Tablespoon butter
- 1 yellow onion, diced
- 2 garlic cloves, minced
- 1 red bell pepper, chopped
- 1 green bell pepper, chopped
- 2 celery stalks, chopped
- 1 jalapeno pepper, chopped (optional)
- 1 cup corn kernels

- 1 can (14-ounce) diced tomatoes
- 2 cups chicken broth
- 1 can (6-ounce) tomato paste
- 1 teaspoon ground cumin
- 1 teaspoon smoked paprika
- 1 Tablespoon fresh cilantro, chopped
- 1 teaspoon salt (to taste)
- 1 teaspoon fresh ground black pepper (to taste)

Instructions:

1. Press Sauté button on Instant Pot. Melt the butter. Add onions and garlic. Sweat for 1 minute.
2. Add ground chicken. Sauté until chicken is brown.
3. Add red and green bell peppers, celery, jalapeno, corn, tomatoes. Stir well.
4. Add tomato paste. Stir well. Add chicken broth. Stir well.
5. Add the spices. Stir well.
6. Press Keep Warm/Cancel setting to stop Sauté mode.
7. Close and seal lid. Press Bean/Chili button. Cook for 30 minutes.
8. Naturally release or quick-release pressure once done. Stir ingredients. Serve.

Delicious Broccoli Cheese Soup
Time: 40 minutes   Servings: 4

Ingredients:

- 1 head broccoli, chopped into florets
- 4 garlic cloves, minced
- 3 cups vegetable broth
- 1 cup heavy cream

- 3 cups cheddar cheese, shredded
- 1 teaspoon salt (to taste)
- 1 teaspoon fresh ground black pepper (to taste)

Instructions:

1. In your Instant Pot, add broccoli florets, garlic, vegetable stock, heavy cream, and shredded cheese. Stir well.
2. Close and seal lid. Press Soup button. Cook for 30 minutes.
3. Naturally release or quick-release pressure when done. Open the lid with care. Stir. Serve.

Tongue-Kicking Jalapeno Popper Soup
Time: 40 minutes   Servings: 4

Ingredients:

- 2 chicken breasts, boneless, skinless
- 2 Tablespoons coconut oil
- 6 slices of bacon, cooked and crumbled
- 4 jalapeno peppers, finely sliced (depending on desired heat level, can leave some seeds in, or remove all the seeds)
- 2 Tablespoons butter
- ½ cup cream cheese, softened

- 1 cup heavy cream
- 2 cups chicken broth
- 2 Tablespoons salsa verde (or green sauce)
- ½ cup cheddar cheese, shredded
- ½ cup mozzarella cheese, shredded
- 1 teaspoon garlic powder
- 1 teaspoon salt (to taste)
- 1 teaspoon black pepper (to taste)

Instructions:

1. Rinse the chicken, pat dry.
2. Press Sauté button on Instant Pot. Heat the coconut oil. Add chicken breasts.
3. Cook until chicken breasts cooked through. Remove and shred chicken with fork.
4. Press Keep Warm/Cancel button to stop Sauté mode.
5. Return chicken to Instant Pot. Add rest of ingredients. Stir well.
6. Close and seal lid. Press Soup button. Cook 30 minutes.
7. Naturally or quick-release pressure when the timer beeps,. Open the lid with care. Stir. Serve.

Southwestern Pork Stew
Time: 40 minutes   Servings: 4

Ingredients:

- 1 pound pork shoulder
- 1 red onion, diced
- 2 garlic cloves, minced
- 2 Tablespoons coconut oil
- 6-ounce can sliced mushrooms
- 1 green bell pepper, chopped
- 1 red bell pepper, chopped
- 4 cups beef broth
- Juice from 1 lime
- ½ cup tomato paste
- 2 teaspoons chili powder
- 2 teaspoons ground cumin
- 1 Tablespoon fresh cilantro, chopped
- 1 teaspoon smoked paprika
- 1 teaspoon salt (to taste)
- 1 teaspoon fresh ground black pepper (to taste)

Instructions:

1. Rinse the pork shoulder, pat dry. Cut into chunks.
2. Press Sauté button on Instant Pot. Heat the coconut oil.
3. Add onion, garlic. Sweat for 1 minute. Add pork shoulder. Brown on all sides.
4. Add mushrooms, bell peppers. Sauté until vegetables have softened.
5. Press Keep Warm/Cancel button to stop Sauté mode.
6. Add rest of ingredients. Stir well. Close and seal lid. Press Soup button. Cook for 30 minutes.
7. When the timer beeps, quick-release or naturally release pressure. Open the lid with care. Stir ingredients. Serve

Spiced Pumpkin and Sausage Soup
Time: 40 minutes   Servings: 4

Ingredients:

- 1 pound pork sausage, chopped
- 2 cups pumpkin puree (not pie filling)
- 2 cups vegetable broth
- 1 cup heavy cream
- 4 Tablespoons butter
- 1 red onion
- 2 garlic cloves, minced
- 4 slices of bacon, cooked and crumbled
- 1 teaspoon onion powder
- 1 teaspoon ground cumin
- 1 teaspoon cinnamon
- 1 teaspoon ginger, grated
- 1 teaspoon salt (to taste)
- 1 teaspoon fresh ground black pepper (to taste)

Instructions:

1. Cook the bacon. Crumble in small pieces and set aside.
2. Press Sauté button on Instant Pot. Melt the butter.
3. Add onion and garlic. Sweat for 1 minute. Add sausage. Sauté until sausage is brown.
4. Add pumpkin puree. Stir well. Add vegetable stock, heavy cream. Stir well.
5. Add seasoning. Stir well. Press Keep Warm/Cancel setting to stop Sauté mode.
6. Close and seal lid. Press Soup button. Cook for 30 minutes.
7. Quick-release or naturally release pressure when done. Open the lid with care. Stir. Top with crumbled bacon. Serve.

Autumn Beef and Vegetable Stew
Time: 45 minutes   Servings: 4

Ingredients:

- 1½ pounds stewing beef chunks
- 4 zucchini, chopped
- 2 carrots, chopped
- 2 cups frozen peas
- 4 cups vegetable broth
- 1 Tablespoon coconut oil
- ½ cup ghee
- 1 red onion, chopped
- 4 garlic cloves, minced
- 2 tomatoes, chopped
- 2 Tablespoons ground cumin
- 1 Tablespoon ground ginger
- 1 teaspoon salt (to taste)
- 1 teaspoon fresh ground black pepper (to taste)

Instructions:

1. Press Sauté button on Instant Pot. Heat the coconut oil. Add onions and garlic. Sweat for 1 minute. Add stewing beef. Brown on all sides. Add zucchini, carrots, and peas.
2. Press Keep Warm/Cancel setting to stop Sauté mode.
3. Add ghee. Stir well. Add vegetable stock. Stir well. Add tomatoes, cumin, ginger, salt and pepper. Stir well.
4. Close and seal lid. Press Meat/Stew button. Cook for 35 minutes.
5. When the timer beeps, quick-release or naturally release pressure. Open the lid with care. Stir ingredients. Spoon into serving bowls.

Splendid Broccoli and Ham Chowder
Time: 50 minutes   Servings: 6

Ingredients:

- 1 head of broccoli
- 1 pound of ham
- 2 Tablespoons coconut oil
- 1 celery stalk, chopped
- 1 yellow onion, chopped
- 4 garlic cloves, minced
- 4 cups vegetable broth
- 1 cup of organic heavy cream
- ¼ cup mozzarella cheese, shredded
- ¼ cup parmesan cheese, shredded
- ¼ cup fresh parsley, chopped
- 1 teaspoon salt (to taste)
- 1 teaspoon fresh ground black pepper (to taste)

Instructions:

1. Rinse the broccoli, chop into florets. Chop ham into chunks.
2. Press Sauté button on Instant Pot. Heat the coconut oil. Add onions and garlic. Sweat for 1 minute. Add celery. Add cauliflower and ham.
3. Sauté until meat is brown and vegetables have softened.
4. Press Keep Warm/Cancel button to stop Sauté mode.
5. Add vegetable stock, heavy cream. Stir well.
6. Add mozzarella cheese, parmesan cheese. Stir well.
7. Close and seal lid. Press Manual button. Cook on High Pressure for 30 minutes.
8. Instant Pot will switch to Keep Warm mode when the timer beeps,.
9. Remain on Keep Warm for 10 minutes.
10. Use Quick-Release when done,. Open the lid with care. Stir ingredients. Serve.

Magnificent Asparagus Stew
Time: 45 minutes   Servings: 4

Ingredients:

- 2 Tablespoons coconut oil
- 1 pound of asparagus
- 1 green bell pepper, chopped
- 1 red bell pepper, chopped
- 2 shallots, chopped
- 4 garlic cloves, minced
- 1 leek, chopped
- 4 cups vegetable broth
- ¼ cup fresh parsley, chopped
- 1 teaspoon salt (to taste)
- 1 teaspoon fresh ground black pepper (to taste)

Instructions:

1. Rinse asparagus, pat dry. Break off woodsy end. Chop asparagus in bite-size pieces.
2. Press Sauté button on Instant Pot. Heat the coconut oil.
3. Add asparagus, bell peppers, shallots, garlic cloves and leeks.
4. Sauté until vegetables have softened. Press Keep Warm/Cancel setting to stop Sauté mode.
5. Add vegetable broth and parsley. Stir well.
6. Close and seal lid. Press Meat/Stew button on Instant Pot. Cook 35 minutes.
7. Quick release pressure when the timer beeps,. Open the lid with care. Stir ingredients. Serve.

Satisfying Turkey Stew
Time: 45 minutes

Servings: 4

Ingredients:

- 4 cups cooked turkey meat, cut in chunks (not ground turkey)
- 4 celery stalks, chopped
- 2 green onions, chopped
- 2 garlic cloves, minced
- 4 carrots, chopped
- 4 cups turkey or vegetable broth
- Zest and juice from ½ lemon
- 2 Tablespoons coconut oil
- 1 Tablespoon coconut flour
- 1 teaspoon salt (to taste)
- 1 teaspoon fresh ground black pepper (to taste)

Instructions:

1. Press Sauté button on Instant Pot. Heat the coconut oil. Add green onions and garlic. Sweat for 1 minute. Add celery and carrots. Sauté until vegetables have softened.
2. Press Keep Warm/Cancel button to end Sauté mode.
3. Add turkey. Stir in coconut flour to coat ingredients.
4. Pour in turkey/vegetable broth, lemon juice, lemon zest, salt, and pepper. Stir.
5. Close and seal lid. Press Meat/Stew button. Cook for 35 minutes.
6. When the timer beeps, set to quick pressure release. Open the lid with care. Stir.
7. Spoon into serving bowls. Serve.

Homemade Vegetable Stock

Time: Around 50 minutes   Servings: 8 cups

Ingredients:

- 8 cups of water
- 2 garlic cloves, minced
- 2 bay leaves
- 8 peppercorns
- 6 sprigs of parsley
- 4 sprigs of thyme
- 4 celery stalks, chopped
- 4 carrots, peeled and chopped
- 2 green onions, sliced
- Any other keto-friendly vegetables (as desired)
- 1 teaspoon of salt (to taste)
- 1 teaspoon of black pepper

Instructions:

- Add all the ingredients inside your Instant Pot. No need to stir the contents.
- Lock the lid and cook at high pressure for 30 minutes. When the cooking is done, allow for a full natural release method. Carefully remove the lid.
- Strain the vegetable stock through a fine-mesh strainer. Transfer to mason jars and place inside your refrigerato Use as needed.

Mulligatawny Soup

Time: 25 minutes   Servings: 10

Ingredients:

- 10 cups of homemade low-sodium chicken stock or turkey stock
- 2 tablespoons of curry powder
- 5 cups of boneless, skinless chicken breasts, cut into bite-sized pieces
- ¼ cup of apple cider vinegar
- 3 cups of celery root, finely chopped
- 2 tablespoons of Swerve sweetener
- ½ cup of sour cream
- ¼ cup of fresh parsley, finely chopped
- Sea salt and freshly cracked black pepper (to taste)

Instructions:

- Add all the ingredients except for the sour cream and fresh parsley.
- Lock the lid and cook at high pressure for 18 minutes. When the cooking is done, naturally release the pressure and carefully remove the lid.
- Stir in the sour cream and fresh parsley. Serve and enjoy!

Turkey Sausage, Pumpkin and Kale Soup

Time: 30 minutes   Servings: 8

Ingredients:

- 1 pound of Italian turkey sausage
- 2 tablespoons of olive oil

- ½ cup of white or brown onion, finely chopped
- 3 cups of pumpkin or butternut squash, chopped
- 4 cups of kale, stemmed and chopped
- 8 cups of homemade low-sodium chicken stock
- Fine sea salt and freshly cracked black pepper (to taste)

Instructions:

- Press the "Sauté" setting on your Instant Pot and add the olive oil. Once hot, add the onions and cook until translucent, stirring frequently.
- Add the turkey sausage and cook until brown, stirring occasionally.
- Add the remaining ingredients and stir until well combined. Lock the lid and cook at high pressure for 15 minutes. When the cooking is done, naturally release the pressure and remove the lid.
- Stir the soup again and season with sea salt and black pepper. Serve and enjoy!

Chili Dog Soup
Time: 30 minutes   Servings: 6

Ingredients:

- 1 ½ pound of ground beef
- 4 hot dogs, sliced
- ¼ cup of low-sugar ketchup
- 2 tablespoons of Dijon mustard
- 1 (28-ounce) can of crushed tomatoes
- ½ cup of mild salsa
- 3 cups of homemade low-sodium beef broth
- 1 teaspoon of chili powder
- 1 tablespoon of ground cumin
- Fine sea salt and freshly cracked black pepper (to taste)

Instructions:

- Add all the ingredients inside your Instant Pot. You don't need to stir.
- Lock the lid and cook at high pressure for 20 minutes. When the cooking is done, naturally release the pressure and carefully remove the lid.
- Press the "Sauté" setting on your Instant Pot and cook until most of the liquid evaporates. Adjust the seasoning if necessary. Serve and enjoy!

Zuppa Toscana with Cauliflower
Time: 25 minutes   Servings: 4

Ingredients:

- 1 pound of ground Italian sausage
- 6 cups of homemade low-sodium chicken stock
- 2 cups of cauliflower florets
- 1 onion, finely chopped
- 1 cup of kale, stemmed and roughly chopped
- 1 (14.5-ounce) can of full-fat coconut milk
- Fine sea salt and freshly cracked black pepper (to taste)

Instructions:

- Press the "Sauté" function on your Instant Pot and add the ground Italian sausage. Cook until brown, stirring occasionally and breaking up the meat with a wooden spoon.
- Add the remaining ingredients except for the kale and coconut milk and stir until well combined.
- Lock the lid and cook at high pressure for 10 minutes. When the cooking is done, naturally release the pressure and remove the lid. Stir in the kale and coconut milk. Cover and sit for 5 minutes or until the kale has wilted. Serve and enjoy!

Andouille Sausage and Cabbage Soup
Time: 20 minutes   Servings: 4

Ingredients:

- 4 andouille sausage links, sliced
- 2 small shallots, finely chopped
- 4 medium garlic cloves, minced
- 8 cups of cabbage, sliced
- 1 cup of carrots, chopped
- 8 cups of homemade low-sodium chicken stock
- 1 teaspoon of fine sea salt
- 1 teaspoon of freshly cracked black pepper

Instructions:

- Add all the ingredients inside your Instant Pot. You do not need to stir.
- Lock the lid and cook at high pressure for 15 minutes. When the cooking is done, naturally release the pressure and carefully remove the lid. Stir the soup and adjust the seasoning if necessary. Serve!

Ham and Green Bean Soup
Time: 20 minutes　　　　Servings: 6

Ingredients:

- 8 cups of homemade low-sodium chicken stock
- 1 large onion, finely chopped
- 1 pound of green beans, cut into bite-sized pieces
- 1 pound of ham, cut into cubes
- Fine sea salt and freshly cracked black pepper (to taste)

Instructions:

- Add all the ingredients inside your Instant Pot. You do not need to stir.
- Lock the lid and cook at high pressure for 10 minutes. When the cooking is done, allow for a full natural release method. Carefully remove the lid.
- Stir the soup and adjust the seasoning if necessary. Serve and enjoy!

Fire-Roasted Tomato and Garlic Soup
Time: 15 minutes　　　　Servings: 8

Ingredients:

- 4 (14.5-ounce) cans of fire-roasted tomatoes, undrained
- 8 garlic cloves, peeled and crushed
- 2 tablespoons of extra-virgin olive oil
- 2 cups of homemade low-sodium chicken stock
- Fine sea salt and freshly cracked black pepper (to taste)

Instructions:

- Press the "Sauté" setting on your Instant Pot and add the olive oil. Once hot, add the crushed garlic and sauté for 1 minute or until fragrant. Be careful not to overcook the garlic.
- Add the remaining ingredients and lock the lid. Cook at high pressure for 8 minutes. When the cooking is done naturally release the pressure and remove the lid.
- Stir the soup again and adjust the seasoning if necessary. If you want, use an immersion blender to puree the soup until smooth. Serve and enjoy!

Pork and Tomato Soup
Time: 30 minutes　　　　Servings: 6

Ingredients:

- 2 pounds of boneless pork ribs, cut into 1-inch pieces
- 2 tablespoons of olive oil
- ½ cup of dry white wine
- 1 small onion, finely chopped
- 2 medium garlic cloves, minced
- 2 cups of homemade low-sodium chicken stock
- 1 (28-ounce) can of crushed tomatoes
- 2 cups of cauliflower rice
- 2 tablespoons of dried oregano
- Fine sea salt and freshly cracked black pepper (to taste)

Instructions:

- Press the "Sauté" setting on your Instant Pot and add the olive oil. Once hot, add the pork pieces and cook until brown.
- Add the onions and garlic cloves. Cook for another 2 minutes.
- Stir in the remaining ingredients and stir until well combined. Lock the lid and cook at high pressure for 20 minutes. When the cooking is done, naturally release the pressure and carefully remove the lid. Serve and enjoy

Spicy Shrimp and Chorizo Soup

Time: 30 minutes   Servings: 6

Ingredients:

- 1 pound of shrimp, peeled and deveined
- 3 tablespoons of olive oil
- 4 medium garlic cloves, minced
- 1 red bell pepper, chopped
- 3 celery stalks, chopped
- 1 medium onion, finely chopped
- 1 pound of chorizo, crumbled
- 1 (28-ounce) can of crushed tomatoes
- 4 cups of homemade low-sodium chicken stock
- Fine sea salt and freshly cracked black pepper (to taste)

Instructions:

- Press the "Sauté" setting on your Instant Pot and add the crumbled chorizo, chopped onions, chopped celery, chopped red bell pepper and minced garlic. Cook for 6 minutes or until the vegetable shave softened, stirring occasionally.
- Add the remaining ingredients and lock the lid. Cook at high pressure for 15 minutes.
- When the cooking is done, naturally release the pressure and carefully remove the lid.Serve and enjoy!

Bacon and Chicken Chowder

Time: 30 minutes   Servings: 6

Ingredients:

- 6 boneless, skinless chicken thighs
- 1 pound of bacon, chopped
- 2 cups of fresh spinach
- 1 (8-ounce) package of cream cheese, softened
- 1 cup of mushrooms
- 4 medium garlic cloves, minced
- 1 medium yellow onion, finely chopped
- 1 teaspoon of fresh thyme
- 1 teaspoon of fine sea salt
- 1 teaspoon of freshly cracked black pepper
- 3 cups of homemade low-sodium chicken stock
- 1 cup of heavy cream

Instructions:

- Press the "Sauté" setting on your Instant Pot and add the bacon. Cook until brown and crispy, stirring frequently. Transfer the bacon to a plate lined with paper towels.
- Add the chopped onions, mushrooms and garlic cloves to the bacon grease. Sauté for 4 minutes or until tender, stirring occasionally.
- Add the chicken thighs, cream cheese and chicken stock inside your Instant Pot. Lock the lid and cook at high pressure for 20 minutes. When the cooking is done, naturally release the pressure and carefully remove the lid.
- Stir in the bacon and remaining ingredients. Cover with a lid and let the chowder sit for 10 minutes. Serve and enjoy!

Cheesy Ham Chowder

Time: 15 minutes   Servings: 4

Ingredients:

- 4 bacon slices, chopped
- ½ medium onion, finely chopped
- 2 garlic cloves, minced
- 2 cups of homemade low-sodium chicken stock
- 1 ½ cup of heavy whipping cream
- 2 cups of pre-cooked ham, cut into cubes
- 2 cups of broccoli florets
- 1 teaspoon of cream cheese
- 1 teaspoon of fresh parsley, finely chopped
- 2 cups of shredded cheddar cheese
- ½ teaspoon of fine sea salt
- ½ teaspoon of freshly cracked black pepper

Instructions:

- Press the "Sauté" setting on your Instant Pot and add the chopped bacon. Cook until brown and crispy, stirring frequently. Transfer the bacon to a plate lined with paper towels.
- Add the chopped onions and minced garlic. Sauté until softened, stirring frequently.
- Add the remaining ingredients except for the cheddar cheese inside your Instant Pot and lock the lid. Cook at high pressure for 8 minutes. When the cooking is done, naturally release the pressure and remove the lid.
- Stir in the cheddar cheese and cook until the cheese has melted, stirring occasionally.Serve and enjoy!

Salmon and Bacon Chowder
Time: 10 minutes   Servings: 4

Ingredients:

- 1 pound of shrimp, peeled and deveined
- ½ pound of bacon strips, chopped
- 1 small onion, finely chopped
- 3 cups of homemade low-sodium chicken stock
- 1 ½ cup of heavy whipping cream
- ½ cup of shredded cheddar cheese
- 2 teaspoons of fine sea salt
- 2 teaspoons of freshly cracked black pepper
- 2 teaspoons of smoked paprika

Instructions:

- Press the "Sauté" function on your Instant Pot and add the bacon. Cook until the bacon has browned, stirring frequently. Transfer the bacon to a plate lined with paper towels.
- Add the chopped onions to the bacon grease. Cook until translucent, stirring frequently.
- Add the chicken stock and shrimp inside your Instant Pot along with the salt, black pepper and smoked paprika.
- Lock the lid and cook at high pressure for 4 minutes. When the cooking is done, quick release or naturally release the pressure. Carefully remove the lid.
- Stir in the heavy whipping cream and cheddar cheese. Return the bacon to the chowder.
- Serve and enjoy!

Pumpkin and Sausage Chowder
Time: 30 minutes   Servings: 8

Ingredients:

- 1 pound of ground sausage
- 6 cups of homemade low-sodium chicken stock
- 1 (15-ounce) can of pureed pumpkin
- 1 teaspoon of fine sea salt
- 1 teaspoon of freshly cracked black pepper
- 3 cups of cauliflower rice
- 1 onion, finely chopped
- 2 medium garlic cloves, minced
- 1 tablespoon of fresh sage, finely minced

Instructions:

- Press the "Sauté" setting on your Instant Pot and add the ground sausage. Once hot, add the sausage or until brown, stirring frequently.
- Add the remaining ingredients and lock the lid. Cook at high pressure for 15 minutes. When the cooking is done, naturally release the pressure and carefully remove the lid. Serve and enjoy!

Homemade Chicken Stock
Time: 1 hour   Servings: 10 cups

Ingredients:

- 2 ½ pounds of chicken carcasses and bones
- 2 tablespoons of extra-virgin olive oil
- 2 onions, quartered
- 2 celery stalks, roughly chopped
- 2 carrots, roughly chopped
- 2 bay leaves
- 4 whole garlic cloves
- 1 teaspoon of whole peppercorns
- 10 cups of water
- 1 tablespoon of apple cider vinegar

Instructions:

- Press the "Sauté" function on your Instant Pot and add the olive oil. Once hot, add the chicken carcasses and bones. Cook for around 2 minutes, stirring occasionally. This is to enhance the flavor of the chicken.
- Turn off the "Sauté" setting and stir in the remaining ingredients. Lock the lid and cook at high pressure for 1 minute. When the cooking is done, naturally release the pressure and carefully remove the lid. Strain the liquid through a fine mesh strainer and transfer to mason jars and refrigerate for future use. Serve and enjoy!

Cabbage Soup
Time: 25 minutes   Servings: 8

Ingredients:

- 2 pounds of lean ground beef
- 1 small or white onion, finely chopped
- 1 large head of cabbage, cored and chopped
- 4 medium garlic cloves, minced
- 3 carrots, chopped
- 3 celery stalks, chopped
- 1 (28-ounce) can of diced tomatoes
- 3 cups of homemade low-sodium chicken stock or vegetable stock
- 1 teaspoon of cumin
- 1 teaspoon of fine sea salt
- 1 teaspoon of freshly cracked black pepper

Instructions:

- Press the "Sauté" function on your Instant Pot and add the ground beef. Cook until brown, breaking up the meat with a wooden spoon as you cook.
- Add the onions and garlic cloves. Cook for another minute or two, stirring frequently.
- Add the remaining ingredients and stir until well combined. Lock the lid and cook at high pressure for 15 minutes. When the cooking is done, quick release the pressure and carefully remove the lid.
- Stir the cabbage soup again and adjust the seasoning as needed. Serve and enjoy!

Creamy Tomato Basil Soup
Time: 25 minutes   Servings: 6

Ingredients:

- 2 large celery stalks, chopped
- 1 medium onion, chopped
- 2 carrots, chopped
- 2 (14.5-ounce) cans of diced tomatoes
- 2 cups of homemade low-sodium chicken stock
- ½ cup of heavy whipping cream
- 1 teaspoon of fine sea salt
- 1 teaspoon of freshly cracked black pepper
- 2 teaspoons of dried basil
- 2 bay leaves
- 2 tablespoons of extra-virgin olive oil

Instructions:

- Press the "Sauté" setting on your Instant Pot and add the extra-virgin olive oil. Once hot, add the chopped onions. Sauté for 4 minutes or until lightly softened, stirring frequently.
- Add the celery and carrots and sauté for another 2 minutes, stirring occasionally.
- Add the remaining ingredients except for the heavy cream. Stir until well combined.
- Lock the lid and cook at high pressure for 15 minutes. When the cooking is done, naturally release the pressure and carefully remove the lid. Use an immersion blender to puree the soup until smooth. Gently stir in the heavy cream and adjust the seasoning if necessary. Serve and enjoy!

Cream of Red Bell Pepper Soup
Time: 30 minutes   Servings: 4

Ingredients:

- 2 ½ pounds of red bell peppers
- 4 tablespoons of coconut oil, melted
- 2 shallots, finely chopped
- 2 medium garlic cloves, peeled and minced
- 3 cups of homemade low-sodium vegetable stock
- 2 teaspoons of red wine vinegar
- ½ teaspoon of cayenne pepper
- 1 teaspoon of fine sea salt
- 1 teaspoon of freshly cracked black pepper
- ½ cup of heavy cream

Instructions:

- Press the "Sauté" function on your Instant Pot and add the coconut oil. Once hot, add the bell peppers, shallots and garlic cloves. Sauté until softened, stirring occasionally.
- Add the remaining ingredients except for the heavy cream.
- Lock the lid and cook at high pressure for 3 minutes. When the cooking is done, quick release the pressure and carefully remove the lid.
- Use an immersion blender to blend the soup until smooth. Stir in the heavy cream and adjust the seasoning if necessary. Serve and enjoy!

Stuffed Pepper Soup
Time: 35 minutes   Servings: 6

Ingredients:

- 1 pound of lean ground beef
- 2 tablespoons of coconut oil
- 1 small onion, finely chopped
- 2 large red bell peppers, seeds removed and chopped
- 1 (28-ounce) can of diced tomatoes
- 1 (14.5-ounce) can of tomato sauce
- 2 cups of homemade low-sodium chicken stock
- 2 cups of cauliflower rice
- 1 teaspoon of garlic powder
- 1 teaspoon of fine sea salt
- 1 teaspoon of freshly cracked black pepper

Instructions:

- Press the "Sauté" function on your Instant Pot and add the coconut oil, ground beef, bell peppers and onions. Cook until the meat has browned and vegetables have softened, stirring frequently.
- Add the remaining ingredients and stir until well combined.
- Lock the lid and cook at high pressure for 15 minutes. When the cooking is done, naturally release the pressure and carefully remove the lid.Stir the soup again and adjust the seasoning if necessary. Serve and enjoy!

Shiitake Mushroom and Asparagus Soup
Time: 35 minutes   Servings: 4

Ingredients:

- 1 pound of asparagus, trimmed and cut into bite-sized pieces
- 1 pound of shiitake mushrooms, sliced
- 4 cups of baby spinach
- 4 tablespoons of coconut oil, melted
- 4 cups of homemade low-sodium chicken or vegetable stock
- 1 bay leaf
- 1 cup of heavy cream (more as needed)
- ¼ cup of fresh parsley, finely chopped
- 1 lemon, juice
- 1 teaspoon of fine sea salt
- 1 teaspoon of freshly cracked black pepper

Instructions:

- Press the "Sauté" setting on your Instant Pot and add the coconut oil. Once hot, add the onions and garlic cloves Sauté until translucent, stirring frequently.
- Add the chopped mushrooms and asparagus. Saute for 3 minutes or until softened, stirring frequently.
- Stir in the remaining ingredients except for the heavy cream. Lock the lid and cook at high pressure for 15 minutes. When the cooking is done, allow for a full natural release pressure method and carefully remove the lid.Stir in the heavy cream and adjust the seasoning if necessary.Serve and enjoy!

Green Chile Chicken Soup
Time: 40 minutes   Servings: 6

Ingredients:

- 3 boneless, skinless chicken breasts
- 1 red bell pepper, seeds removed and chopped
- 2 tablespoons of coconut oil, melted
- 1 onion, finely chopped
- 3 celery stalks, chopped
- 4 garlic cloves, peeled and minced
- 4 cups of homemade low-sodium chicken stock
- 1 (16-ounce) jar of salsa verde
- 2 (4-ounce) cans of diced green chiles, undrained
- 1 tablespoon of ground cumin
- 1 tablespoon of oregano
- 1 teaspoon of fine sea salt
- 1 teaspoon of freshly cracked black pepper
- ¼ cup of fresh cilantro, finely chopped

Instructions:

- Press the "Sauté" function on your Instant Pot and add the coconut oil. Once hot, add the chicken breasts and sear on both sides until brown.
- Gently stir in the remaining ingredients. Lock the lid and cook at high pressure for 15 minutes. When the cooking is done, allow for a full natural release method. Carefully remove the lid.
- Transfer the chicken to a cutting board and shred using two forks. Stir the shredded chicken into the soup and adjust the seasoning if necessary. Serve and enjoy!

Egg Drop Soup

Time: 15 minutes   Servings: 4

Ingredients:

- 4 cups of homemade low-sodium chicken stock
- 5 large organic eggs, beaten
- 3 fresh scallions, chopped
- 1 teaspoon of toasted sesame oil
- 1 tablespoon of fresh ginger, minced
- 1 teaspoon of garlic powder
- 1 teaspoon of fine sea salt
- 1 teaspoon of freshly cracked black pepper
- 1 teaspoon of arrowroot powder or xanthan gum
- A drop of yellow food coloring.

Instructions:

- Add all the ingredients inside your Instant Pot except for the arrowroot powder and give a good stir.
- Lock the lid and cook at high pressure for 3 minutes. When the cooking is done, naturally release the pressure and carefully remove the lid. Stir in the yellow food coloring and arrowroot powder. Cook until the liquid thickens, stirring occasionally. Serve and enjoy!

Vegetable Cream Soup

Time: 35 minutes   Servings: 6

Ingredients:

- 1 pound of cauliflower florets
- 1 pound of broccoli florets
- 1 bunch of kale or spinach, roughly chopped
- 2 celery ribs, chopped
- 4 tablespoons of extra-virgin olive oil
- 2 medium garlic cloves, minced
- 1 medium red onion, roughly chopped
- 10 cups of homemade low-sodium vegetable stock
- 1 cup of heavy cream (more as needed)
- 1 teaspoon of fin sea salt
- 1 tablespoon of Dijon mustard
- 1 tablespoon of fresh parsley, finely chopped

Instructions:

- Press the "Sauté" function on your Instant Pot and add the olive oil. Once hot, add the onions and garlic cloves. Sauté until translucent, stirring frequently.
- Add the celery, cauliflower florets, and broccoli florets. Cook for 2 minutes, stirring frequently.
- Add the remaining ingredients except for the heavy cream inside your Instant Pot. Lock the lid and cook at high pressure for 15 minutes.When the cooking is done, naturally release the pressure and carefully remove the lid.
- Use an immersion blender to puree the soup until smooth. Gently stir in the heavy cream and adjust the seasoning if necessary. Serve and enjoy!

Beef and Mushroom Soup

Time: 25 minutes   Servings: 4

Ingredients:

- 1 pound of ground beef
- 1 pound of mushrooms, sliced
- 2 tablespoons of coconut oil, melted
- 1 small onion, finely chopped
- 4 garlic cloves, peeled and minced
- 1 teaspoon of fine sea salt
- 1 teaspoon of freshly cracked black pepper
- 2 cups of homemade low-sodium beef broth

Instructions:

- Press the "Sauté" function on your Instant Pot and add the coconut oil. Once the coconut oil is hot, add the ground beef, onions and garlic. Cook until the brown, stirring occasionally.
- Add the remaining ingredients and lock the lid. Cook at high pressure for 12 minutes. When the cooking is done, naturally release the pressure and carefully remove the lid.
- Stir the soup again and adjust the seasoning if necessary. Serve and enjoy!

Columbian Creamy Avocado Soup

Time: 20 minutes   Servings: 4

Ingredients:

- 4 tablespoons of avocado oil
- 1 shallot, finely chopped
- 1 garlic clove, minced
- 4 cups of homemade low-sodium chicken stock
- 4 medium ripe avocados, peeled and mashed
- 1 tablespoon of freshly squeezed lime juice
- 2 cups of heavy cream
- 1 teaspoon of fine sea salt
- 1 teaspoon of freshly cracked black pepper
- ¼ cup of fresh cilantro, chopped

Instructions:

- Press the "Sauté" setting on your Instant Pot and add the avocado oil. Once hot, add the chopped shallots and minced garlic. Sauté for 3 minutes, stirring frequently.
- Add the chicken stock, lime juice, avocados and seasonings. Lock the lid and cook at high pressure for 3 minutes. When the cooking is done, naturally release the pressure and remove the lid.
- Use an immersion blender to puree the soup until smooth. Stir in the heavy cream and fresh cilantro. Serve and enjoy!

Chicken Avocado Soup
Time: 20 minutes   Servings: 4

Ingredients:

- 2 pounds of boneless, skinless chicken thighs
- 1 green onions, finely chopped
- 1 jalapeno pepper, seeds remove and chopped
- 4 cups of homemade low-sodium chicken stock
- 2 tablespoons of extra-virgin olive oil
- 6 garlic cloves, peeled and minced
- 2 teaspoons of ground cumin
- ½ cup of fresh cilantro, chopped
- 2 limes, freshly squeezed juice
- 2 large avocados, pitted, peeled and mashed

Instructions:

- Press the "Sauté" setting on your Instant Pot and add the olive oil. Once hot, add the chicken thighs and sear for 4 minutes per side or until brown.
- Add the remaining ingredients except for the heavy cream and avocados. Lock the lid and cook at high pressure for 8 minutes. When the cooking is done, quick release the pressure and remove the lid.
- Transfer the chicken to a cutting board and shred using two forks.
- Use an immersion blender to blend the contents inside your Instant Pot. Stir in the mashed avocados, heavy cream and shredded chicken. Serve and enjoy!

Hot Avocado Curry with Shrimp
Time: 20 minutes   Servings: 2

Ingredients:

- ½ pound of shrimp, peeled and deveined
- 2 cups of homemade low-sodium chicken stock
- 1 (14-ounce) can of coconut milk
- 2 avocados, ripe, pitted, peeled and cut into quarters
- ½ teaspoon of cayenne pepper
- 1 teaspoon of fin sea salt
- 1 tablespoon of freshly squeezed lime juice

Instructions:

- In a blender, add all the ingredients except for the shrimp. Blend until smooth and creamy.
- Pour in the mixture inside your Instant Pot along with the shrimp.
- Lock the lid and cook at high pressure for 3 minutes. When the cooking is done, quick release the pressure and remove the lid. Adjust the seasoning if necessary. Serve and enjoy!

Lamb and Herb Bone Broth
Time: 1 hour and 30 minutes   Servings: 8 cups

Ingredients:

- 1 pound of lamb bones
- 1 large onion, quartered

- 3 medium carrots, cut into chunks
- 3 celery stalks, roughly chopped
- 4 whole garlic cloves
- 4 fresh sprigs of rosemary
- 5 fresh sprigs of thyme
- 8 cups of water

Instructions:

- Add all the ingredients inside your Instant Pot. Lock the lid and cook at high pressure for 50 minutes. When the cooking is done, naturally release the pressure and remove the lid.
- Strain the liquid through a fine mesh strainer. Transfer the liquid to mason jars. Refrigerate and use as needed.

Turmeric Beef Bone Broth

Time: 2 hours   Servings: 10 cups

Instructions:

- 4 pounds of beef bones
- 3 carrots, cut into chunks
- 3 celery stalks, cut into large pieces
- 2 onions, roughly chopped or quartered
- 6 whole garlic cloves, peeled
- 10 fresh sprigs of parsley
- 2 tablespoons of apple cider vinegar
- 1 tablespoon of turmeric

Instructions:

- Add all the ingredients inside your Instant Pot. Lock the lid and cook at high pressure for 2 hours minutes. When the cooking is done, naturally release the pressure and remove the lid.
- Strain the liquid using a fine mesh strainer. Transfer the liquid to mason jars. Serve and enjoy!

Steak Cabbage Soup

Time: 35 minutes   Servings: 8

Ingredients:

- 1 pound of sirloin steak, cut into strips
- 1 celery stalk, chopped
- 2 large carrots, finely chopped
- 1 large onion, finely chopped
- 2 tablespoons of extra-virgin olive oil
- 1 small green cabbage, cored and chopped
- 3 tablespoons of fresh parsley, finely chopped
- 2 teaspoons of dried thyme
- 2 teaspoons of dried rosemary
- 1 (28-ounce) can of diced or crushed tomatoes
- 4 cups of homemade low-sodium beef broth

Instructions:

- Press the "Sauté" setting on your Instant Pot and add the olive oil. Once hot, add the steak strips and cook until brown.
- Add the chopped carrots, celery and onions. Cook for 4 to 6 minutes, stirring frequently.
- Add the remaining ingredients and stir until well combined.
- Lock the lid and cook at high pressure for 20 minutes. When the cooking is done, naturally release the pressure and remove the lid. Serve and enjoy!

Thai Shrimp Soup

Time: 20 minutes   Servings: 6

Ingredients:

- 2 tablespoons of unsalted butter
- ½ pound of medium shrimp, peeled and deveined
- ½ yellow onion, peeled and finely chopped
- 2 garlic cloves, minced
- 4 cups of homemade low-sodium chicken stock
- 2 tablespoons of freshly squeezed lime juice
- 2 tablespoons of fish sauce
- 2 teaspoons of red curry paste
- 1 tablespoon of coconut aminos
- 1 stalk of lemongrass, finely chopped
- 1 cup of white mushrooms, sliced
- 1 tablespoon of fresh ginger, minced
- 1 teaspoon of fine sea salt

Instructions:

- Press the "Sauté" setting on your Instant Pot and add 1 tablespoon of butter. Once hot, add the shrimp and cook until the shrimp becomes pink and opaque.
- Add another tablespoon of butter. Add the chopped onions and garlic. Sauté for 3 minutes or until translucent, stirring frequently.
- Add the remaining ingredients and stir until well combined. Lock the lid and cook at high pressure for 5 minutes. When the cooking is done, naturally release the pressure for 5 minutes, then quick release the remaining pressure. Carefully remove the lid.
- Press the "Sauté" setting on your Instant Pot and cook until most of the liquid evaporates.
- Serve and enjoy!

Beef and Broccoli Zoodle Soup
Time: 4 hours and 10 minutes   Servings: 6

Ingredients:

- 2 tablespoons of olive oil
- 3 tablespoons of fresh ginger, finely minced
- 2 garlic cloves, peeled and minced
- 1 ½ pounds of sirloin steaks, cut into 1-inch pieces
- 2 cups of broccoli florets
- 1 cup of cremini mushrooms, sliced

- 6 cups of homemade low-sodium beef broth
- ¼ cup of apple cider vinegar
- ¼ cup of coconut aminos
- ¼ cup of buffalo hot sauce
- 1 large zucchini, spiralized
- 1 small onion, finely chopped

Instructions:

- Press the "Sauté" setting on your Instant Pot and add oil. Once hot, add the ginger, garlic and steak. Cook until the beef is lightly brown, stirring frequently.
- Add the remaining ingredients except for the spiralized zucchini. Stir until well combined.
- Lock the lid and cook at high pressure for 8 minutes. When the cooking is done, quick release the pressure and remove the lid.
- Stir in the spiralized zucchini. Serve and enjoy!

Chicken Enchilada Soup
Time: 35 minutes   Servings: 4

Ingredients:

- 1 pound of boneless, skinless chicken breasts
- 1 tablespoon of olive oil
- 1 large onion, finely chopped
- 3 garlic cloves, minced
- 1 large red bell pepper, chopped
- 1 large jalapeno, chopped
- 1 (14.5-ounce) can of tomato sauce

- 1 tablespoon of chili powder
- 1 tablespoon of chipotle pepper in adobo sauce, minced
- 2 teaspoons of ground cumin
- 1 teaspoon of fine sea salt
- 1 teaspoon of freshly cracked black pepper
- 3 cups of homemade low-sodium chicken stock

Instructions:

- Press the "Sauté" setting on your Instant Pot and add the olive oil. Once hot, add the chopped onions, minced garlic, bell pepper and jalapeno. Sauté for 4 minutes or until softened, stirring frequently.
- Add the remaining ingredients and stir until well combined.
- Lock the lid and cook at high pressure for 20 minutes. When the cooking is done, naturally release the pressure and remove the lid.
- Transfer the chicken to a cutting board and shred using two forks. Return the shredded chicken to the inner pot and stir. Serve and enjoy!

Brussel Sprouts and Sausage Soup
Time: 30 minutes   Servings: 4

Ingredients:

- 1 pound of brussel sprouts, trimmed and cut half lengthwise
- 1 medium cauliflower, cut into florets

- ½ pound of andouille sausage, sliced
- 2 bay leaves
- 4 cups of homemade low-sodium chicken stock
- 2 (14.5-ounce) can of diced tomatoes
- 1 medium onion, finely chopped
- 2 medium garlic cloves, minced
- 2 tablespoons of extra-virgin olive oil
- 1 teaspoon of fine sea salt
- 1 teaspoon of freshly cracked black pepper

Instructions:

- Press the "Sauté" function on your Instant Pot and add the olive oil. Once hot, add the chopped onions and garlic cloves. Sauté until translucent, stirring occasionally.
- Add the sliced sausage and cook for another 3 minutes, stirring frequently.
- Add the remaining ingredients and lock the lid. Cook at high pressure for 10 minutes. When the cooking is done, naturally release the pressure and carefully remove the lid.
- Stir the soup again and adjust the seasoning as needed. Serve and enjoy!

Creamy Celery Soup
Time: 45 minutes   Servings: 4

Ingredients:

- 4 cups of celery with leaves, roughly chopped
- 4 tablespoons of extra-virgin olive oil
- 1 onion, finely chopped
- 2 leeks, finely chopped
- 4 medium garlic cloves, peeled and minced
- 5 cups of homemade low-sodium chicken stock
- 1 teaspoon of fine sea salt
- 1 teaspoon of freshly cracked black pepper
- 2 cups of heavy cream
- 1 tablespoon of fresh parsley, finely chopped

Instructions:

- Press the "Sauté" setting on your Instant Pot and add the olive oil. Once hot, add the chopped onions, leeks, chopped celery and minced garlic. Sauté until translucent, stirring frequently.
- Add the remaining ingredients except for the heavy cream.
- Lock the lid and cook at high pressure for 10 minutes. When the cooking is done, naturally release the pressure and carefully remove the lid.
- Use an immersion blender to blend the contents until smooth.
- Gently stir in the heavy cream and adjust the seasoning if necessary. Serve and enjoy!

Smoked Sausage and Cheddar Beer Soup
Time: 30 minutes   Servings: 14

Ingredients:

- 1 pound of smoked sausage, sliced
- 4 cups of homemade low-sodium beef broth
- 12-ounces of gluten-free, keto-friendly beer
- 1 cup of carrots, chopped
- 1 cup of celery, chopped
- 1 small onion, finely chopped
- 4 medium garlic cloves, minced
- 1 teaspoon of crushed red pepper flakes
- 1 teaspoon of fine sea salt
- ½ teaspoon of freshly cracked black pepper
- 1 cup of heavy cream
- 1 (8-ounce) package of cream cheese
- 2 cups of cheddar cheese, shredded

Instructions:

- Add the sliced smoked sausage, beef broth, beer, chopped carrots, chopped onions, chopped celery and minced garlic inside your Instant Pot.
- Lock the lid and cook at high pressure for 10 minutes. When the cooking is done, naturally release the pressure and carefully remove the lid.
- Stir in the red pepper flakes, salt, black pepper, heavy cream, cream cheese and shredded cheddar cheese. Allow the cheese to melt, stirring frequently. Serve and enjoy!

Spinach and Artichoke Soup
Time: 10 minutes   Servings: 6

Ingredients:

- 4 cups of baby spinach
- 2 (14-ounce) cans of artichoke hearts
- 1 tablespoon of butter
- 2 slices of provolone cheese
- ¼ cup of cheddar cheese.
- ½ small onion, finely chopped

- 2 tablespoons of sour cream
- 2 cups of homemade low-sodium vegetable stock
- ½ cup of heavy cream
- ½ teaspoon of fine sea salt
- ½ teaspoon of freshly cracked black pepper

Instructions:

- Add all the ingredients inside your Instant Pot and give a good stir.
- Lock the lid and cook at high pressure for 5 minutes. When the cooking is done, naturally release the pressure and remove the lid.
- Use an immersion blender to puree the soup until smooth. Adjust the seasoning if necessary.
- Serve and enjoy!

Crab Soup
Time: 15 minutes   Servings: 4

Ingredients:

- 1 pound of crab meat
- 6 tablespoons of butter
- 1 tablespoon of cooking sherry

- 2 cups of almond milk
- 2 cups of heavy whipping cream

Instructions:

- Add all the ingredients inside your Instant Pot. Stir until well combined.
- Lock the lid and cook at high pressure for 5 minutes. When the cooking is done, quick release the pressure and remove the lid. Serve and enjoy!

Brown Butter Mushroom Soup
Time: 13 minutes   Servings: 6

Ingredients:

- 1 pound of mushrooms, sliced
- 2 tablespoons of fresh sage, chopped
- 4 cups of homemade low-sodium chicken stock or vegetable stock

- 6 tablespoons of butter
- ½ teaspoon of fine sea salt
- ½ teaspoon of freshly cracked black pepper
- ½ cup of heavy cream

Instructions:

- Press the "Sauté "setting on your Instant Pot and add the butter. Once hot, add the mushrooms and sauté for 4 minutes or until brown, stirring occasionally.
- Add the chicken stock and lock the lid. Cook at high pressure for 3 minutes. When the cooking is done, naturally release the pressure and carefully remove the lid.
- Use an immersion blender to puree the soup until smooth. Stir in the heavy cream, sea salt, black pepper and chopped fresh sage. Serve and enjoy!

Lobster Chowder
Time: 15 minutes   Servings: 6

Ingredients:

- 6 bacon slices, chopped
- 1 small onion, finely chopped
- ¼ cup of coconut oil
- 2 cups of homemade low-sodium lobster stock
- 2 cups of cauliflower florets
- 3 cups of almond milk or coconut milk

- 2 cups of cooked lobster milk, chopped
- 1 teaspoon of fine sea salt
- 1 teaspoon of freshly cracked black pepper
- 2 tablespoons of fresh parsley, finely chopped
- 2 tablespoons of apple cider vinegar
- ¼ teaspoon of xanthan gum

Instructions:

- Press the "Sauté" setting on your Instant Pot and add the coconut oil, chopped bacon and onion. Cook for 4 minutes or until the onions have softened, stirring frequently.
- Add the remaining ingredients and stir until well combined. Lock the lid and cook at high pressure for 3 minutes. When the cooking is done, naturally release the pressure and remove the lid. Serve and enjoy!

Creamy Chicken and Mushroom Soup
Time: 30 minutes   Servings: 8

Ingredients:

- 1 pound of boneless, skinless chicken breast
- 2 tablespoons of olive oil
- 1 large onion, finely chopped
- 1 cup of celery, chopped
- 6 garlic cloves, minced
- 2 cups of mushrooms, sliced
- 1 teaspoon of fresh rosemary, chopped
- 1 teaspoon of dried thyme
- 1/3 cup of dry sherry
- 8 cups of homemade low-sodium chicken stock
- 2/3 cups of heavy cream
- ¼ cup of fresh parsley, finely chopped
- Sea salt and freshly cracked black pepper (for taste)

Instructions:

- Press the "Sauté" function on your Instant Pot and add the olive oil. Once hot, add the chopped onions, chopped celery and minced garlic. Sauté for 3 minutes or until softened, stirring frequently. Add the mushrooms and sauté for another 2 minutes, stirring frequently.
- Add the remaining ingredients except for the heavy cream. Lock the lid and cook at high pressure for 15 minutes. When the cooking is done, naturally release the pressure and carefully remove the lid.
- Transfer the chicken to a cutting board and shred using two forks. Return the shredded chicken to the soup along with the heavy cream. Stir until well combined and adjust the seasoning if necessary. Serve and enjoy!

Beef Stroganoff Soup
Time: 30 minutes   Servings: 4

Ingredients:

- 2 pounds of beef sirloin steak, cut into strips
- 1 pound of brown mushrooms, sliced
- ¼ cup of butter
- 2 medium garlic cloves
- 1 medium onion, finely chopped
- 5 cups of homemade low-sodium beef broth
- 1 ½ cup of sour cream or heavy cream
- Sea salt and freshly cracked black pepper (to taste)

Instructions:

- Press the "Sauté" setting on your Instant Pot and add the butter. Once hot, add the sirloin strips and cook for 4 minutes or until brown. Add the mushrooms, garlic cloves and onions. Cook for 4 minutes or until slightly softened, stirring frequently.
- Return the sirloin strips along with the beef broth. Lock the lid and cook at high pressure for 20 minutes. When the cooking is done, naturally release the pressure and remove the lid.
- Stir in the sour cream and season with salt and black pepper. Serve and enjoy!

Thai Curried Butternut Squash Soup
Time: 25 minutes   Servings: 6

Ingredients:

- 1 small onion, finely chopped
- 1 tablespoon of coconut oil
- 2 medium garlic cloves, minced
- 2 tablespoons of red curry paste
- ¼ teaspoon of cayenne pepper
- 3 cups of homemade low-sodium chicken stock
- 1 (15-ounce) can of coconut milk
- 1 pound of butternut squash, peeled, seeds removed and cut into chunks
- ¼ cup of fresh cilantro, finely chopped
- Sea salt and freshly cracked black pepper (to taste)

Instructions:

- Press the "Sauté" setting on your Instant Pot and add the coconut oil. Once hot, add the chopped onions and minced garlic. Sauté for 4 minutes or until translucent, stirring frequently.
- Add the cayenne pepper and red curry paste. Sauté for another minute or until fragrant, stirring frequently.
- Add the remaining ingredients and stir until well combined. Lock the lid and cook at high pressure for 8 minutes. When the cooking is done, naturally release the pressure and remove the lid. Use an immersion blender to puree the soup until smooth.
- Stir in the fresh cilantro and season with salt and pepper. Serve and enjoy!

Cauliflower and Leek Soup with Coconut Cream
Time: 20 minutes   Servings: 2

Ingredients:

- 1 large leek, chopped
- 1 small cauliflower, chopped
- ½ cup of coconut cream
- 3 cups of homemade low-sodium chicken stock
- Sea salt and freshly cracked black pepper

Instructions:

- Add all the ingredients inside your Instant Pot except for the coconut cream.
- Lock the lid and cook at high pressure for 10 minutes. When the cooking is done, naturally release the pressure and remove the lid.
- Use an immersion blender and puree the contents until smooth.
- Gently stir in the coconut cream and adjust the seasoning if necessary. Serve and enjoy!

Creamy Cauliflower Soup
Time: 25 minutes   Servings: 6

Ingredients:

- 1 large cauliflower head, cut into florets
- 2 tablespoons of butter
- 1 tablespoon of olive oil
- 1 white onion, finely chopped
- 3 celery stalks, chopped
- 3 carrots, chopped
- 4 medium garlic cloves, minced
- 1 teaspoon of dried thyme
- 2 tablespoons of arrowroot powder
- 2 cups of homemade low-sodium chicken stock
- 2 cups of heavy whipping cream

Instructions:

- Press the "Sauté" setting on your Instant Pot and add the butter and olive oil. Once hot, add the chopped onions, garlic cloves, carrots and celery. Sauté for 4 minutes or until softened, stirring frequently.
- Pour in the chicken stock and dried thyme. Lock the lid and cook at high pressure for 10 minutes. When the cooking is done, naturally release the pressure and remove the lid.
- Stir in the heavy cream and arrowroot powder. Continue to cook until thickens, stirring occasionally. Serve and enjoy!

Creamy Leek and Salmon Soup
Time: 15 minutes   Servings: 4

Ingredients:

- 1 pound of boneless salmon fillets, cut into bite-sized pieces
- 2 tablespoons of avocado oil or extra-virgin olive oil
- 4 leeks, trimmed and sliced
- 3 medium garlic cloves, minced
- 6 cups of homemade low-sodium seafood stock or chicken stock
- 2 teaspoons of dried thyme
- 2 cups of heavy cream
- 1 teaspoon of fine sea salt
- 1 teaspoon of freshly cracked black pepper

Instructions:

- Press the "Sauté" setting on your Instant Pot and add the avocado oil. Once hot, add the leeks and garlic cloves. Sauté until almost softened, stirring frequently.

- Add the remaining ingredients except for the heavy cream. Lock the lid and cook at high pressure for 4 minutes. When the cooking is done, naturally release the pressure and remove the lid.
- Gently stir in the heavy cream and adjust the seasoning if necessary. Serve and enjoy!

Asparagus Soup with Parmesan Cheese and Lemon
Time: 30 minutes   Servings: 6

Ingredients:

- 2 pounds of asparagus, trimmed and cut into bite-sized pieces
- 3 tablespoons of butter
- 2 medium white or yellow onions, finely chopped
- 3 medium garlic cloves, peeled and crushed
- 6 cups of homemade low-sodium chicken stock
- 1 teaspoon of fine sea salt
- 1 teaspoon of freshly cracked black pepper
- 2 tablespoons of freshly squeezed lemon juice
- ½ teaspoon of fresh lemon zest
- ½ cup of shredded Parmigiano-Reggiano or shredded mozzarella cheese
- ¼ cup of fresh basil, chopped

Instructions:

- Press the "Sauté" setting on your Instant Pot and add the butter. Once melted, add the chopped onions, crushed garlic and lemon zest. Sauté for 4 minutes or until softened, stirring frequently.
- Add the asparagus and sauté for a minute or two, stirring frequently. Turn off the "Sauté" setting and add the chicken stock, salt, black pepper, lemon juice and fresh basil.
- Lock the lid and cook at high pressure for 15 minutes. When the cooking is done, naturally release the pressure and remove the lid.
- Use an immersion blender to puree the asparagus until smooth. Stir in the shredded cheese and allow to melt, stirring occasionally. Adjust the seasoning if necessary. Serve and enjoy!

Hearty Green Soup
Time: 20 minutes   Servings: 4

Ingredients:

- 1 medium broccoli head, cut into florets
- 1 medium cauliflower head, cut into florets
- 3 zucchinis, chopped
- 3 leeks, chopped
- 1 medium white or yellow onion, finely chopped
- ½ cup of butter
- 2 cups of homemade low-sodium chicken stock
- 1 cup of heavy cream
- Sea salt and freshly cracked black pepper (to taste)

Instructions:

- Press the "Sauté" function on your Instant Pot and add the butter. Once hot, add the chopped onions, chopped leeks, chopped zucchini, broccoli and cauliflower. Sauté for 4 minutes, stirring frequently.
- Add the chicken stock and lock the lid. Cook at high pressure for 5 minutes. When the cooking is done, naturally release the pressure and carefully remove the lid.
- Use an immersion blender to puree the soup until smooth. Season with sea salt and freshly cracked black pepper. Gently stir in the heavy cream. Serve and enjoy!

Creamy Pumpkin Soup
Time: 20 minutes   Servings: 6

Ingredients:

- 2 (13-ounce) cans of pumpkin
- 2 cups of homemade low-sodium chicken stock
- 1 cup of coconut cream
- 1 teaspoon of onion powder
- 1 teaspoon of smoked paprika
- 1 teaspoon of fine sea salt
- 1 teaspoon of freshly cracked black pepper
- 1 teaspoon of garlic powder
- 1 teaspoon of ground cinnamon

Instructions:

- Add all the ingredients except for the coconut cream inside your Instant Pot and give a good stir. Lock the lid and cook at high pressure for 8 minutes.
- When the cooking is done, naturally release the pressure and remove the lid.
- Use an immersion blender to puree the soup until smooth. Stir in the coconut cream.Serve and enjoy!

Italian Wedding Soup
Time: 25 minutes   Servings: 4

Meatball Ingredients:

- 1 pound of ground beef
- 1 teaspoon of fine sea salt
- 1 teaspoon of freshly cracked black pepper

- 1 teaspoon of garlic powder
- 2 tablespoons of fresh parsley, finely chopped

Soup Ingredients:

- 2 tablespoons of extra-virgin olive oil
- 2 tablespoons of fresh parsley, finely chopped
- 1 beaten egg
- 3 cups of baby spinach

- 6 cups of homemade low-sodium bone broth
- 2 medium garlic cloves, minced
- 2 celery stalks, chopped
- ½ onion, finely chopped

Instructions:

- In a large bowl, add all the meatball ingredients and mix with your hands until well combined. Form meatballs and set aside.
- Press the "Sauté" function on your Instant Pot and add the olive oil. Once hot, add the chopped onions, garlic cloves and celery. Sauté for 2 minutes, stirring frequently.
- Add the meatballs and remaining soup ingredients inside your Instant Pot. Lock the lid and cook at high pressure for 15 minutes. When the cooking is done, naturally release the pressure and remove the lid. Serve and enjoy!

Slow-Cooked Vegetable and Beef Soup
Time: 6 hours   Servings: 12

Ingredients:

- 4 bacon slices, roughly chopped
- 2 pounds of beef stew meat, cut into 1-inch pieces
- 2 tablespoons of red wine vinegar
- 4 cups of homemade low-sodium beef broth
- 1 medium yellow onion, finely chopped
- 1 small celeriac, finely chopped
- ¼ cup of carrots, chopped

- 1 (28-ounce) can of diced tomatoes
- 1 (6-ounce) can of tomato paste
- 2 medium garlic cloves, minced
- ½ teaspoon of dried rosemary
- ½ teaspoon of dried thyme
- 1 teaspoon of fine sea salt
- ½ teaspoon of freshly cracked black pepper

Instructions:"

- Press the "Sauté" setting on your Instant Pot and add the chopped bacon. Cook until brown and crispy. Transfer to a plate lined with paper towels.
- Add the beef meat and cook until brown, stirring occasionally.
- Add the remaining ingredients and stir until well combined. Lock the lid and press the "Slow Cook" button and set the time to 8 hours. Remove the lid and adjust the seasoning if necessary. Serve and enjoy!

Turmeric Chicken Soup
Time: 30 minutes   Servings: 4

Ingredients:

- 2 teaspoons of turmeric powder
- 1 teaspoon of cumin powder
- 3 boneless, skinless chicken thighs
- 4 tablespoons of extra-virgin olive oil

- 1 small onion, finely chopped
- 1 cup of carrots, chopped
- 1 cup of cauliflower florets
- 1 cup of broccoli florets

- 5 cups of homemade low-sodium bone broth or vegetable broth
- 1 bay leaf

- 1 teaspoon of fresh ginger, finely grated
- 2 cups of chard, stems removed and sliced
- ½ cup of coconut milk

Instructions:

- Press the "Sauté" setting on your Instant Pot and add 2 tablespoons of olive oil. Once hot, add the chicken thighs and sear for 2 minutes per side or until brown. Remove and set aside.
- Add the remaining tablespoons of olive oil. Add the chopped vegetables and sauté for 4 minutes or until slightly softened, stirring frequently.
- Add the remaining ingredients except for the coconut milk inside your Instant Pot.
- Lock the lid and cook at high pressure for 15 minutes. When the cooking is done, naturally release the pressure and remove the lid.
- Transfer the chicken to a cutting board and shred using two forks. Return the shredded chicken to the soup along with the coconut milk. Stir and add more turmeric as needed. Serve and enjoy!

Chicken Avocado Lime Soup

Time: 30 minutes   Servings: 4

Ingredients:

- 2 pounds of boneless, skinless chicken thighs
- 2 tablespoons of avocado oil
- 1 cup of green onions, finely chopped
- 2 jalapenos, seeds removed and minced
- 6 cups of homemade low-sodium chicken stock
- 2 Roma tomatoes, finely chopped

- 1/3 cup of fresh cilantro, chopped
- 1 teaspoon of fine sea salt
- 1 teaspoon of freshly cracked black pepper
- 3 tablespoons of freshly squeezed lime juice
- 3 medium avocados, peeled and finely chopped

Instructions:

- Press the "Sauté" setting on your Instant Pot and add the 1 tablespoon of avocado oil. Once hot, add the chicken thighs and sear for 2 minutes per side or until brown. Remove and set aside.
- Add the remaining tablespoon of avocado oil to the pot and add the chopped green onions and jalapenos. Sauté for 2 minutes or until tender, stirring frequently.
- Return the chicken stock along with the stock. Lock the lid and cook at high pressure for 15 minutes. When the cooking is done, naturally release the pressure and remove the lid.
- Stir in the lime juice, chopped avocados, salt, black pepper, tomatoes and fresh cilantro.
- Serve and enjoy!

Chicken and Cauliflower Rice Soup

Time: 50 minutes   Servings: 6

Ingredients:

- 1 pound of boneless, skinless chicken breasts
- 2 celery stalks, chopped
- 2 carrots, chopped
- 1 small onion, finely chopped
- 2 tablespoons of olive oil
- 4 cups of homemade low-sodium chicken stock

- 1 teaspoon of fresh thyme, finely chopped
- 1 teaspoon of fine sea salt
- 1 teaspoon of freshly cracked black pepper
- 2 cups of cauliflower rice
- 2 cups of coconut cream

Instructions:

- Press the "Sauté" setting on your Instant Pot and add 1 tablespoon of olive oil. Once hot, add the chicken breasts and sear for 3 minutes or until brown. Remove and set aside.
- Add the remaining tablespoon of olive oil along with the vegetables. Sauté for 4 minutes or until tender, stirring frequently.
- Return the chicken along with the chicken stock. Lock the lid and cook at high pressure for 15 minutes. When the cooking is done, naturally release the pressure and remove the lid.
- Transfer the chicken to a cutting board and shred using two forks.
- Return the shredded chicken and remaining ingredients inside your Instant Pot. Allow the soup to get heated through, stirring occasionally. Serve and enjoy!

Pumpkin and Beef Stew

Time: 1 hour   Servings: 6

Ingredients:

- 2 tablespoons of olive oil
- 1 pound of beef stew meat, cut into bite-sized pieces
- 1 pound of pumpkin, peeled and cut into bite-sized pieces
- 4 cups of homemade low-sodium beef broth
- 1 (14.5-ounce) can of diced tomatoes, undrained

- 1 (6-ounce) can of tomato paste
- 2 bay leaves
- 2 garlic cloves, minced
- 1 large onion, finely chopped
- ½ teaspoon of chili powder
- 1 teaspoon of fine sea salt
- 1 teaspoon of freshly cracked black pepper

Instructions:

- Press the "Sauté" function on your Instant Pot and add the olive oil. Once hot, add the beef meat, onions and garlic. Sauté until the beef has browned and onions are tender, stirring frequently.
- Add the beef broth and lock the lid. Cook at high pressure for 30 minutes. When the cooking is done, naturally release the pressure and remove the lid.
- Stir in the pumpkin and remaining ingredients. Lock the lid and cook at high pressure for 10 minutes. When the cooking is done, naturally release the pressure and carefully remove the lid.Serve and enjoy!

Smoky Eggplant Soup

Time: 15 minutes   Servings: 4

Ingredients:

- 2 pounds of eggplants, peeled and chopped
- 5 tablespoons of extra-virgin olive oil
- 1 large white or yellow onion, finely chopped
- 1 teaspoon of fine sea salt
- 1 teaspoon of freshly cracked black pepper

- 6 cups of homemade low-sodium chicken stock
- ½ teaspoon of cayenne pepper
- 1 lemon, juice and zest
- 2 tablespoons of fresh parsley, finely chopped

Instructions:

- Press the "Sauté" setting on your Instant Pot and add the olive oil. Once hot, add the chopped onions and minced garlic. Sauté until translucent, stirring occasionally.
- Add the remaining ingredients and stir until well combined.
- Lock the lid and cook at high pressure for 10 minutes. When the cooking is done, naturally release the pressure and remove the lid.
- Use an immersion blender to puree the soup until smooth. Stir the contents again and adjust the seasoning as needed. Serve and enjoy!

Butternut Squash Soup

Time: 45 minutes   Servings: 4

Ingredients:

- 1 (3-pound) butternut squash, peeled and cut into cubes
- 1 large onion, finely chopped
- 2 medium garlic cloves, minced
- 4 tablespoons of extra-virgin olive oil
- 2 tablespoons of tomato paste

- 4 cups of homemade low-sodium chicken or vegetable stock
- 1 cup of coconut cream
- 1 tablespoon of curry powder
- 1 teaspoon of fine sea salt
- 1 teaspoon of freshly cracked black pepper
- 1 teaspoon of pumpkin pie spice

Instructions:

- Press the "Sauté" setting on your Instant Pot and add the olive oil. Once hot, add the onion, garlic, and curry powder. Sauté for 4 minutes or until fragrant, stirring occasionally
- Add the remaining ingredients except for the coconut cream.

- Lock the lid and cook at high pressure for 30 minutes. When the cooking is done, naturally release the pressure and carefully remove the lid.
- Use an immersion blender to puree the soup until smooth.
- Gently stir in the coconut cream and adjust the seasoning if necessary. Serve and enjoy!

Creamy Tomato Soup
Time: 20 minutes   Servings: 4

Ingredients:

- 1 medium onion, finely chopped
- 4 garlic cloves, minced
- 1 (28-ounce) can of diced tomatoes
- 2 tablespoons of extra-virgin olive oil
- 1 tablespoon of dried oregano
- 1 tablespoon of dried basil

- 1 cup of homemade low-sodium chicken or vegetable stock
- ½ cup of coconut cream or heavy cream
- 1 teaspoon of apple cider vinegar
- 1 teaspoon of fine sea salt
- 1 teaspoon of freshly cracked black pepper

Instructions:

- Press the "Sauté" setting on your Instant Pot and add the olive oil. Once hot, add the chopped onions and minced garlic. Saute for 4 minutes, stirring frequently.
- Add the remaining ingredients except for the cram. Lock the lid and cook at high pressure for 15 minutes. When the cooking is done, naturally release the pressure and remove the lid.
- Use an immersion blender to puree the soup until smooth. Stir in the cream. Serve and enjoy!

Creamy Garlic Chicken Soup
Time: 20 minutes   Servings: 4

Ingredients:

- 2 large boneless, skinless chicken breasts
- 3 cups of chicken broth
- 4 garlic cloves, minced
- 4-ounces of cream cheese, softened
- 2 tablespoons of butter
- 2 tablespoons of olive oil or coconut oil

- 1 tablespoon of parsley, freshly chopped
- 1 tablespoon of garlic powder
- 2 teaspoons of onion powder
- 1 teaspoon of salt
- 1 teaspoon of black pepper

Instructions:

- Press the "Sauté" setting on your Instant Pot and add the olive oil. Once hot, add the chicken breasts and sear for 4 minutes per side or until brown. Remove the chicken and add the minced garlic. Sauté for 1 minute or until fragrant, stirring frequently.
- Return the chicken and add all the ingredients and stir until well combined. Lock the lid and cook at high pressure for 15 minutes. When the cooking is done, naturally release the pressure and remove the lid.
- Transfer the chicken to a cutting board and shred using two forks. Return to the soup. Serve and enjoy!

Cauliflower Parmesan Soup
Time: 15 minutes   Servings: 6

Ingredients:

- 4 tablespoons of olive oil or coconut oil
- 4 garlic cloves, minced
- 4 cups of homemade low-sodium chicken stock
- 1 onion, finely chopped
- 1 leek, chopped

- 2 large cauliflower heads, cut into florets
- ½ cup of parmesan cheese, grated
- 1 teaspoon of fine sea salt
- 1 teaspoon of freshly cracked black pepper
- 2 tablespoons of fresh thyme, finely chopped

Instructions:

- Press the "Sauté" function on your Instant Pot and add olive oil. Once hot, add the chopped onions, leeks and garlic cloves. Sauté until softened, stirring occasionally.
- Add the cauliflower florets and cook for another minute. Turn off the "Sauté" setting on your Instant Pot.

- Add the remaining ingredients except for the parmesan cheese and stir until well combined. Lock the lid and cook at high pressure for 12 minutes. When the cooking is done, naturally release or quick release the pressure. Remove the lid.
- Use an immersion blender to puree the soup until smooth. Stir in the parmesan cheese and allow to melt. Adjust the seasoning if necessary. Serve and enjoy!

Broccoli and Cheesy Soup
Time: 25 minutes   Servings: 4

Ingredients:

- 3 cups of homemade low-sodium chicken stock
- 4 cups of broccoli, cut into florets
- 3 cups of heavy cream
- 3 cups of cheddar cheese, shredded
- 1 cup of water

Instructions:

- Add 1 cup of water and a steamer basket inside your Instant Pot. Place the broccoli in the basket and lock the lid. Cook at high pressure for 3 minutes. When the cooking is done, quick release the pressure and remove the lid.
- Discard the steamer basket and water. Add the broccoli to the inner pot.
- Press the "Sauté" function on your Instant Pot and add the heavy cream. Allow the heavy cream to get heated through.
- Lock the lid and cook at high pressure for 1 minute. When the cooking is done, quick release the pressure and remove the lid.
- Stir in the shredded cheddar cheese and allow to melt. Serve and enjoy!

Italian-Style Broccoli Cheese Soup
Time: 30 minutes   Servings: 4

Ingredients:

- 3 broccoli stalks, chopped
- 1 large white onion, finely chopped
- 1 cup of matchsticks carrots
- 3 large garlic cloves, peeled and minced
- 3 cups of homemade low-sodium chicken stock
- 1 tablespoon of Italian parsley, minced
- 1 teaspoon of dried oregano
- 1 teaspoon of crushed red pepper flakes
- ¼ cup of heavy whipping cream
- 1 cup of shredded Mozzarella cheese
- 1 cup of shredded Italian cheese mix
- ¼ cup of parmesan cheese, finely grated
- ¼ cup of almond flour

Instructions:

- Add the chopped broccoli, onion, carrots, garlic, salt, black pepper and chicken stock inside your Instant Pot. Lock the lid and cook at high pressure for 3 minutes. When the cooking is done, naturally release the pressure and remove the lid.
- Press the "Sauté" function on your Instant Pot and set to the lowest setting. Add the cheeses, parsley, dried oregano, crushed red pepper flakes and almond flour. Cook until the cheese has melted and the liquid thickens, stirring frequently. Serve and enjoy!

Winter Kale Vegetable Soup
Time: 20 minutes   Servings: 6

Ingredients:

- 1 pound of baby carrots, roughly chopped
- 5 celery stalks, chopped
- 5 cups of kale, stemmed and roughly chopped
- 2 tablespoons of ghee
- 2 tablespoons of olive oil
- 1 onion, finely chopped
- 9 cups of homemade low-sodium chicken stock or vegetable stock
- 1 tablespoon of fresh thyme, chopped
- 3 bay leaves
- 1 teaspoon of fine sea salt
- 1 teaspoon of freshly cracked black pepper

Instructions:

- Press the "Sauté" function on your Instant Pot and add the olive oil. Once hot, add the chopped onions and minced garlic cloves. Cook until fragrant, stirring frequently.
- Add the other vegetables and sauté for another minute. Add the remaining ingredients and lock the lid. Cook at high pressure for 15 minutes. When the cooking is done, quick release the pressure and remove the lid. Serve and enjoy!

Sausage and Kale Soup
Time: 25 minutes   Servings: 6

Ingredients:

- 2 tablespoons of extra-virgin olive oil
- 1 pound of Andouille sausage, chopped
- 1 onion, finely chopped
- 3 garlic cloves, peeled and minced
- 1 cup of mushrooms, chopped
- 5 cups of homemade low-sodium chicken stock
- 1 cup of dry white wine

- 1 tablespoon of dried basil
- 4 cups of kale, stemmed and roughly chopped
- 2 tablespoons of apple cider vinegar
- 2 tablespoons of fresh thyme, finely chopped
- 1 teaspoon of fine sea salt
- 1 teaspoon of freshly cracked black pepper

Instructions:

- Press the "Sauté" function on your Instant Pot and add the olive oil. Add the chopped onions and minced garlic. Sauté until softened, stirring frequently. Add the Andouille sausage and cook for 4 minutes, stirring frequently. Add the remaining ingredients and lock the lid. Cook at high pressure for 8 minutes. When the cooking is done, quick release the pressure and remove the lid. Adjust the seasoning if necessary. Serve and enjoy!

Mushroom and Chicken Coconut Soup
Time: 1 hour and 10 minutes   Servings: 4

Ingredients:

- 4 boneless, skinless chicken breasts
- 4 tablespoons of extra-virgin olive oil.
- 1 large onion, finely chopped
- 6 cups of homemade low-sodium chicken stock
- 2 cups of shiitake mushrooms, chopped
- 4 medium garlic cloves, peeled and minced
- 1 (14-ounce) can of coconut milk

- 1 (14.5-ounce) can of diced tomatoes
- ½ cup of fresh basil, chopped
- 1 tablespoon of red curry paste
- 2 tablespoons of fish sauce
- 1 teaspoon of fine sea salt
- 1 teaspoon of freshly cracked black pepper

Instructions:

- Press the "Sauté" setting on your Instant Pot add the olive oil. Once the oil is hot, add the chicken breast and sear until brown on both sides. Remove and set aside.
- Add the onions, mushrooms and garlic cloves. Sauté until the vegetables have softened, stirring frequently.
- Add the remaining ingredients except for the coconut milk inside your Instant Pot and stir until well combined. Lock the lid and cook at high pressure for 15 minutes. When the cooking is done, naturally release the pressure and remove the lid.
- Transfer the chicken to a cutting board and shred using two forks. Return the shredded chicken to the soup along with the coconut milk. Adjust the seasoning if necessary. Serve and enjoy!

Part 6: Fish and Seafood Recipes

Spicy Spirited Lemon Salmon
Time: 20 minutes   Servings: 4

Ingredients:

- 4 salmon fillets
- Juice from 2 lemons + slices for garnish
- 1 cup of water
- 1 Tablespoon paprika
- 1 teaspoon cayenne pepper
- 1 teaspoon salt (to taste)
- 1 teaspoon fresh ground black pepper (to taste)

Instructions:

1. Rinse the salmon, pat dry.
2. In a bowl, combine salt, pepper, paprika, cayenne pepper.
3. Drizzle lemon juice over salmon fillet. Season with spice mixture. Turn over fillet, repeat on other side.
4. Add 1 cup of water to Instant Pot. Place trivet inside. Place fillets on trivet.
5. Close and seal cover. Press Manual button. Cook at High Pressure for 10 minutes.
6. Quick-Release the pressure when done. Open the lid with care. Serve.

Awesome Coconut Shrimp Curry
Time: 35 minutes   Servings: 4

Ingredients:

- 1 pound shrimp, peeled and deveined
- 1 Tablespoon coconut oil
- 4 garlic cloves, minced
- Juice from 1 lime
- 1 teaspoon salt
- 1 teaspoon fresh ground black pepper
- 4 tomatoes, chopped
- 1 red bell pepper, sliced
- 10-ounces coconut milk
- ½ cup fresh cilantro, chopped

Instructions:

1. Press Sauté mode on Instant Pot. Heat the coconut oil.
2. Season shrimp with lime juice, salt and pepper. Sauté garlic for 1 minute.
3. Add shrimp. Cook 2 – 4 minutes per side. Add bell peppers and tomatoes. Stir well.
4. Press Keep Warm/Cancel button to cancel Sauté mode. Add coconut milk. Stir well.
5. Close and seal lid. Press Manual setting. Cook at High Pressure for 25 minutes.
6. Quick-Release the pressure when done. Open the lid with care.
7. Garnish with fresh cilantro. Serve.

Wondrous Mediterranean Fish
Time: 25 minutes   Servings: 4

Ingredients:

- 4 fish fillets (any kind)
- 1 pound cherry tomatoes, halved
- 1 cup green olives, pitted
- 2 garlic cloves, minced
- 1 cup of water
- 1 teaspoon coconut oil
- 1 Tablespoon fresh thyme, chopped
- 1 teaspoon fresh parsley
- 1 teaspoon salt (to taste)
- 1 teaspoon fresh ground black pepper (to taste)

Instructions:

1. Pour 1 cup of water in Instant Pot. Cover trivet in foil.
2. On a flat surface, rub fish fillets with garlic. Season with salt, pepper and thyme.
3. Place olives and cherry tomatoes along bottom of Instant Pot. Place fillets on trivet.
4. Close and seal lid. Press Manual button. Cook at High Pressure for 15 minutes.
5. Release pressure naturally when done. Open the lid with care.
6. Place the fish with the ingredients. Stir to coat them.
7. Plate the fillets. Top with fresh parsley. Serve.

Wild Alaskan Cod
Time: 25 minutes   Servings: 4

Ingredients:

- 4 wild Alaskan cod fillets
- 4 cups cherry tomatoes, halved
- 4 garlic cloves, minced
- 4 Tablespoons butter, melted
- 1 Tablespoon coconut oil
- ¼ cup of fresh cilantro, chopped
- 1 teaspoon salt (to taste)
- 1 teaspoon fresh ground black pepper (to taste)

Instructions:

1. On a flat surface, rub garlic over cod fillets. Season with salt and pepper.
2. Cover trivet with foil. Add 1 cup of water to Instant Pot. Place trivet inside.
3. Place tomatoes along bottom of Instant Pot. Season with salt and pepper.
4. Place salmon fillets on trivet.
5. Pour melted butter and coconut oil over cod fillets and tomatoes.
6. Close and seal lid. Press Manual switch. Cook at High Pressure for 15 minutes.
7. When the timer beeps, quick-release pressure. Open the lid with care.
8. Plate the fillets. Top with tomatoes and fresh cilantro. Serve.

Stunning Shrimp and Sausage Gumbo
Time: 35 minutes   Servings: 4

Ingredients:

- 1 pound shrimp, peeled and deveined
- 1 pound lean sausage, thinly sliced
- 1 red bell pepper, chopped
- 1 yellow onion, chopped
- 1 garlic clove, minced
- 1 celery stalk, chopped
- 2 cups chicken broth
- ½ cup fresh parsley, chopped
- 2 Tablespoons coconut oil
- 2 Tablespoons Cajun seasoning
- 1 teaspoon salt (to taste)
- 1 teaspoon fresh ground black pepper (to taste)

Instructions:

1. Press Sauté button on Instant Pot. Heat the coconut oil.
2. Sauté onion and garlic for 1 minute.
3. Add sausage and shrimp. Cook until golden brown.
4. Add bell pepper and celery. Season with Cajun spice. Stir well.
5. Press Keep Warm/Cancel setting to stop Sauté mode.
6. Add 2 cups of chicken broth. Stir well.
7. Close and seal lid. Press Meat/Stew button. Adjust to cook for 25 minutes.
8. When the timer beeps, quick-release or naturally release pressure. Open the lid with care. Stir well. Serve.

Appetizing Steamed Crab Legs
Time: 20 minutes   Servings: 4

Ingredients:

- 2 pounds frozen crab legs
- 2 cups of water
- 4 Tablespoons butter, melted
- Juice from 1 lemon
- 1 teaspoon salt (to taste)
- 1 teaspoon fresh ground black pepper (to taste)

Instructions:

1. In a small bowl, combine melted butter, lemon juice, salt and pepper.
2. Add 2 cups of water to Instant Pot. Cover trivet in foil. Place trivet in Instant Pot.
3. Place crab legs in single layer on trivet. Pour half butter mixture over crab.
4. Close and seal lid. Press Manual button. Cook at High Pressure for 10 minutes.
5. Quick-release the pressure when done. Open the lid with care.
6. Plate the crab legs. Pour remaining butter mixture over crab. Serve.

Mouthwatering Parmesan Cod
Time: 30 minutes   Servings: 4

Ingredients:

- 4 cod fillets
- 4 green onions, minced
- 4 garlic cloves, minced
- ½ cup of parmesan cheese, grated
- 1 cup low-carb mayonnaise

- 1 teaspoon Worcestershire sauce
- 2 cups of water
- 1 teaspoon salt (to taste)
- 1 teaspoon fresh ground black pepper (to taste)

Instructions:

1. Add 2 cups of water in Instant Pot. Cover trivet with foil.
2. In a bowl, add green onions, garlic cloves, parmesan cheese, mayonnaise, Worcestershire sauce, salt, and black pepper. Stir well. Coat cod fillets with mixture. Place on trivet.
3. Close and seal lid. Press Manual button. Cook at High Pressure for 20 minutes.
4. Quick-Release the pressure when done. Open the lid with care.
5. Let the cod rest for 5 minutes before removing. Serve.

Lovely Tilapia Fillets
Time: 25 minutes   Servings: 4

Ingredients:

- 4 boneless, tilapia fillets
- ½ cup parmesan cheese, grated
- 4 Tablespoons low-carb mayonnaise
- ¼ cup ghee, melted
- 2 cups of water
- 1 teaspoon fresh basil, chopped

- 1 teaspoon onion powder
- Juice from ½ lemon
- 1 teaspoon garlic powder
- 1 teaspoon salt (to taste)
- 1 teaspoon fresh ground black pepper (to taste)

Instructions:

1. Pour 2 cups of water in Instant Pot. Cover trivet with foil.
2. In a bowl, combine parmesan cheese, mayonnaise, ghee, basil, lemon juice, and seasonings. Coat tilapia fillets with mixture. Place the tilapia fillets on trivet.
3. Close and seal lid. Press Manual button. Cook at High Pressure for 15 minutes.
4. Quick-Release the pressure when done. Open the lid with care.
5. Allow the fish to rest for 5 minutes before removing. Serve.

Generous Orange Trout Fillets
Time: 25 minutes   Servings: 4

Ingredients:

- 4 trout fillets
- 4 garlic cloves
- Zest and juice from 1 orange
- ¼ cup fresh parsley, chopped
- 1 cup pecans, roasted and chopped
- 1 Tablespoon ghee

- 2 cups of water
- 1 Tablespoon coconut oil
- 1 teaspoon salt (to taste)
- 1 teaspoon fresh ground black pepper (to taste)

Instructions:

1. Pour 2 cups of water in Instant Pot. Cover trivet with foil.
2. Combine orange juice and zest, garlic, parsley, ghee, coconut oil, salt, and pepper in a bowl. Stir well. Cover trout with mixture. Place trout fillets on trivet.
3. Close and seal lid. Press Manual button. Cook at High Pressure for 15 minutes.
4. Quick-Release the pressure when done. Open the lid with care. Plate the fillets. Serve.

Intriguing Oysters
Time: 30 minutes   Servings: 4

Ingredients:

- 1 pound oysters, shucked

- 4 garlic cloves, minced

- ¼ cup fresh parsley, chopped
- 1 teaspoon paprika
- Juice from 1 lemon + slices for garnish
- 2 Tablespoons ghee, melted

- 2 cups of water
- 1 teaspoon salt (to taste)
- 1 teaspoon fresh ground black pepper (to taste)

Instructions:

1. Rinse the oysters.
2. In a bowl, combine garlic, parsley, paprika, lemon juice, ghee, salt, and black pepper.
3. Place the oysters in Instant Pot. Pour mixture over the oysters.
4. Close and seal the lid. Press Manual setting. Cook at High Pressure 20 minutes.
5. Quick-Release the pressure when done. Open the lid with care.
6. Serve. Top with lemon wedges.

Robust Halibut Fillets
Time: 30 minutes   Servings: 4

Ingredients:

- 4 halibut fillets
- 6 garlic cloves, minced
- 4 green onions, chopped
- ¼ cup low-carb mayonnaise
- ¼ cup ghee, melted
- ¼ cup fresh parmesan cheese, grated
- ¼ cup mozzarella cheese, grated

- 1 teaspoon salt (to taste)
- 1 teaspoon fresh ground black pepper (to taste)
- Zest and juice from 1 lime
- 2 cups of water
- 1 lemon sliced for garnish
- Fresh parsley for garnish

Instructions:

1. Pour 2 cups of water in Instant Pot. Cover trivet with foil.
2. In a large mixing bowl, add the garlic, green onions, mayonnaise, ghee, cheeses, lime juice, lime zest, salt, and pepper. Stir well.
3. Coat the halibut fillets with the mixture. Place halibut on trivet.
4. Close and seal lid. Press Manual button. Cook at High Pressure for 20 minutes.
5. Once done, quick-release or naturally release pressure. Open the lid with care.
6. Plate the halibut. Top with fresh parsley, lemon slices. Serve.

Fantastic Chili Lime Cod
Time: 30 minutes   Servings: 4

Ingredients:

- 4 cod fillets, shredded
- 1 can (14-oucne) diced tomatoes
- 4 garlic cloves, minced
- 1 celery stalk, chopped
- 1 yellow onion, chopped
- 1 Tablespoon rice wine vinegar
- ½ cup low-carb mayonnaise

- ¼ cup fresh parsley, chopped
- Zest and juice from 1 lime
- 1 cup vegetable stock
- 1 Tablespoon coconut oil
- 1 teaspoon paprika
- 1 teaspoon salt
- 1 teaspoon fresh ground black pepper

Instructions:

1. Press Sauté mode on Instant Pot. Heat the coconut oil.
2. Add onion and garlic. Sauté for 1 minute. Add the celery and shredded cod.
3. Press Keep Warm/Cancel setting to stop Sauté mode.
4. Add diced tomatoes, mayonnaise, rice wine vinegar, parsley, lime juice, lime zest, and seasoning. Stir well.
5. Close and seal lid. Press Manual switch. Cook at High Pressure for 20 minutes.
6. Once done, quickly or naturally release pressure. Open the lid with care. Stir. Serve.

Delicious Cauliflower Risotto and Salmon
Time: 30 minutes   Servings: 4

Ingredients:

- 4 salmon fillets, shredded
- 1 pound asparagus, stemmed and chopped
- 1 head cauliflower, chopped into florets
- 8-ounce coconut cream, unsweetened
- 1 Tablespoon fresh or dried rosemary, chopped
- 2 teaspoons fresh or dried thyme, chopped
- ½ cup parmesan cheese, shredded
- 1 cup chicken broth
- 1 Tablespoon coconut oil
- 2 teaspoons salt (to taste)
- 1 teaspoon fresh ground black pepper (to taste)

Instructions:

1. In a food processor, add cauliflower florets. Pulse until rice-like consistency. Remove and set aside.
2. Press Sauté button on Instant Pot. Add the coconut oil, cauliflower rice, asparagus, and shredded salmon fillet. Cook until light brown and tender.
3. Press the Keep Warm/Cancel setting to stop the Sauté mode.
4. Add remaining ingredients. Stir well.
5. Close and seal lid. Press Manual button. Cook at High Pressure for 20 minutes.
6. Once done, naturally or quick-release pressure. Open the lid with care. Stir well. Serve.

Tender Ginger Sesame Glaze Salmon
Time: 25 minutes   Servings: 4

Ingredients:

- 4 salmon fillets
- 4 garlic cloves, minced
- 1 Tablespoon fish sauce
- 1 Tablespoon fresh ginger, grated
- 1 Tablespoon sugar-free ketchup
- 2 Tablespoons white wine
- 1 Tablespoon rice vinegar
- 2 Tablespoons soy sauce
- 2 teaspoons sesame oil
- 2 cups of water

Instructions:

1. In a bowl, combine garlic, fish sauce, ginger, ketchup, white wine, rice vinegar, soy sauce, and sesame oil.
2. In a large Ziploc bag, add the sauce and salmon fillets. Marinate for 6 – 10 hours.
3. Pour 2 cups of water in Instant Pot. Cover trivet in foil. Place trivet in Instant Pot.
4. Place marinated salmon fillet on trivet.
5. Close and seal lid. Press Manual button. Cook at High Pressure for 15 minutes.
6. Once done, naturally release pressure. Open the lid with care. Serve.

Homemade Seafood Stock
Time: 50 minutes   Servings: 4

Ingredients:

- 4 cups of water
- 4 pounds of fish bones, pieces and shrimp shells.
- ½ cup of fresh parsley
- 1 celery stalk, cut into 3 pieces
- 1 carrot, cut into 3 pieces
- 1 onion, quartered
- 2 bay leaves

Instructions:

- Add all the ingredients inside your Instant Pot. Lock the lid and cook at high pressure for 30 minutes. When the cooking is done, naturally release the pressure and remove the lid.
- Strain the liquid and transfer to jars for future use. Serve and enjoy!

Homemade Lobster Stock
Time: 50 minutes   Servings: 7 cups of lobster stock

Ingredients:

- 1/3 cup of olive oil
- Shells and legs from lobsters, cut into large pieces
- 2 medium onions, quartered
- 6 whole garlic cloves, peeled
- 1 bay leaf
- 5 fresh sprigs of thyme
- 2 cups of dry white wine
- 1 (14-ounce) can of whole peeled tomatoes
- 6 cups of water

Instructions:

- Press the "Sauté" function on your Instant Pot and add the olive oil. Once hot, add the lobster shells, legs, onions, garlic cloves, bay leaf, and fresh sprigs of thyme. Sauté for 3 minutes, stirring occasionally.
- Add the remaining ingredients and lock the lid. Cook at high pressure for 40 minutes. When the cooking is done, naturally release the pressure and remove the lid.
- Strain the liquid and transfer to jars for future use. Serve and enjoy!

10-Minute Salmon

Time: 10 minutes   Servings: 4

Ingredients:

- 4 salmon fillets, frozen or fresh
- 4 tablespoons of extra-virgin olive oil
- ½ cup of fresh parsley or dill, finely chopped
- 1 cup of water
- 3 medium lemons, juice and sliced

Instructions:

- Add ¼ cup of freshly squeezed lemon juice along with 1 cup of water inside your Instant Pot. Place a trivet or a steamer rack inside as well.
- Add the salmon fillets on top of the steamer rack or trivet. Sprinkle with fresh parsley or dill and add lemon slices on top. Lock the lid and cook at high pressure for 5 minutes.
- When the timer beeps, quick release the pressure and remove the lid. Serve and enjoy!

Tilapia Fillet with Miso Butter and Greens

Time: 15 minutes   Servings: 2

Ingredients:

- 2 (6-ounce) tilapia fish fillets
- 1-inch piece of whole fresh ginger, peeled and finely minced
- 1 cup of homemade low-sodium vegetable broth or chicken broth
- 1 whole garlic clove, peeled and finely sliced
- 1 teaspoon of coconut aminos
- ½ teaspoon of fine sea salt
- ½ teaspoon of freshly cracked black pepper
- 1 tablespoon of butter
- 1 ½ teaspoon of miso paste
- 1 lemon, fresh juice
- 1 bunch of kale

Instructions:

- Add the vegetable broth, ginger and garlic. Place a trivet on top and lay a sheet of aluminum foil on top.
- Lay the tilapia fillets on the sheet of foil. Drizzle with coconut aminos, sea salt, freshly cracked black pepper.
- Lock the lid and cook at high pressure for 4 minutes. When the cooking is done, quick release the pressure and remove the lid.
- Squeeze the lemon juice over the salmon fillets. Remove the fish and trivet from your Instant Pot.
- Press the "Sauté" function on your Instant Pot. Add the kale and cook until wilted. Turn off "Sauté" function In a small bowl, add the butter and miso paste. Mix well.
- Serve the tilapia with fresh greens and miso butter. Enjoy!

Tomato Basil Tilapia

Time: 5 minutes   Servings: 4

Ingredients:

- 4 (4-ounce) tilapia fillets, frozen
- 3 Roma tomatoes, finely diced
- 2 medium garlic cloves, peeled and minced
- ¼ cup of fresh basil, chopped
- 2 tablespoons of extra-virgin olive oil
- ½ teaspoon of fine sea salt
- ½ teaspoon of freshly cracked black pepper

Instructions:

- Add 1 cup of water and a steamer basket inside your Instant Pot. Place the tilapia fillets on top. Lock the lid and cook at high pressure for 4 minutes. When done, quick release the pressure and remove the lid. Discard the liquid and remove the trivet.
- In a bowl, add the diced tomatoes, minced garlic, chopped basil, olive oil, sea salt and black pepper. Stir well.
- Top the tilapia fillets with the tomato mixture. Serve and enjoy!

Haddock with Spinach and Cauliflower Rice
Time: 15 minutes   Servings: 4

Ingredients:

- 1 pound of haddock fillets, frozen
- 2 cups of frozen spinach
- 2 tablespoons of extra-virgin olive oil

- 1 teaspoon of fine sea salt
- 1 teaspoon of freshly cracked black pepper
- 2 cups of cauliflower rice

Lemon Garlic Mayonnaise Ingredients:

- 2 tablespoons of mayonnaise
- 2 teaspoons of freshly squeezed lemon juice

- 1 teaspoon of minced garlic

Instructions:

- In a small bowl, add the mayonnaise, lemon juice and garlic. Stir well and set aside.
- Add 1 cup of water and a trivet inside your Instant Pot.
- In a heat-safe dish that fits inside your Instant Pot, add the cauliflower rice and spinach. Place the haddock fillets on top.
- Season the haddock fillets with sea salt and black pepper. Drizzle with olive oil.
- Place the dish on top of the trivet and lock the lid.
- Cook at high pressure for 6 minutes. When the cooking is done, quick release the pressure and remove the lid. Serve and enjoy!

Zoodles with White Clam Sauce
Time: 20 minutes   Servings: 4

Ingredients:

- 2 pounds of small clams
- 3 large zucchinis, spiralized
- ¼ cup of unsalted butter
- 2 tablespoons of extra-virgin olive oil
- 1 tablespoon of garlic, minced
- ½ cup of dry white wine

- 2 tablespoons of freshly squeezed lemon juice
- 1 teaspoon of lemon zest
- 1 teaspoon of fine sea salt
- ¼ teaspoon of freshly cracked black pepper
- ¼ cup of fresh parsley, finely chopped

Instructions:

- Press the "Sauté" setting on your Instant Pot and add the olive oil and butter. Once hot, add the minced garlic and sauté for 2 minutes or until fragrant, stirring frequently.
- Add the dry white wine and lemon juice. Cook for 2 minutes or until most of the liquid evaporates, stirring frequently.
- Add the clams and cook for 3 minutes or until the clams has opened up.
- Turn off the "Sauté" setting on your Instant Pot and stir in the spiralized zucchini. Stir until well coated with liquid.
- Stir in the lemon zest and fresh parsley. Season with sea salt and freshly cracked black pepper. Serve and enjoy!

Oysters Stew with Spinach and Chorizo
Time: 15 minutes   Servings: 4

Ingredients:

- 2 tablespoons of extra-virgin olive oil
- 6-ouncse of chorizo sausage, cut into ¼-inch pieces

- 1 medium onion, finely chopped
- 1 cup of oysters, shucked
- 3 cups of spinach

- 1 ½ cup of almond milk
- 1 cup of heavy whipping cream

- 1 teaspoon of fine sea salt
- 1 teaspoon of freshly cracked black pepper

Instructions:

- Press the "Sauté" setting on your Instant Pot and add the olive oil. Once hot, add the chorizo and cook for 3 to 4 minutes or until brown, stirring occasionally.
- Transfer the chorizo to a plate lined with paper towels.
- Add the chopped onions and sauté until translucent, stirring occasionally.
- Add the remaining ingredients and cook for 2 to 3 minutes or until the oysters have opened up, stirring occasionally. Serve and enjoy!

Buttered Cod
Time: 10 minutes   Servings: 4

Ingredients:

- 1 ½ pounds of cod fillets, cut into pieces
- 6 tablespoons of unsalted butter
- ¼ teaspoon of garlic powder

- ½ teaspoon of fine sea salt
- ¼ teaspoon of freshly cracked black pepper
- 1 teaspoon of smoked paprika

Instructions:

- In a small bowl, add the garlic powder, sea salt, black pepper and smoked paprika.
- Season the cod pieces with the seasoning.
- Press the "Sauté" setting on your Instant Pot and add 2 tablespoons of butter. Once melted, add the cod fillets and sauté for 2 minutes per side.
- Turn off the "Sauté" setting on your Instant Pot and top the cod fillets with butter. Cover with a lid and sit for 4 minutes. Serve and enjoy!

Nutrition information per serving:

- Calories: 298
- Fat: 19g

- Net Carbs: 5g
- Protein: 31g

Lemon Butter Tilapia
Time: 20 minutes   Servings: 4

Ingredients:

- 4 (6-ounce) tilapia fillets
- ¼ cup of unsalted butter, melted
- 3 medium garlic cloves, minced
- 3 tablespoons of freshly squeezed lemon juice

- 1 teaspoon of lemon zest
- 2 tablespoons of fresh parsley, finely chopped
- Fine sea salt and freshly cracked black pepper (to taste)

Instructions:

- Add 1 cup of water and a trivet inside your Instant Pot. Grease a baking dish that fits inside your Instant Pot with nonstick cooking spray.
- In a small bowl, add the melted butter, minced garlic, lemon juice, lemon zest, fresh parsley, sea salt and freshly cracked black pepper. Mix well.
- Place the tilapia fillets onto the baking dish and pour in the mixture.
- Place the baking dish on top of the trivet. Lock the lid and cook at high pressure for 4 minutes. When the cooking is done, quick release the pressure and carefully remove the lid. Serve and enjoy!

Cucumber and Salmon Salad
Time: 15 minutes   Servings: 2

Ingredients:

- ½ pound of salmon fillets
- 1 tablespoon of extra-virgin olive oil
- 1 cup of cherry tomatoes, chopped

- 2 cups of cucumber, diced
- 3 tablespoons of fresh cilantro, chopped
- 1 cup of water

Instructions:

- Add 1 cup of water and a trivet inside your Instant Pot. Place the salmon fillets on top of the trivet. Lock the lid and cook at high pressure for 3 minutes. When the cooking is done, quick release the pressure and carefully remove the lid.
- Transfer the salmon to a cutting board and cut into small pieces.
- In a large bowl, add the salmon pieces, olive oil, cherry tomatoes, diced cucumber and fresh cilantro. Stir until well combined. Serve and enjoy!

Crabs Legs with Chipotle and Lime Butter Sauce
Time: 20 minutes   Servings: 3

Ingredients:

- 2 pounds of crab legs
- 1 packet of crab boil seasoning
- ½ cup of unsalted butter
- 1 teaspoon of red chilies, chopped
- 1 tablespoon of canned chipotles, chopped
- 1 tablespoon of ground coriander

- ½ teaspoon of fine sea salt
- ½ teaspoon of freshly cracked black pepper
- 2 tablespoons of freshly squeezed lime juice
- ¼ cup of fresh parsley, chopped
- Around 4 cups of water

Instructions:

- Add the crab legs, crab boil seasoning and water inside your Instant Pot. Lock the lid and cook at high pressure for 5 minutes. When the cooking is done, quick release the pressure and carefully remove the lid.
- Transfer the crab legs to a plate and discard the water.
- Press the "Sauté" setting on your Instant Pot and add the butter. Once melted, add the red chilies, chipotles, ground coriander, sea salt, black pepper, lime juice and chopped fresh parsley. Sauté until the butter has melted, stirring frequently.
- Spoon the butter sauce over the crab legs. Serve and enjoy!

Crab Cakes with Roasted Red Pepper Sauce
Time: 25 minutes   Servings: 8

Ingredients:

- 2 tablespoons of coconut oil, melted
- 1 cup of lump crab meat
- 1 large egg organic egg, beaten
- 2 teaspoons of Dijon mustard
- 1 tablespoon of freshly squeezed lemon juice

- 2 teaspoons of old bay seasoning
- 2 tablespoons of fresh parsley, finely chopped
- 1 tablespoon of coconut flour
- Fine sea salt and freshly cracked black pepper (to taste)

Roasted Red Pepper Sauce Ingredients:

- 1 (16-ounce) jar of roasted red peppers, drained
- ¼ cup of extra-virgin olive oil
- 2 tablespoons of shallots, finely chopped

- 2 medium garlic cloves, minced
- 2 tablespoons of fresh basil, chopped
- 1 lemon, juice and zest

Instructions:

- In a large bowl, add the crab meat, beaten egg, Dijon mustard, lemon juice, old bay seasoning, fresh parsley, coconut flour, sea salt and freshly cracked black pepper. Mix well using your hands.
- Form the mixture into crab cakes.
- Press the "Sauté' setting on your Instant Pot and add the coconut oil. Once hot, add the crab cakes and cook for 2 to 3 minutes on each side or until golden brown. Transfer the crab cakes to a plate lined with paper towels.
- In a blender, add the roasted red pepper sauce. Blend until smooth. Spoon the sauce over the crab cakes. Serve and enjoy!

Spicy Mussels in Tomato Chorizo Broth
Time: 15 minutes   Servings: 6

Ingredients:

- 2 pounds of mussels, cleaned and debearded
- 1 pound of chorizo
- 3 medium garlic cloves, minced
- 1 (14-ounce) can of diced tomatoes

- 1 cup of white wine
- ¼ teaspoon of dried thyme
- Fine sea salt and freshly cracked black pepper (to taste)

Instructions:

- Add all the ingredients inside your Instant Pot. Lock the lid and cook at high pressure for 5 minutes. When the cooking is done, quick release the pressure and carefully remove the lid. Serve and enjoy!

Indian Fish Curry
Time: 15 minutes   Servings: 4

Ingredients:

- 1 ½ pound of haddock or cod fish fillets, cut into 2-inch pieces
- 2 tablespoons of coconut oil
- 1 small onion, finely chopped
- 2 medium garlic cloves, peeled and minced
- 1 (14.5-ounce) can of diced tomatoes
- 1-inch piece of ginger, peeled and minced
- 1 small jalapeno pepper, sliced
- 1 teaspoon of ground coriander

- ¼ teaspoon of ground cumin
- ½ teaspoon of turmeric
- ½ teaspoon of freshly cracked black pepper
- 1 teaspoon of fine sea salt
- 2 tablespoons of water
- 1 cup of coconut milk
- 10 curry leaves
- 1 teaspoon of fresh lemon juice

Instructions:

- Press the "Sauté" function on your Instant Pot and add the coconut oil. Once hot, add the onions, garlic and ginger. Sauté until softened, stirring occasionally.
- Add the curry leaves along with the rest of the seasonings. Sauté for another 20 seconds. Turn off "Sauté" function.
- Deglaze your Instant Pot with 2 tablespoons of water.
- Gently stir in the coconut milk, fish pieces and the remaining ingredients.
- Lock the lid and cook at high pressure for 2 minutes. When the cooking is done, quick release the pressure and remove the lid. Serve and enjoy!

Lemon and Dill Fish Packets
Time: 7 minutes   Servings: 2

Ingredients:

- 2 (6-ounce) tilapia or cod fish fillets
- ½ teaspoon of fine sea salt
- ½ teaspoon of freshly cracked black pepper
- ½ teaspoon of garlic powder

- 2 fresh sprigs of dill
- 1 medium lemon, cut into 4 slices
- 2 tablespoons of butter

Instructions:

- Lay out 2 pieces of parchment paper.
- Add 1 fish fillet on each parchment paper and season with salt, black pepper and garlic powder.
- Add 1 fresh sprig of dill, 2 slices of lemon and 1 tablespoon of butter per parchment paper. Carefully wrap the parchment paper and seal.
- Add 1 cup of water and a trivet inside your Instant Pot. Place the fish packet on top and lock the lid. Cook at high pressure for 5 minutes.
- When the cooking is done, quick release the pressure and remove the lid. Unfold the packet.
- Serve and enjoy!

Tilapia and Pesto Fish Packet
Time: 9 minutes   Servings: 4

Ingredients:

- 1 cup of pesto
- 4 (6-ounce) tilapia fish fillets
- 4 tablespoons of tomato paste
- ½ cup of white onion, finely chopped

- 1 teaspoon of fine sea salt
- ½ teaspoon of freshly cracked black pepper
- 1 medium lemon, sliced

Instructions:

- Place each fillet onto a piece of parchment paper.
- Divide and add the tomato paste, onion, pesto, salt black pepper and lemon slices per parchment paper.
- Fold and tightly wrap each parchment paper.
- Add 1 cup of water and a trivet inside your Instant Pot. Place the salmon fillets on top of the trivet.
- Lock the lid and cook at high pressure for 4 minutes. When done, quick release the pressure and remove the lid.

Tuscan Fish Packets
Time: 10 minutes   Servings: 4

Ingredients:

- 4 (6-ounce) white fish fillets
- 1 medium cauliflower head, cut into florets
- 4 plum tomatoes, chopped
- 1 small zucchini, chopped
- 1 medium red onion, finely chopped

- 2 medium garlic cloves, peeled and crushed
- 4 tablespoons of olive oil
- 1 teaspoon of fine sea salt
- 1 teaspoon of freshly cracked black pepper
- 1 medium lemon, sliced

Instructions:

- Prepare four separate sheets of parchment paper or aluminum foil.
- Place a fish fillet onto each piece of parchment paper and season with salt and black pepper. Per each fish packet: Evenly divide and add the cauliflower florets, tomatoes, zucchini, red onion, garlic cloves, coconut oil and lemon slices.
- Fold the packet and ensure the edges are tightly seal.
- Add 2 cups of water and a trivet inside your Instant Pot.
- Place the fish packets onto the trivet. Lock the lid and cook at high pressure for 5 minutes.
- When the cooking is done, quick release the pressure and remove the lid.
- Unfold the fish packets and enjoy!

Salmon with Garlic Butter and Asparagus
Time: 10 minutes   Servings: 3

Ingredients:

- 1 pound of salmon fillet, cut into 3 separate pieces
- 1 pound of asparagus stalks
- ¼ cup of freshly squeezed lemon juice

- 3 tablespoons of butter
- 2 tablespoons of garlic, peeled and minced
- ½ teaspoon of fine sea salt
- ½ teaspoon of freshly cracked black pepper

Instructions:

- Lay 3 separate pieces of aluminum foil or parchment paper onto a flat surface.
- Place salmon fillet onto each sheet of foil.
- Divide and add the asparagus stalks, lemon juice, butter, garlic, salt and black pepper.
- Tightly wrap the foil and ensure the edges are seal.
- Pour 1 ½ cup of water and a trivet inside your Instant Pot. Place the fish packet on top.
- Lock the lid and cook at high pressure for 4 minutes. When done, quick release the remove the lid. Serve and enjoy!

Sweet and Spicy Red Snapper
Time: 25 minutes   Servings: 2

Ingredients:

- 1 pound of red snapper filets

- 1/8 teaspoon of freshly cracked black pepper

- 1/8 teaspoon of fine sea salt
- 1 medium lime, juice

- 3 tablespoons of truvia low-carb brown sugar
- 1 ½ tablespoon of siracha hot sauce

Instructions:

- Add 1 cup of water and a steamer rack inside your Instant Pot. Place the red snapper filets on the steamer rack.
- Lock the lid and cook at high pressure for 5 minutes. When the cooking is done, quick release the pressure and remove the lid.
- In a bowl, add the brown sugar, siracha hot sauce, lime juice, salt and black pepper. Mix well. Drizzle the sauce over the red snapper fillets. Serve and enjoy!

Pressure-Cooked Octopus
Time: 25 minutes   Servings: 6

Ingredients:

- 1 (2 pound) whole octopus, rinsed

- Around 2 to 3 cups of water

Instructions:

- Add the octopus and enough water inside your Instant Pot.
- Lock the lid and cook at high pressure for 15 minutes. When the cooking is done, quick release the pressure and remove the lid. Cut the tentacles into pieces and serve. Enjoy!

Garlic Butter Shrimp
Time: 20 minutes   Servings: 4

Ingredients:

- 1 pound of shrimp, peeled and deveined
- 6 tablespoons of butter
- 1 tablespoon of olive oil
- 5 medium garlic cloves, crushed
- ½ cup of homemade low-sodium seafood stock or chicken stock

- 2 tablespoons of freshly squeezed lemon juice
- 2 tablespoons of fresh parsley, finely chopped
- ½ teaspoon of fine sea salt
- ½ teaspoon of freshly cracked black pepper

Instructions:

- Press the "Sauté" function on your Instant Pot and add the butter and olive oil. Once hot, add the garlic cloves and sauté for 1 minute, stirring occasionally.
- Add the remaining ingredients and lock the lid. Cook at high pressure for 2 minutes. When the cooking is done, quick release the pressure and remove the lid. Serve and enjoy!

Tilapia with Pesto Veggies
Time: 15 minutes   Servings: 4

Ingredients:

- 4 (7-ounce) tilapia fillets, fresh or frozen
- 4 lemon slices
- ¼ cup of homemade pesto
- ½ teaspoon of fine sea salt

- ½ teaspoon of freshly cracked black pepper
- 4 to 6 cups of mixed and chopped summer vegetables (such as zucchini, bell peppers, or cherry tomatoes)

Instructions:

- In a large bowl, add the summer vegetables and pesto. Gently stir until well combined.
- Lay 4 large sheets of aluminum foil and evenly add the vegetables.
- Top the vegetables with the tilapia fish fillets. Place lemon slices on top and season with salt and black pepper. Tightly wrap the aluminum foil and ensure the edges are sealed.
- Add 2 cups of water and a trivet inside your Instant Pot. Place the packet on top of the trivet.
- Lock the lid and cook at high pressure for 5 minutes. When the cooking is done, quick release the pressure and remove the lid. Serve and enjoy!

Halibut with Coconut Creamed Kale
Time: 10 minutes   Servings: 2

Ingredients:

- 1 (6-ounce) halibut fillet
- ½ lemon, slices
- 1 bunch of kale, ribs removed and roughly chopped
- ½ to 1 cup of coconut milk or coconut cream
- ½ teaspoon of fine sea salt
- ½ teaspoon of freshly cracked black pepper

Instructions:

- Season the halibut fillet with salt and black pepper.
- Add the kale and coconut milk inside your Instant Pot. Give a gentle stir.
- Add a trivet inside your Instant Pot and place the halibut fillet on top. Place the lemon slices on top.
- Lock the lid and cook at high pressure for 5 minutes. When the cooking is done, quick release the pressure and carefully remove the lid.Spoon the creamed kale on top of the halibut fillet. Serve and enjoy!

Salmon and Broccoli Foil Packets
Time: 30 minutes   Servings: 2

Ingredients:

- 2 (6-ounce) salmon fillets
- 4 tablespoons of extra-virgin olive oil
- 2 cups of broccoli florets
- 1 lemon, halved

Instructions:

- Lay two sheets of aluminum foil onto a flat surface. Place the salmon fillets onto each pieces of foil. Add 1 cup of broccoli, 1 lemon half and 2 tablespoons of extra-virgin olive oil per each packet.
- Tightly wrap the fish packets and ensure the edges are sealed.
- Add 2 cups of water and a steamer rack or trivet inside your Instant Pot. Place the fish packets onto the trivet.
- Lock the lid and cook at high pressure for 5 minutes. When the cooking is done, naturally release the pressure and remove the lid. Serve and enjoy!

Seafood Stuffed Peppers
Time: 25 minutes   Servings: 4

Ingredients:

- 4 medium green bell peppers, tops removed and inner portions scooped out
- 4 tablespoons of olive oil
- 1 small onion, finely chopped
- 2 celery stalks, chopped
- ¼ cup of fresh parsley, finely chopped
- ½ pound of lump crabmeat
- ½ pound of shrimp, peeled and deveined
- ½ pound of ground Italian sausage
- ½ cup of cheddar cheese or mozzarella cheese, shredded
- Fine sea salt and freshly cracked black pepper (to taste)

Instructions:

- Press the "Sauté" function on your Instant Pot and add the olive oil. Once hot, add the onions, celery and ground Italian sausage. Cook until the sausage is brown and vegetables are tender, stirring occasionally. Transfer to a large bowl.Add the fresh parsley, crabmeat and shrimp. Mix until well combined.Divide and spoon the mixture into the peppers. Add 1 cup of water and a trivet inside your Instant Pot.
- Place the bell peppers on the trivet and sprinkle with the cheese. Lock the lid and cook at high pressure for 12 minutes. When done, quick release the pressure and carefully remove the lid.Serve and enjoy!

Best Ever Seafood Chili
Time: 20 minutes   Servings: 6

Ingredients:

120

- 1 pound of small shrimp, peeled and deveined
- ½ pound of scallops, cleaned
- 2 large fish steaks, cut into bite-sized pieces
- 1 pound of mussels
- ½ pound of clams
- 2 tablespoons of olive oil or coconut oil

- 1 (14.5-ounce) can of diced tomatoes, undrained
- 3 cups of homemade low-sodium fish stock or clam juice
- 1 large yellow onion, finely chopped
- 1 jalapeno pepper, seeds removed and chopped
- 3 sweet bell peppers (green, yellow or red) bell peppers, seeded and chopped

Seasoning Ingredients:

- 1 teaspoon of ground cumin
- 1 tablespoon of dried oregano
- 2 teaspoons of garlic powder
- 2 teaspoons of smoked paprika

- 2 tablespoons of chili powder
- 1 teaspoon of ground coriander
- 1 teaspoon of fine sea salt
- 1 teaspoon of freshly cracked black pepper

Instructions:

- Press the "Sauté" setting on your Instant Pot and add the olive oil. Once hot, add the chopped onions, jalapeno and bell pepper. Sauté for 4 to 6 minutes or until softened, stirring occasionally.
- Add the remaining ingredients inside your Instant Pot and stir until well combined. Lock the lid and cook at high pressure for 6 minutes. When the cooking is done, naturally release the pressure for 10 minutes, then quick release the remaining pressure. Carefully remove the lid.
- Check if the mussels and clams are open. Serve and enjoy!

Crab Cakes
Time: 15 minutes   Servings: 2

Ingredients:

- 1 cup of lump crab meat
- ¼ onion, finely chopped
- ¼ cup of red bell pepper, finely chopped
- ¼ cup of almond flour
- 1 large organic egg

- 2 tablespoons of mayonnaise
- 1 teaspoon of old bay seasoning
- ¼ teaspoon of freshly cracked black pepper
- 2 tablespoons of olive oil

Tartar Sauce Ingredients:

- ¼ cup of mayonnaise
- 1 tablespoon of fresh lemon juice
- ½ tablespoon of dill pickle, finely chopped
- ½ tablespoon of white onion, finely chopped

- 1 teaspoon of swerve sweetener
- ½ teaspoon of Dijon mustard
- ½ teaspoon of smoked or sweet paprika

Instructions:

- In a bowl, add the tartar sauce ingredients. Stir until well combined and refrigerate.
- In another bowl, add all the crab cake ingredients except for the olive oil and mix until well combined. Form the crab cake mixture with 6 patties.
- Press the "Sauté" function on your Instant Pot and add the olive oil. Once hot and working in batches, add the crab cakes and cook for 3 minutes on each side or until golden brown. Serve and enjoy!

Hot Jalapeno-Tuna Salad
Time: 10 minutes   Servings: 2

Ingredients:

- 2 (5-ounce) can of chunk light tuna
- ½ cup of Kalamata olives, pitted and sliced
- 1 large jalapeno pepper, seeds removed and finely minced
- 2 medium garlic cloves, peeled and minced
- 1 medium cucumber, finely diced
- 1 tablespoon of coconut oil, melted

- 4 green scallions, thinly sliced
- 3 tablespoons of sugar-free mayonnaise
- ¼ teaspoon of dry mustard powder
- 1 tablespoon of fresh parsley, finely chopped
- ¼ teaspoon of fine sea salt (more to taste)
- ¼ teaspoon of freshly cracked black pepper (more to taste)

Instructions:

- Press the "Sauté" feature on your Instant Pot and add the coconut oil. Once hot, add the garlic cloves and sauté for 1 minute or until fragrant, stirring occasionally.
- Set to the lowest setting and add the jalapeno, can tuna and olives. Sauté until well heated through. Remove the contents and refrigerate. Allow to cool for a couple of hours.
- Once cooled, add all the ingredients to a large bowl and stir until well combined.Serve!

Barramundi en Papillote

Time: 10 minutes   Servings: 4

Ingredients:

- 4 barramundi fish fillets, fresh
- 4 lemons, thinly sliced
- 1 large shallot, thinly sliced
- 2-inch pieces of ginger, peeled and julienned
- 2 orange and yellow bell pepper, seeds removed and julienned
- 1 jalapeno, thinly sliced
- ½ teaspoon of fine sea salt
- ½ teaspoon of freshly cracked black pepper
- ¼ cup of fresh cilantro, chopped

Instructions:

- Lay 4 pieces of parchment paper onto a flat surface.
- Season the barramundi fish fillets with sea salt and black pepper.
- For each fish packet: divide and add the barramundi fish fillets, lemon slices, sliced shallots, julienned ginger, julienned bell pepper and sliced jalapeno.
- Wrap the fish packet and fold the edges
- Add 2 cups of water and a trivet inside your Instant Pot. Place the fish packet on top.
- Lock the lid and cook at high pressure for 5 minutes. When the cooking is done, quick release the pressure and remove the lid.
- Unwrap the fish fillets and top with fresh cilantro. Serve and enjoy!

Brazilian Fish Stew

Time: 40 minutes   Servings: 6

Fish Ingredients:

- 1 ½ pound of boneless cod or halibut fish fillets, cut into bite-sized pieces
- 1 tablespoon of freshly squeezed lemon juice
- 1 tablespoon of fresh parsley, finely chopped

Stew Ingredients:

- 1 medium onion, finely chopped
- 1 medium red bell pepper, sliced
- 5 medium garlic cloves, minced
- 1 (14-ounce) can of crushed tomatoes
- 1 cup of homemade low-sodium seafood broth
- 2 tablespoons of extra-virgin olive oil
- 1 tablespoon of ground cumin
- 1 tablespoon of smoked or regular paprika
- 1 teaspoon of fine sea salt
- ½ teaspoon of freshly cracked black pepper
- ½ teaspoon of ground cayenne pepper

Instructions:

- Add all the stew ingredients inside your Instant Pot and give a good stir.
- Lock the lid and cook at high pressure for 10 minutes. When done, naturally release the pressure for 10 minutes then quick release the remaining pressure. Carefully remove the lid.
- Press the "Sauté" function on your Instant Pot and cook for 10 minutes or until the sauce lightly thickens.
- Add the fish pieces, lemon juice and parsley. Cook for 5 minutes or until the sauce thickens, stirring occasionally. Serve and enjoy!

Provencal Fish Stew

Time: 25 minutes   Servings: 4

Ingredients:

- 4 tablespoons of extra-virgin olive oil
- 1 medium onion, finely chopped

- 1 medium zucchini, chopped
- 2 medium garlic cloves, skins removed and minced
- 1 teaspoon of fine sea salt
- 1 teaspoon of freshly cracked black pepper
- ½ cup of dry white wine
- 1 (28-ounce) can of diced or crushed tomatoes
- 3 cups of homemade low-sodium fish stock or chicken stock
- 2 teaspoons of fresh thyme
- 1 medium head of cauliflower, cut into florets
- 1 ½ pounds of cod or halibut fish fillets, cut into bite-sized pieces

Instructions:

- Press the "Sauté" setting on your Instant Pot and add the onion and garlic. Sauté for 6 minutes or until translucent, stirring occasionally.
- Add the remaining ingredients except for the cauliflower and sauté for 3 minutes.
- Deglaze your Instant Pot with the dry white wine and continue to cook until most of the liquid evaporates.
- Pour in the crushed tomatoes and stock. Lock the lid and cook at high pressure for 6 minutes.
- When the cooking is done, quick release the pressure and remove the lid.
- Press the "Sauté" function on your Instant Pot and stir in the fish pieces. Cook for 5 minutes or until the fish is cooked through. Serve and enjoy!

Seafood Chowder
Time: 30 minutes   Servings: 4

Ingredients:

- 1 pound of fresh white fish, cut into bite-sized pieces
- 1 pound of shrimp, peeled and deveined
- 1 cup of crab meat, chopped
- 1 large onion, finely chopped
- 2 garlic cloves, peeled and minced
- 4 medium bacon slices, chopped
- 1 daikon radish, peeled and chopped
- 2 cups of homemade low-sodium fish or chicken stock
- 1 ½ cup of full-fat coconut milk
- 2 tablespoons of extra-virgin olive oil
- ½ teaspoon of fine sea salt
- ½ teaspoon of freshly cracked black pepper

Instructions:

- Press the "Sauté" function on your Instant Pot and add the bacon slices. Cook until brown and crispy. Transfer to a plate lined with paper towels.
- Add the onions and garlic cloves. Sauté until translucent, stirring occasionally.
- Add the remaining ingredients except for the coconut milk and stir until well combined. Lock the lid and cook at high pressure for 4 minutes. When the cooking is done, quick release the pressure and remove the lid.
- Give the chowder a stir and add in the coconut milk. Adjust the seasoning if necessary.
- Serve and enjoy!

Cioppino Seafood Stew
Time: 30 minutes   Servings: 6

Ingredients:

- 2 (6-ounce) boneless tilapia fillets, cut into bite-sized pieces
- 3 cups of shrimps, bay scallops and mussels
- 1 (14-ounce) can of crushed tomatoes
- 1 (14-ounce) can of fire-roasted tomatoes
- ¼ cup of extra-virgin olive oil
- 1 cup of white or yellow onion, finely chopped
- 1 cup of carrots, chopped
- 1 cup of bell pepper, chopped
- 2 cups of homemade low-sodium seafood stock or chicken stock
- 2 bay leaves
- 1 tablespoon of tomato paste
- 2 tablespoons of minced garlic
- 2 teaspoons of toasted fennel seeds
- 1 teaspoon of dried oregano
- 2 teaspoons of fine sea salt
- 1 teaspoon of red pepper flakes

Instructions:

- Press the "Sauté" function on your Instant Pot and add the olive oil. Once hot, add the onion, chopped carrot, chopped bell pepper and garlic. Sauté until translucent, stirring occasionally.
- Add the remaining ingredients inside your Instant Pot and give a good stir. Lock the lid and cook at high pressure for 15 minutes. When the cooking is done, quick release the pressure and remove the lid.

- Adjust the seasoning if necessary and stir the cioppino stew again. Serve and enjoy!

Shrimp and Fish Stew
Time: 30 minutes   Servings: 4

Ingredients:

- 2 tablespoons of olive oil
- 1 large yellow or white onion, finely chopped
- 6 medium garlic cloves, crushed
- 1 (15-ounce) can of crushed tomatoes
- 4 tablespoons of tomato paste
- ½ cup of fresh parsley, finely chopped
- 2 teaspoons of Italian seasoning
- ½ pound of fresh cherry tomatoes, cut in half

- 1 cup of clam juice
- ½ cup of dry white wine
- 3 cups of homemade low-sodium fish stock or chicken stock
- 2 pounds of boneless white fish, frozen
- ½ pound of frozen shrimp, peeled and deveined
- 1 teaspoon of fine sea salt
- 1 teaspoon of freshly cracked black pepper

Instructions:

- Press the "Sauté" function on your Instant Pot and add the olive oil. Once hot, add the onions and crushed garlic Sauté for 6 minutes or until tranluscne.t
- Add the remaining ingredients inside your Instant Pot and lock the lid. Cook at high pressure for 10 minutes.
- When the timer beeps, naturally release the pressure and remove the lid. Carefully use a fork to break up the fish and adjust the seasoning if necessary Serve and enjoy!

Greek Fish Stew
Time: 15 minutes   Servings: 6

Ingredients:

- 6 tablespoons of olive oil
- 1 onion, thinly sliced
- 1 medium leek, thinly sliced
- 2 large garlic cloves, crushed
- 5 large celery stalks, thinly sliced
- 3 cups of dry white wine
- 1 ½ pound of boneless white fish, cut into bite-sized pieces

- 2 pounds of mussels, scrubbed
- 2 cups of homemade low-sodium fish stock or chicken stock
- 2 tablespoons of fresh parsley, finely chopped
- 2 tablespoons of fresh thyme, finely chopped
- 1 teaspoon of fine sea salt
- 1 teaspoon of freshly cracked black pepper

Instructions:

- Press the "Sauté" function on your Instant Pot and add the olive oil. Once hot, add the onions, leeks, and garlic. Sauté until translucent.
- Add the remaining ingredients and stir until well combined.
- Lock the lid and cook at high pressure for 8 minutes.
- When done, naturally release the pressure and remove the lid. Serve and enjoy!

Portuguese-Style Fish Stew
Time: 15 minutes   Servings: 4

Ingredients:

- 2 pounds of boneless, skinless sea bass, cut into 2-inch pieces
- 3 tablespoon of coconut oil
- 2 bay leaves
- 2 teaspoons of smoked or sweet paprika
- 1 small onion, thinly sliced
- 1 small green bell pepper, seeds removed and thinly sliced

- 1 (14.5-ounce) can of diced tomatoes
- 1 (14.5-ounce) can of crushed tomatoes
- 2 cups of homemade low-sodium chicken stock or fish stock
- 1 medium garlic clove, minced
- ¼ cup of fresh cilantro
- 1 teaspoon of fine sea salt
- 1 teaspoon of freshly cracked black pepper

Instructions:

- Press the "Sauté" setting on your Instant Pot and add the coconut oil. Once hot, add the onions and garlic. Sauté until translucent.
- Add the remaining ingredients except for the sea bass inside your Instant Pot.
- Lock the lid and cook at high pressure for 6 minutes. When done, quick release or naturally release the pressure and remove the lid.
- Press the "Sauté" function on your Instant Pot and add the fish pieces. Cook for 5 minutes or until the fish is cooked through. Serve and enjoy!

Southwestern Cilantro Fish Stew
Time: 15 minutes   Servings: 6

Ingredients:

- 2 tablespoons of extra-virgin olive oil
- 1 large white or yellow onion, peeled and finely chopped
- 1 cup of carrots, thinly sliced
- 3 medium garlic cloves, minced
- 1 jalapeno pepper, sliced
- 4 cups of homemade low-sodium chicken stock
- 2 cups of cauliflower florets, chopped
- 1 cup of dry white wine
- 1 cup of fresh cilantro, chopped
- 1 (15-ounce) can of crushed tomatoes
- 1 pound of halibut, cut into 2-inch pieces
- ½ pound of large shrimp, peeled and deveined

Instructions:

- Press the "Sauté" function on your Instant Pot and add the olive oil. Once hot, add all the vegetables and sauté for 6 minutes or until softened.
- Add the remaining ingredients except for the halibut pieces and shrimp. Give a good stir and lock the lid. Cook at high pressure for 6 minutes. When done, naturally release or quick release the pressure. Carefully remove the lid.
- Press the "Sauté" setting on your Instant Pot and add the halibut pieces and shrimp. Cook until the fish and shrimp is cooked through, stirring occasionally. Serve and enjoy!

Sicilian-Style Fish Stew
Time: 45 minutes   Servings: 6

Ingredients:

- 3 tablespoons of olive oil
- 1 large white or yellow onion, finely chopped
- 4 large garlic cloves, peeled and crushed
- 1 teaspoon of fine sea salt
- 1 teaspoon of freshly cracked black pepper
- 2 celery stalks, chopped
- 1 cup of keto-friendly red wine
- 1 (28-ounce) can of plum tomatoes, undrained
- 3 cups of homemade low-sodium fish stock or chicken stock
- 2 tablespoons of capers
- 2 pounds of white fish fillets, cut into chunks
- ½ cup of fresh cilantro, chopped

Instructions:

- Press the "Sauté" function on your Instant Pot and add the olive oil. Once hot, add the onions and garlic cloves. Sauté for 5 minutes or until translucent.
- Deglaze your Instant Pot with the red wine and add the remaining ingredients.
- Lock the lid and cook at high pressure for 8 minutes. When done, naturally release or quick release the pressure. Carefully remove the lid.Serve and enjoy!

Cajun Salmon with Alfredo Sauce
Time: 25 minutes   Servings: 4

Ingredients:

- 4 (6-ounce) tilapia fillets, frozen
- 1 tablespoon of Cajun seasoning
- 4 tablespoons of unsalted butter
- 1 cup of heavy cream
- ½ teaspoon of garlic powder
- ½ teaspoon of onion powder
- ½ teaspoon of freshly cracked black pepper
- ½ teaspoon of fine sea salt

- 1 cup of parmesan cheese, grated

Instructions:

- In a heat-proof dish that can fit inside your Instant Pot, add the heavy cream, Cajun seasoning, butter, garlic powder, onion powder, black pepper, salt and grated parmesan cheese. Stir well.
- Place the frozen tilapia fillets on the dish.
- Add 2 cups of water and a trivet inside your Instant Pot.
- Place the dish on top of the trivet.
- Lock the lid and cook at high pressure for 6 minutes. When the cooking is done, quick release the pressure and remove the lid. Serve and enjoy!

Alaskan Cod with Olives, Fennel and Cauliflower
Time: 20 minutes   Servings: 3

Ingredients:

- 2 tablespoons of extra-virgin olive oil
- 1 pound of Alaskan cod fillet, cut into chunks
- ½ medium white or yellow onion, chopped
- 6 garlic cloves, peeled and minced
- 1 ½ cups of homemade low-sodium chicken stock or fish stock

- ½ cup of green, black or Kalamata olives, pitted and chopped
- ¼ cups of tomato puree
- 1 head of cauliflower, cut into florets
- 1 head of fennel, chopped
- ¼ bunch of fresh basil
- 1 medium lemon, juice

Instructions:

- Press the "Sauté" setting on your Instant Pot and add the onions and garlic. Sauté for 5 minutes or until translucent.
- Deglaze your Instant Pot with the chicken stock.
- Add the remaining ingredients except for the fish and lock the lid. Cook at low pressure for 10 minutes. When the cooking is done, quick release the pressure and remove the lid.
- Press the "Sauté" setting on your Instant Pot and add the Alaskan cod fillets. Cook for 4 minutes or until the fish is cooked through. Serve and enjoy!

Coconut Fish Curry
Time: 10 minutes   Servings: 4

Ingredients:

- 1 ½ pounds of white fish fillets, cut into bite-sized pieces
- 1 cup of cherry tomatoes, halved
- 2 medium red bell peppers, seeds remove and chopped
- 2 medium onions, thinly sliced
- 4 garlic cloves, minced
- 1-inch piece of fresh ginger, peeled and minced

- 1 teaspoon of fine sea salt
- 2 tablespoons of olive oil
- 1 teaspoon of freshly cracked black pepper
- 2 cups of unsweetened coconut milk
- 3 tablespoons of madras curry powder
- 1 lemon, freshly squeezed juice
- 2 cups of cauliflower rice (for serving)

Instructions:

- Press the "Sauté" setting on your Instant Pot and add the olive oil. Once hot, add the onions, ginger, garlic cloves and red bell pepper. Sauté for 4 to 5 minutes or until translucent.
- Add the remaining ingredients and gently stir until well combined.
- Lock the lid and cook at high pressure for 3 minutes. When done, quick release the pressure and remove the lid. Serve and enjoy with cauliflower rice!

Cod Platter
Time: 15 minutes   Servings: 6

Ingredients:

- 1 ½ pound of fresh cod fillets
- 12 cherry tomatoes, cut in half
- 2 garlic cloves, minced
- 1 medium yellow bell pepper, seeds removed and chopped

- 3 tablespoons of olive oil
- 1 tablespoon of fresh rosemary, minced
- 1 tablespoon of fresh oregano, minced
- 1 teaspoon of fine sea salt
- 1 teaspoon of freshly cracked black pepper

Instructions:

- In a bowl, add the tomatoes, minced garlic, yellow bell pepper, rosemary, oregano, salt and black pepper.
- Press the "Sauté" function on your Instant Pot and add the olive oil. Add the vegetable mixture. Sauté for 1 minute, stirring occasionally.
- Add the cod fillets on top of the vegetables. Lock the lid and cook at high pressure for 3 minutes. When done, quick release the pressure and remove the lid. Serve and enjoy!

Fish Tacos

Time: 10 minutes   Servings: 2

Ingredients:

- 2 tilapia fillets
- 1 teaspoon of olive oil
- A pinch of fine sea salt
- 2 teaspoons of smoked or sweet paprika
- 1 lime, juice

- 2 fresh sprigs of thyme
- Lettuce leaves (for serving)
- Avocado slices (for serving)
- Diced tomatoes (for serving)
- Sour cream (for serving)

Instructions:

- Lay parchment paper on your counter and add the tilapia fillets. Season with sea salt and paprika. Drizzle with olive oil and lime juice. Wrap the parchment paper.
- Place 2 cups of water and a trivet inside your Instant Pot. Place the parchment paper on top of the trivet.
- Lock the lid and cook at high pressure for 8 minutes. When done, quick release the pressure and remove the lid.
- Transfer the fish to a cutting board and shred using two forks.
- Assemble each taco onto lettuce leaves along with avocado slices, diced tomatoes and sour cream. Serve and enjoy!

Lime and White Pepper Salmon

Time: 15 minutes   Servings: 4

Ingredients:

- 1 pound of skin-on salmon fillets
- 1 tablespoon of butter
- ½ teaspoon of fine sea salt

- ½ teaspoon of white pepper
- 1 lime, sliced
- A few sprigs of fresh herbs such as parsley, dill, thyme or tarragon

Instructions:

- Add 1 cup of water and herbs inside your Instant Pot. Place a steamer rack inside.
- Season the salmon fillets with sea salt and white pepper.
- Place the salmon fillets on top of the steamer rack. Place the lime slices on top.
- Lock the lid and cook at high pressure for 4 minutes. When done, quick release the pressure and remove the lid. Serve and enjoy!

Simple Wild Alaskan Cod

Time: 10 minutes   Servings: 4

Ingredients:

- 1 large Alaskan cod fillet
- 1 cup of cherry tomatoes, halved
- ½ teaspoon of fine sea salt
- ½ teaspoon of freshly cracked black pepper

- 1 medium garlic clove, peeled and crushed
- 1 medium lemon, fresh juice and lemon zest
- 2 tablespoons of unsalted butter, melted

Instructions:

- In an oven-safe dish that can fit inside your Instant Pot. Add a layer of halved cherry tomatoes.
- Place the Alaskan cod fillet on top of the fillet and season with sea salt, freshly cracked black pepper, crushed garlic, lemon juice and lemon zest. Drizzle with the melted butter.
- Add 1 cup of water and a trivet inside your Instant Pot. Place the dish on top of the trivet and lock the lid. Cook at high pressure for 5 minutes. When done, quick release the pressure and remove the lid. Serve and enjoy!

Lobster Tails
Time: 10 minutes   Servings: 4

Ingredients:

- 4 (4-ounce) lobster tails
- 1 cup of water

- 4 tablespoons of unsalted butter, melted

Instructions:

- Add 1 cup of water and a trivet inside your Instant Pot. Place the lobster tails on top of the trivet.
- Lock the lid and press the "Steam" function. Set the time to 2 minutes and press start.
- When the timer beeps, remove the lid and brush with melted butter. Serve and enjoy!

Lobster with Lemon-Herb Butter
Time: 5 minutes   Servings: 4

Ingredients:

- 1 (2 pound) whole lobsters, killed and prepared
- ¾ cups of butter, melted
- 2 teaspoons of freshly squeezed lemon juice
- 2 teaspoons of fresh Italian parsley, finely chopped

- 2 teaspoons of fresh chives, finely chopped
- 2 teaspoons of fresh basil, finely chopped
- ¼ teaspoon of fine sea salt
- 3 cups of water

Instructions:

- Add 3 cups of water and a trivet inside your Instant Pot. Place the lobster on top of the trivet.
- Lock the lid and cook at high pressure for 3 minutes. When the cooking is done, quick release the pressure and remove the lid.
- In a bowl, add the melted butter, lemon juice, fresh herbs and sea salt. Mix well.
- Drizzle the butter sauce over the lobster. Serve and enjoy!

Lobster Cauliflower Risotto
Time: 5 minutes   Servings: 2

Ingredients:

- ½ pound of lobster meat
- 2 tablespoons of unsalted butter
- 1 tablespoon of extra-virgin olive oil
- 1 large shallot, finely chopped
- 3 medium garlic cloves, peeled and minced

- 1 cup of cauliflower rice
- 2 cups of homemade low-sodium lobster stock
- 3 tablespoons of mascarpone cheese
- ½ teaspoon of fine sea salt
- ½ teaspoon of freshly cracked black pepper

Instructions:

- Press the "Sauté" function on your Instant Pot and add the unsalted butter and olive oil. Once hot, add the chopped shallots and minced garlic. Sauté until translucent, stirring occasionally.
- Add the cauliflower rice and lobster stock inside your Instant Pot.
- Gently stir in the lobster meat. Lock the lid and cook at high pressure for 2 minutes.
- When the cooking is done, naturally release the pressure and remove the lid.
- Gently stir in the remaining ingredients.Serve and enjoy!

Lobster Bisque

Time: 10 minutes   Servings: 4

Ingredients:

- 4 (4-ounce) lobster tails
- 4 cups of homemade low-sodium lobster stock
- 3 tablespoons of extra-virgin olive oil
- 1 (28-ounce) can of diced tomatoes
- 2 shallots, finely chopped
- 1 medium garlic clove, minced
- 1 cup of carrots, chopped
- 1 cup of celery, chopped
- 1 tablespoon of old bay seasoning
- 1 teaspoon of dried dill
- 1 teaspoon of freshly cracked black pepper
- ½ teaspoon of smoked paprika or regular paprika
- 1 pint of heavy whipping cream

Instructions:

- Press the "Sauté" function on your Instant Pot and add the extra-virgin olive oil. One hot, add the chopped shallots and garlic. Sauté for 4 minutes or until translucent, stirring occasionally.
- Add the chopped celery and carrots. Sauté for another 2 minutes, stirring occasionally.
- Add the diced tomatoes, lobster stock, old bay seasoning, dried dill, black pepper and paprika. Gently stir in the lobster tails.
- Lock the lid and cook at high pressure for 4 minutes. When the cooking is done, naturally release the pressure and remove the lid.
- Remove the lobster tails and carefully remove the flesh form the tails. Set aside.
- Use an immersion blender to blend the contents of the Instant Pot until smooth. Gently stir in the lobster meat along with the heavy cream. Serve and enjoy!

Lobster Deviled Eggs

Time: 15 minutes   Servings: 8

Ingredients:

- 8 large organic egg
- 1 (8-ounce) lobster tail
- ¼ cup of mayonnaise
- 2 teaspoons of freshly squeezed lemon juice
- 1 tablespoon of Dijon mustard
- ¼ teaspoon of freshly cracked black pepper
- 1/8 teaspoon of fine sea salt
- 1 celery stalk, finely chopped
- 2 teaspoons of unsalted butter
- Smoked paprika (for garnishing)

Instructions:

- Add 1 cup of water and a steamer rack inside your Instant Pot. Place the eggs on the steamer rack along with the lobster tail.
- Lock the lid and cook at low pressure for 8 minutes. When the cooking is done, quick release the pressure and remove the lid.
- Transfer the eggs and lobster tails to an ice bath. Peel the eggs and set aside. Remove the flesh from the lobster tail and finely chop the lobster.
- Cut the eggs in half and transfer the eggs to a bowl.
- In the bowl with the egg yolks, add the lobster meat, mayonnaise, lemon juice, Dijon mustard, black pepper, salt, celery and unsalted butter. Stir until combined.
- Spoon the yolk mixture onto each egg half and sprinkle with paprika. Serve and enjoy!

Southwestern Lobster Chili

Time: 20 minutes   Servings: 6

Ingredients:

- 2 ½ pounds of lobster meat
- 6 slices of bacon, chopped
- 2 cups of homemade low-sodium lobster stock
- 1 (28-ounce) can of crushed or diced tomatoes
- 4 medium Roma tomatoes, finely chopped
- 1 red or green bell pepper, seeds removed and chopped
- 1 red onion, finely chopped
- 4 medium garlic cloves, peeled and minced
- 1 teaspoon of dried oregano
- 1 teaspoon of ground cumin
- 3 tablespoons of chili powder
- ½ teaspoon of fine sea salt
- ½ teaspoon of freshly cracked black pepper

Instructions:

- Press the "Sauté" function on your Instant Pot and add the chopped bacon. Cook until the bacon is brown and crispy. Transfer the bacon to a plate lined with paper towels.
- Add the onion and garlic to the bacon grease and sauté for 4 to 6 minutes or until translucent, stirring occasionally.
- Add the lobster stuck, crushed tomatoes, chopped tomatoes, bell pepper, dried oregano, ground cumin, chili powder, sea salt and black pepper. Give a good stir.
- Lock the lid and cook at high pressure for 5 minutes. When the cooking is done, naturally release the pressure and remove the lid.
- Press the "Sauté" function on your Instant Pot and add the lobster meat and chopped bacon. Cook for 3 to 5 minutes or until the lobster is cooked through. Serve and enjoy!

Wild-Caught Crab Legs
Time: 3 minutes   Servings: 4

Ingredients:

- 2 pounds of wild-caught crab legs
- 1 cup of water

- 1/3 cup of unsalted butter, melted
- 2 tablespoons of freshly squeezed lemon juice

Instructions:

- Add 1 cup of water and a trivet inside your Instant Pot.
- Place the crab legs on the trivet and lock the lid.
- Cook at high pressure for 3 minutes. When the cooking is done, quick release the pressure.
- In a bowl, add the unsalted butter and lemon juice. Mix well.
- Spoon the butter-lemon sauce over the crab legs. Serve and enjoy!

Shrimp Boil
Time: 10 minutes   Servings: 6

Ingredients:

- 1 large cauliflower head, cut into florets
- 1 andouille sausage, thinly sliced
- 2 tablespoons of coconut oil
- 1 medium white or yellow onion, roughly chopped
- 1 red bell pepper, seeds removed and chopped
- ¼ cup of unsalted butter

- 1 ½ pounds of shrimp, peeled and deveined
- 3 garlic cloves, peeled and minced
- 2 tablespoons of fresh parsley, finely chopped
- 1 tablespoon of freshly squeezed lemon juice
- 4 teaspoons of old bay seasoning
- 1 tablespoon of hot sauce
- 2 cups of homemade low-sodium seafood stock

Instructions:

- Add all the ingredients inside your Instant Pot and stir until well combined.
- Lock the lid and cook at high pressure for 5 minutes.
- When the cooking is done, naturally release the pressure and remove the lid.
- Serve and enjoy!

Steamed Clams in Wine Garlic Sauce
Time: 20 minutes   Servings: 4

Ingredients:

- 5 pounds of live clams
- 1 ½ cup of dry white wine
- 1 stick of unsalted butter
- 10 garlic cloves, peeled and minced

- 2 teaspoons of fine sea salt
- ½ cup of fresh parsley, chopped
- 1 tablespoon of freshly squeezed lemon juice

Instructions:

- Press the "Sauté" function on your Instant Pot and add half of the stick of butter. Once hot, add the minced garlic and sauté for 1 minute.
- Add the dry white wine and live clams. Lock the lid and press the "Steam" setting and set the time for 1 minute.
- When the timer beeps, remove the lid. Press the "Sauté" setting on your Instant Pot and add the remaining stick of butter, salt, fresh parsley and fresh lemon juice. Serve and enjoy!

Steamed Clams in Spicy Tomato Sauce
Time: 30 minutes   Servings: 6

Ingredients:

- 2 pounds of fresh clams
- 2 tablespoons of extra-virgin olive oil
- 1 cup of dry white wine
- 1 small onion, finely chopped
- 4 medium garlic cloves, minced
- 1 (28-ounce) can of chopped tomatoes, undrained
- 1 teaspoon of fresh thyme
- 1 teaspoon of fine sea salt
- 1 teaspoon of red pepper flakes
- 1 teaspoon of freshly cracked black pepper
- 4 tablespoons of fresh parsley, finely chopped
- ½ cup of homemade low-sodium clam juice or seafood stock

Instructions:

- Add the clams onto a steamer basket.
- Press the "Sauté" function on your Instant Pot and add the olive oil.
- Once hot, add the chopped onions and minced garlic. Sauté for 5 minutes or until softened, stirring occasionally.
- Add the clams and remaining ingredients inside your Instant Pot. Give a gentle stir.
- Lock the lid and cook at high pressure for 6 minutes. When done, naturally release the pressure and remove the lid. Serve and enjoy!

Thai Coconut Clams
Time: 30 minutes   Servings: 6

Ingredients:

- 3 shallots, sliced
- 1 stalk of fresh lemongrass core, chopped
- 1 tablespoon of coconut oil
- ½ cup of homemade low-sodium seafood stock
- 1 1-inch piece of fresh ginger, peeled and julienned
- 2 jalapeno peppers, seeds removed and sliced
- ½ cup of full-fat coconut milk
- 2 pounds of clams, cleaned
- ½ teaspoon of fine sea salt
- ½ teaspoon of freshly cracked black pepper
- 1 scallion, chopped
- ½ cup of fresh cilantro, chopped

Instructions:

- Press the "Sauté" function on your Instant Pot and add the coconut oil. Once hot, add the sliced shallots and sauté for 3 to 5 minutes or until softened, stirring occasionally.
- Add the chopped lemongrass core, ginger and jalapenos to the pot. Sauté for 1 minute, stirring occasionally.
- Add the remaining ingredients except for the fresh cilantro.
- Lock the lid and cook at high pressure for 2 minutes. When the cooking is done, quick release the pressure and remove the lid.
- Ladle into serving bowls and top with fresh cilantro Serve and enjoy!

Red Clam Sauce
Time: 25 minutes   Servings: 4

Ingredients:

- 2 (6.5-ounce) cans of chopped clams, undrained
- 1 (14.5-ounce) can of diced tomatoes, undrained
- 1 (6-ounce) can of tomato paste
- 2 medium garlic cloves, minced
- 1 medium onion, finely chopped
- 1 tablespoon of extra-virgin olive oil
- ¼ cup of fresh parsley, finely chopped
- 1 bay leaf
- 1 teaspoon of dried basil
- ½ teaspoon of dried thyme

Instructions:

- Press the "Sauté" function on your Instant Pot and add the olive oil. Once hot, add the onions and garlic. Sauté for 2 minutes or until tender, stirring occasionally.
- Add the remaining ingredients and stir until well combined.
- Lock the lid and cook at high pressure for 3 minutes. When the cooking is done, naturally release the pressure and remove the lid.
- Remove the bay leaf and adjust the seasoning if necessary. Serve and enjoy!

Crawfish Boil
Time: 15 minutes   Servings: 6

Ingredients:

- 4 pounds of crawfish
- 1 cup of water
- 3 tablespoons of Louisiana Crawfish Boil
- 6 tablespoons of butter, melted
- 1 tablespoon of garlic, minced
- 1/8 teaspoon of Cajun seasoning
- 5 drops of hot sauce

Instructions:

- Press the "Sauté" function on your Instant Pot and add the butter. Once melted, add the minced garlic and sauté for 1 minute, stirring occasionally.
- Add the remaining ingredients except for the crawfish inside your Instant Pot.
- Lock the lid and cook at high pressure for 5 minutes.
- When the cooking is done, quick release the pressure and carefully remove the lid.
- Gently stir in the crawfish and lock the lid. Cook at high pressure for 3 minutes. When the cooking is done, quick release the pressure and remove the lid. Serve and enjoy!

Shrimp Etouffee
Time: 30 minutes   Servings: 6

Ingredients:

- 2 pounds of shrimp, peeled and deveined
- 1 tablespoon of creole seasoning
- 4 tablespoons of butter, melted
- ¼ cup of almond flour
- 1 cup of onions, finely chopped
- 1 cup of green bell pepper, finely chopped
- 1 cup of celery, chopped
- 2 cups of homemade low-sodium seafood stock
- 1 cup of tomatoes, chopped
- 1 tablespoon of tomato puree
- 1 tablespoon of sherry
- 1 teaspoon of Worcestershire sauce
- 1 teaspoon of freshly squeezed lemon juice
- 1 tablespoon of garlic, minced
- ½ teaspoon of freshly cracked black pepper
- ½ teaspoon of fine sea salt

Instructions:

- Press the "Sauté" function on your Instant Pot and add the butter. Once melted, add the flour and cook until the butter has blended with the flour, stirring frequently.
- Add the chopped onions, chopped bell pepper, chopped celery, and minced garlic. Sauté the vegetables for 5 minutes or until softened.
- Stir in the creole seasoning, salt and black pepper.
- Add the remaining ingredients inside your Instant Pot. Give a good stir and lock the lid. Cook at high pressure for 10 minutes. When the cooking is done, quick release the pressure and carefully remove the lid. Serve and enjoy!

Tuna Cauliflower Risotto
Time: 12 minutes   Servings: 4

Ingredients:

- 2 cups of canned tuna chunks
- 2 tablespoons of unsalted butter
- 1 cup of cauliflower rice
- 1 small onion, finely chopped

- 2 medium garlic cloves, peeled and minced
- 1 lemon, juice and zest
- 1 ½ cup of homemade low-sodium seafood stock
- 1/3 cups of parmesan cheese, finely grated

Instructions:

- Press the "Sauté" function on your Instant Pot and add the butter and tuna. Sauté for 2 minutes, stirring occasionally.
- Add the chopped onion and minced garlic. Saut é for 3 minutes, stirring occasionally.
- Add the cauliflower rice and mix well. Add the remaining ingredients except for the parmesan cheese.
- Lock the lid and cook at high pressure for 2 minutes. When the cooking is done, quick release the pressure and remove the lid.
- Stir in the grated parmesan cheese. Serve and enjoy!

Tuna Cauliflower Casserole
Time: 25 minutes   Servings: 10

Ingredients:

- 1 large head of cauliflower, cut into florets
- 1 cup of mushrooms, finely chopped
- 2 tablespoons of extra-virgin olive oil
- 1 cup of yellow or white onion, finely chopped
- 1 cup of celery stalk, finely chopped
- 1 (10-ounce) can of tuna
- 1 (10.5-ounce) cream of mushroom soup
- 1 (10.5-ounce) cream of celery soup
- 1 teaspoon of fine sea salt
- ½ teaspoon of freshly cracked black pepper
- 4 cups of homemade low-sodium seafood stock
- 4-ounces of cream cheese, softened and cubed

Instructions:

- Press the "Sauté" function on your Instant Pot and add the olive oil. Once hot, add the onions, celery stalk, mushrooms and cauliflower florets. Sauté for 5 minutes or until the vegetables are fragrant, stirring occasionally.
- Add the remaining ingredients except for the cream cheese inside your Instant Pot and stir until well combined.
- Lock the lid and cook at high pressure for 2 minutes. When the cooking is done, quick release the pressure and remove the lid. Gently stir in the cream cheese. Serve and enjoy!

Salmon Patties
Time: 10 minutes   Servings: 6

Ingredients:

- 1 pound of salmon fillets
- 1 cup of white or yellow onion, finely chopped
- ½ red bell pepper, seeds removed and chopped
- 3 tablespoons of unsalted butter, melted
- 1 cup of crushed pork rinds
- 2 large eggs, beaten
- 3 tablespoons of mayonnaise
- 1 teaspoon of Worcestershire sauce
- ¼ cup of fresh parsley, finely chopped

Instructions:

- In a large bowl, add all the salmon patty ingredients and stir until well combined.
- Form the salmon mixture into 6 separate patties.
- Wrap the salmon patties with aluminum foil.
- Add 2 cups of water and a trivet inside your Instant Pot. Place the salmon patties on top of the trivet. Lock the lid and cook at high pressure for 6 minutes.
- When the cooking is done, quick release the pressure and remove the lid.
- Unwrap the salmon patties and enjoy!

Cajun Crab Casserole
Time: 18 minutes   Servings: 6

Ingredients:

- 2 tablespoons of extra-virgin olive oil
- 1 medium yellow onion, finely chopped
- ½ cup of celery, chopped
- 1 ¼ cups of mayonnaise

- 4 large organic eggs
- 1 ¼ cup of shredded cheddar cheese
- 1 (15-ounce) can of crab meat, drained
- 2 teaspoons of paprika
- ¼ teaspoons of cayenne pepper
- ½ teaspoon of fine sea salt
- ½ teaspoon of freshly cracked black pepper

Instructions:

- Press the "Sauté" function on your Instant Pot and add olive oil. Once hot, add the onions and celery. Sauté until translucent, stirring occasionally.
- Remove the contents and set aside. In a large bowl, add the cooked onions and celery. Add the remaining ingredients but reserve ½ cup of cheddar cheese.
- Transfer the crab mixture to a greased baking dish that fits inside your Instant Pot.. Place the cheddar cheese on top and cover with aluminum foil.
- Add 2 cups of water and a trivet inside your Instant Pot. Place the baking dish on top of the trivet.
- Lock the lid and cook at high pressure for 6 minutes. When the cooking is done, quick release the pressure. Carefully remove the lid. Serve and enjoy!

Oyster Stew
Time: 10 minutes   Servings: 4

Ingredients:

- 1 pint of full-fat coconut milk or heavy whipping cream
- 1 cup of homemade low-sodium seafood stock
- 1 cup of celery, chopped
- 2 (10-ounce) jars of shucked oysters, undrained
- 2 tablespoons of unsalted butter, coconut oil or other cooking fat
- 2 tablespoons of shallot, finely chopped
- 2 medium garlic cloves, peeled and minced
- ½ teaspoon of fine sea salt
- ½ teaspoon of white pepper
- 2 tablespoons of fresh parsley, chopped

Instructions:

- Press the "Sauté" setting on your Instant Pot add the butter. Once hot, add the shallots, garlic and celery. Sauté for 4 minutes or until softened, stirring occasionally.
- Add the oysters, coconut milk and seafood stock. Lock the lid and cook at low pressure for 6 minutes.
- When the cooking is done, quick release the pressure and remove the lid. Season with sea salt, white pepper and fresh parsley. Serve and enjoy!

Part 7: Appetizers and Side Dishes Recipes

Ultimate Corn on the Cob
Time: 15 minutes   Servings: 4

Ingredients:

- 8 corn on the cob
- 2 cups of water
- 2 teaspoons low-carb brown sugar
- 1 teaspoon salt (to taste)
- 1 teaspoon fresh ground black pepper (to taste)

Instructions:

1. Pour 2 cups of water in Instant Pot. Place corn in steamer basket. Place basket in Instant Pot.
2. Close and seal lid. Press Manual button. Cook at High Pressure for 5 minutes.
3. When the timer beeps, naturally release pressure. Open the lid with care.
4. Sprinkle with brown sugar. Serve.

Tangy Steamed Artichokes
Time: 25 minutes   Servings: 2

Ingredients:

- 2 artichokes
- Juice from 1 lemon
- 2 Tablespoons low-carb mayonnaise
- 2 cups of water
- 1 teaspoon paprika
- 1 teaspoon salt (to taste)
- 1 teaspoon fresh ground black pepper (to taste)

Instructions:

1. Wash and trim artichokes. Pour 2 cups of water in Instant Pot.
2. Place artichokes in steamer basket. Place basket in Instant Pot.
3. Close and seal lid. Press Manual switch. Cook at High Pressure for 10 minutes.
4. Release pressure naturally when done. Open the lid with care.
5. In a bowl, combine mayonnaise, lemon juice, paprika, salt, and black pepper. Spread on artichokes. Serve.

Succulent Sausage and Cheese Dip
Time: 10 minutes   Servings: 4

Ingredients:

- 1 pound ground Italian sausage
- ¼ cup green onions, chopped
- 1 cup cream cheese, softened
- 1 cup mozzarella cheese, shredded
- 1 cup cheddar cheese, shredded
- 1 cup vegetable broth
- 2 cups canned diced tomatoes
- 2 Tablespoons ghee, melted

Instructions:

1. Press Sauté button on Instant Pot. Heat the ghee.
2. Sauté Italian sausage and green onions, until sausage is brown.
3. Add remaining ingredients. Stir well.
4. Close and seal lid. Press Manual button. Cook at High Pressure for 5 minutes.
5. When the timer beeps, naturally release pressure. Open the lid with care. Serve.

Zesty Onion and Cauliflower Dip
Time: 20 minutes   Servings: 4

Ingredients:

- 1 head cauliflower, minced
- 1 cup chicken broth
- 1 ¼ cup low-carb mayonnaise
- 1 onion, chopped
- 1 cup cream cheese, softened
- 1 teaspoon Chili powder
- 1 teaspoon ground cumin
- 1 teaspoon garlic powder
- 1 teaspoon salt (to taste)
- 1 teaspoon fresh ground black pepper (to taste)

Instructions:

1. Add all ingredients to Instant Pot. Stir well. Using a hand blender, blend ingredients.
2. Close and seal lid. Press Manual button. Cook at High Pressure for 10 minutes.
3. When the timer beeps, naturally release pressure, Open the lid with care. Stir ingredients.
4. Serve.

Ravishing Mushrooms and Sausage Gravy

Time: 15 minutes   Servings: 4

Ingredients:

- 1 pound Italian ground sausage
- 2 Tablespoons coconut oil
- 1 yellow onion, diced
- 2 garlic cloves, minced
- 2 cups mushrooms, chopped
- 1 red bell pepper, minced
- 2 Tablespoons ghee, melted
- ⅓ cup coconut flour
- 3½ cups coconut milk, unsweetened
- ½ cup organic heavy cream
- 1 teaspoon salt (to taste)
- 1 teaspoon fresh ground black pepper (to taste)

Instructions:

1. Press Sauté button on Instant Pot. Heat the coconut oil. Sauté onion and garlic for 2 minutes.
2. Add the Italian sausage. Cook until brown.
3. Add mushrooms, bell peppers and sauté until soft. Season with salt and pepper.
4. Press Keep Warm/Cancel button to end Sauté mode.
5. In a small saucepan, over medium heat, melt the ghee. Add the flour. Whisk in coconut milk and heavy cream. Continue stirring until thickens.
6. Add flour mixture to Instant Pot. Stir well.
7. Close and seal lid. Press Manual button. Cook at High Pressure for 10 minutes.
8. When the timer beeps, naturally release pressure. Open the lid with care. Serve.

Flawless Cranberry Sauce

Time: 20 minutes   Servings: 4

Ingredients:

- 12-ounces fresh cranberries
- ¼ cup red wine
- 1 Tablespoon granulated Splenda
- Juice from 1 orange
- ⅛ teaspoon salt

Instructions:

1. Add all ingredients to Instant Pot. Stir well.
2. Close and seal lid. Press Manual switch. Cook at High Pressure for 2 minutes.
3. When the timer beeps, naturally release pressure. Open the lid with care.
4. Crush the cranberries with a fork or masher. Stir again. Serve warm or cold.

Perfect Marinara Sauce

Time: 15 minutes   Servings: 2

Ingredients:

- 2 (14-ounce) cans diced tomatoes
- 2 Tablespoons red wine vinegar
- ¼ cup coconut oil
- 1 teaspoon onion powder
- 1 teaspoon garlic powder
- 1 Tablespoon fresh oregano, chopped
- 1 Tablespoon fresh basil, chopped
- 1 Tablespoon fresh parsley, chopped
- 1 teaspoon salt
- 1 teaspoon fresh ground black pepper

Instructions:

1. Add the ingredients to Instant Pot. Stir well.
2. Close and seal lid. Press Manual button. Cook at High Pressure for 8 minutes.
3. When the timer beeps, naturally release pressure. Open the lid with care.
4. Puree mixture with immersion blender. Serve.

Very Cheesy Cheese Sauce
Time: 10 minutes   Servings: 2

Ingredients:

- 2 Tablespoons ghee
- ½ cup cream cheese, softened
- 1 cup cheddar cheese, grated
- 1 cup mozzarella cheese, grated

- 2 Tablespoons water (or coconut milk)
- ½ cup heavy whipping cream
- 1 teaspoon of salt

Instructions:

1. Press Sauté button on Instant Pot. Melt the ghee.
2. Add cream cheese, cheddar cheese, mozzarella cheese, water or/coconut milk, heavy whipping cream, and salt. Stir constantly until melted.
3. Press Keep Warm/Cancel button to end sauté mode.
4. Close and seal lid. Press Manual switch. Cook at High Pressure for 4 minutes.
5. Quick-release or naturally release pressure when done. Open the lid with care. Stir. Serve.

Best Homemade Alfredo Sauce
Time: 15 minutes   Servings: 2

Ingredients:

- 1 cup coconut milk
- 2 cups Parmesan cheese, grated
- 1 onion, chopped
- 1 teaspoon of salt
- ½ lemon, juice
- ¼ cup + 1 Tablespoon nutritional yeast

- 2 Tablespoons ghee
- 1 teaspoon garlic powder
- 1 teaspoon ground nutmeg
- 1 teaspoon salt
- 1 teaspoon fresh ground black pepper

Instructions:

1. Press Sauté button on Instant Pot. Heat the ghee.
2. Sauté the garlic and onion until become translucent.
3. Add coconut milk, parmesan cheese, nutritional yeast, lemon juice, and seasonings. Stir constantly until smooth.
4. Press Keep Warm/Cancel button. Cook at High Pressure for 6 minutes.
5. Quick-release or naturally release pressure when done. Open the lid with care. Stir. Serve.

Hot Dogs with a Twist
Time: 10 minutes   Servings: 4

Ingredients:

- 8 hot dogs
- 1 cup low-carb beer

- 8 ketogenic hot dog buns (for serving)

Instructions:

1. Place the hot dogs in Instant Pot. Pour beer over the hot dogs.
2. Close and seal the lid. Press Manual button. Cook at High Pressure for 5 minutes.
3. Quick-Release the pressure when done. Open the lid with care. Serve, on buns or alone.

Knockout Asparagus and Shrimp Mix
Time: 10 minutes   Servings: 4

Ingredients:

- 1 pound asparagus, trimmed and chopped
- 1 pound shrimp, peeled and deveined
- 2 Tablespoons ghee, melted

- 2 cups of water
- 1 teaspoon salt (to taste)
- 1 teaspoon fresh ground black pepper (to taste)

Instructions:

1. Pour 2 cups of water in Instant Pot.
2. Place shrimp and asparagus in steamer basket. Drizzle melted ghee over shrimp and asparagus. Season with salt and pepper. Place basket in Instant Pot.
3. Close and seal lid. Press Manual button. Cook at High Pressure for 6 minutes.
4. When the timer beeps, release pressure naturally. Open the lid with care. Serve.

Heavenly Stuffed Bell Peppers
Time: 30 minutes   Servings: 4

Ingredients:

- 1 pound lean ground beef
- 1 teaspoon coconut oil
- 4 medium to large bell peppers, de-seeded, tops sliced off
- 1 avocado, chopped
- Juice from 1 lime
- 1 jalapeno, minced (depending on heat level, remove or leave seeds)
- 2 green onions, chopped
- 2 cups of water
- 1 cup mixed cheeses, shredded
- 2 teaspoons chili powder
- 1 teaspoon garlic powder
- 1 teaspoon ground cumin
- 1 teaspoon salt (to taste)
- 1 teaspoon fresh ground black pepper (to taste)

Instructions:

1. Press Sauté button on Instant Pot. Heat the coconut oil.
2. Sauté ground beef until no longer pink; drain.
3. Place ground beef in a bowl. Add green onions, jalapeno, and seasoning. Stir well.
4. Stuff mixture in bell peppers.
5. Pour 2 cups of water in Instant Pot. Place stuffed peppers in steamer basket. Top with shredded cheese.
6. Close and seal lid. Press Manual button. Cook at High Pressure for 15 minutes.
7. When done, naturally release pressure. Open the lid with care. Serve.

Delicious Broccoli and Garlic Combo
Time: 15 minutes   Servings: 4

Ingredients:

- 1 broccoli head, chopped into florets
- 2 Tablespoons coconut oil
- 6 garlic cloves, minced
- 2 cups of water
- 1 teaspoon salt (to taste)
- 1 teaspoon black pepper (to taste)

Instructions:

1. Press Sauté button on Instant Pot. Heat the coconut oil.
2. Sauté garlic for 2 minutes. Add the broccoli. Cook until softened. Set aside.
3. Press Keep Warm/Cancel button to end Sauté mode.
4. Pour 2 cups of water in Instant Pot. Place garlic and broccoli florets in steamer basket. Season with salt and black pepper.
5. Close and seal lid. Press Manual button. Cook at High Pressure for 10 minutes.
6. When done, naturally release pressure. Open the lid with care.
7. Transfer to a bowl. Stir well. Serve.

Hollywood Collard Greens and Bacon
Time: 15 minutes   Servings: 4

Ingredients:

- 1 pound collard greens, trimmed and chopped
- ¼ pound bacon, chopped
- ½ cup ghee, melted
- 1 teaspoon salt
- 1 teaspoon fresh ground black pepper

Instructions:

1. Press Sauté button on Instant Pot. Melt 1 tablespoon of ghee. Add the bacon. Sauté until bacon is brown and crispy. Press Keep Warm/Cancel button to end Sauté mode.
2. Add collard greens, rest of the ghee, salt and pepper. Stir well.

3. Close and seal lid. Press Manual button. Cook at High Pressure for 10 minutes.
4. When done, naturally release pressure. Open the lid with care. Stir. Serve.

Godly Kale Delish
Time: 15 minutes   Servings: 4

Ingredients:

- 1 bunch of kale, trimmed and chopped
- 1 red onion, thinly sliced
- 4 garlic cloves, minced
- 1 cup pine nuts, roughly chopped
- 1 cup vegetable broth
- 1 Tablespoon ghee, melted

- 2 Tablespoons coconut oil
- 1 Tablespoon balsamic vinegar
- 1 teaspoon red pepper flakes
- 1 teaspoon salt
- 1 teaspoon fresh ground black pepper

Instructions:

1. Press Sauté button on Instant Pot. Heat the coconut oil.
2. Sauté onion and garlic until translucent. Press Keep Warm/Cancel button to end Sauté mode.
3. Add kale, pine nuts, melted ghee, balsamic vinegar, pine nuts, red pepper flakes, salt and pepper. Stir well. Close and seal lid. Press Manual button. Cook at High Pressure for 8 minutes.
4. Quick-Release the pressure when done. Open the lid with care.
5. Adjust seasoning if needed. Serve.

Roasted Brussel Sprouts
Time: 20 minutes   Servings: 4

Ingredients:

- 2 tablespoons of coconut oil, melted
- 1 pound of whole brussel sprouts, trimmed
- 1 medium onion, roughly chopped

- ½ cup of homemade low-sodium vegetable stock
- Fine sea salt and freshly cracked black pepper (to taste)

Instructions:

- Press the "Sauté" function on your Instant Pot and add the olive oil. Once hot, add the onions and sauté for 2 minutes or until translucent, stirring occasionally.
- Add the brussel sprouts and cook for another minute. Season with sea salt and black pepper.
- Pour in the vegetable stock and lock the lid. Cook at high pressure for 3 minutes. When the cooking is done, quick release the pressure and carefully remove the lid. Serve and enjoy!

Creamy Brussel Sprouts with Garlic Cream Cheese
Time: 10 minutes   Servings: 8

Ingredients:

- 2 tablespoons of unsalted butter
- 2 pounds of brussel sprouts, trimmed and cut half lengthwise
- 5 medium garlic cloves, peeled and minced
- 1 ½ cup of homemade low-sodium vegetable stock or chicken stock

- ¾ cup of cream cheese, softened
- ¼ cup of parmesan checsc, grated
- Fine sea salt and freshly cracked black pepper (to taste)

Instructions:

- Add all the ingredients except for the parmesan inside your Instant Pot. Lock the lid and cook at high pressure for 2 minutes. When the cooking is done, quick release the pressure and carefully remove the lid. Stir in the grated parmesan cheese and cover with the lid. Sit for 5 minutes or until the sauce thickens. Give another good stir. Serve and enjoy!

Brussel Sprouts with Cranberries and Balsamic Vinegar

Time: 25 minutes   Servings: 12

Ingredients:

- 3 pounds of brussel sprouts, trimmed and halved
- ½ cup of extra-virgin olive oil
- 1 cup of dried cranberries
- ¾ cups of balsamic vinegar
- 1 cup of water
- Fine sea salt and freshly cracked black pepper (to taste)

Instructions:

- Add 1 cup of water and a steamer basket inside your Instant Pot. Add the brussel sprouts in the steamer basket.
- Lock the lid and cook at high pressure for 3 minutes.
- When the cooking is done, quick release the pressure and remove the lid. Remove the steamer basket and discard the water.
- Transfer the brussel sprouts to a baking sheet lined with aluminum foil. Add the dried cranberries. Drizzle with the cranberries, extra-virgin olive oil and balsamic vinegar. Sprinkle with sea salt and freshly cracked black pepper.
- Set your oven to 370 degrees Fahrenheit. Place inside your oven and bake for around 5 minutes. Toss until well combined. Serve and enjoy!

Spaghetti Squash

Time: 25 minutes   Servings: 2

Ingredients:

- 1 (2 pound) spaghetti squash, cut half lengthwise
- 1 cup of water

Instructions:

- Add 1 cup of water and a steamer basket or trivet inside your Instant Pot. Place the squash on top. Lock the lid and cook at high pressure for 7 minutes.
- When the cooking is done, manually release the pressure and remove the lid.
- Shred the spaghetti squash using two forks. Serve and enjoy!

Balsamic Sautéed Asparagus with Bacon

Time: 20 minutes   Servings: 4

Ingredients:

- 1 pound of asparagus, trimmed and cut into 2-inch pieces
- 4 medium slices of bacon, chopped
- ½ cup of homemade low-sodium chicken stock
- 1 tablespoon of balsamic vinegar
- ½ teaspoon of granulated erythritol
- 2 tablespoons of parmesan cheese, finely grated
- Fine sea salt and freshly cracked black pepper (to taste)

Instructions:

- Press the "Sauté" setting on your Instant Pot and add the bacon. Cook until brown and crispy, stirring occasionally.
- Add the asparagus, chicken stock, balsamic vinegar, granulated erythritol, sea salt and black pepper. Cook for 5 minutes or until most of the liquid evaporates, stirring frequently.
- Transfer the asparagus to a serving platter. Sprinkle with parmesan cheese. Serve and enjoy!

Spinach Crab Dip

Time: 45 minutes   Servings: 8

Ingredients:

- 4-ounces of frozen chopped spinach
- 3 (6-ounce) cans of crabmeat, drained
- 1/3 cup of homemade mayonnaise
- ¼ cup of full-fat coconut milk

- 2 tablespoons of almond flour
- 2 tablespoons of nutritional yeast
- 2 tablespoons of unsalted butter or ghee
- 1 medium red onion, finely chopped
- 3 medium garlic cloves, minced
- 1 teaspoon of old bay seasoning
- 2 green onions, finely chopped
- Fine sea salt and freshly cracked black pepper (to taste)

Instructions:

- Press the "Sauté" setting on your Instant Pot and add the butter. Once melted, add the chopped red onion and sauté until tender, stirring occasionally.
- Add the remaining ingredients. Lock the lid and cook at high pressure for 10 minutes.
- When the cooking is done, naturally release the pressure for 5 minutes, then quick release the remaining pressure. Carefully remove the lid. Serve and enjoy!

Sautéed Greens
Time: 5 minutes   Servings: 1

Ingredients:

- 3 large handfuls of leafy greens (arugula, kale, mustard, etc.)
- 4 tablespoons of unsalted butter
- 3 medium bacon slices, chopped
- 2 tablespoons of toasted nuts or seeds
- Fine sea salt and freshly cracked black pepper (to taste)

Instructions:

- Press the "Sauté" setting on your Instant Pot and add the chopped bacon. Cook until brown and crispy, stirring occasionally.
- Add the butter and cook until melted. Add the leafy greens and continue to cook until wilted, stirring occasionally.
- Stir in the toasted nuts, sea salt and freshly cracked black pepper. Serve and enjoy!

Bacon Brussel Sprouts
Time: 10 minutes   Servings: 4

Ingredients:

- 1 pound of fresh brussel sprouts, trimmed
- 6 slices of bacon, roughly chopped
- ½ white onion, finely chopped
- 2 medium garlic cloves, peeled and minced
- 1 tablespoon of olive oil
- 1 cup of water
- Fine sea salt and freshly cracked black pepper (to taste)

Instructions:

- Add 1 cup of water and a steamer basket inside your Instant Pot. Place the brussel sprouts in the basket.
- Lock the lid and cook at high pressure for 3 minutes.
- When the cooking is done, quick release the pressure and remove the lid.
- Remove the steamer basket and discard the water.
- Press the "Sauté" setting on your Instant Pot and add the olive oil. Once hot, add the chopped bacon. Cook until brown and crispy, stirring occasionally.
- Add the chopped onions and minced garlic. Sauté until translucent, stirring occasionally. Remove and set aside.
- Add the brussel sprouts and sauté for a couple more minutes, stirring occasionally.Serve and enjoy!

Simple Broccoli
Time: 10 minutes   Servings: 8

Ingredients:

- 1 pound of broccoli florets
- 1 teaspoon of fine sea salt
- ½ teaspoon of freshly cracked black pepper
- 1 tablespoon of butter, melted

Instructions:

- Add 1 cup of water and a steamer basket inside your Instant Pot. Place the broccoli florets on the steamer basket
- Lock the lid and cook at high pressure for 0 minutes. When the cooking is done, quick release the pressure and remove the lid.
- Drizzle the melted butter. Season with sea salt and black pepper. Serve and enjoy!

Simple Cauliflower Florets
Time: 15 minutes   Servings: 8

Ingredients:

- 2 pounds of cauliflower florets
- 1 teaspoon of fine sea salt
- 1 teaspoon of freshly cracked black pepper
- 1 tablespoon of coconut oil, melted

Instructions:

- In a bowl, add the cauliflower florets, sea salt, freshly cracked black pepper and coconut oil. Toss until well coated.
- Add 1 cup of water and a steamer basket inside your Instant Pot. Place the cauliflower florets on the basket.
- Lock the lid and cook at high pressure for 0 minutes. When the cooking is done, quick release the pressure and remove the lid. Serve and enjoy!

Beet Salad with Arugula, Candied Walnuts and Goat Cheese
Time: 20 minutes   Servings: 6

Salad Ingredients:

- 6 cups of arugula
- 2-ounces of goat cheese, crumbled

Salad Dressing Ingredients:

- 3 tablespoons of balsamic vinegar
- 4 tablespoons of olive oil
- 1 teaspoon of Dijon mustard
- 1 medium garlic clove, peeled and minced

Candied Walnut Ingredients:

- 1 tablespoon of unsalted butter
- 1 cup of walnuts, roughly chopped
- 1 tablespoon of truvia low-carb brown sugar or erythritol

Beets Ingredients:

- 6 medium beets, rinsed and trimmed

Instructions:

- Prepare the salad dressing: In a small bowl, add all the salad dressing ingredients. Mix until well combined.
- In a frying pan over medium heat, add all the walnuts ingredients. Continue to cook until the sweetener has combined with the walnuts. Continue to toss until well combined. Transfer to a baking sheet lined with parchment paper.
- Add 1 cup of water and a steamer basket inside your Instant Pot. Place the beets in the steamer basket.
- Lock the lid and cook at high pressure for 15 minutes. When the cooking is done, quick release the pressure and remove the lid. Remove the steamer basket and allow the beets to cool.
- Peel the beets and cut into ½-inch pieces.
- In a large bowl, add the beets, walnuts, goat cheese and drizzle with the balsamic vinegar. Toss until well combined.

Braised Kale with Jalapenos and Onions
Time: 30 minutes   Servings: 6

Ingredients:

- 1 sweet onions, peeled and thinly sliced
- 1 jalapeno pepper, thinly sliced
- 2 medium garlic cloves, minced
- 2 cups of homemade low-sodium vegetable stock
- ½ cup of apple cider vinegar
- ½ cup of sugar-free maple syrup

- ¼ cup of extra-virgin olive oil
- Fine sea salt and freshly cracked black pepper (to taste)

Instructions:

- Add all the ingredients inside your Instant Pot and stir until well combined.
- Lock the lid and cook at high pressure for 15 minutes. When the cooking is done, manually release the pressure and carefully remove the lid. Serve and enjoy!

Kale Stir-Fry
Time: 25 minutes   Servings: 4

Ingredients:

- 3 shallots, finely chopped
- A large bunch of baby spinach (more as needed)
- 2 tablespoons of water
- 2 teaspoons of olive oil
- 1 teaspoon of mustard seeds
- 2 teaspoons of cumin seeds
- ½ teaspoon of chili powder
- ¼ teaspoon of turmeric powder
- Fine sea salt and freshly cracked black pepper (to taste)

Instructions:

- Press the "Sauté" setting on your Instant Pot and add the olive oil. Once hot, add the cumin seeds and mustard seeds. Sauté for 10 seconds, stirring frequently.
- Add the chopped shallots and sauté for 1 minute, stirring frequently.
- Add the remaining ingredients and lock the lid. Press the "Steam" setting and set the time to 1 minute.
- When the timer beeps, quick release the pressure and remove the lid.
- Press the "Sauté" setting on your Instant Pot and continue to cook for another 2 to 3 minutes, stirring frequently. Serve and enjoy!

Green Beans
Time: 15 minutes   Servings: 4

Ingredients:

- 1 pound of green beans, cleaned and ends trimmed
- 1 cup of water
- Fine sea salt and freshly cracked black pepper (to taste)

Instructions:

- Add 1 cup of water and a steamer basket inside your Instant Pot. Place the green beans inside your steamerbaske.t
- Lock the lid and cook at high pressure for 0 minutes. When the timer beeps, manually release the pressure and remove the lid.
- Season the green beans with sea salt and freshly cracked black pepper. Serve and enjoy!

Garlic Butter Green Beans
Time: 5 minutes   Servings: 4

Ingredients:

- 1 pound of fresh green beans, cleaned and trimmed
- 4 tablespoons of unsalted butter
- 4 medium garlic cloves, peeled and minced
- 1 cup of water
- Fine sea salt and freshly cracked black pepper (to taste)

Instructions:

- Add 1 cup of water and a steamer basket inside your Instant Pot. Add the green beans, garlic, unsalted butter, sea salt and black pepper.
- Lock the lid and cook at low pressure for 5 minutes. When the cooking is done, manually release the pressure and carefully remove the lid. Serve and enjoy!

Blue Cheese Asparagus
Time: 7 minutes   Servings: 4

Ingredients:

- 1 pound of asparagus spears, trimmed
- 1 tablespoon of balsamic vinegar
- 1 tablespoon of extra-virgin olive oil
- 2 tablespoons of blue cheese, crumbled
- 2 tablespoons of walnuts, chopped
- 1 cup of water
- Fine sea salt and freshly cracked black pepper (to taste)

Instructions:

- Add 1 cup of water and a steamer basket inside your Instant Pot. Place the asparagus onto the steamer basket.
- Lock the lid and cook at high pressure for 1 minute. When the cooking is done, manually release the pressure and remove the lid.
- Season with sea salt and freshly cracked black pepper.
- Transfer the asparagus to a serving platter and top with olive oil, balsamic vinegar, crumbled cheese, chopped walnuts.

Okra Stir-Fry
Time: 20 minutes   Servings: 2

Ingredients:

- 1 pound of okra, cut into ½-inch pieces
- 1 medium onion, sliced
- 1 large tomato, finely chopped
- 1 tablespoon of extra-virgin olive oil
- ½ teaspoon of cumin seeds
- 3 medium garlic cloves, minced
- Fine sea salt and freshly cracked black pepper (to taste)

Instructions:

- Press the "Sauté" setting on your Instant Pot and add the olive oil. Once hot, add the cumin seeds and minced garlic. Sauté for 30 seconds, stirring frequently.
- Add the sliced onions and sauté for another 3 minutes, stirring occasionally.
- Add the chopped tomatoes, sea salt and freshly cracked black pepper. Lock the lid and cook at low pressure for 2 minutes. Remove the lid.
- Stir in the okra pieces and allow to be well heated. Serve and enjoy!

Steamed Asparagus
Time: 6 minutes   Servings: 4

Ingredients:

- 1 pound of asparagus spears, trimmed
- 1 cup of water
- Fine sea salt and freshly cracked black pepper (to taste)

Instructions:

- Add a trivet and 1 cup of water inside your Instant Pot. Place the asparagus on top of the trivet.
- Lock the lid and cook at low pressure for 0 minutes. When the cooking is done, quick release the pressure and remove the lid. Season with sea salt and black pepper. Serve and enjoy!

Garlic and Parmesan Asparagus
Time: 10 minutes   Servings: 4

Ingredients:

- 1 pound of asparagus, trimmed
- 3 medium garlic cloves, minced
- 1 cup of water
- 3 tablespoons of unsalted butter
- 3 tablespoons of parmesan cheese, grated
- Fine sea salt and freshly cracked black pepper (to taste)

Instructions:

- Add 1 cup of water and a trivet inside your Instant Pot.
- Lay a sheet of aluminum foil onto a flat surface. Place the asparagus, garlic, and butter. Wrap and place inside your Instant Pot. Lock the lid and cook at high pressure for 8 minutes.
- When the cooking is done, quick release the pressure and remove the lid. Unwrap the foil and sprinkle with parmesan cheese. Serve and enjoy!

Sesame Garlic Broccolini
Time: 10 minutes   Servings: 4

Ingredients:

- 2 bunches of broccolini
- 2 tablespoons of toasted sesame oil
- 1 teaspoon of garlic sea salt
- 1 lemon, juiced

Instructions:

- Add 1 cup of water and a steamer basket inside your Instant Pot. Place the broccolini on top.
- Lock the lid and cook at high pressure for 2 minutes. When the cooking is done, quick release the pressure and remove the lid.
- Drizzle with sesame oil, garlic sea salt and lemon juice.Serve and enjoy!

Southern Collard Greens
Time: 30 minutes   Servings: 8

Ingredients:

- 16-ounces of collard greens
- 1 small onion, finely chopped
- 2 tablespoons of olive oil
- 2 bacon slices, uncooked and chopped
- 4-ounces of ham, sliced and chopped
- 1/3 cup of apple cider vinegar
- ¾ cups of homemade low-sodium chicken stock
- Fine sea salt and freshly cracked black pepper (to taste)

Instructions:

- Press the "Sauté" Setting on your Instant Pot and add the olive oil. Once hot, add the chopped bacon and ham. Cook for 4 to 5 minutes, stirring occasionally.
- Add the onions and continue to cook until golden, stirring occasionally.
- Add the remaining ingredients inside your Instant Pot and stir until well combined. Lock the lid and cook at high pressure for 5 minutes. When the cooking is done, naturally release the pressure for 5 minutes, then quick release the remaining pressure. Carefully remove the lid. Serve and enjoy!

Sauerkraut
Time: 25 minutes   Servings: 8

Ingredients:

- ½ cup of homemade low-sodium chicken stock
- 2 (14.5-ounces) cans of shredded sauerkraut
- ¾ teaspoons of caraway seeds
- 1 small onion, finely chopped
- 3 medium slices of bacon, chopped
- ½ teaspoon of fine sea salt
- ½ teaspoon of freshly cracked black pepper

Instructions:

- Press the "Sauté" setting on your Instant Pot and add the chopped bacon. Continue to cook for 4 minutes or until almost brown, stirring frequently.
- Add the chopped onions and continue to cook for 5 to 6 minutes or until golden brown, stirring occasionally.
- Add the remaining ingredients. Lock the lid and cook at high pressure for 10 minutes.
- When the cooking is done, naturally release the pressure for 10 minutes, then quick release the remaining pressure. Carefully remove the lid. Serve and enjoy!

Okra Gumbo

Time: 30 minutes   Servings: 4

Ingredients:

- 2 celery stalks, chopped
- 1 medium onion, finely chopped
- 2 cups of okra, chopped
- 1 green bell pepper, chopped
- 5 medium garlic cloves, peeled and minced
- 2 bay leaves
- 1 teaspoon of smoked paprika

- 1 teaspoon of dried thyme
- 1 to 2 teaspoons of Cajun seasoning
- 1 tablespoon of Worcestershire sauce
- 4 cups of homemade low-sodium vegetable stock
- Fine sea salt and freshly cracked black pepper (to taste)

Roux Ingredients:

- ½ cup of olive oil

- ½ cup of almond or coconut flour

Instructions:

- Press the "Sauté" setting on your Instant Pot and add the olive oil and flour. Cook for 30 seconds, whisking frequently.
- Add the chopped onions, chopped celery and chopped bell peppers. Cook for another 5 minutes, stirring occasionally.
- Stir in the remaining ingredients until well combined. Lock the lid and cook at high pressure for 10 minutes. When done, quick release the pressure and remove the lid. Serve and enjoy!

Glazed Bok Choy

Time: 10 minutes   Servings: 6

Ingredients:

- 1 pound of bok choy
- ½ cup of water
- 1-inch piece of fresh ginger, peeled and minced
- 1 medium garlic clove, peeled and minced

- 3 tablespoons of coconut aminos
- 1 tablespoon of dry white wine
- 1 tablespoon of olive oil

Instructions:

- Press the "Sauté" setting on your Instant Pot and add the olive oil. Once hot, add the ginger and garlic. Sauté for 1 minute, stirring frequently.
- Add the bok choy and water inside your Instant Pot. Lock the lid and cook at high pressure for 5 minutes. In another bowl, add the coconut aminos and white wine. Mix well.
- Quick release the Instant Pot and remove the lid. Stir in the mixture. Serve and enjoy!

Bacon Wrapped Asparagus

Time: 15 minutes   Servings: 3

Ingredients:

- 12 asparagus spears
- 6 slices of bacon
- ½ cup of heavy cream

- 1 cup of water
- Fine sea salt and freshly cracked black pepper (to taste)

Instructions:

- Add 1 cup of water and a trivet inside your Instant Pot.
- Spread the heavy cream over the asparagus and season with sea salt and black pepper.
- Divide your asparagus spears into 3 separate portions.
- Wrap 2 slices of bacon onto each asparagus group. Place the asparagus onto the trivet.
- Lock the lid and cook at high pressure for 3 minutes. When the cooking is done, naturally release the pressure and remove the lid. Serve and enjoy!

Simple Cauliflower Rice
Time: 5 minutes   Servings: 4

Ingredients:

- 1 large head of cauliflower, cut into florets
- 2 tablespoons of extra-virgin olive oil
- 1 teaspoon of fine sea salt
- 1 tablespoon of fresh parsley, finely chopped
- ¼ teaspoon of cumin
- ¼ teaspoon of turmeric
- ¼ teaspoon of smoked paprika

Instructions:

- Add 1 cup of water and a steamer basket inside your Instant Pot. Place the cauliflower on the steamer basket. Lock the lid.
- Cook at high pressure for 1 minute. When the cooking is done, quick release the pressure and remove the lid. Transfer the cauliflower to a food processor. Pulse until rice-like consistency. Add the olive oil, salt, cumin, turmeric, and smoked paprika. Give another pulse. Serve and enjoy!

Creamy Mashed Cauliflower with Kale
Time: 15 minutes   Servings: 4

Ingredients:

- 2 pounds of cauliflower florets
- 1 cup of homemade low-sodium chicken stock
- ¼ cup of unsalted butter, melted
- 3 cups of fresh kale, stemmed and roughly chopped
- 4 medium garlic cloves, crushed
- 2 scallions, chopped
- 1 cup of heavy whipping cream (more if needed)
- 1 teaspoon of fine sea salt
- 1 teaspoon of freshly cracked black pepper

Instructions:

- Add 1 cup of water and a steamer basket inside your Instant Pot. Place the cauliflower in the steamer basket.
- Lock the lid and cook at high pressure for 4 minutes. When the cooking is done, quick release the pressure and remove the lid.
- Remove the steamer basket and discard the water. Add the cauliflower florets inside your inner pot.
- Add the remaining ingredients except for the immersion blender. Use a potato masher to blend the cauliflower until smooth.
- Stir in the kale. Lock the lid and cook at high pressure for 1 minutes. When the cooking is done, quick release the pressure and remove the lid. Serve and enjoy!

Coconut Cream and Herbed Mashed Potatoes
Time: 15 minutes   Servings: 6

Ingredients:

- 2 pounds of cauliflower florets
- 1 small onion, finely chopped
- 4 whole garlic cloves, peeled and crushed
- 1 ½ pounds of fresh rosemary
- 2 tablespoons of fresh parsley, finely chopped
- 2 tablespoons of coconut oil, melted
- 1 ½ cup of coconut milk or coconut cream
- 1 teaspoon of fine sea salt
- 1 teaspoon of freshly cracked black pepper

Instructions:

- Add 1 cup of water and a steamer basket inside your Instant Pot. Place the cauliflower florets and the rosemary onto the steamer basket.
- Lock the lid and cook at high pressure for 4 minutes. When the cooking is done, quick release the pressure and remove the lid.
- Discard the water and remove the steamer basket. Place the cauliflower florets inside the inner pot along with the remaining ingredients. Use a potato masher to mash the cauliflower until smooth. Serve and enjoy!

Creamy Mozzarella Mashed Cauliflower
Time: 20 minutes   Servings: 4

Ingredients:

- 1 large head of cauliflower, chopped
- 1 cup of homemade low-sodium chicken stock
- 4 whole garlic cloves, peeled
- 6 fresh sprigs of thyme
- ½ cup of shredded mozzarella cheese
- ½ cup of plain Greek yogurt
- ½ teaspoon of fine sea salt
- ½ teaspoon of freshly cracked black pepper

Instructions:

- Add the chicken stock, garlic cloves and fresh sprigs of thyme.
- Add a trivet inside the Instant Pot and place a cauliflower on top. Lock the lid and cook at high pressure for 12 minutes. When the cooking is done, quick release the pressure and remove the lid.
- Discard the liquid and remove the trivet. Return the cauliflower inside your Instant Pot along with the mozzarella cheese, Greek yogurt, salt and freshly cracked black pepper.
- Use an immersion blender to blend the cauliflower until smooth. Serve and enjoy!

Creamed Spinach
Time: 10 minutes   Servings: 4

Ingredients:

- 1 pound of fresh spinach
- ¼ cup of unsalted butter
- ½ cup of heavy whipping cream
- ½ teaspoon of onion powder
- ½ teaspoon of garlic powder
- 1 teaspoon of fine sea salt
- 1 teaspoon of freshly cracked black pepper
- 4 tablespoons of parmesan cheese, finely grated

Instructions:

- Press the "Sauté" function on your Instant Pot and add the butter and spinach. Sauté until the spinach has wilted, stirring frequently.
- Add the heavy whipping cream. Lock the lid and cook at high pressure for 3 minutes. When the cooking is done, quick release the pressure and carefully remove the lid.
- Stir in the grated parmesan cheese and allow to melt. Season with the onion powder, garlic powder, sea salt and freshly cracked black pepper. Serve and enjoy!

Spinach Saag
Time: 25 minutes   Servings: 4

Ingredients:

- 1 pound of spinach
- 1 pound of mustard leaves
- 4 tablespoons of ghee
- 2-inch fresh piece of ginger, peeled and finely minced
- 4 medium garlic cloves, minced
- 2 teaspoons of fine sea salt
- 1 teaspoon of coriander
- 1 teaspoon of ground cumin
- 1 teaspoon of garam masala
- ½ teaspoon of turmeric
- ½ teaspoon of cayenne pepper
- ½ teaspoon of freshly cracked black pepper

Instructions;

- Press the "Sauté" setting on your Instant Pot and add the ghee. Once hot, add the onion, garlic, ginger and seasonings. Sauté until translucent, stirring frequently.
- Add the spinach and mustard greens. Lock the lid and cook at high pressure for 15 minutes.
- When the cooking is done, quick release the pressure and remove the lid.
- Use an immersion blender to blend the contents to your desired consistency. Serve and enjoy!

Stuffed Mushrooms
Time: 30 minutes   Servings: 20

Ingredients:

- Around 40 mushrooms, stemmed
- 1 pound of ground sausage

- 1 medium onion, finely chopped
- 2 garlic cloves, peeled and minced
- 1 (8-ounce) package of cream cheese, softened
- 2 large eggs, beaten
- 1 cup of shredded mozzarella cheese
- 1/3 cup of homemade low-sodium vegetable broth
- Fine sea salt and freshly cracked black pepper (to taste)

Instructions:

- Press the "Sauté" function on your Instant Pot and add the ground sausage. Cook until the sausage has browned, breaking up the meat with a wooden spoon.
- Add the chopped onions and minced garlic. Cook for another 3 minutes or until softened, stirring occasionally.
- Add the sausage mixture to a large bowl. Stir in the cream cheese, egg yolks and shredded mozzarella cheese, reserve some of the mozzarella cheese.
- Spoon the sausage mixture into the mushrooms.
- Add the vegetable broth in your inner pot. Place the mushrooms to the inner pot and sprinkle with the shredded mozzarella cheese.
- Lock the lid and cook at high pressure for 5 minutes. When the cooking is done, quick release the pressure and carefully remove the lid. Serve and enjoy!

Balsamic Mushrooms
Time: 15 minutes   Servings: 4

Ingredients:

- 1/3 cup of extra-virgin olive oil
- 3 medium garlic cloves, minced
- 1 pound of fresh mushrooms, sliced
- 3 tablespoons of balsamic vinegar
- 3 tablespoons of red wine
- Fine sea salt and freshly cracked black pepper (to taste)

Instructions:

- Press the "Sauté" setting on your Instant Pot and add the olive oil. Once hot, add the minced garlic cloves and mushrooms. Sauté for 3 minutes or until softened, stirring frequently.
- Turn off the "Sauté' setting on your Instant Pot. Stir in the balsamic vinegar, red wine, sea salt and freshly cracked black pepper. Stir until well coated, stirring occasionally. Serve and enjoy!

Garlic Mushrooms with Butter Sauce
Time: 20 minutes   Servings: 2

Ingredients:

- 1 pound of small button mushrooms
- 2 tablespoons of extra-virgin olive oil
- 2 tablespoons of unsalted butter
- 1 teaspoon of fresh thyme
- 2 medium garlic cloves, minced
- 2 tablespoons of fresh parsley, finely chopped
- Fine sea salt and freshly cracked black pepper (to taste)

Instructions:

- Press the "Sauté" setting on your Instant Pot and add the olive oil. Once hot, add the mushrooms, caps down and sauté for 5 minutes.
- Add the remaining ingredients and lock the lid. Cook at high pressure for 12 minutes. When the cooking is done, naturally release the pressure for 5 minutes, then quick release the remaining pressure. Carefully remove the lid.
- Transfer the mushrooms to a serving platter and spoon with the butter sauce. Serve and enjoy!

Sri Lankan Coconut Cabbage
Time: 25 minutes   Servings: 4

Ingredients:

- 1 medium cabbage, chopped
- 1 tablespoon of turmeric powder
- 1 tablespoon of curry powder
- 1 teaspoon of mustard powder
- 1 medium onion, finely chopped
- 2 medium garlic cloves, peeled and crushed

- 1 medium carrot, sliced
- 2 tablespoons of freshly squeezed lemon juice
- ½ cup of desiccated unsweetened coconut
- 2 tablespoons of olive oil
- 1/3 cups of water

Instructions:

- Press the "Sauté" setting on your Instant Pot and add the oil. Once hot, add the chopped onions and sauté until tender, stirring occasionally.
- Add the crushed garlic and all seasonings. Sauté for another 30 seconds.
- Add the remaining ingredients. Lock the lid and cook at high pressure for 5 minutes. When the cooking is done, quick release the pressure and carefully remove the lid. Serve and enjoy!

Unstuffed Cabbage Bowls
Time: 30 minutes   Servings: 4

Ingredients:

- 1 pound of ground beef
- 1 tablespoon of olive oil
- 1 medium onion, finely chopped
- 4 medium garlic cloves, minced
- 1 red bell pepper, finely chopped
- 1 medium cabbage head, chopped
- 1 cup of cauliflower rice
- 1 cup of homemade low-sodium beef broth
- 1 (8-ounce) can of tomato paste

Instructions:

- Press the "Sauté" setting on your Instant Pot and add the olive oil. Once hot, add the ground beef, onions, garlic and bell peppers. Sauté until the beef is no longer pink.
- Add the beef broth and tomato paste. Lock the lid and cook at high pressure for 15 minutes.
- Quick release the pressure and remove the lid.
- Stir in the cauliflower rice and cabbage. Lock the lid and cook for 3 minutes at high pressure. Quick release. Serve and enjoy!

Sausage Cabbage Bowls
Time: 35 minutes   Servings: 6

Ingredients:

- 12 cups of thinly sliced cabbage
- ¼ cup of fresh parsley, finely chopped
- 1 pound of Italian chicken sausage
- 1 tablespoon of olive oil
- 1 yellow onion, finely chopped
- 3 medium garlic cloves, minced
- 1 teaspoon of smoked paprika
- 1 teaspoon of dried oregano
- 1 ¼ cup of homemade low-sodium chicken broth
- 1 cup of diced tomatoes
- ½ cup of cauliflower rice
- ½ teaspoon of fine sea salt
- ½ teaspoon of freshly cracked black pepper

Instructions:

- Press the "Sauté" setting on your Instant Pot and add the olive oil. Once hot, add the chicken sausage and onions. Cook until the sausage is brow and the onions are tender, stirring occasionally.
- Stir in the minced garlic, smoked paprika, dried oregano, sea salt and freshly cracked black pepper. Cook for another 30 seconds, stirring frequently.
- Add the chicken broth and diced tomatoes. Stir until well combined.
- Lock the lid and cook at high pressure for 12 minutes. When the cooking is done, naturally release the pressure and carefully remove the lid.
- Stir in the cauliflower rice and cabbage. Lock the lid and cook at high pressure for 3 minutes. When the cooking is done, manually release the pressure and carefully remove the lid.
- Stir in the fresh parsley. Serve and enjoy!

Steamed Artichokes
Time: 30 minutes   Servings: 4

Ingredients:

- 4 large artichokes, trimmed
- 1 cup of water
- 1 bay leaf

- 2 whole garlic cloves
- 1 fresh medium lemon, juice

Instructions:

- Prepare your artichokes: Cut the tops of the artichokes and remove the stems and outer leaves.
- Add the water, bay leaves, garlic cloves inside your Instant Pot. Place a steamer basket inside.
- Squeeze the lemon juice over the artichokes and place on top of the steamer basket.
- Lock the lid and cook at high pressure for 10 minutes. When the cooking is done, quick release the pressure and carefully remove the lid.
- Remove the artichokes from your Instant Pot. Serve and enjoy!

Artichokes with Jalapeno Dip

Time: 20 minutes   Servings: 4

Ingredients:

- 4 medium artichokes
- 1 cup of water
- 1 tablespoon of extra-virgin olive oil

- 1 tablespoon of freshly squeezed lemon juice
- 1 tablespoon of dried rosemary
- A small pinch of fine sea salt and freshly cracked black pepper (to taste)

Jalapeno Dip Ingredients:

- ½ cup of jalapenos, chopped
- ½ cup of cream cheese

- ½ cup of Greek yogurt
- 2 tablespoons of fresh parsley, finely chopped

Instructions:

- Prepare your artichokes: Cut the tops of the artichokes and remove the stems and outer leaves.
- Add 1 cup of water and a steamer rack inside your Instant Pot. Place the artichokes on top of the steamer rack.
- Drizzle with the olive oil and lemon juice. Season with dried rosemary, sea salt and black pepper.
- Lock the lid and cook at high pressure for 10 minutes. When the cooking is done, quick release the pressure and remove the lid.
- In a food processor, add all the jalapeno dip ingredients. Pulse until well combined. Transfer to a serving bowl.
- Serve the artichokes with the jalapeno dip. Serve and enjoy!

Italian Stuffed Artichokes

Time: 20 minutes   Servings: 3

Ingredients:

- 3 artichokes
- 1 cup of pork rinds, finely crushed
- ¼ cup of sour cream
- 3 tablespoons of parmesan cheese, finely grated

- 1 tablespoon of fresh parsley, finely chopped
- 1 tablespoon of garlic, minced
- 1 cup of shredded mozzarella cheese
- A small pinch of fine sea salt and freshly cracked black pepper

Instructions:

- Prepare your artichokes: Cut the tops of the artichokes and remove the stems and outer leaves. In a bowl, add the crushed pork rinds, sour cream, parmesan cheese, parsley, minced garlic, shredded cheese, sea salt and freshly cracked black pepper. Mix well and spoon the stuffing inside the artichokes.
- Add 1 cup of water and a steamer rack inside your Instant Pot. Place the artichokes on top.
- Lock the lid and cook at high pressure for 15 minutes. When the cooking is done, quick release the pressure and carefully remove the lid. Serve and enjoy!

Artichokes with Creamy Herb Dip

Time: 20 minutes   Servings: 2

Artichoke Ingredients:

- 2 large artichokes
- 2 tablespoons of freshly squeezed lemon juice
- 2 tablespoons of extra-virgin olive oil

Creamy Herb Dip Ingredients:

- ½ cup of plain Greek yogurt
- 1-ounce of cream cheese, softened
- 1 tablespoon of mayonnaise
- 1 tablespoon of fresh parsley, finely chopped
- 1 tablespoon of fresh chives
- A small pinch of fine sea salt and freshly cracked black pepper

Instructions:

- Prepare your artichokes: Cut the tops of the artichokes and remove the stems and outer leaves. In a bowl, add all the creamy herb dip ingredients and stir until well combined. Refrigerate and set aside.
- Add 1 cup of water and a steamer basket inside your Instant Pot. Place the artichokes on top. Lock the lid and cook at high pressure for 10 minutes.
- When the cooking is done, naturally release the pressure and serve the artichokes along with the dip. Serve and enjoy!

Tuscan-Style Baby Artichokes
Time: 10 minutes   Servings: 4

Ingredients:

- Around 9 baby artichokes, washed and trimmed
- ½ cup of dry white wine
- 2 tablespoons of freshly squeezed lemon juice
- 1 medium garlic clove, minced
- 1 teaspoon of garlic powder
- 1 teaspoon of fine sea salt
- 1 cup of water
- ¼ cup of extra-virgin olive oil
- ½ cup of Parmesan cheese, finely grated

Instructions:

- Prepare your artichokes: Cut the tops of the artichokes and remove the stems and outer leaves.
- Cut the artichokes lengthwise into 4 slices for each artichoke.
- Press the "Sauté" Setting on your Instant Pot and add the olive oil. Once hot, add the artichokes and garlic. Sauté for a couple of minutes, stirring frequently.
- Add the remaining ingredients except for the parmesan cheese inside your Instant Pot. Lock the lid and cook at high pressure for 5 minutes. When the cooking is done, quick release the pressure and carefully remove the lid
- Remove the artichokes from your Instant Pot and place into a large bowl. Add the grated cheese and toss until well combined. Serve and enjoy!

Artichokes with Lemon Chive Butter
Time: 20 minutes   Servings: 3

Ingredients:

- 3 large artichokes
- 1 lemon, wedged
- 3 tablespoons of freshly squeezed lemon juice
- ¼ teaspoon of fresh lemon zest
- 4 tablespoons of unsalted butter, melted
- 2 tablespoons of olive oil or coconut oil
- 2 tablespoons of fresh chives, minced
- A small pinch of fine sea salt

Instructions:

- Prepare your artichokes: Cut the tops of the artichokes and remove the stems and outer leaves.
- Pour 1 cup of water and a steamer basket inside your Instant Pot. Place the artichokes on top of the steamer basket.
- Lock the lid and cook at high pressure for 13 minutes. When the cooking is done, naturally release the pressure for 10 minutes, then quick release the remaining pressure. Carefully remove the lid.
- In a small bowl, add the olive oil, unsalted butter, lemon juice, lemon zest, fresh chives, and fine sea salt. Mix well. Serve the artichokes with the lemon-chive butter. Enjoy!

Parmesan Garlic Artichokes

Time: 15 minutes   Servings: 4

Ingredients:

- 4 artichokes, washed and prepared
- 4 medium garlic cloves, peeled and minced
- 2 tablespoons of olive oil
- ¼ cup of parmesan cheese, finely grated or shredded
- ½ cup of homemade low-sodium vegetable stock or chicken stock

Instructions:

- Prepare your artichokes: Cut the tops of the artichokes and remove the stems and outer leaves.
- Top each artichoke with 1 minced garlic and drizzle with olive oil.
- Sprinkle with parmesan cheese
- Pour ½ cup of vegetable stock and a steamer basket inside your Instant Pot. Place the artichokes on the steamer basket.
- Place the artichokes on top. Lock the lid and press the "Steam" setting and set the time for 10 minutes.
- When the cooking is done, quick release the pressure and remove the lid. Serve and enjoy!

Sautéed Radishes

Time: 15 minutes   Servings: 4

Ingredients:

- 1 pound of radishes, quartered
- 2 tablespoons of unsalted butter

Instructions:

- Press the "Sauté" setting on your Instant Pot and set to medium setting.
- Add the butter. Once melted, add the radishes and sauté for 10 to 15 minutes or until tender.
- Serve and enjoy!

Part 8: Dessert and Snacks Recipes

Delectable Brownie Cake
Time: 25 minutes   Servings: 6

Ingredients:

- 4 Tablespoons butter, softened
- 2 eggs
- 1 cup of water
- ⅛ teaspoon salt
- ⅓ cup coconut flour (or almond meal)
- ⅓ cup cocoa powder, unsweetened
- ⅓ cup granulated Splenda
- ⅓ cup dark chocolate chips
- ⅓ cup chopped nuts (optional)

Instructions:

1. In a bowl, combine butter, eggs, water, coconut flour, cocoa powder, salt, and granulated Splenda. Stir well, but don't overmix.
2. Grease a 6-inch pan, suitable for Instant Pot, with non-stick cooking spray.
3. Pour brownie mixture in pan. Cover with aluminum foil.
4. Pour water in Instant Pot. Place a trivet inside. Place cake pan on trivet.
5. Close and seal lid. Press Manual button. Cook at High Pressure for 20 minutes.
6. Release pressure naturally when done. Open the lid with care.
7. Remove pan from Instant Pot. Allow to cool 15 minutes before slicing.

Healthy Corn Pudding
Time: 20 minutes   Servings: 4

Ingredients:

- 2 (14-ounce) cans of creamed corn
- 2 cups of water
- 2 cups coconut milk
- 2 Tablespoons granulated Splenda
- 2 large eggs
- 2 Tablespoons coconut flour
- ⅛ teaspoon salt
- 1 Tablespoon butter, softened

Instructions:

1. Pour 2 cups of water in Instant Pot. Place trivet inside.
2. Set to Simmer. Bring to a boil.
3. In a bowl, combine creamed corn, coconut milk, Splenda, eggs, coconut flour, salt, and butter. Stir well. Grease a baking dish, suitable for Instant Pot, with non-stick cooking spray.
4. Pour corn mixture in baking dish. Cover with aluminum foil. Place baking dish on trivet.
5. Close and seal lid. Press Manual button. Cook on High Pressure for 20 minutes.
6. Quick-release or naturally release pressure when done. Open the lid with care.
7. Remove corn pudding. Allow to cool before serving.

Lovely Cinnamon Baked Apples
Time: 10 minutes   Servings: 4

Ingredients:

- 6 apples, cored and sliced (or chopped)
- ½ cup plump golden raisins
- ½ cup nuts, chopped (your choice)
- 1 teaspoon pure cinnamon powder
- 3 packets raw stevia
- 1 teaspoon apple pie spice
- 3 Tablespoons butter, softened

Instructions:

In your Instant Pot, combine apples, raisins, nuts, cinnamon powder, stevia, apple pie spice, and butter. Stir well. Close and seal lid. Press Manual button. Cook at High Pressure for 10 minutes. Release pressure naturally when done. Open the lid with care. Serve.

Delicious Peach Cobbler
Time: 20 minutes   Servings: 4

Ingredients:

- 8 peaches, peeled and chopped
- 2 Tablespoons butter, softened
- ½ cup coconut flour
- 1 teaspoon vanilla extract
- ¼ cup granulated Splenda
- ¼ cup low-carb brown sugar
- 1 teaspoon pure cinnamon
- 1 teaspoon lime juice
- 1 cup coconut milk

Instructions:

1. In your Instant Pot, place peaches in single layer along bottom.
2. In a large bowl, combine coconut milk, butter, vanilla extract, coconut flour, brown sugar, and Splenda. Stir well. Pour mixture over peaches.
3. Close and seal lid. Press Manual button. Cook on High Pressure for 10 minutes.
4. Release pressure naturally when done. Open the lid with care.
5. Spoon into bowls.

Creamy Chocolate Pudding
Time: 20 minutes   Servings: 2

Ingredients:

- 1 cup organic coconut milk
- 1½ cups organic heavy cream
- 2 Tablespoons cocoa powder, unsweetened
- ½ teaspoon stevia powder extract
- 1 Tablespoons raw, organic honey
- 8-ounce bittersweet dark chocolate, chopped
- 2 large eggs
- 2 Tablespoons butter, softened
- ⅓ cup coconut flour
- ¼ cup granulated Splenda
- ⅓ cup low-carb brown sugar
- 2 teaspoons vanilla extract
- ¼ teaspoon cinnamon
- ⅛ teaspoon salt
- 2 Tablespoons of water

Instructions:

1. In a saucepan, add coconut milk, heavy cream, cocoa powder, stevia powder extract, and honey. Stir well. Simmer 3 minutes.
2. Remove saucepan from heat. Add dark chocolate. Stir until melted. Set aside. Let it cool slightly before adding to rest of mixture.
3. In a large bowl, combine eggs, coconut flour, brown sugar, Splenda, vanilla extract, cinnamon, butter, and salt. Stir well. Add chocolate mixture to batter. Stir well. Pour 2 cups of water in Instant Pot. Place trivet inside.
4. Grease a pan, suitable for Instant Pot, with non-stick cooking spray.
5. Pour batter in pan. Cover with aluminum foil. Place on trivet.
6. Close and seal lid. Press Manual button. Cook at High Pressure for 10 minutes.
7. Release pressure naturally when done. Open the lid with care.
8. Remove pan from Instant Pot. Allow to cool. Serve.

Just as Filling Cauliflower Rice Pudding
Time: 20 minutes   Servings: 2

Ingredients:

- 1 head cauliflower
- 2 cups coconut milk
- 1 cup heavy cream
- 4 teaspoons cinnamon powder
- 1 teaspoon granulated Splenda
- 1 teaspoon pure stevia extract
- 1 teaspoon pure vanilla extract
- ½ teaspoon salt

Instructions:

1. Chop up cauliflower. Place pieces in food processor.
2. Pulse until cauliflower is rice-like consistency. Pour cauliflower rice in Instant Pot.
3. Add coconut milk, cinnamon, Splenda, stevia extract, vanilla extract, and salt. Stir well.
4. Close and seal lid. Press Porridge button. Cook at High Pressure for 20 minutes.
5. When done, allow pressure to release naturally for 10 minutes.
6. After 10 minutes, press the Cancel button. Open the lid with care.
7. To finish off, add cream and vanilla extract. Stir well. Serve in bowls.

Almost-Famous Chocolate Lava Cake
Time: 15 minutes   Servings: 4

Ingredients:

- ⅓ cup granulated Splenda
- 2 Tablespoons butter, softened
- ¼ cup coconut milk
- ¼ cup coconut flour (or any ketogenic alternatives)
- 1 large egg
- 1 Tablespoon cocoa powder, unsweetened
- Zest from ½ a lime
- ½ teaspoon baking powder
- ⅛ teaspoon salt
- 1 cup of water
- 4 ramekins

Instructions:

1. In a bowl, combine eggs, Splenda, butter, milk, coconut flour, egg, cocoa powder, lime zest, baking powder, and salt. Stir well.
2. Grease 4 ramekins with non-stick cooking spray. Divide batter evenly in 4 ramekins.
3. Pour 2 cups of water in Instant Pot. Place trivet inside. Place ramekins on trivet.
4. Close and seal lid. Press Manual button. Cook at High Pressure for 7 minutes.
5. When done, allow pressure to release naturally. Remove ramekins.
6. Allow lava cakes to cool 5 minutes. Serve.

Irresistible Lemon Cheesecake
Time: 30 minutes (plus 6 hours for refrigerating)   Servings: 4

Ingredients:

- 1½ cups low-carb graham crackers (approximately 10-12 crackers)
- 2 teaspoons low-carb brown sugar
- 2 Tablespoons butter, melted
- 1 Tablespoon almond flour
- 1 package (16-ounce) cream cheese, softened
- ½ cup granulated sugar
- 1 teaspoon vanilla extract
- 2 large eggs
- ½ cup heavy whipping cream
- Zest and juice from 1 lemon

Instructions:

1. In a food processor, add graham crackers, brown sugar, and butter.
2. Pulse until well blended, almost sand-like consistency.
3. Grease a 6-inch cheesecake pan with non-stick cooking spray.
4. Press crust mixture into bottom of pan firmly. Place in freezer for 10 minutes to harden.
5. In a separate bowl, combine cream cheese, granulated sugar, heavy cream, eggs, almond flour, zest and juice from lemon, and vanilla extract.
6. Stir vigorously or blend with hand mixer until smooth.
7. Pour filling over crust. Cover cheesecake pan with aluminum foil.
8. Pour 2 cups of water in Instant Pot. Place trivet inside. Place pan on trivet.
9. Close and seal lid. Press Manual button. Cook at High Pressure for 20 minutes.
10. Once done, naturally release pressure. Open the lid with care.
11. Allow cheesecake to rest in Instant Pot for 20 minutes.
12. Transfer cheesecake to refrigerator. Cool for 6 hours or overnight.
13. Top with whip cream and fresh lemon zest when serving.

Berry Bliss Cheesecake
Time: 30 minutes (plus 6 hours for refrigerating)   Servings: 4

Ingredients:

- 1½ cups low-carb graham crackers (approximately 10-12 crackers)
- 1 Tablespoon granulated Splenda
- 4 Tablespoons butter, melted
- 2 packages (16-ounce) cream cheese, softened:
- 1 cup granulated Splenda
- 3 large eggs
- ¼ cup sour cream
- Zest and juice from 1 lemon
- 1 teaspoon vanilla extract
- 1 cup heavy whipping cream
- 4 cups mixed fresh berries (keto-friendly, your choice)

Instructions:

1. Mash half the berries with a fork. Set aside.
2. In a food processor, add graham crackers, granulated Splenda, melted butter.
3. Pulse until sand-like consistency.
4. Grease 6-inch cheesecake pan, to fit Instant Pot, with non-stick cooking spray.
5. Press crust mixture into bottom of pan. Place in freezer 10 minutes to harden.
6. In a separate bowl, combine cream cheese, Splenda, eggs, sour cream, zest and juice from lemon, vanilla and heavy cream. Add crushed mixed berries.
7. Stir vigorously or blend with hand mixer until smooth.
8. Pour mixture over crust. Cover cheesecake pan with aluminum foil.
9. Pour 2 cups of water in Instant Pot. Place trivet inside. Place pan on trivet.
10. Close and seal lid. Press Manual button. Cook at High Pressure for 20 minutes.
11. Once done, naturally release pressure. Open the lid with care.
12. Allow cheesecake to rest for 20 minutes in Instant Pot.
13. Transfer cheesecake to refrigerator. Cool for 6 hours or overnight.
14. Top with rest of fresh berries when serving.

Fantastic Bread Pudding
Time: 25 minutes   Servings: 4

Ingredients:

- 6 slices low-carb day-old/stale bread, cut into cubes
- 1½ cups unsweetened almond milk
- 4 Tablespoons unsalted butter
- 3 large eggs
- ¼ cup granulated Splenda
- ¾ cup low-carb dark chocolate chips
- 1 teaspoon vanilla extract
- 1 cup plump golden raisins
- Zest from 1 lemon
- 2 cups of water

Instructions:

1. In a small bowl, combine eggs, Splenda and almond milk. Whisk until combined.
2. Melt the butter.
3. In a large bowl, add the bread. Pour melted butter over bread.
4. Add lemon zest, chocolate chips, and raisins. Pour liquid mixture over bread. Stir well.
5. Grease baking dish, to fit Instant Pot, with non-stick cooking spray.
6. Pour in bread mixture. Cover with aluminum foil.
7. Pour 2 cups of water in Instant Pot. Place trivet inside. Place dish on trivet.
8. Close and seal lid. Press Manual button. Cook at High Pressure for 20 minutes.
9. Release pressure naturally when done. Open the lid with care.
10. Allow bread pudding to rest 15 minutes in Instant Pot. Serve.

Spice Cake
Time: 1 hour and 10 minutes   Servings: 10

Ingredients:

- 2 cups of almond flour or coconut flour
- ½ cup of erythritol or keto-friendly sweeteners
- 1 teaspoon of baking soda
- 1 teaspoon of organic ground ginger
- 1 teaspoon of baking powder
- ¼ teaspoon of ground cloves
- ½ teaspoon of fine sea salt
- 2 large organic eggs, beaten
- 1/3 cup of unsalted butter or coconut butter, melted
- 1/3 cup of water
- ½ teaspoon of pure vanilla extract
- 3 tablespoons of toasted pecans or toasted walnuts, roughly chopped

Instructions:

- Grease a 7-inch oven-safe baking pan with nonstick cooking spray.
- Add 1 cup of water and a trivet to your Instant Pot.
- In a large bowl, add the almond flour, erythritol, baking soda, baking powder, ground ginger, ground cloves and sea salt.
- Stir in the beaten eggs, melted butter, water and pure vanilla extract until well combined.
- Transfer the cake batter to a baking pan and smooth on top. Sprinkle with toasted pecans or walnuts and cover with aluminum foil. Place on top of your trivet.

- Close and seal the lid; cook at high pressure for 40 minutes.
- When the cooking is done, naturally release the pressure and carefully remove the lid.
- Remove the aluminum foil and allow the cake to cool. Serve and enjoy!

Chocolate Zucchini Brownies
Time: 50 minutes   Servings: 4

Ingredients:

- 2/3 cups of almond flour or coconut flour
- ¾ cups of unsweetened cocoa powder
- ¼ teaspoon of baking soda or baking powder
- ¼ teaspoon of fine sea salt
- 1 cup of zucchini, finely grated
- 1 cup of erythritol or swerve sweetener
- 2 large eggs, beaten
- 1 teaspoon of pure vanilla extract
- ½ cup of unsalted butter, melted

Instructions:

- In a bowl, add the almond flour, cocoa powder, baking soda and fine sea salt. Mix until well combined.
- In another bowl, add the erythritol and the grated zucchini. Stir until well combined.
- Stir in the large eggs, pure vanilla extract and unsalted butter. Mix well.
- Grease a dish that fits inside your Instant Pot. Add the brownie batter to the dish and tightly cover with aluminum foil.
- Add 1 cup of water and a trivet inside your Instant Pot. Place the dish on top of the trivet. Lock the lid and cook at high pressure for 45 minutes. When the cooking is done, quick release the pressure and carefully remove the lid.
- Remove the dish from your Instant Pot and allow to cool Serve and enjoy!

Blueberry Syrup
Time: 22 minutes   Servings: 10

Ingredients:

- 2 ½ cups of fresh or frozen blueberries
- ¼ cup of powdered erythritol
- ½ cup of water
- 1 teaspoon of freshly squeezed lemon juice

Instructions:

- Add all the ingredients inside your Instant Pot.
- Lock the lid and cook at high pressure for 4 minutes. When the cooking is done, naturally release the pressure for 5 minutes, then quick release the remaining pressure. Carefully remove the lid.
- If not already thickened, press the "Sauté" setting on your Instant Pot and continue to cook until thicken and syrupy, stirring frequently. Serve and enjoy!

Pumpkin Pie Cauliflower Mug Cake
Time: 15 minutes   Servings: 4

Ingredients:

- ½ cup of cauliflower, steamed and mashed
- 2/3 cups of coconut flour
- 1 large egg, beaten
- 1 teaspoon of pure vanilla extract
- 2 tablespoons of sugar-free syrup
- 2 teaspoons of pumpkin pie spice

Instructions:

- Add 1 cup of water and a trivet inside your Instant Pot.
- In a large bowl, add the mashed cauliflower, coconut flour, egg, vanilla extract, syrup and pumpkin pie spice. Stir until well combined.
- Grease a mason jar with nonstick cooking spray and add the mixture.
- Place the mason jars on top and lock the lid. Cook at low pressure for 8 minutes.
- When the cooking is done, quick release the pressure and remove the lid. Allow the cake to cool. Serve and enjoy!

Blueberry Cheesecake

Time: 50 minutes   Servings: 12

Crust Ingredients:

- 1 ¼ cup of almond flour
- 2-ounces of unsalted butter, melted
- 2 tablespoons of granulated erythritol
- ½ teaspoon of pure vanilla extract

Filling Ingredients:

- 20-ounces of cream cheese, softened
- ½ cup of heavy whipping cream
- 2 large eggs
- 1 egg yolk
- 1 tablespoon of erythritol
- 1 teaspoon of fresh lemon zest
- ½ teaspoon of vanilla extract
- 2-ounces of fresh blueberries

Instructions:

- In a food processor, add all the crust ingredients and pulse until well combined.
- Grease a springform pan that will fit inside your Instant Pot with nonstick cooking spray and line with parchment paper. Press the crust onto the pan.Pour the batter inside the springform pan and cover with aluminum foil.
- Add 1 cup of water and a trivet inside your Instant Pot. Place the springform pan on top.
- Lock the lid and cook at high pressure for 25 minutes. When the cooking is done, naturally release the pressure for 10 minutes, then quick release the remaining pressure. Carefully remove the lid. Serve and enjoy!

Candied Almonds

Time: 10 minutes   Servings: 6

Ingredients:

- 2 ½ cups of almonds
- ¼ cups of granulated erythritol
- ¼ cup of water
- 1 tablespoon of cinnamon
- ½ teaspoon of pure vanilla extract
- ½ teaspoon of fine sea salt

Instructions:

- Press the "Sauté" setting on your Instant Pot and add the water, erythritol, cinnamon, pure vanilla extract and fine sea salt. Mix well and stir until well blended.
- Once the liquid starts to slightly boil, add the almonds. Stir until well coated with the liquid. Continue to cook for 3 to 4 minutes or until the almonds have blended with the liquid. Serve and enjoy!

Dark Chocolate Nuts

Time: 35 minutes   Servings: 16

Ingredients:

- 4 cups of mixed keto-friendly nuts
- ½ cup of granulated erythritol
- 2 teaspoons of pure vanilla extract
- 2 teaspoons of cinnamon
- ½ teaspoon of nutmeg
- ½ teaspoon of fine sea salt
- ¾ cups of unsweetened dark chocolate, shaved
- ½ cup of water
- 3 tablespoons of unsweetened cocoa powder

Instructions:

- Press the "Sauté" setting on your Instant Pot and add the nuts, pure vanilla extract, cinnamon, nutmeg and fine sea salt. Continue to cook for 8 minutes or until the mixed nuts are tender, stirring frequently.
- Add 1/2 cup of water and stir until well combined. Lock the lid and cook at high pressure for 10 minutes.
- When the cooking is done, quick release the pressure and remove the lid.
- Preheat your oven to 375 degrees Fahrenheit. Transfer the nuts to a baking sheet lined with aluminum foil.
- Place the baking sheet inside your oven and roast for 5 to 10 minutes. Sprinkle the dark chocolate over the nuts and allow to melt.
- Sprinkle the unsweetened cocoa powder and stir until well coated. Serve and enjoy!

Pumpkin Spice Candied Walnuts

Time: 45 minutes   Servings: 16

Ingredients:

- 8 cups of walnuts, chopped or cut in half
- 1 ½ cup of maple sugar-free syrup
- ½ cup of water
- 3 tablespoons of pureed pumpkin
- 1 teaspoon of fine sea salt
- 2 tablespoons of pumpkin pie spice
- ½ cup of granulated erythritol or swerve sweetener

Instructions:

- Preheat your oven to 360 degrees Fahrenheit and line a baking sheet with aluminum foil.
- Press the "Sauté "setting on your Instant Pot.
- Place the walnuts inside your Instant Pot. Add the maple syrup, pureed pumpkin, fin sea salt and pumpkin spice Toss until well combined. Cook for 10 minutes, stirring occasionally.
- Lock the lid and cook at high pressure for 10 minutes. When the cooking is done, naturally release the pressure for 10 minutes, then quick release the remaining pressure. Carefully remove the lid.
- Line a baking sheet with parchment paper and grease with nonstick cooking spray.
- Spread the walnut mixture onto the baking sheet and place inside your oven. Bake for 15 minutes, stirring every so often.
- Sprinkle the erythritol and toss until well coated. Allow to cool. Serve and enjoy!

Mini Mochaccino Cheesecakes

Time: 20 minutes   Servings: 6

Crust Ingredients:

- 1 ½ cup of almond flour
- ¼ cup of unsalted butter, melted
- ¼ cup of unsweetened cocoa powder
- 2 tablespoons of erythritol or swerve sweetener

Filling Ingredients:

- 6-ounces of cream cheese, softened
- 1 tablespoon of sour cream
- ¼ teaspoon of pure vanilla extract
- 2 teaspoons of Instant espresso powder
- ¼ cup of granulated erythritol or swerve sweetener
- 1 large egg

Instructions:

- Grease cupcake liners with nonstick cooking spray.
- In a food processor, add all the crust ingredients and pulse until well combined.
- Divide and press the mixture to cupcake liners.
- In a large bowl, using an electric mixer, add all the filling ingredients and mix until smooth.
- Divide and spoon the cheesecake filling into the cupcake liners.
- Add 1 cup of water and a steamer rack inside your Instant Pot. Place the cheesecake on top of the rack.
- Lock the lid and cook at high pressure for 20 minutes. When the cooking is done, quick release the pressure and remove the lid.
- Remove the cheesecakes from the cake and allow to cool. Serve and enjoy!

Cinnamon Swirl Bread

Time: 45 minutes   Servings: 10

Ingredients:

- 4 large eggs, separated
- 2 tablespoons of unsalted butter, melted
- 2 tablespoons of unsalted butter, softened
- 1 teaspoon of pure vanilla extract
- 4-ounces of cream cheese, softened
- 12 drops of liquid stevia
- 1 teaspoon of baking powder or baking soda
- 1 cup of coconut flour
- 1 ½ teaspoon of cinnamon
- ¼ cups of granulated erythritol
- ¼ teaspoon of cream of tarter

Instructions:

- Grease a loaf pan that will fit inside your Instant Pot with nonstick cooking spray.
- In a large bowl, add the egg whites. In a second bowl, add the egg yolks.
- Use an electric mixer to mix the ¼ teaspoon of cream of tartar with the egg whites. Beat well and set aside.
- In the second bowl, add the 2 tablespoons of softened butter, pure vanilla extract, softened cream cheese, 12 drops of stevia and egg yolks. Beat well until combined.
- Add1/2 teaspoon of cinnamon, baking soda or baking powder, and coconut flour. Continue to beat until combined.
- In a small bowl, add the 2 tablespoons of melted butter, granulated erythritol, and the remaining teaspoon of cinnamon. Stir until well combined.
- Add the egg white mixture to the egg yolk mixture. Gently stir until well combined.
- Add the half of the mixture into the loaf pan. Top with the cinnamon-butter mixture.
- Add the remaining loaf batter to the pan. Use a knife to make swirls.
- Add 2 cups of water and a trivet inside your Instant Pot. Place the loaf pan on top. Cover the pan with aluminum foil.
- Lock the lid and cook at high pressure for 50 minutes. When the cooking is done, naturally release the pressure and remove the lid. Serve and enjoy!

Pumpkin Brownies
Time: 1 hour and 30 minutes   Servings: 16

Ingredients:

- ¼ cup of coconut oil or ghee, melted
- ½ cup of pureed pumpkin
- ¼ cup of sugar-free maple syrup
- ¼ cup of erythritol or swerve sweetener
- ¾ cups of unsweetened cocoa powder

- 3 large organic eggs, beaten
- 1 teaspoon of pumpkin pie spice
- ¼ teaspoon of fine sea salt
- 1 cup of water (to help build up pressure)

Instructions:

- In a large bowl, add all the ingredients and stir until well combined.
- Add the batter to a brownie pan that will fit inside your Instant Pot. Tightly cover with aluminum foil.
- Add 1 cup of water and a trivet inside your Instant Pot. Place the brownie pan on top of the trivet.
- Lock the lid and cook at high pressure for 40 minutes. When the cooking is done, quick release the pressure and carefully remove the lid.
- Allow the brownie pan to cool and slice into servings. Serve and enjoy!

Bacon Jam
Time: 30 minutes   Servings: 32

Ingredients:

- 1 pound of bacon, chopped
- 1 large yellow onion, finely chopped
- 4 medium garlic cloves, peeled and crushed
- ¼ cup of apple cider vinegar
- ½ cup of sugar-free maple syrup

- 1 teaspoon of adobo sauce
- 1 chipotle in adobo sauce, minced
- ½ teaspoon of sweet paprika
- 1 tablespoon of instant espresso powder
- ½ cup of pure filtered water

Instructions:

- Press the "Sauté" setting on your Instant Pot and add the chopped bacon and onions. Continue to cook for 3 to 5 or until the bacon has browned and onions are translucent, stirring frequently.
- Add the crushed garlic and continue to cook for another minute.
- Discard the bacon grease.
- Stir in the remaining ingredients. Lock the lid and cook at high pressure for 10 minutes.
- When the cooking is done, manually release the pressure and remove the lid.
- Use an immersion blender to blend the contents until smooth and thick.
- Spoon the jam to mason jars. Serve and enjoy!

Carrot Pudding
Time: 15 minutes   Servings: 10

Ingredients:

- 1 pound of carrots, peeled and finely grated
- ½ cup of unsweetened coconut milk
- ¼ cup of water
- ½ cup of erythritol or swerve sweetener
- 4 tablespoons of coconut oil or ghee

Instructions:

- Add all the ingredients except for the erythritol inside your Instant Pot and stir until well combined.
- Lock the lid and cook at high pressure for 1 minute. When the cooking is done, manually release the pressure and remove the lid.
- Press the "Sauté" setting on your instant Pot and add the erythritol. Continue to cook or until thickened, stirring frequently. Serve and enjoy!

Lemon Pudding Cups
Time: 11 minutes   Servings: 4

Ingredients:

- 3 cups of unsweetened coconut milk
- 2 to 4 drops of lemon essential oil
- 2 tablespoons of gelatin
- ¼ cup of freshly squeezed lemon juice
- 2 tablespoons of fresh lemon zest
- ½ cup of sugar-free maple syrup
- 3 tablespoons of coconut oil, melted
- 3 large eggs

Instructions:

- In a blender, add the unsweetened coconut milk, lemon juice, lemon zest, syrup, coconut oil and eggs. Blend until smooth.
- Add the lemon essential oil and continue to blend until smooth.
- Add the gelatin and blend until smooth.
- Divide and pour the mixture into heat-safe glass jars. Add a lid to the glass jars or tightly cover with aluminum foil.
- Pour 1 cup of water and a trivet inside your Instant Pot. Place the glass jars on top of the trivet.
- Lock the lid and cook at high pressure for 5 minutes. When the cooking is done, manually release the pressure and remove the lid. Serve and enjoy!

Chocolate Pudding Cake
Time: 35 minutes   Servings: 6

Ingredients:

- 3 large organic eggs
- 1 cup of almond flour or coconut flour
- 1/3 cups of unsweetened cocoa powder
- ¾ cups of unsweetened coconut milk
- 1 stick of unsalted butter, softened
- 2 tablespoons of Swerve sweetener
- 1 teaspoon of pure vanilla extract
- 1 teaspoon of baking powder or baking soda

Chocolate Sauce Ingredients:

- 1 tablespoon of granulated Swerve
- ¼ cups of unsweetened cocoa powder
- 1 cup of boiling hot unsweetened milk or water

Instructions:

- In a large bowl, add the almond flour, Swerve sweetener, cocoa powder and baking powder. Stir until well combined.
- Stir in the coconut milk, softened butter and vanilla extract until smooth.
- Beat in the 3 eggs to the batter.
- Grease a cake pan suitable for your Instant Pot with nonstick cooking spray and spoon in the batter.
- In another bowl, add the granulated swerve, cocoa powder, and unsweetened milk. Mix well.
- Pour the sauce over the cake batter and cover with aluminum foil.
- Add 1 cup of water and a trivet to your Instant Pot. Place the cake pan on top.
- Close and seal the lid; cook at high pressure for 30 minutes.

- When the cooking is done, quick release the pressure and carefully remove the lid.
- Remove the aluminum foil off the pan and allow to cool. Serve and enjoy!

Pumpkin Cheesecake with Sour Cream Topping
Time: 1 hour and 25 minutes   Servings: 10

Cheesecake Crust Ingredients:

- 1 ½ cup of almond flour
- 2 tablespoons of granulated erythritol or Swerve
- 1/3 cups of unsalted butter, melted

Pumpkin Cheesecake Filling Ingredients:

- 2 (8-ounce) packages of cream cheese, softened and cut into cubes
- 2/3 cups of canned pureed pumpkin
- 1 cup of granulated erythritol or Swerve
- 2 large organic eggs
- 2 tablespoons of heavy whipping cream
- 1 teaspoon of pumpkin pie spice
- ½ teaspoon of organic ground cinnamon
- 1 teaspoon of pure vanilla extract
- A pinch of fine sea salt

Sour Cream Topping Ingredients:

- 2/3 cups of organic sour cream
- 3 tablespoons of granulated erythritol
- ½ teaspoon of pure vanilla extract

Instructions:

- Place parchment paper on the bottom of a springform pan that fits inside your Instant Pot. Spray with nonstick cooking spray.
- In a bowl, add all the cheesecake crust ingredients and stir until well combined. Add to the springform pan and firmly press.
- In another bowl, use a hand-mixer to blend all the cheesecake filling ingredients until smooth.
- Add the cheesecake filling to the springform pan and cover with aluminum foil.
- Pour 1 ½ cup of water and place a trivet inside your Instant Pot. Place the springform pan on top of the trivet.
- Lock the lid and cook at high pressure for 55 minutes. When the cooking is done, naturally release the pressure and remove the lid.
- Remove the cheesecake from your Instant Pot and allow to cool.
- Meanwhile, in a bowl, add all the sour cream topping ingredients and stir until well combined. Spread the sour cream topping on top of the cheesecake. Serve and enjoy!

Berry Mug Cake
Time: 5 minutes   Servings: 1

Ingredients:

- 2 tablespoons of almond flour
- 1 tablespoon of coconut flour
- 1/8 teaspoon of baking soda
- 1 tablespoon of erythritol
- 1 large egg
- ½ teaspoon of vanilla extract
- 1 tablespoon of coconut oil, melted
- 1 teaspoon of stevia
- 1 cup of mixed berries, fresh or frozen

Instructions:

- Grease a ramekin with nonstick cooking spray.
- Add all the ingredients except for the blueberries inside the ramekin until well combined.
- Top with the blueberries and wrap with aluminum foil.
- Add 1 cup of water and a trivet to your Instant Pot. Place the ramekin on top; close and seal the lid.
- Cook at high pressure for 7 minutes. Once done, naturally release the pressure and remove the lid. Serve and enjoy!

Lemon Cheesecake
Time: 35 minutes   Servings: 6

Crust Ingredients:

- ¾ cups of almond flour
- 2 tablespoons of powdered erythritol
- 2 tablespoons of unsalted butter, melted
- A small pinch of fine sea salt

Filling Ingredients:

- 1 pound of softened cream cheese
- 2/3 cups of powdered erythritol
- ¼ cups of freshly squeezed lemon juice
- 1 teaspoon of fresh lemon zest
- 1 teaspoon of lemon extract
- 2 large organic eggs, beaten
- 2 tablespoons of heavy whipping cream

Instructions:

- Line a 7-inch springform pan with parchment paper and spray with nonstick cooking spray.
- In a bowl, add all the crust ingredients and stir until well combined.
- Add the almond mixture to the springform pan and firmly press.
- In another bowl, add all the filling ingredients and use a hand mixer to mix well.
- Add and spread the filling into the springform pan and cover with aluminum foil.
- Pour 1 cup of water and add a trivet inside your Instant Pot. Place the springform pan on top of the trivet.
- Lock the lid and cook at high pressure for 35 minutes. When the cooking is done, naturally release the pressure and remove the lid.
- Remove the cheesecake and refrigerate for 4 hours or overnight. Serve and enjoy!

Cream Cheese Pound Cake
Time: 50 minutes   Servings: 8

Ingredients:

- 4-ounces of cream cheese, softened
- 4 tablespoons of unsalted butter, softened
- ¼ cup of swerve sweetener
- 4 large eggs
- ¼ cup of sour cream
- 2 cups of almond flour
- 2 teaspoons of baking powder or baking soda
- 1 teaspoon of almond extract

Instructions:

- Add 2 cups of water and a trivet inside your Instant Pot.
- Grease a half-size bundt pan with nonstick cooking spray.
- In a large bowl, add the cream cheese, butter, eggs and swerve. Beat until well combined.
- Beat in the almond extract, eggs and sour cream.
- Beat in the almond flour and baking powder until well combined.
- Transfer the batter to the pan and cover with aluminum foil.
- Place the pan on top of the trivet. Lock the lid and cook at high pressure for 35 minutes. When the cooking is done, naturally release the pressure and remove the lid. Serve and enjoy!

Italian Cream Cake
Time: 45 minutes   Servings: 12

Cake Ingredients:

- 1 cup of sour cream
- 1 teaspoon of baking soda
- 1 cup of unsalted butter
- 2 cups of swerve Confectioners' sugar
- 5 large organic eggs
- 2 teaspoons of pure vanilla extract
- 1 cup of unsweetened coconut flakes
- 1 teaspoon of baking powder
- 2 ½ cups of almond flour

Frosting Ingredients:

- 1 (8-ounce) package of cream cheese, softened
- ½ cup of unsalted butter, softened
- 1 teaspoon of pure vanilla extract
- 2 cups of Swerve confectioners
- 2 tablespoons of heavy whipping cream
- ½ cup of walnuts or pecans, chopped
- 1 cup of unsweetened coconut flakes

Instructions:

- Add 1 cup of water and a trivet inside your Instant Pot.
- Place parchment paper on a 7-inch springform pan and grease with nonstick cooking spray.

- In a bowl, add all the cake ingredients and gently stir until well combined.
- Add the batter to the springform pan and place on top of the trivet. Cover with a piece of foil.
- Lock the lid and cook at high pressure for 35 minutes. When the cooking is done, naturally release the pressure and remove the lid. Remove the cake from the springform pan and allow to cool.
- In a medium bowl, add all the frosting ingredients and stir until well combined. Spread the Italian cream on the cake. Serve and enjoy!

Pound Cake

Time: 50 minutes   Servings: 16

Ingredients:

- 2 ½ cups of almond flour or coconut flour
- ½ cup of softened unsalted butter
- 1 ½ cups of erythritol
- 8 large organic eggs
- 1 ½ teaspoons of pure vanilla extract
- ½ teaspoons of fresh lemon extract
- ½ teaspoons of fine sea salt
- 1 (8-ounce) package of cream cheese, softened
- 1 ½ teaspoon of baking powder

Glaze Ingredients:

- ¼ cup of powdered erythritol
- 3 tablespoons of heavy whipping cream
- ½ teaspoon of pure vanilla extract

Instructions:

- In a bowl, add all the glaze ingredients and stir until well combined. Refrigerate and set aside.
- In a large bowl, add the cream cheese and butter. Beat well.
- Add the remaining cake ingredients and stir until well combined.
- Line a 7-inch springform pan with parchment paper and grease with nonstick cooking spray.
- Add the cake ingredients to the springform pan and spread evenly. Cover with aluminum foil.
- Add 2 cups of water and a trivet inside your Instant Pot. Place the cake on top and lock the lid.
- Cook at high pressure for 35 minutes. When the cooking is done, naturally release the pressure and remove the lid. Remove the cake from the springform pan and allow to cool.
- Spread the glaze over the cake. Serve and enjoy!

Chocolate Zucchini Bundt Cake

Time: 50 minutes   Servings: 16

Ingredients:

- 3 cups of almond flour or coconut flour
- 1 ½ cups of powdered erythritol or powdered swerve
- ½ cups of unsweetened cacao powder
- 2 teaspoons of baking powder
- ½ teaspoon of fine sea salt
- 6 large organic eggs
- ½ cup of unsalted butter, melted
- 2 medium zucchinis, peeled and pureed
- 2 teaspoons of pure vanilla extract

Frosting Ingredients:

- ¼ cup of coconut oil
- ½ cup of cacao powder

Instructions:

- Grease a half-size bundt cake pan with nonstick cooking spray.
- In a large bowl, add all the cake ingredients and gently stir until well combined. Add the cake batter to the bundt pan and evenly smooth on top. Cover with aluminum foil.
- Add 2 cups of water and a trivet inside your Instant Pot. Place the bundt cake pan on top of the trivet. Lock the lid and cook at high pressure for 30 minutes at high pressure.
- When the cooking is done, naturally release the pressure for 10 minutes, then quick release the remaining pressure. Carefully remove the lid and remove the cake pan.
- Allow the cake to cool and remove from the bundt pan.
- To make the frosting, add the coconut oil and cacao powder and mix well. Spread the frosting over the cake. Serve and enjoy!

Pumpkin Bundt Cake
Time: 40 minutes   Servings: 4

Pumpkin Cake Ingredients:

- 3 cups of almond flour or coconut flour
- ½ cups of unsalted butter, melted
- 6 large organic eggs
- 1 cup of pumpkin puree

- 2 teaspoons of pure vanilla extract
- 2 teaspoons of pumpkin pie spice
- ½ teaspoon of fine sea salt
- 2 teaspoons of baking powder

Glaze Ingredients:

- ¼ cup of unsalted butter
- ½ cup of powdered erythritol or swerve sweetener

- 1 teaspoon of organic cinnamon powder
- 1 teaspoons of pure vanilla extract

Instructions:

- Grease a half-size bundt cake pan with nonstick cooking spray.
- In a large bowl, add all the pumpkin cake ingredients and stir until well combined.
- Transfer the batter to a cake pan and cover with aluminum foil.
- Add 2 cups of water and a trivet inside your Instant Pot. Place the cake pan on top of the trivet and lock the lid. Cook at high pressure for 25 minutes.
- When the cooking is done, naturally release the pressure for 10 minutes, then quick release the remaining pressure. Carefully remove the lid and remove the cake from the pan. Allow to cool.
- In another bowl, add all the glaze ingredients: unsalted butter, powdered erythritol, cinnamon, and pure vanilla extract. Mix well.
- Spread the glaze ingredients over the pumpkin cake. Serve and enjoy!

Italian Ricotta Cheesecake
Time: 2 hours and 30 minutes   Servings: 8

Ingredients:

- 8-ounces of cream cheese, softened
- 15-ounces of ricotta cheese milk, drained
- 1 cup of granulated erythritol
- 1 teaspoon of arrowroot powder

- A small pinch of fine sea salt
- 1 teaspoon of pure vanilla extract
- 1 lemon, juice and zest
- 2 large eggs

Instructions:

- Grease a 7-inch springform pan with nonstick cooking spray.
- In a large bowl, add all the ingredients and beat until smooth. Pour the cheesecake batter into the prepared springform pan.
- Add 2 cups of water and a trivet inside your Instant Pot. Place the springform pan on top of the trivet and tightly cover with aluminum foil.
- Lock the lid and cook at high pressure for 20 minutes with a full natural release pressure method.
- Remove the springform pan from your Instant Pot and refrigerate until cool and set.Serve and enjoy!

Birthday Cake
Time: 50 minutes   Servings: 16

Ingredients:

- 1 ½ cup of almond flour or coconut flour
- 2 ½ teaspoons of baking powder
- ¼ teaspoon of baking soda
- ½ teaspoon of fine sea salt
- 8 tablespoons of unsalted butter, softened

- 1 ½ cup of erythritol or swerve sweetener
- 1 teaspoon of vanilla extract
- 1 large organic egg
- ½ cup of sour cream
- 3 tablespoons of cake sprinkles (optional)

Buttercream Ingredients:

- 4 cups of erythritol
- 3 sticks of unsalted butter

- 3 tablespoons of heavy crema

Instructions:

- Line a 7-inch cake pan with parchment paper and grease with nonstick cooking spray.
- In a large bowl, add all the cake ingredients and beat until well combined.
- In another bowl, add all the buttercream ingredients and beat until smooth. Refrigerate and set aside.
- Transfer the cake batter to the cake pan and spread evenly on top.
- Add 2 cups of water and a trivet inside your Instant Pot. Place the cake pan on top of the trivet and cover with aluminum foil.
- Lock the lid and cook at high pressure for 40 minutes. When the cooking is done, quick release the pressure and remove the lid.
- Remove the cake from the pan and allow to cool.
- Slice the cake in half to create a total of two layers.
- Spread the buttercream on top of one half and carefully place on top of the second.
- Spread the rest of the buttercream on top of the cake and all around. Decorate with sprinkles if you like. Serve and enjoy!

Chocolate Pudding
Time: 25 minutes   Servings: 6

Ingredients:

- 4-ounces of unsweetened chocolate, chopped
- 1 ½ cup of heavy whipping cream
- 4 egg yolks
- 1/3 cup of truvia low-carb brown sugar or erythritol
- 1 tablespoon of unsweetened cocoa powder
- 1 teaspoon of pure vanilla extract
- 1 teaspoon of fine sea salt

Instructions:

- In a medium saucepan over medium heat, add the heavy whipping cream. Allow to heat through. Once hot enough, stir in the chopped chocolate and allow to melt. Stir until smooth.
- In a large bowl, whisk in the egg yolks, sweetener, unsweetened cocoa powder, pure vanilla extract and fine sea salt.
- Slowly whisk in the chocolate mixture until well blended.
- Strain the mixture into a mason jar or soufflé dish. Tightly cover with aluminum foil.
- Add 1 cup of water and a trivet inside your Instant Pot. Place the mason jars or dish on top. Lock the lid and cook at low pressure for 22 minutes.
- When the cooking is done, naturally release the pressure for 5 minutes, then quick release the remaining pressure. Remove the lid.
- Remove the dish from your Instant Pot and remove the aluminum foil.
- Cover and place inside your refrigerator. Serve and enjoy!

Vanilla Bean Pudding
Time: 35 minutes   Servings: 1

Ingredients:

- 1 cup of heavy whipping cream
- 1 vanilla bean
- 3 large egg yolks
- 3 tablespoons of erythritol or swerve sweetener

Instructions:

- In a medium saucepan over low heat, add the heavy cream and allow to heat through. Once warm, add to a large bowl.
- Split the vanilla beans and spoon out the seeds. Stir in the vanilla.
- In another mixing bowl, add the egg yolks and swerve sweetener. Mix well.
- Combine the egg mixture to the heavy cream and mix well.
- Strain the mixture to ramekins or custard cups.
- Add 2 cups of water and a trivet inside your Instant Pot. Place the ramekins on top and cover with aluminum foil.
- Lock the lid and cook at low pressure for 22 minutes. When the cooking is done, naturally release the pressure for 5 minutes, then quick release the remaining pressure. Remove the lid. Serve and enjoy!

Red Velvet Cake
Time: 40 minutes   Servings: 12

Ingredients:

- ¼ cup of butter, softened
- ½ cup of swerve sweetener or erythritol
- 4 large eggs
- 1 teaspoon of pure vanilla extract
- 2 tablespoons of unsweetened cocoa powder
- 1 teaspoon of baking powder

- 1 teaspoon of baking soda
- 2/3 cups of almond flour
- 1/3 cup of coconut flour
- ¼ cup of plain yogurt
- Red food coloring

Cream Cheese Frosting Ingredients:

- 1 (8-ounce) package of cream cheese, softened
- ¼ cup of unsalted butter, softened

- ¾ cups of powdered erythritol or other sweeteners
- ½ teaspoon of pure vanilla extract

Instructions:

- Grease a cake pan with nonstick cooking spray and add 2 cups of water.
- In a large bowl, add all the cake ingredients and beat until well combined.
- Pour the cake batter to the greased pan and tightly cover with aluminum foil.
- Place the cake pan on top of the trivet. Lock the lid and cook at high pressure for 35 minutes. When the cooking is done, naturally release the pressure and remove the lid.
- Check if the cake is done using a toothpick.
- In another bowl, add the cream cheese ingredients and stir until well combined. Spoon the frosting over the cake. Serve and enjoy!

Pumpkin Pie Spice Cupcakes
Time: 35 minutes   Servings: 6

Cupcake Ingredients:

- ½ cup of pureed pumpkin
- ½ cup of whey protein
- ½ cup of almond flour
- ½ cup of erythritol or swerve sweetener
- 1 teaspoon of baking powder or baking soda
- 1 teaspoon of cinnamon
- ½ teaspoon of allspice

- ¼ teaspoon of ground ginger
- ¼ teaspoon of cardamom powder
- ¼ teaspoon of nutmeg
- ¼ teaspoon of ground cloves
- ¼ cup of coconut oil
- 1 tablespoon of apple cider vinegar

Cream Cheese Frosting Ingredients:

- 1 (8-ounce) package of cream cheese
- ½ cup of heavy whipping cream

- ½ cup of powdered erythritol
- ½ teaspoon of pure vanilla extract

Instructions:

- In a large bowl, add all the cupcake ingredients and stir until well combined.
- In another bowl, add all the cream cheese ingredients and stir until well combined. Set aside.
- Grease 6 cupcake liners with nonstick cooking spray. Spoon the cupcake batter onto the liners.
- Add 1 cup of water and a steamer rack inside your Instant Pot. Add the cupcake liners on top of the steamer rack.
- Lock the lid and cook at high pressure for 25 minutes. When the cooking is done, naturally release the pressure for 10 minutes, then quick release the remaining pressure. Carefully remove the lid.
- Remove the cupcakes from your pot and spoon the cream cheese frosting on top. Serve and enjoy!

Chocolate Zucchini Muffin Bites
Time: 40 minutes   Servings: Around 24 to 30 muffins

Ingredients:

- 2 large organic eggs

- 1 cup of evaporated cane juice

- ½ cup of coconut oil
- 2 teaspoons of pure vanilla extract
- 1 tablespoon of unsalted butter
- 3 tablespoons of unsweetened cocoa powder
- 1 cup of almond flour
- ½ teaspoon of baking powder or baking soda

- ¼ teaspoon of fine sea salt
- ¾ teaspoon of ground cinnamon
- 1 cup of finely grated zucchini
- 1/3 cup of unsweetened chocolate chips
- 1 water (to build pressure)

Instructions:

- In a large bowl, add all the ingredients and beat until well combined.
- Add 1 cup of water and a trivet inside your Instant Pot. Spoon the batter into silicone muffin cups. Place on top of the trivet.
- Lock the lid and cook at high pressure for 8 minutes. When the cooking is done, naturally release the pressure and carefully remove the lid.
- Remove the cupcakes from your Instant Pot and check if muffin bites are done using a toothpick. Serve and enjoy!

Coconut Flour Cupcakes
Time: 30 minutes   Servings: 4

Cupcake Ingredients:

- ¼ cup of coconut flour
- ½ teaspoon of baking powder
- ¼ teaspoon of fine sea salt
- ½ teaspoon of pure vanilla extract
- ½ teaspoon of coconut extract

- 2 tablespoons of unsweetened non-dairy milk
- 3 tablespoons of unsalted butter, melted
- ¼ cup of powdered erythritol or swerve sweetener
- 3 large organic eggs
- 2 tablespoons of unsweetened coconut, shredded

Frosting Ingredients:

- ¼ cup of heavy whipping cream
- ¼ cup of unsalted butter, softened
- ½ teaspoon of pure vanilla extract
- ½-ounces of cream cheese, softened

- 2 tablespoons of powdered erythritol
- ¼ teaspoon of xanthan gum
- 12 drops of liquid stevia

Instructions:

- In a large bowl, dad all the cupcake ingredients and stir until well combined.
- Grease silicone cupcake liners with nonstick cooking spray. Add 1 cup of water and a trivet inside your Instant Pot.
- Spoon the cupcake batter onto the silicone cupcake liners.
- Place the cupcake liners on top of the trivet. Lock the lid and cook at high pressure for 9 minutes. When the cooking is done, remove the lid and allow to cool for 20 minutes.
- Meanwhile, add the frosting ingredients and stir until well combined. Spoon the frosting on top of the cupcakes. Serve and enjoy!

Chocolate Cupcakes with Vanilla Buttercream
Time: 20 minutes   Servings: 6

Cupcake Ingredients:

- 1 ¼ cup of coconut flour
- ¼ cup of unsweetened cocoa powder
- 2 teaspoons of baking powder
- ½ teaspoon of baking soda
- 1 teaspoon of fresh lime zest

- 2 large organic eggs
- ¼ cup of erythritol or swerve sweetener
- 3 tablespoons of unsalted butter, melted
- ½ teaspoon of pure vanilla extract
- A small pinch of fine sea salt

Vanilla Buttercream Ingredients:

- 1 cup of powdered erythritol or other powdered sweeteners
- 1/3 cup of unsalted butter, softened

- ½ teaspoon of pure vanilla extract
- 2 teaspoons of almond milk

Instructions:

- In a large bowl, add the coconut flour, cocoa powder, baking powder, baking soda, fine sea salt and erythritol. Mix until well combined.
- In another bowl, add the lime zest, eggs, butter and vanilla extract. Mix well.
- Pour the wet ingredients to the dry ingredients. Stir until well combined.
- Spoon the cupcake batter into greased cupcake liners.
- Add 1 cup of water and a trivet inside your Instant Pot. Lock the lid and cook at high pressure for 9 minutes. When the cooking is done, quick release the pressure and remove the lid. Remove the cupcakes from your Instant Pot and allow to cool for 20 minutes. Serve and enjoy!

Chocolate Mousse
Time: 30 minutes   Servings: 6

Ingredients:

- 4 egg yolks
- ½ cup of swerve sweetener
- ¼ cup of water
- ¼ cup of cacao powder

- 1 cup of heavy whipping cream
- ½ cup of non-dairy milk
- ¼ teaspoon of fine sea salt
- ½ teaspoon of pure vanilla extract

Instructions:

- In a bowl, add the egg yolks and whisk.
- In a saucepan over low heat, add the swerve sweetener, water and cacao powder. Whisk until melted.
- Add the heavy whipping cream and non-dairy milk. Allow to get heated through until warm.
- Stir in the sea salt and pure vanilla extract.
- In a bowl, add the eggs and 1 tablespoon of the chocolate mixture. Mix well.
- Whisk in the remaining chocolate mixture. Divide and pour the chocolate mixture into ramekins or mason jars.
- Add 1 ½ cup of water and a trivet inside your Instant Pot. Place the ramekins on top of the trivet and cover with aluminum foil.
- Lock the lid and cook at high pressure for 6 minutes. When the cooking is done, manually release the pressure and carefully remove the lid. Serve and enjoy!

Cinnamon Coffee and Sour Cream Cake
Time: 1 hour   Servings: 12

Cake Ingredients:

- 2 cups of almond flour
- 1 cup of erythritol or swerve sweetener
- 1 tablespoon of baking powder or baking soda
- 2 teaspoons of organic ground cinnamon
- 1 teaspoon of fine sea salt

- ¼ teaspoon of nutmeg
- ½ cup of unsalted butter, melted
- 1 cup of sour cream
- 2 large organic eggs

Streusel Topping Ingredients:

- 1 cup of almond flour
- ½ cup of coconut flour
- ½ cup of swerve sweetener

- ½ cup of pecans
- ½ cup of unsalted butter, thinly sliced
- ¼ teaspoon of fine sea salt

Instructions:

- In a small bowl, add all the streusel topping ingredients. Stir well or until well combined or resembles crumb-like consistency. Set aside.
- In a large mixing bowl, add all the cake ingredients and stir until well combined.
- Grease a cake pan that can fit inside your Instant Pot. Add the cake batter and gently press the streusel topping on top. Cover with aluminum foil.
- Add 2 cups of water and a trivet inside your Instant Pot. Lock the lid and cook at high pressure for 40 minutes.
- When the cooking is done, allow for a natural release for 10 minutes, then quick release the remaining pressure. Carefully remove the lid.
- Remove the cake from your Instant Pot and slice. Serve and enjoy!

Butternut Squash Cake

Time: 50 minutes   Servings: 8

Butternut Squash Cake Ingredients:

- 3 large organic eggs
- 1 ½ cup of erythritol or swerve sweetener
- ¾ cups of unsalted butter, softened
- ½ cups of walnuts, chopped
- 2 cups of shredded butternut squash
- ½ teaspoon of fine sea salt

- ½ teaspoon of ground ginger
- ½ teaspoon of cinnamon
- ½ teaspoon of fine sea salt
- 2 ½ cups of almond flour
- ¾ cups of buttermilk

Frosting Ingredients:

- ½ cup of unsalted butter, softened
- 4-ounces of cream cheese, softened
- 4 cups of powdered erythritol

- 2 to 4 tablespoons of non-dairy milk
- ½ cup of walnuts, chopped

Instructions:

- Grease a baking pan that fits inside your Instant Pot with nonstick cooking spray and line with parchment paper.
- Add 2 cups of water and a trivet inside your Instant Pot.
- In a large bowl, add all the butternut cake ingredients except for the squash and chopped walnuts. Stir until well combined and smooth. Gently stir in the squash along with the walnuts.
- Pour the batter onto the baking pan and place inside your Instant Pot. Lock the lid and cook at high pressure for 20 minutes.
- In a bowl, add all the frosting ingredients and stir until well smooth. Set aside.
- When the cooking is done, naturally release the pressure and carefully remove the lid.
- Gently spoon the frosting over the cake. Serve and enjoy!

Chocolate Pots De Crème

Time: 35 minutes   Servings: 6

Ingredients:

- 1 ½ cup of heavy whipping cream
- ½ cup of non-dairy milk
- 5 egg yolks from 5 large eggs
- ¼ cup of swerve sweetener or erythritol

- 8-ounces of unsweetened chocolate, melted
- A small pinch of fine sea salt
- A dollop of whipped cream (for decoration)
- Grated unsweetened chocolate (for decoration)

Instructions:

- In a saucepan over medium-low heat, add the heavy whipping cream and non-dairy milk. Bring to a simmer and remove from the heat.
- In a large bowl, add the egg yolks, sweetener and sea salt. Whisk well.
- Whisk in the cream mixture and the melted chocolate until well blended.
- Divide and pour the mixture into 6 custard cups or ramekins.
- Add 1 cup of water and a trivet inside your Instant Pot. Layer and place the custard cups on top of the trivet. Lock the lid and cook at high pressure for 6 minutes.
- When the cooking is done, naturally release the pressure for 15 minutes, then quick release the remaining pressure. Carefully remove the lid.
- Remove the custard cups and top with the whipped cream and grated chocolate. Serve and enjoy!

Lime Curd

Time: 10 minutes   Servings: Around 20 ounces

Ingredients:

- 6 tablespoons of unsalted butter, softened
- 1 cup of erythritol
- 2 large eggs

- 2 large egg yolks
- 2/3 cups of freshly squeezed lime juice
- 2 teaspoons of fresh lime zest

Instructions:

- In a food processor, add the butter and erythritol. Pulse until well combined.
- Gradually add the eggs and egg yolks into the food processor and blend for 1 minute.
- Add and blend the lime juice.
- Divide and add the mixture to three mason jars. Cover with aluminum foil.
- Add 2 cups of water and a trivet inside your Instant Pot. Place the mason jars on top.
- Lock the lid and cook at high pressure for 10 minutes.
- When the cooking is done, naturally release the pressure for 10 minutes, then quick release the remaining pressure. Carefully remove the lid.
- Remove the mason jars from your Instant Pot and stir in the lime zest. Add the lids and place inside your refrigerator. It will take around 20 minutes or until the curd thickens.

Coconut Custard
Time: 35 minutes   Servings: 4

Ingredients:

- 1 cup of unsweetened coconut milk
- 3 large eggs
- 1/3 cup of swerve sweetener or erythritol

Instructions:

- In a blender, add the eggs, coconut milk and sweetener. Blend until well combined.
- Pour the contents into a heat-safe bowl that will fit inside your Instant Pot. Tightly cover with a sheet of aluminum foil.
- Add 2 cups of water and a trivet inside your Instant Pot. Place the bowl on top of the trivet.
- Lock the lid and cook at high pressure for 30 minutes. When done, naturally release the pressure and remove the lid.
- Place the mason jars inside your refrigerator and allow 20 hours to thicken. Serve and enjoy!

Blueberry Crisp
Time: 30 minutes   Servings: 4

Ingredients:

- 4 cups of blueberries, fresh or frozen
- 1 cup of pecans
- ½ cup of almond meal
- 4 tablespoons of unsalted butter, softened
- 4 tablespoons of swerve sweetener or erythritol
- 4 tablespoons of ground flax
- 1 teaspoon of cinnamon
- 1 teaspoon of pure vanilla extract
- ½ teaspoon of fine sea salt
- 1 cup of water

Instructions:

- In a food processor, add all the ingredients except for the blueberries and water. Pulse until well combined and crumbled.
- Divide and add the blueberries to 4 ramekins. Top with the pecan mixture.
- Add 1 cup of water and a trivet inside your Instant Pot. Place the ramekins on top of the rack and cover with aluminum foil.
- Lock the lid and cook at high pressure for 10 minutes.
- When the cooking is done, naturally release the pressure for 10 minutes, then quick release the remaining pressure. Carefully remove the lid. Serve and enjoy!

White Chocolate Bundt Cake
Time: 1 hour and 30 minutes   Servings: 4

Ingredients:

- ½ teaspoon of baking powder or baking soda
- ½ cup + 1 tablespoon of almond flour
- A small pinch of fine sea salt
- 1/3 cup of Swerve sweetener or erythritol
- 1 large egg
- 1 teaspoon of pure vanilla extract
- ¼ teaspoon of almond extract
- 2-ounces of unsweetened white chocolate, melted
- ¼ cup of sour cream

- 1-ounce of cherries, finely chopped
- 5 tablespoons of unsalted butter

Instructions:

- Add 1 cup of water and a trivet inside your Instant Pot.
- Grease a half-size bundt cake with nonstick cooking spray.
- In a bowl, add all the ingredients and beat until well combined.
- Transfer the batter to the bundt cake pan and tightly cover with aluminum foil. Place on top of the trivet. Lock the lid and cook at high pressure for 25 minutes.
- When the cooking is done, quick release the pressure and carefully remove the lid.
- Remove the cake from the bundt pan and allow to cool. Serve and enjoy!

Pecan Chocolate Chip Cake

Time: 35 minutes   Servings: 6

Cake Ingredients:

- 2 cups of almond flour or coconut flour
- 1/3 cup of sour cream
- ¼ cup of coconut oil
- ¼ cup of cold water
- 1 tablespoon of truvia low-carb brown sugar
- 2 large eggs
- ½ cup of pecans, chopped
- ½ cup of unsweetened chocolate chips

Chocolate Topping Ingredients:

- ½ cup of unsweetened chocolate chips
- 3 tablespoons of heavy cream

Instructions:

- In a large bowl, add all the cake ingredients except for the chopped pecan and chocolate chips. Stir until well combined.
- Grease a half size bundt cake pan with nonstick cooking spray and add all the cake ingredients except for the chopped pecan and chocolate chips. Stir until well combined.
- Pour the cake batter to the bundt pan and tightly cover with aluminum foil.
- Add 1 cup of water and a trivet inside your Instant Pot. Place the bundt pan on top of the trivet.
- Lock the lid and cook at high pressure for 25 minutes. When the cooking is done, naturally release the pressure for 15 minutes, then quick release the remaining pressure. Carefully remove the lid.
- Remove the cake from the bundt pan.
- In a small bowl, add the chocolate chips and 1 tablespoon of heavy cream. Microwave for 30 seconds.
- Add the remaining tablespoons of heavy cream and mix until smooth. Spoon the topping on top of the cake. Serve and enjoy!

Turtle Cheesecake

Time: 40 minutes   Servings: 6

Crust Ingredients:

- 1 ½ cup of pecans, roughly chopped
- 2 tablespoons of almond flour
- ¼ cup of erythritol or swerve sweetener
- 1 teaspoon of cinnamon
- 6 tablespoons of unsalted butter, melted

Filling Ingredients:

- 2 (8-ounce) package of cream cheese, softened
- 2/3 cups of swerve sweetener or erythritol
- 2 large eggs
- ¼ cup of sour cream
- 1 teaspoon of pure vanilla extract
- ½ cup of pecans

Instructions:

- In a food processor, add the pecans and pulse until fine.
- Add the almond flour, erythritol, cinnamon and unsalted butter. Continue to pulse until well combined.
- Line a springform pan with parchment paper and grease with parchment paper.
- Add the almond mixture to the pan and press firmly down.
- In a large bowl, add the filling ingredients except for the pecans and stir until well combined.
- Add the filling ingredient into the cake pan. Cover with aluminum foil.
- Add 2 cups of water and a trivet inside your Instant Pot. Place the cake pan on top.

- Lock the lid and cook at high pressure for 35 minutes. When the cooking is done, naturally release the pressure and remove the lid.
- Remove the cake from your Instant Pot and remove the aluminum foil.. Top with the pecans.
- Place inside your refrigerator and allow to cool. Serve and enjoy!

Chocolate Birthday Cake with Buttercream
Time: 40 minutes   Servings: 6

Cake Ingredients:

- ½ cup of unsweetened dark chocolate, roughly chopped
- 2 large organic eggs
- ½ cup of coconut cream
- 2 tablespoons of unsweetened cacao powder
- ½ cup of coconut flour or almond flour
- 2 teaspoons of baking powder
- ¼ teaspoon of fine sea salt
- 30 drops of liquid stevia (more or less if necessary)

Vanilla Buttercream Ingredients:

- ½ pound of unsalted butter, softened
- 3 scoops of MCT powder
- 1 teaspoon of pure vanilla extract

Instructions:

- Line a 7-inch cake pan with parchment paper and grease with nonstick cooking spray.
- In a microwavable safe bowl, add the chocolate and microwave for 30 seconds. Add the coconut cream and stir until smooth.
- In a large bowl, add the chocolate and cake ingredients. Stir until well combined.
- Transfer the cake batter to the cake pan and cover with aluminum foil.
- Add 2 cups of water and a trivet inside your Instant Pot. Place the cake pan on top of the trivet.
- Lock the lid and cook at high pressure for 35 minutes. When the cooking is done, naturally release the pressure and carefully remove the lid. Remove the cake from the pan and allow to cool.
- In another bowl, add all the vanilla buttercream ingredients and gently blend. Spread the buttercream on the cake. Serve and enjoy!

Carrot Cake
Time: 1 hour and 5 minutes   Servings: 10

Cake Ingredients:

- 3 cups of almond flour or coconut flour
- 1 ½ cups of powdered erythritol or swerve sweetener
- 2 teaspoons of baking powder
- 2 teaspoons of organic cinnamon powder
- ½ teaspoon of fine sea salt
- 6 large organic eggs
- ½ cup of unsalted butter, melted
- ¼ cup of unsweetened almond milk or coconut milk
- 2 cups of carrots, finely grated
- 2 teaspoons of pure vanilla extract

Frosting Ingredients:

- 1 (8-ounce) package of cream cheese, softened
- 3 tablespoons of Greek yogurt
- 1/3 cups of powdered erythritol

Instructions:

- In a bowl, add the almond flour, erythritol, baking powder, cinnamon powder, and sea salt. Stir until well combined.
- In a second bowl, add the eggs, butter, almond milk, grated carrots and vanilla extract. Stir until well combined.
- Add the wet ingredients to the dry ingredients and stir until smooth.
- Line a springform pan with parchment paper and grease with nonstick cooking spray. Grease with nonstick cooking spray.
- Add 2 cups of water and a trivet inside your Instant Pot. Place the cake on top of the trivet and cover with aluminum foil.
- Lock the lid and cook at high pressure for 20 minutes. When the cooking is done, naturally release the pressure and remove the lid. Carefully remove the cake from the cake pan and allow to cool.

- In another bowl, add all the cream cheese, Greek yogurt and powdered erythritol. Beat until smooth and spread evenly on the cake. Serve and enjoy!

Caramel Cake
Time: 50 minutes   Servings: 12

Cake Ingredients:

- 2 ½ cups of almond flour
- ¼ cups of coconut flour
- ¼ cups of unflavored whey protein powder
- 1 tablespoon of baking powder
- ½ teaspoon of fine sea salt
- 2/3 cups of swerve sweetener or erythritol
- ½ cup of unsalted butter, softened
- 1 teaspoon of pure vanilla extract
- ¾ cups of unsweetened almond milk
- 4 large organic eggs,

Caramel Sauce Ingredients:

- ¼ cup of butter
- 3 tablespoons of truvia low-carb brown sugar
- 3 tablespoons of Bocha sweet
- 2 tablespoons of water
- ¼ teaspoon of fine sea salt
- ¼ teaspoon of xanthan gum
- ½ cup of heavy whipping cream

Instructions:

- To make the caramel sauce: In a medium saucepan over medium-high heat, add all the caramel sauce ingredients and bring to a boil. Stir well until thickened. Refrigerate and set aside.
- Line a 7-inch springform pan with parchment paper and grease with nonstick cooking spray.
- In a large bowl, add all the cake ingredients and beat until well combined. Add the batter to the springform pan and spread. Cover with aluminum foil.
- Add 2 cups of water and a trivet inside your Instant Pot. Place the cake on top and lock the lid. Cook at high pressure for 35 minutes. When the cooking is done, naturally release the pressure and remove the lid. Remove the cake from your Instant Pot and allow to cool.
- Gently spread the caramel sauce over the cake. Serve and enjoy!

Chocolate Lava Cake
Time: 10 minutes   Servings: 2

Ingredients:

- 4 tablespoons of unsweetened cocoa powder
- 2 tablespoons of granulated erythritol
- A small pinch of fine sea salt
- 2 tablespoons of heavy whipping cream
- ¼ teaspoon of pure vanilla extract
- 2 organic pasteurized eggs
- 2 tablespoons of unsalted butter, melted
- ½ teaspoon of baking powder

Instructions:

- Grease 2 ramekins with nonstick cooking spray. Add 2 cups of water and a trivet inside your Instant Pot.
- In a medium bowl, add the unsweetened cocoa powder, erythritol, baking powder and fine sea salt. Stir well.
- In another bowl, add the melted butter, heavy whipping cream, vanilla extract and eggs. Mix well.
- Combine the wet ingredients with the dry ingredients. Stir until smooth.
- Divide the batter and pour into two ramekins. Cover with aluminum foil and place on the trivet.
- Lock the lid and cook at high pressure for 4 minutes. When the cooking is done, quick release the pressure and remove the lid. Serve and enjoy!

Brownie Cups
Time: 35 minutes   Servings: 4

Ingredients:

- 2/3 cups of sugar-free chocolate chips
- 6 tablespoons of salted butter
- 3 large organic eggs
- 2/3 cups of erythritol
- 3 ½ tablespoons of almond flour or coconut flour
- 1 teaspoon of pure vanilla extract

Instructions:

- Grease 4 ramekins with nonstick cooking spray and set aside.
- In a small saucepan over medium-low heat, add the butter and chocolate chips. Stir until well melted. Remove and set aside.
- In a large bowl, add all the ingredients and gently blend until well combined.
- Divide and fill the ramekins halfway full. Add 2 cups of water and a trivet inside your Instant Pot. Place the ramekins on top and cover with foil.
- Lock the lid and cook at high pressure for 9 minutes. When done, quick release the pressure and remove the lid. Remove the ramekins and allow to cool. Serve and enjoy!

Molten Brownie Pudding
Time: 50 minutes   Servings: 4

Ingredients:

- 1 ½ cup of water
- 7 tablespoons of unsalted butter, melted
- 1 cup of erythritol or swerve sweetener
- 2 large organic eggs
- ¼ cup of almond flour

- ¼ cup + 2 tablespoons of unsweetened cocoa powder
- 1 teaspoon of pure vanilla extract
- ½ cup of unsweetened chocolate chips
- A small pinch of fine sea salt

Instructions:

- Add 1 ½ cup of water and a trivet inside your Instant Pot.
- Spread 1 tablespoon of butter onto a baking or soufflé dish.
- In a large bowl, add the 6 tablespoons of butter, erythritol, eggs, almond flour, cocoa powder, pure vanilla extract, fine sea salt. Beat until well combined.
- Transfer the mixture to the dish and top with the unsweetened chocolate chips.
- Place on top of the trivet and cover with aluminum foil.
- Lock the lid and cook at high pressure for 30 minutes. When the cooking is done, manually release the pressure and remove the lid. Serve and enjoy!

Nutella Lava Cakes
Time: 2 minutes   Servings: 2

Ingredients:

- 1 large organic egg
- 1 egg yolk
- 2 tablespoons of erythritol or swerve sweetener

- 1/3 cup of Nutella spread
- 2 tablespoons of almond flour

Instructions:

- In a medium bowl, add the egg and egg yolk. Whisk well until smooth.
- Whisk in the erythritol or swerve sweetener.
- Add the Nutella spread and continue to whisk until smooth. Whisk in the flour or until smooth.
- Grease 2 ramekins with nonstick cooking spray and add the batter.
- Pour 1 cup of water and add a trivet inside your Instant Pot. Place the ramekins on top of the trivet. Cover with aluminum foil. Lock the lid and cook at high pressure for 9 minutes. When the cooking is done, quick release the pressure and remove the lid. Serve and enjoy!

Fudgy Chocolate Brownies
Time: 50 minutes   Servings: 8

Ingredients:

- ½ cup of unsalted butter, melted
- 2/3 cups of swerve sweetener or erythritol
- 3 large organic eggs
- ½ teaspoon of pure vanilla extract

- ½ cup of almond flour
- 1/3 cup of unsweetened cocoa powder
- 1 tablespoon of gelatin
- ½ teaspoon of baking powder

- ¼ teaspoon of fine sea salt
- ¼ cup of water
- 1/3 cups of unsweetened chocolate chips

Instructions:

- In a large bowl, add all the ingredients and stir until well combined.
- Grease a baking pan that fits inside your Instant Pot and line with parchment paper.
- Add the brownie batter to the baking pan and cover with aluminum foil.
- Pour 1 cup of water and a trivet inside your Instant Pot. Place the baking pan on top. Lock the lid and cook at high pressure for 40 minutes. When the cooking is done, naturally release the pressure for 10 minutes, then quick release the remaining pressure. Carefully remove the lid. Slice into servings and allow to cool. Serve and enjoy!

Keto Orange Semolina Cake
Time: 50 minutes   Servings: 8

Cake Ingredients:

- 1 cup of fine semolina
- ½ cup of erythritol or swerve sweetener
- 1 teaspoon of cardamom powder
- ½ cup of non-dairy yogurt
- ¾ cups of non-dairy milk
- 3 tablespoons of unsalted butter, melted
- ½ teaspoon of baking powder
- ½ teaspoon of baking soda
- 1 tablespoon of almonds, sliced
- 1 tablespoon of pistachios, sliced
- ¼ teaspoon of fresh orange zest

Orange Syrup Ingredients:

- 1 orange, juice and zest
- ½ cup of water
- ½ cup of Swerve sweetener and erythritol

Instructions:

- Grease a 6-inch cake pan with nonstick cooking spray.
- Add 2 cups of water and a trivet inside your Instant Pot. Press the "Sauté" setting on your Instant Pot and allow the water to be heated.
- In a large bowl, add the semolina, erythritol and cardamom powder. Stir until well combined. Stir in the non-dairy yogurt and non-dairy milk. Mix well. Finally, stir in the melted butter. Allow the cake batter to sit for 10 minutes.
- Once the time is up, mix in the baking soda, baking powder and the orange zest.
- Transfer the cake batter to the greased pan. Cover with aluminum foil. Place on top of the trivet. Lock the lid and press the "Steam" setting and set the time to 22 minutes. When the timer beeps, remove the lid.
- In a saucepan over medium heat, add the orange juice, orange zest, and swerve sweetener. Bring to a boil and stir until well combined. Reduce the heat and allow to cook for a couple more minutes, stirring frequently.
- Pour the syrup over the cake. Serve and enjoy!

Crème Brulee
Time: 15 minutes   Servings: 6

Ingredients:

- 2 cups of heavy whipping cream
- 6 egg yolks
- 5 tablespoons of erythritol
- 1 tablespoon of pure vanilla extract

Instructions:

- In a bowl, add all the ingredients and stir until well combined.
- Add the mixture into 6 small ramekins and cover with aluminum foil.
- Add 1 cup of water and place a trivet inside your Instant Pot. Place the ramekins on top of the trivet.
- Lock the lid and cook at high pressure for 9 minutes. When done, naturally release the pressure and remove the lid.
- Remove the lid and allow to cool. Serve and enjoy!

Mini Chocolate Cake

Time: 15 minutes   Servings: 2

Ingredients:

- 2 tablespoons of Splenda, stevia or other keto-friendly sweeteners
- 2 large organic eggs
- 2 tablespoons of organic heavy cream or unsweetened coconut cream
- ½ teaspoon of baking soda or baking powder
- 1 teaspoon of pure vanilla extract
- ¼ cup of unsweetened cocoa powder

Instructions:

- In a small bowl, add the unsweetened cocoa powder, Splenda and baking soda. Mix well.
- Stir in the eggs, heavy cream and vanilla extract.
- Grease 2 ramekins with nonstick cooking spray.
- Distribute and fill each ramekin with the mixture.
- Add 1 cup of water and a trivet to your Instant Pot. Place the ramekins on top and cover with aluminum foil.
- Close and seal the lid; cook at high pressure for 9 minutes.
- When your Instant Pot beeps, quick release the pressure and remove the lid.
- Carefully remove the ramekins and allow to cool. Serve and enjoy!

Part 9: Vegetarian and Vegan Recipes

Unbelievable Zucchini with Avocado Sauce
Time: 15 minutes   Servings: 4

Ingredients:

- 2 pounds of zucchini, chopped
- 2 avocados, chopped
- Juice from 1 lime
- 1 shallot, chopped
- 2 garlic cloves, minced
- 1 cup of water
- 2 Tablespoons coconut oil
- ¼ cup fresh basil, chopped
- 1 teaspoon salt (to taste)
- 1 teaspoon fresh ground black pepper (to taste)

Instructions:

1. Press Sauté mode on Instant Pot. Heat the coconut oil.
2. Sauté garlic and shallots for 1 minute. Press Keep Warm/Cancel setting to stop Sauté mode.
3. Add zucchini, avocado, basil, salt, and black pepper. Stir well. Add the water. Stir well.
4. Close and seal lid. Press Manual setting. Cook at High Pressure for 5 minutes.
5. Quick-release or naturally release pressure. Open the lid with care. Stir ingredients.
6. Allow to cool down or refrigerate overnight.

Awesome Vegan Patties
Time: 15 minutes   Servings: 2

Ingredients:

- 2 cups mushrooms, chopped
- 1 onion, chopped
- 2 garlic cloves, minced
- 1 cup vegetable broth
- 1 Tablespoon ghee, melted
- 2 Tablespoons fresh basil, chopped
- 1 Tablespoon fresh oregano, chopped
- 1 teaspoon salt
- 1 teaspoon fresh ground black pepper
- 1 teaspoon fresh ginger, grated
- 2 ketogenic hamburger buns (to serve)
- 1 cup mixed lettuce (topping)

Instructions:

1. Press Sauté button on Instant Pot. Cover trivet in foil.
2. Add melted ghee, garlic cloves, onion, mushrooms, and ginger. Sauté until vegetables become translucent. Press Keep Warm/Cancel setting to stop Sauté mode.
3. Add vegetable stock, basil, oregano, salt, and black pepper. Stir well.
4. Close and seal lid. Press Manual switch. Cook at High Pressure for 6 minutes.
5. Quick-release pressure when the timer goes off,. Allow to cool.
6. Mash ingredients with a fork or masher until smooth when cooled off. Form into patties.
7. Pour 2 cups of water in Instant Pot. Place trivet inside. Place patties on trivet.
8. Close and seal lid. Press Manual button. Cook at High Pressure for 7 minutes. Serve.

Scrumptious Brussels Sprouts
Time: 15 minutes   Servings: 4

Ingredients:

- 1 pound Brussels sprouts
- 2 Tablespoons coconut oil
- 1 teaspoon salt
- 1 teaspoon fresh ground black pepper

Instructions:

1. Add 2 cups of water in Instant Pot. Place trivet in Instant Pot. Place steamer basket on top.
2. Add Brussels sprouts to steamer basket. Drizzle with coconut oil; sprinkle with salt and black pepper. Close and seal lid. Press Manual switch. Cook at High Pressure for 7 minutes.
3. When done, quickly release pressure. Open the lid with care. Serve.

Wonderful Eggplant Lasagna
Time: 30 minutes   Servings: 4

Ingredients:

- 1 pound of eggplant, sliced
- 4 garlic cloves, minced
- 2 Tablespoons coconut oil
- Juice from 1 lemon
- 1 cup vegetable broth
- 6 cups low-carb tomato sauce
- 1 cup mozzarella cheese, shredded
- 1 cup parmesan cheese, grated
- 1 cup ricotta cheese
- 1 Tablespoon fresh basil leaves, chopped
- 1 Tablespoon fresh oregano, chopped
- 1 Tablespoon paprika
- 1 teaspoon salt
- 1 teaspoon fresh ground black pepper

Instructions:

1. Grease a baking dish with non-stick cooking spray.
2. In a bowl, combine the cheeses and herbs.
3. In a separate bowl, add and season the eggplants with garlic cloves, lemon juice, paprika, salt, and black pepper.
4. Layer baking dish with eggplant slices, tomato sauce. Sprinkle mixed cheeses. Repeat.
5. Cover baking dish with aluminum foil.
6. Add 2 cups of water. Place trivet in Instant Pot. Place dish on trivet.
7. Close and seal lid. Press Manual switch. Cook at High Pressure for 25 minutes.
8. When done, naturally release or quickly release pressure. Open the lid with care. Serve.

Won't Know it's Vegan Chili
Time: 35 minutes   Servings: 4

Ingredients:

- 1 eggplant, chopped
- 1 jalapeno, chopped
- 1 red bell pepper, chopped
- 1 green bell pepper, chopped
- 1 zucchini, chopped
- 4 garlic cloves, minced
- 1 onion, chopped
- ½ pound mushrooms, chopped
- 2 Tablespoons coconut oil
- 2 cups vegetable broth
- 1 can (6-ounce) tomato paste
- 1 can (14-oucne) diced tomatoes
- 1 Tablespoon Chili powder
- 1 teaspoon ground cumin
- 1 teaspoon salt (to taste)
- 1 teaspoon fresh ground black pepper (to taste)

Instructions:

1. Press Sauté button on Instant Pot. Heat the coconut oil.
2. Add eggplant, jalapeno, bell peppers, zucchinis, garlic cloves, onion, and mushrooms. Sauté until vegetables become soft.
3. Press Keep Warm/Cancel setting to stop Sauté mode. Add tomato paste. Stir well.
4. Add vegetable broth, diced tomatoes, and seasonings. Stir well.
5. Close and seal lid. Press Bean/Chili button. Cook for 30 minutes. Naturally release or quick-release pressure when complete. Stir chili. Adjust seasoning if necessary. Serve.

Buddha's Tofu and Broccoli Delight
Time: 15 minutes   Servings: 4

Ingredients:

- 1 pound of tofu, extra firm, chopped into cubes
- 1 broccoli head, chopped into florets
- 1 onion, chopped
- 1 carrot, chopped
- 4 garlic cloves, minced
- 2 Tablespoons low-carb brown sugar
- 1 Tablespoon fresh ginger, grated
- 1 Tablespoon rice vinegar
- 1 cup vegetable broth
- 2 scallions, chopped
- 2 Tablespoons coconut oil
- 1 teaspoon salt (to taste)
- 1 teaspoon fresh ground black pepper (to taste)

Instructions:

1. Press Sauté button on Instant Pot. Heat the coconut oil.
2. Sauté garlic and onion for 2 minutes. Add broccoli florets and tofu. Sauté for 3 minutes.

3. Press Keep Warm/Cancel button to end Sauté mode. Add remaining ingredients. Stir well.
4. Close and seal lid. Press Manual setting. Cook at High Pressure for 6 minutes.
5. When the timer beeps, quick-release pressure. Open the lid with care. Serve.

Special Spicy Almond Tofu

Time: 25 minutes   Servings: 4

Ingredients:

- 1 pound extra firm tofu, chopped into cubes
- 1 cauliflower head, chopped into florets
- 1 broccoli head, chopped into florets
- 1 cup almonds, roughly chopped
- 2 Tablespoons low-carb soy sauce
- 2 Tablespoons green Chili Sauce

- 2 Tablespoons coconut oil
- 1 teaspoon garlic powder
- 1 teaspoon onion powder
- 1 teaspoon salt (to taste)
- 1 teaspoon fresh ground black pepper (to taste)

Instructions:

1. Press Sauté button on Instant Pot. Heat the coconut oil.
2. Add tofu, cauliflower florets, and broccoli florets. Sauté until fork tender.
3. Press Keep Warm/Cancel setting to end Sauté mode.
4. Add remaining ingredients to Instant Pot. Stir well.
5. Close and seal lid. Press Manual switch. Cook at High Pressure for 10 minutes.
6. When the timer beeps, naturally release or quickly release pressure. Open the lid with care. Stir ingredients. Serve.

Fresh Garlic and Sweet Potato Mash

Time: 20 minutes   Servings: 4

Ingredients:

- 2 pounds sweet potatoes, chopped
- 1 head cauliflower, chopped into florets
- 4 garlic cloves, minced
- 2 TablespCauliflower oons coconut oil

- 1 teaspoon salt (to taste)
- 1 teaspoon fresh ground black pepper (to taste)
- 2 cups of water

Instructions:

1. Press Sauté button on Instant Pot. Heat the coconut oil.
2. Sauté sweet potatoes, cauliflower, and garlic. Sauté until almost tender.
3. Press Keep Warm/Cancel button to end Sauté mode. Add the water to your ingredients.
4. Close and seal lid. Press Manual switch. Cook at High Pressure for 10 minutes.
5. When the timer beeps, quick-release pressure. Mash ingredients in Pot until smooth.
6. Serve.

Everyday Bold Beet and Caper Salad

Servings: 2   Time: 30 minutes

Ingredients:

- 4 beets, sliced
- 4 carrots, sliced
- 1 cup pine nuts, chopped

- 2 Tablespoons rice wine vinegar
- 1 cup of water

Dressi

ng Ingredients:

- 1 Tablespoon coconut oil, melted and cooled
- ¼ cup fresh parsley, chopped
- 2 garlic cloves, minced

- 2 Tablespoons capers
- 4-ounces goat cheese, crumbled
- 1 teaspoon salt
- 1 teaspoon fresh ground black pepper

Instructions:

1. Pour 1 cup of water in Instant Pot. Place a trivet inside; place steamer basket on top.

2. Add sliced beets, pine nuts, and carrots to steamer basket.
3. Drizzle with rice wine vinegar.
4. Close and seal lid. Press Manual setting. Cook at High Pressure for 20 minutes.
5. As it cooks, in a large bowl, combine dressing ingredients. Stir well. Set aside.
6. When done, naturally release pressure. Open the lid with care.
7. In a large bowl, combine the beets and carrots with dressing. Stir until coated. Serve.

Fragrant Zucchini Mix
Servings: 4   Time: 15 minutes

Ingredients:

- 2 pounds zucchini, roughly chopped
- 1 broccoli head, chopped into florets
- 1 red onion, chopped
- 2 garlic cloves, minced
- 2 Tablespoons coconut oil

- 1 cup of water
- 2 cups fresh basil, chopped
- 1 teaspoon salt (to taste)
- 1 teaspoon fresh ground black pepper (to tastes)

Instructions:

1. Press Sauté button on Instant Pot. Heat the coconut oil. Sauté onion and garlic for 1 minute.
2. Add broccoli florets and zucchini. Sauté until the vegetables become soft.
3. Press Keep Warm/Cancel setting to end Sauté mode.
4. Add remaining ingredients to vegetables. Stir well.
5. Close and seal lid. Press Manual switch. Cook at High Pressure for 7 minutes.
6. When the timer goes off, quick-release pressure. Open the lid with care. Serve.

Not Your Average Mushroom Risotto
Time: 15 minutes   Servings: 2

Ingredients:

- 2 pounds cremini mushrooms, chopped
- 1 pound extra firm tofu, chopped into cubes
- Bunch of baby spinach, freshly chopped
- 1 Tablespoon ghee
- 1 Tablespoon nutritional yeast
- 4 garlic cloves, minced
- ⅓ cup parmesan cheese, shredded
- 1 red onion, chopped

- 2 Tablespoons coconut oil
- ¼ cup dry white wine
- 3 cups vegetable broth
- Zest and juice from 1 lemon
- 1 teaspoon fresh thyme, chopped
- 1 teaspoon salt (to taste)
- 1 teaspoon fresh ground black pepper (to taste)

Instructions:

1. Press Sauté button on Instant Pot. Melt the ghee. Sauté garlic and onion for 1 minute.
2. Add tofu and mushrooms. Cook until softened. Press Keep Warm/Cancel button to end Sauté mode. Add remaining ingredients. Stir well.
3. Close and seal lid. Press Manual setting. Cook at High Pressure for 8 minutes.
4. Quick-Release the pressure when done. Open the lid with care. Serve.

Classic Deviled Eggs
Time: 35 minutes   Servings: 6

Ingredients:

- 1 (8-ounce) package of cream cheese, softened
- ½ cup of sugar-free pizza sauce

- 1 cup of mozzarella cheese, shredded
- ½ teaspoon of dried basil

Instructions:

- Add the cream cheese to the bottom of a baking dish that will fit inside your Instant Pot.
- Spread the pizza sauce and sprinkle with the shredded cheese. Add the dried basil.
- Add 2 cups of water and a trivet inside your Instant Pot. Place the dish on top of the trivet and cover with aluminum foil.

- Lock the lid and cook at high pressure for 20 minutes. When the cooking is done, quick release the pressure and remove the lid. Serve and enjoy!

Sausage Queso

Time: 40 minutes   Servings: 8

Ingredients:

- 1 pound of ground sausage
- 1 tablespoon of extra-virgin olive oil
- 1 large jalapeno pepper, seeds removed and finely chopped
- 1 (12-ounce) can of low-carb beer

- 1 (10-ounce) can of diced tomatoes with green chilies
- 2 cups of cheddar cheese, shredded
- 2 cups of Monterey jack cheese, shredded
- 1 teaspoon of chili powder or cayenne pepper
- ½ teaspoon of ground cumin

Instructions:

- Press the "Sauté" setting on your Instant Pot and add the olive oil. Once hot, add the chopped onions and jalapeno. Cook for 3 minutes, stirring frequently.
- Add the chili powder and cumin and cook for another 2 minutes, stirring occasionally. Transfer the contents to a plate lined with paper towels and set aside.
- Add the ground sausage and cook until brown and no longer pink. Turn off the "Sauté" setting. Discard the grease and clean your Instant Pot otherwise, the queso will come out brown.
- Add the onions and sausage to your Instant Pot. Stir in the beer and diced tomatoes. Lock the lid and cook at high pressure for 5 minutes. When the cooking is done, naturally release the pressure for 5 minutes, then quick release the remaining pressure. Carefully remove the lid.
- Stir in the shredded cheddar cheese and shredded Monterey jack cheese. Stir until the cheese has melted. Serve and enjoy!

Buffalo Ranch Chicken Dip

Time: 45 minutes   Servings: 8

Ingredients:

- 3 boneless, skinless chicken breasts
- 1 (8-ounce) package of cream cheese, softened
- 1 cup of buffalo sauce

- 1 ½ cup of cheddar cheese, shredded
- Fine sea salt and freshly cracked black pepper (to taste)

Instructions:

- Add all the ingredients inside your Instant Pot. Lock the lid and cook at high pressure for 15 minutes.
- When the cooking has done, quick release the pressure and remove the lid.
- Transfer the chicken to a cutting board and shred using two forks. Return the shredded chicken to your Instant Pot and stir until well combined. Serve and enjoy!

Cauliflower Salad

Time: 30 minutes   Servings: 5

Ingredients:

- 1 head of cauliflower, chopped
- 4 large hard-boiled eggs
- 1 to 1 ½ cup of plain Greek yogurt
- 1 tablespoon of white wine vinegar
- 1 tablespoon of yellow mustard

- 2 celery stalks, chopped
- ½ small onion, finely chopped
- 1 cup of water
- Fine sea salt and freshly cracked black pepper (to taste)

Instructions:

- Prepare your eggs by hard boiling either on a saucepan or inside your Instant Pot. Peel and chop.
- Add 1 cup of water and a steamer basket inside your Instant Pot. Add the cauliflower inside.
- Lock the lid and cook at high pressure for 5 minutes. When the cooking is done, quick release the pressure and remove the lid.

- Transfer the cauliflower to a large bowl along with the remaining ingredients. Stir until well combined. Serve and enjoy!

Garlic Parmesan Zoodles
Time: 5 minutes   Servings: 4

Ingredients:

- 2 summer squash, peeled and spiralized
- 2 large zucchinis, peeled and spiralized
- 1 tablespoon of extra-virgin olive oil
- 2 medium garlic cloves, minced
- 2 cups of grape tomatoes, halved

- 1 bunch of fresh basil, torn
- 2 tablespoons of parmesan cheese, grated
- 2 tablespoons of pine nuts
- ½ teaspoon of fine sea salt
- ½ teaspoon of freshly cracked black pepper

Instructions:

- Press the "Sauté" setting on your Instant Pot and add the olive oil. Once hot, add the minced garlic and sauté for 1 minute or until fragrant, stirring frequently.
- Add the spiralized zucchini and spiralized squash. Stir until the spiralized zoodles are coated with the garlic and olive oil.
- Turn off the "Sauté" setting on your Instant Pot. Stir in the remaining ingredients until well combined. Serve and enjoy!

Thai Tofu Red Curry
Time: 20 minutes   Servings: 4

Ingredients:

- 1 (14-ounce) package of extra-firm tofu, drained and cut into cubes
- 2 tablespoons of coconut oil
- 2 to 3 tablespoons of Thai red curry paste
- 1 (14-ounce) can of full-fat coconut milk

- 1 bell pepper, cubed
- 1 small onion, finely chopped
- 2 medium limes, juiced
- Fine sea salt and freshly cracked black pepper (to taste)

Instructions:

- Press the "Sauté" setting on your Instant Pot and add the coconut oil.
- Once hot, add the Thai red curry paste. Sauté for 2 minutes.
- Pour in the coconut milk and mix until well combined. Continue to cook for 2 to 3 minutes.
- Press the "Sauté" setting on your Instant Pot and mixed in the remaining ingredients.
- Lock the lid and cook at low pressure for 3 minutes. When the cooking is done, quick release the pressure and carefully remove the lid. Serve and enjoy on top with cauliflower.

Ratatouille
Time: 40 minutes   Servings: 8

Ingredients:

- 3 cups of eggplants, cut into ¼-inch pieces
- 3 cups of zucchini, cut into ¼-inch pieces
- 6 medium garlic cloves, peeled and minced
- 2 medium bell peppers, seeds remove and chopped
- 5 whole basil leaves
- 1 tablespoon of capers

- 2 ½ cups of diced tomatoes
- 1 tablespoon of fresh parsley, finely chopped
- 1 teaspoon of balsamic vinegar
- ½ teaspoon of crushed red pepper flakes
- 2 teaspoons of fine sea salt
- 1 teaspoon of freshly cracked black pepper
- 1 medium onion, finely chopped

Instructions:

- Press the "Sauté" setting on your Instant Pot and add the oil. Once hot, onions and cook for 5 minutes or until translucent, stirring occasionally.
- Add the zucchini and garlic. Sauté for another 3 minutes.
- Add the bell pepper and sauté for 3 minutes. Stir in the basil leaves.

- Add the eggplant and continue to sauté for another 2 minutes, stirring occasionally.
- Add all the ingredients, tomatoes and seasonings inside your Instant Pot. Lock the lid and cook at high pressure for 8 minutes. When the cooking is done, manually release the pressure and carefully remove the lid. Serve and enjoy!

Mushroom Bourguignon
Time: 20 minutes   Servings: 6

Ingredients:

- 1 large onion, finely chopped
- 3 medium garlic cloves, minced
- 2 carrots, cut into bite-sized pieces
- 5 cups of button mushrooms, chopped
- 1 cup of red wine
- 4 tablespoons of red wine
- 1 teaspoon of dried marjoram

- 1 cup of homemade low-sodium vegetable stock
- 3 teaspoons of dried thyme, dried basil, dried rosemary, dried oregano
- 1 tablespoon of almond flour mixed with 2 tablespoons of water
- Fine sea salt and freshly cracked black pepper (to taste)

Instructions:

- Press the "Sauté" setting on your Instant Pot and add the onions. Cook for 3 minutes or until translucent, stirring frequently.
- Add the minced garlic, mushrooms and carrots. Continue to cook for 3 minutes, stirring occasionally. Add the tomato paste and continue to cook for another minute.
- Deglaze your Instant Pot with the red wine and vegetable stock.
- Add the dried herbs, marjoram, sea salt and freshly cracked black pepper. Lock the lid and cook at high pressure for 8 minutes. When the cooking is done, naturally release the pressure and remove the lid.
- Press the "Sauté" setting again and stir in the almond flour. Continue to cook until the liquid has thickened, stirring frequently. Serve and enjoy!

Vegan BBQ Meatballs
Time: 20 minutes   Servings: 4

Ingredients:

- ¼ cup of vegetable stock
- 2 pounds of frozen vegan meatballs
- 1 ½ cup of sugar-free barbecue sauce
- 1 (14-ounce) can of cranberry sauce

- 1 tablespoon of almond flour mixed with 1 tablespoon of water
- Fine sea salt and freshly cracked black pepper (to taste)

Instructions:

- Add the vegetable stock, meatballs, barbecue sauce, cranberry sauce inside your Instant Pot. Lock the lid and cook at high pressure for 5 minutes.
- When the cooking is done, naturally release the pressure for 5 minutes, then quick release the remaining pressure. Carefully remove the lid.
- Stir in the almond flour mixture. Press the "Sauté" setting and cook until the liquid has thickened, stirring frequently. Serve and enjoy!

Cauliflower Pav Bhaji
Time: 10 minutes   Servings: 4

Ingredients:

- 2 pounds of cauliflower, cut into florets
- 2 tablespoons of butter
- 1 medium onion, finely chopped
- 5 large garlic cloves, minced
- 1 tablespoon of garam masala
- 1 tablespoon of fresh ginger, grated
- 1 teaspoon of fine sea salt

- ½ teaspoon of ground turmeric
- ½ teaspoon of chili powder
- ¼ teaspoon of ground fenugreek
- 5 tablespoons of organic tomato paste
- ½ tablespoon of freshly squeezed lemon juice
- Fine sea salt and freshly cracked black pepper (to taste)

Instructions:

- Press the "Sauté" setting on your Instant Pot and add the butter. Once hot, add the chopped onions and cook for 2 to 3 minutes or until translucent, stirring frequently.
- Add the minced garlic, grated ginger and seasonings. Cook for 1 minute, stirring frequently.
- Add the remaining ingredients. Lock the lid and cook at high pressure for 2 minutes.
- When the cooking is done, quick release the pressure and carefully remove the lid. Serve and enjoy!

Spaghetti Squash with Mushroom Ragu
Time: 1 hour   Servings: 4

Ingredients:

- 1 (3-pound) spaghetti squash, cut in half and seeds removed
- 1 cup of homemade low-sodium vegetable stock

- 1 fresh sprig of rosemary
- ½ tablespoon of fine sea salt

Ragu Ingredients:

- 2 tablespoons of olive oil
- 1 medium onion, finely chopped
- 2 medium garlic cloves, peeled and minced
- 1 cup of mushrooms, chopped

- 1 (28-ounce) can of diced tomatoes, undrained
- 3 bay leaves
- Fine sea salt and freshly cracked black pepper (to taste)

Instructions:

- Add all the squash ingredients inside your Instant Pot. Lock the lid and cook at high pressure for 6 minutes. When the cooking is done, quick release the pressure and remove the lid.
- Transfer the squash to a cutting board and shred using two forks.
- Discard the liquid from your Instant Pot.
- Press the "Sauté" setting on your Instant Pot and add the olive oil. Once hot, add the chopped onions, garlic cloves and mushrooms. Sauté until softened, stirring frequently.
- Add the diced tomatoes, bay leaves, sea salt and freshly cracked black pepper. Lock the lid and cook at high pressure for 3 minutes. When the cooking is done, naturally release the pressure and remove the lid. Ladle the sauce on top of the spaghetti squash. Serve and enjoy!

Cauliflower Macaroni and Cheese
Time: 15 minutes   Servings: 4

Ingredients:

- 1 pound of cauliflower, florets
- 4-ounces of cream cheese, softened
- 1 cup of heavy cream
- 1 cup of cheddar cheese, shredded

- ½ cup of mozzarella cheese, shredded
- ½ teaspoon of cayenne pepper
- 3 tablespoons of unsalted butter
- Fine sea salt and freshly cracked black pepper (to taste)

Instructions:

- In a large heat-safe bowl that will fit inside your Instant Pot, add all the ingredients and toss until well combined. Cover with aluminum foil.
- Add 1 cup of water and a trivet inside your Instant Pot. Place the bowl on top. Lock the lid and cook at high pressure for 5 minutes. When the cooking is done, naturally release the pressure for 10 minutes, then quick release the remaining pressure. Carefully remove the lid. Preheat your broiler and transfer the bowl inside. Broi until the cheese has browned on top. Serve and enjoy!

Green Coconut Curry
Time: 30 minutes   Servings: 4

Ingredients:

- 1 medium cauliflower head, chopped
- 1 cup of radishes, chopped

- 1 cup of asparagus spears, trimmed and choppec
- 1 medium broccoli head, chopped

- 1 medium red bell pepper, seeds remove and sliced
- 2 tablespoons of green curry paste
- 1 teaspoon of onion powder
- 1 teaspoon of garlic powder

- 1 cup of unsweetened coconut milk
- 2 cups + ½ cup of homemade low-sodium vegetable stock
- Fine sea salt and freshly cracked black pepper (to taste)

Instructions:

- Add ½ cup of vegetable stock and all the vegetables inside your Instant Pot.
- Lock the lid and cook at high pressure for 3 minutes. Quick release the pressure and remove the lid.
- Press the "Sauté" setting in your Instant Pot and stir in the remaining ingredients. Cook until the thickened, stirring frequently. Serve and enjoy!

Carrot Medley

Time: 20 minutes   Servings: 10

Ingredients:

- 2 tablespoons of olive oil
- 1 white onion, finely chopped
- 3 pounds of cauliflower, cut into florets
- 2 pounds of baby carrots

- 1 ½ cup of vegetable stock
- 1 teaspoon of Italian seasoning or herbs mixed
- Fine sea salt and freshly cracked black pepper (to taste)

Instructions:

- Press the "Sauté" setting on your Instant Pot and add the oil and onions. Sauté for 5 minutes.
- Add the baby carrots and sauté for another 5 minutes. Stir in the remaining ingredients.
- Lock the lid and cook at high pressure for 5 minutes. When the cooking is done, naturally release the pressure for 10 minutes, then quick release the remaining pressure. Carefully remove the lid.
- Serve and enjoy!

Cauliflower Queso

Time: 25 minutes   Servings: 8

Ingredients:

- 2 cups of cauliflower florets
- 1 cup of homemade low-sodium vegetable stock
- ¼ cup of raw cashes
- ¾ cups of carrots, peeled and sliced
- ¼ cup of nutritional yeast
- 2 (10-ounce) cans of diced tomatoes with green chiles, undrained

- ½ teaspoon of smoked or sweet paprika
- ¼ teaspoon of mustard powder
- ¼ teaspoon of jalapeno powder
- ½ cup of red bell pepper, chopped
- 2 tablespoons of red onion, minced
- ¼ cup of fresh cilantro, chopped

Instructions:

- Add the cauliflower florets, vegetable stock, carrots and raw cashews inside your Instant Pot. Lock the lid and cook at high pressure for 5 minutes. Quick release the pressure and remove the lid.
- Strain the contents and set aside. In a blender, add the liquid along with the nutritional yeast, 1 can of diced tomatoes, paprika, mustard powder and jalapeno powder. Blend until smooth and transfer to a large bowl. Stir in the bell peppers, onions and fresh cilantro. Serve and enjoy!

Ginger Garlic Vegan Stir Fry

Time: 20 minutes   Servings: 4

Ingredients:

- 1 tablespoon of olive oil
- 1 cup of broccoli, chopped
- ½ cup of green bell pepper, chopped
- ½ cup of red bell pepper, chopped

- 1 bunch of asparagus, trimmed and cut into bite-sized pieces
- ½ cup of onions, finely chopped
- 2 medium garlic cloves, minced
- 1 tablespoon of fresh ginger, peeled and grated

- 1/8 cup of coconut aminos
- Fine sea salt and freshly cracked black pepper (to taste)

Instructions:

- Press the "Sauté" setting on your Instant Pot and add the oil. Once hot, add all the vegetable and continue to cook for 4 to 5 minutes or until softened, stirring frequently.
- Drizzle with the coconut aminos, sea salt and black pepper. Serve an enjoy!

Mushroom Bulgogi Lettuce Wraps
Time: 1 hour   Servings: 6

Ingredients:

- 1 medium yellow onion, sliced
- 1 pound of portobello mushrooms, sliced
- ¼ cup of sugar-free maple syrup
- 2 tablespoons of Frank's red hot sauce
- 1 tablespoon of fresh ginger, minced
- 1 tablespoon of garlic, minced
- ¼ cup of coconut aminos
- 2 tablespoons of dry white wine
- Fine sea salt and freshly cracked black pepper (to taste)
- Lettuce leaves (for serving)

Instructions:

- Add all the ingredients except for the lettuce leaves inside your Instant Pot.
- Lock the lid and cook at high pressure for 20 minutes. When the cooking is done, naturally release the pressure for 10 minutes, then quick release the remaining pressure. Carefully remove the lid.
- Spoon the mushroom bulgogi onto lettuce leaves. Serve and enjoy!

Cream of Mushroom Soup
Time: 30 minutes   Servings: 6

Ingredients:

- 3 cups of cremini mushrooms, sliced
- 1 cup of shiitake mushrooms, sliced
- 1 yellow onion, finely chopped
- 4 tablespoons of unsalted butter
- 1/3 cup of dry white wine
- 1 bay leaf
- 5 fresh sprigs of thyme
- 6 cups of homemade low-sodium vegetable stock
- 1 cup of heavy cream
- Fine sea salt and freshly cracked black pepper (to taste)

Instructions:

- Press the "Sauté" function on your Instant Pot and add the 4 tablespoons of butter. Once hot, add the chopped onions and cook for 5 minutes or until translucent, stirring occasionally.
- Add the garlic and cook for another fragrant, stirring occasionally.
- Add the chopped mushrooms and sauté for another 8 minutes, stirring occasionally.
- Add the remaining ingredients except for the heavy cream. Lock the lid and cook at high pressure for 5 minutes. When the cooking is done, naturally release the pressure for 5 minutes, then quick release the remaining pressure. Carefully remove the lid.
- Gently stir in the heavy cream and adjust the seasoning if necessary. Serve and enjoy!

Parmesan Radish
Time: 20 minutes   Servings: 4

Ingredients:

- 1 pound of radishes, trimmed and halved
- 4 tablespoons of olive oil
- 1 teaspoon of dried thyme
- Fine sea salt and freshly cracked black pepper
- ½ cup of parmesan cheese, grated

Instructions:

- In a large bowl, add all the ingredients except for the cheese and stir until well combined.

- Add 2 cups of water and a steamer basket inside your Instant Pot.
- Add the radishes on the steamer basket. Lock the lid and cook at high pressure for 10 minutes. When done, quick release the pressure and remove the lid.
- Transfer the radishes to a baking dish. Sprinkle the parmesan cheese.
- Transfer the baking dish to a preheated oven and bake until the cheese has melted. Serve and enjoy!

Garlic and Broccoli
Time: 10 minutes   Servings: 4

Ingredients:

- 4 cups of broccoli florets
- ½ cup of water
- 6 medium garlic cloves, peeled and crushed
- 2 tablespoons of coconut oil or extra-virgin olive oil
- Fine sea salt and freshly cracked black pepper (to taste)

Instructions:

- Add the water and a steamer rack inside your Instant Pot. Place the broccoli florets on the steamer rack.
- Lock the lid and press the steam button. Set the time for 2 minutes.
- When the cooking is done, quick release the pressure and remove the lid. Transfer the broccoli to an ice bath to stop the cooking process. Discard the water and remove the steamer basket from your Instant Pot.
- Press the "Sauté" setting on your Instant Pot and add the olive oil.
- Once hot, add the minced garlic and cook until fragrant, stirring frequently.
- Add the broccoli, sea salt and freshly cracked black pepper. Continue to cook until tender, stirring occasionally. Serve and enjoy!

Portobello Mushroom Stir-Fry
Time: 20 minutes   Servings: 4

Ingredients:

- 2 tablespoons of olive oil
- 2 portobello mushrooms, thinly sliced
- 1 medium red bell pepper, thinly sliced
- 1 cup of broccolini, chopped
- 1 cup of green onions, chopped
- 2 medium garlic cloves, minced
- 2 teaspoons of ginger, peeled and grated
- 3 tablespoons of freshly squeezed lime juice
- 1 tablespoon of water
- 3 tablespoons of sugar-free maple syrup
- 3 tablespoons of coconut amino
- Fine sea salt and freshly cracked black pepper (to taste)

Instructions:

- Press the "Sauté" setting on your Instant Pot and add the oil. Once hot, add all the vegetable and continue to cook for 4 to 5 minutes or until softened, stirring frequently.
- In a bowl, add the lime juice, maple syrup and coconut aminos. Mix well.
- Drizzle with the sauce, sea salt and black pepper. Continue to cook for a couple more minutes, stirring frequently. Serve an enjoy!

Tomato Zucchini Stir-Fry
Time: 20 minutes   Servings: 4

Ingredients:

- 2 medium zucchinis, chopped
- 2 medium yellow squash, sliced lengthwise and sliced
- 1 large onion, finely chopped
- 3 medium garlic cloves
- 1 (28-ounce) can of diced tomatoes
- 1 teaspoon of dried thyme
- 3 tablespoons of coconut aminos
- 1 tablespoon of olive oil
- Fine sea salt and freshly cracked black pepper (to taste)

Instructions:

- Press the "Sauté" setting on your Instant Pot and add the olive oil. Once hot, add the chopped onions and minced garlic. Sauté until fragrant, stirring frequently.
- Add the zucchini and squash. Sauté for another minute, stirring frequently.
- Add the remaining ingredients and stir until well combined. Continue to sauté until most of the liquid evaporates, stirring constantly. Serve an enjoy!

Mushroom Masala

Time: 30 minutes   Servings: 3

Ingredients:

- 1 cup of sliced white onions
- 1 cup of spinach, chopped
- ¼ cup of raw cashews, soaked
- 2 large tomatoes, diced
- 1 teaspoon of garam masala
- ½ teaspoon of smoked paprika
- ¼ teaspoon of turmeric

- 1 teaspoon of dried fenugreek leaves
- 1 tablespoon of extra-virgin olive oil
- ½ large onion, finely chopped
- 5 medium garlic cloves
- 1-inch piece of fresh ginger, peeled
- Fine sea salt and freshly cracked black pepper (to taste)

Instructions:

- In a blender, add the chopped onions, garlic, ginger, and a couple of tablespoons of water. Blend until smooth.
- Press the "Sauté" setting on your Instant Pot and add the onion mixture. Sauté for 3 minutes, stirring frequently.
- Add the tomatoes in the blender and blend until smooth. Stir into the instant pot along with the seasonings.
- Add the mushrooms. Lock the lid and cook at high pressure for 6 minutes. When the cooking is done, naturally release the pressure for 10 minutes, then quick release the remaining pressure.
- Stir in the remaining ingredients and press the "Sauté" setting on your Instant Pot. Continue to cook until thickens, stirring frequently. Serve and enjoy!

Mushroom Stroganoff

Time: 20 minutes   Servings: 6

Ingredients:

- 3 pounds of cremini, shiitake or brown mushrooms, sliced
- ¼ cup of extra-virgin olive oil
- 1 small onion, finely chopped
- 2 garlic cloves, peeled and crushed
- 2 teaspoons of dried thyme

- ¼ cup of tomato paste
- ¼ cup of red wine vinegar
- 2 cups of homemade low-sodium beef broth
- 1 cup of sour cream
- Fine sea salt and freshly cracked black pepper (to taste)

Instructions:

- Press the "Sauté" setting on your Instant Pot and add the olive oil. Once hot, add the chopped onions, crushed garlic, mushrooms, sea salt and freshly cracked black pepper. Sauté for 6 to 8 minutes, stirring frequently.
- Add the remaining ingredients inside your Instant Pot. Lock the lid and cook at high pressure for 5 minutes. When the cooking is done, quick release the pressure and carefully remove the lid.
- Stir in the sour cream. Press the "Sauté" setting on your Instant Pot and continue to cook until most of the liquid evaporates, stirring frequently. Serve and enjoy!

Cauliflower Tikka Masala

Time: 10 minutes   Servings: 4

Ingredients:

- 1 small cauliflower, cut into florets
- ½ cup of plain Greek yogurt
- 1 (28-ounce) can of diced tomatoes, undrained
- ¼ teaspoon of ground cumin
- ½ teaspoon of ground chili
- 1 teaspoon of turmeric

- 2 teaspoons of garam masala
- 2 teaspoons of dried fenugreek
- 1 tablespoon of ginger, freshly grated
- 3 medium garlic cloves, minced
- 1 medium onion, finely chopped
- 2 tablespoons of olive oil

- Fine sea salt and freshly cracked black pepper (to taste)

Instructions:

- Press the "Sauté" setting on your Instant Pot and add the olive oil. Once hot, add the chopped onion, garlic and ginger. Cook until softened, stirring occasionally.
- Add all the seasonings and cook for another 1 minute, stirring frequently.
- Add the remaining ingredients except for the Greek yogurt and stir until well combined. Lock the lid and cook at high pressure for 2 minutes. When the cooking is done, naturally release the pressure for 10 minutes, then quick release the remaining pressure. Carefully remove the lid. Gently stir in the Greek yogurt. Serve and enjoy!

Cabbage with Turkey Sausage
Time: 40 minutes   Servings: 4

Ingredients:

- 1 pound of turkey sausage, sliced
- 1 head of green cabbage, cored and chopped
- 1 medium onion, finely chopped
- 2 medium garlic cloves, peeled and minced
- 1 tablespoon of balsamic vinegar
- 1 tablespoon of Dijon mustard
- 1 tablespoon of olive oil
- Fine sea salt and freshly cracked black pepper (to taste)

Instructions:

- Press the "Sauté" setting on your Instant Pot and add the olive oil. Once hot, add the sausage and onions. Cook until the onions are tender, stirring occasionally.
- Add the chopped cabbage along with the remaining ingredients inside your Instant Pot. Continue to cook until the cabbage has wilted down, stirring frequently. Serve and enjoy!

Red Cabbage with Cream Sauce
Time: 20 minutes   Servings: 6

Ingredients:

- 2 pounds of cabbage, chopped
- 1 cup of coconut milk
- 2 tablespoons of fresh parsley, finely chopped
- 2 teaspoons of fine sea salt
- 1 medium onion, finely chopped
- 2 cups of homemade low-sodium vegetable broth
- 1 tablespoon of olive oil

Instructions:

- Press the "Sauté" setting on your Instant Pot and add the olive oil. Once hot, add the chopped onions and cook until tender, stirring occasionally.
- Add the vegetable broth and cabbage inside your Instant Pot. Lock the lid and cook at high pressure for 4 minutes. When the cooking is done, quick release the pressure and carefully remove the lid.
- Press the "Sauté" setting on your Instant Pot and stir in the sea salt, fresh parsley and coconut milk. Continue to cook for around 3 to 4 minutes, stirring frequently. Serve and enjoy!

Artichokes with Lemon Tarragon Sauce
Time: 30 minutes   Servings: 4

Ingredients:

- 4 (6-ounce) cans of artichokes, trimmed and cut
- 1 lemon, sliced
- 1 lemon, juice and zest
- 2 cups of homemade low-sodium vegetable stock
- 1 tablespoon of tarragon leaves, finely chopped
- 1 celery stalk, chopped
- ½ cup of extra-virgin olive oil
- 1 teaspoon of fine sea salt

Instructions:

- Add the lemon slices, artichokes, and vegetable stock inside your Instant Pot. Lock the lid and cook at high pressure for 15 minutes. When the cooking is done, naturally release the pressure and carefully remove the lid.

- In a blender, add the olive oil, celery, sea salt, tarragon leaves, lemon juice, and lemon zest. Blend until smooth. Transfer to small dish. Serve the artichokes with the sauce.

Vegan Sloppy Joes
Time: 50 minutes   Servings: 6

Ingredients:

- ½ cup of hulled hemp seeds
- 1 cup of hulled pumpkin seeds
- 1 cup of walnuts, chopped
- 1 (6-ounce) can of tomato paste
- ½ tablespoon of garlic powder
- 1 teaspoon of onion powder
- 1 tablespoon of Worcestershire sauce

- 1 tablespoon of Dijon mustard
- 1 tablespoon of apple cider vinegar
- 1 tablespoon of erythritol sweetener
- 2 cups of homemade low-sodium vegetable stock
- Fine sea salt and freshly cracked black pepper (to taste)

Instructions:

- Add all the ingredients inside your Instant Pot and stir until well combined. Lock the lid and cook at high pressure for 30 minutes.
- When the cooking is done, naturally release the pressure and remove the lid.
- If there is still liquid, press the "Sauté" setting on your Instant Pot and cook until almost all of the liquid has bene absorbed, stirring occasionally. Serve and enjoy!

Cauliflower Gumbo
Time: 20 minutes   Servings: 4

Ingredients:

- 1 large head of cauliflower, cut into florets
- 2 cups of chopped okra, frozen or fresh
- 1 medium jalapeno, chopped
- 2 tablespoons of extra-virgin olive oil
- 1 medium red onion, finely chopped
- 3 medium garlic cloves, minced
- 1 cup of red bell pepper, chopped

- 2 celery stalks, chopped
- 1 (14.5-ounce) can of diced tomatoes
- 1 (6-ounce) can of tomato paste
- 2 tablespoons of apple cider vinegar
- 3 cups of homemade low-sodium vegetable stock or chicken stock
- Fine sea salt and freshly cracked black pepper (to taste)

Instructions:

- Press the "Sauté" setting on your Instant Pot and add the olive oil. Once hot, add the chopped onions, minced garlic, chopped bell pepper, and chopped celery. Sauté for 5 minutes or until softened, stirring frequently.
- Add the remaining ingredients and stir until well combined.
- Lock the lid and cook at high pressure for 12 minutes. When the cooking is done, naturally release the pressure and carefully remove the lid. Serve and enjoy!

Vegetarian Butter Chicken
Time: 15 minutes   Servings: 6

Ingredients:

- 1 ½ cup of dry soy curls
- 6 garlic cloves, minced
- 1 (14.5-ounce) can of diced tomatoes
- 1 teaspoon of turmeric
- 1 teaspoon of paprika
- 1 teaspoon of garam masala

- 1 teaspoon of ground cumin
- 1 cup of water
- ½ cup of butter, cubed
- ½ cup of heavy cream
- Fine sea salt and freshly cracked black pepper (to taste)

Instructions:

- Add the water, seasonings, tomatoes and soy curls inside your Instant Pot. Lock the lid and cook at high pressure for 6 minutes. When the cooking is done, naturally release the pressure for 10 minutes, then quick release the remaining pressure. Carefully remove the lid.
- Press the "Sauté" function on your Instant Pot and stir in the butter and heavy cream. Allow the butter to melt, stirring occasionally.

Portobello Pot Roast

Time: 40 minutes   Servings: 6

Ingredients:

- 1 pound of baby mushrooms
- 1 pound of cauliflower florets
- 2 cups of pearl onions
- 2 large carrots, cut into bite-sized pieces
- 4 garlic cloves, peeled and minced
- 3 sprigs of fresh thyme
- 3 cups of homemade low-sodium vegetable stock
- ½ cup of dry red wine
- 1 (6-ounce) can of tomato paste
- 2 tablespoons of Worcestershire sauce
- 2 tablespoons of almond flour mixed with 2 tablespoons of water
- Fine sea salt and freshly cracked black pepper (to taste)

Instructions:

- Add all the ingredients inside your Instant Pot except for the almond flour. Lock the lid and cook at high pressure for 20 minutes. When the cooking is done, naturally release the pressure and carefully remove the lid.
- Stir in the almond mixture and gently stir. Continue to cook until the liquid thickens, stirring frequently. Serve and enjoy!

Meatless Chili

Time: 30 minutes   Servings: 4

Ingredients:

- 3 tablespoons of extra-virgin olive oil
- ½ large onion, finely chopped
- 3 celery stalks, chopped
- 4 medium garlic cloves, minced
- 1 bay leaf
- 2 sprigs of fresh thyme
- 1 pound of white cremini mushrooms, sliced
- 1 cup of walnuts, chopped
- ½ cup of pumpkin puree
- 1 ½ tablespoon of coconut aminos
- 1 ½ tablespoon of apple cider vinegar
- 2 tablespoons of nutritional yeast
- 3 cups of homemade low-sodium vegetable stock
- 1 teaspoon of ground cumin
- Fine sea salt and freshly cracked black pepper (to taste)

Instructions:

- Press the "Sauté" setting on your Instant Pot and add the olive oil. Once hot, add the onions, garlic and celery. Sauté for 4 minutes or until tender, stirring occasionally.
- Add the mushrooms and cook until softened, stirring frequently.
- Add the remaining ingredients inside your Instant Pot and stir until well combined. Lock the lid and cook at high pressure for 20 minutes. When the cooking is done, allow for a full natural release method. Carefully remove the lid. Serve and enjoy!

Vegan Cauliflower Burritos

Time: 30 minutes   Servings: 8

Burrito Filling Ingredients:

- 3 tablespoons of olive oil
- 1 medium red onion, finely chopped
- 1 red bell pepper, chopped
- 3 medium garlic cloves, minced
- 2 cups of cauliflower, chopped
- 1 cup of cauliflower
- 1 (12-ounce) jar of salsa
- 1 cup of kale, finely chopped
- 2 cups of homemade low-sodium vegetable stock

- 1 teaspoon of ground cumin
- 2 teaspoons of chili powder

- 1 teaspoon of smoked or regular paprika
- 1 teaspoon of fine sea salt

Assembling Ingredients:

- Lettuce leaves (chopped)

- 1 to 2 avocados, sliced or diced

Instructions:

- Press the "Sauté" Setting on your Instant Pot and add the olive oil. Once hot, add the chopped onions and minced garlic. Sauté for 3 minutes, stirring frequently.
- Add the remaining burrito filling ingredients. Lock the lid and cook at high pressure for 10 minutes. When the cooking is done, naturally release the pressure and carefully remove the lid. If there is still liquid inside your Instant Pot, press the "Sauté" setting and cook until most of the liquid evaporates, stirring frequently. Spoon the mixture into lettuce leaves and enjoy!

Zucchini Noodles with Garlic, Lemon and Parmesan
Time: 10 minutes   Servings: 2

Ingredients:

- 2 tablespoons of olive oil
- 2 garlic cloves, minced
- ½ lemon, zest and juice
- 2 large zucchinis, peeled and spiralized

- 1 tablespoon of mint, finely sliced
- 4 tablespoons of parmesan, grated
- 1 teaspoon of salt
- 1 teaspoon of black pepper

Instructions:

- Press the "Sauté" function and add the olive oil. Once hot, add the minced garlic, lemon zest, salt and black pepper. Cook for 1 minute or until fragrant, stirring frequently. Turn off the "Sauté" setting.
- Add the spiralized zucchini and drizzle with lemon juice. Sauté for 20 to 30 seconds, stirring occasionally. Do not cook the zucchini noodles otherwise you will result in a soggy texture.
- Stir in the sliced mint and grated parmesan. Serve and enjoy!

Part 10: Ketogenic Mediterranean Diet Recipes

Keto Chicken Posole Verde
Time: 1 hour   Servings: 6

Ingredients:

- 2 pounds of boneless, skinless chicken breasts, cut into cubes
- 1 pound of cauliflower florets, chopped
- 1 pound of tomatillos, roughly chopped
- 1 small onion, roughly chopped
- 2 teaspoons of dried oregano
- 1 lime, juice and zest

- 1 large jalapeno pepper, roughly chopped
- 1 large poblano pepper, roughly chopped
- 1 bunch of fresh cilantros, roughly chopped
- 1 teaspoon of ground cumin
- 3 cups of homemade low-sodium chicken stock
- 1 teaspoon of fine sea salt
- 1 teaspoon of freshly cracked black pepper

Instructions:

- In a food processor, add the tomatillos, poblano pepper, jalapeno, garlic, lime juice and cilantro. Pulse until smooth.
- Press the "sauté" function on your Instant Pot and add the olive oil. Cook the chicken until brown and remove.
- Add the onions and cook until lightly softened. Return the chicken and season with salt, black pepper, oregano, and cumin.
- Add the salsa verde, cauliflower and chicken stock. Lock the lid and cook at high pressure for 20 minutes.
- When the cooking is done, quick release the pressure and remove the lid. Serve and enjoy!

Cabbage Detox Soup
Time: 30 minutes   Servings: 6

Ingredients:

- 3 cups of green cabbage, chopped
- 2 ½ cups of homemade low-sodium vegetable stock
- 1 (14.5-ounce) can of diced tomatoes
- 1 small cauliflower, chopped
- 3 stalks of celery, chopped

- 1 onion, finely chopped
- 2 medium garlic cloves, minced
- 2 tablespoons of apple cider vinegar
- 1 tablespoon of freshly squeezed lemon juice
- 2 teaspoons of dried sage

Instructions:

- Add all the ingredients inside your Instant Pot.
- Lock the lid and cook at high pressure for 15 minutes.
- When the cooking is done, naturally release the pressure and remove the lid. Serve and enjoy!

Sicilian-Style Chicken Cacciatore
Time: 1 hour   Servings: 4

Ingredients:

- 4 chicken thighs
- 2 tablespoons of extra-virgin olive oil
- 3 celery stalks, chopped
- ½ red onion, finely chopped
- ½ cup of fresh mushrooms, sliced
- 6 garlic cloves, peeled and minced
- 1 (14-ounce) can of Italian diced tomatoes

- 2 teaspoons of herbes de Provence
- 3 cups of homemade low-sodium chicken stock
- 1 (6-ounce) can of tomato paste
- ½ cup of red wine
- 1 teaspoon of fine sea salt
- 1 teaspoon of freshly cracked black pepper
- Fresh cilantro, chopped

Instructions:

- Press the "Sauté" function on your Instant Pot and add the olive oil. Once hot, add the chicken thighs and cook for 6 minutes per side or until brown. Transfer the chicken to a plate lined with paper towels. Add the chopped mushrooms, celery and onions to your Instant Pot. Sauté for 5 minutes or until softened, stirring occasionally.

195

- Add the chicken to your Instant Pot along with the stewed tomatoes, red wine and tomato paste. Sprinkle herbes de provence, sea salt and black pepper.
- Add the chicken stock and lock the lid. Cook at high pressure for 15 minutes. When the cooking is done, naturally release the pressure and remove the lid.
- Transfer to serving plates and top with fresh cilantro. Serve and enjoy!

Yardbird Chili with Cauliflower

Time: 1 hour and 45 minutes   Servings: 6

Ingredients:

- 1 pound of chicken breasts, cut into bite-sized pieces
- 1 medium cauliflower, cut into florets
- 2 tablespoons of extra-virgin olive oil
- 1 medium onion, finely chopped
- 4 medium garlic cloves, peeled and minced
- 2 cups of homemade low-sodium chicken stock
- 2 (4-ounce) cans of green chiles, undrained
- 1 tablespoon of fresh or dried oregano
- 1 teaspoon of ground cumin

Instructions:

- Press the "Sauté" function on your Instant Pot and add the olive oil. Once hot, add the chicken pieces and cook until brown, stirring occasionally.
- Add the chopped onion and minced garlic. Sauté until softened, stirring occasionally.
- Add the remaining ingredients and give a good stir. Lock the lid and cook at high pressure for 20 minutes. When the cooking is done, naturally release the pressure and remove the lid.
- Serve and enjoy!

Mediterranean Chicken Orzo

Time: 20 minutes   Servings: 6

Ingredients:

- 6 boneless, skinless chicken thighs, cut into bite-sized pieces
- 2 cups of homemade low-sodium chicken stock
- 2 Roma tomatoes, chopped
- 1 cup of green olives, pitted and chopped
- 1 cup of ripe olives, pitted and sliced
- 1 small red onion, finely chopped
- 1 tablespoon of fresh lemon zest
- 3 tablespoons of freshly squeezed lemon juice
- 2 tablespoons of butter
- 1 tablespoon of herbes de Provence
- 1 cup of low-carb orzo pasta

Instructions:

- Add all the ingredients except for the orzo inside your Instant Pot.
- Lock the lid and cook at high pressure for 8 minutes. When the timer beeps, quick release the pressure and remove the lid.
- Add the orzo and lock the lid. Cook at high pressure for 3 minutes. When done, naturally release the pressure for 5 minutes, then quick-release the remaining pressure. Remove the lid. Serve and enjoy!

Middle-Eastern Lamb Stew

Time: 1 hour and 15 minutes   Servings: 4

Ingredients:

- 2 tablespoons of extra-virgin olive oil
- 2 pounds of lamb stew meat, cut into bite-sized pieces
- 1 onion, finely chopped
- 6 medium garlic cloves, peeled and minced
- 2 tablespoons of tomato paste
- ¼ cup of red wine vinegar or apple cider vinegar
- 1 teaspoon of sea salt
- 1 teaspoon of freshly cracked black pepper
- 1 teaspoon of cumin
- 1 teaspoon of coriander
- 1 teaspoon of turmeric
- 1 ¼ cups of chicken stock
- 2 cups of cauliflower florets, chopped

Instructions:

- Press the "Sauté" function on your Instant Pot and add the olive oil. Once hot, add the lamb, minced garlic and all seasonings. Cook until brown, stirring occasionally.
- Add the remaining ingredients and lock the lid.
- Cook at high pressure for 50 minutes. When done, naturally release the pressure and carefully remove the lid. Serve and enjoy!

Mediterranean Lamb Stew

Time: 1 hour and 30 minutes   Servings: 6

Ingredients:

- 2 pounds of lamb shoulder or lamb stew meat, cut into bite-sized pieces
- 2 tablespoons of extra-virgin olive oil
- 1 teaspoon of fine sea salt
- 1 teaspoon of freshly cracked black pepper
- ½ cup of leeks, sliced
- ½ cup of carrots, chopped
- ½ cup of celery, chopped
- ½ cup of fennel, finely chopped
- 1 onion, finely chopped
- 1 teaspoon of dried rosemary
- 1 (28-ounce) can of crushed tomatoes
- 2 cups of cauliflower florets
- 2 cups of homemade low-sodium beef broth
- 1 bay leaf

Instructions:

- Press the "Sauté" function on your Instant Pot and add the olive oil and lamb stew meat. Cook for 6 minutes or until brown. Remove and set the meat aside.
- Add the chopped onion, carrots, leeks, celery and fennel. Cook for 4 minutes, stirring occasionally.
- Return the lamb stew meat and the remaining ingredients to your Instant Pot.
- Lock the lid and cook at high pressure for 45 minutes.
- When the cooking is done, naturally release the pressure and remove the lid. Serve and enjoy!

Mediterranean Lamb Shanks

Time: 50 minutes   Servings: 3

Ingredients:

- 3 lamb shanks
- ¼ cup of extra-virgin olive oil
- 1 medium onion, chopped
- 2 bay leaves
- 2 cups of low-carb, keto-friendly red wine
- 4 cups of homemade low-sodium beef broth
- 3 tablespoons of almond flour
- ¼ cup of fresh Italian parsley, chopped
- 1 teaspoon of fine sea salt
- 1 teaspoon of freshly cracked black pepper

Instructions:

- Season the lamb shanks with sea salt and black pepper/
- Press the "Sauté" function on your Instant Pot and add the olive oil.
- Once hot, brown the lamb shanks on both sides. Remove and set aside.
- Add the onions and sauté until softened.
- Deglaze your Instant Pot with red wine and return to the lamb shanks along with the beef broth. Lock the lid and cook at high pressure for 30 minutes.
- When the cooking is done, naturally release the pressure and remove the lid.
- Press the "Sauté' function on your Instant Pot and sprinkle with the almond flour. Allow the liquid to thicken. Serve and enjoy!

Tuna and Olive Salad

Time: 15 minutes   Servings: 4

Ingredients:

- 1 medium cauliflower head, cut into florets
- 2 large organic eggs
- 3 tablespoons of olive oil
- ¼ cup of pickles, finely chopped
- 2 tablespoons of red wine vinegar
- ½ cup of green olives, pitted and sliced
- 1 medium roasted red pepper, chopped
- 2 tablespoons of fresh parsley

- 1 (10-ounce) can of tuna, drained
- 1 cup of baby arugula, lettuce, baby spinach or kale

Instructions:

- Add 2 cups of water and a steamer basket to your Instant Pot. Place the eggs and cauliflower on top. Lock the lid and cook at high pressure for 8 minutes. When the cooking is done, quick release the pressure. Transfer the eggs to an ice bath. Peel and dice.
- In a large bowl, add all the ingredients and stir until well combined. Serve and enjoy!

Cheddar Cheese and Kale Frittata
Time: 25 minutes   Servings: 6

Ingredients:

- 6 large organic eggs
- 2 tablespoons of heavy whipping cream
- ½ teaspoon of nutmeg, finely grated
- 1 ½ cups of kale, stemmed and roughly chopped
- ¼ cup of cheddar cheese, shredded
- ½ teaspoon of fine sea salt
- ½ teaspoon of freshly cracked black pepper
- 1 cup of water

Instructions:

- Add all the ingredients and stir until well combined.
- Grease an oven-safe dish that fits inside your Instant Pot or a round metal bowl. Add the egg mixture. Add 1 cup of water and a trivet inside your Instant Pot. Place the dish on top and cover with aluminum foil.
- Lock the lid and cook at high pressure for 10 minutes. When the cooking is done, quick release the pressure and remove the lid. Serve and enjoy!

Beef Steak Salad
Time: 1 hour   Servings: 4

Ingredients:

- 1 pound of boneless rib-eye steak
- 1 cup of fresh arugula, baby spinach or kale
- 1 large tomato, diced
- ¼ cup of goat cheese
- ¼ cup of mixed almonds, walnuts, hazelnuts, chopped
- 3 tablespoons of olive oil
- 2 cups of homemade low-sodium beef broth
- 2 tablespoons of red wine vinegar
- 1 tablespoon of Italian seasoning

Instructions:

- In a bowl, add the red wine vinegar and Italian seasoning. Mix well.
- Brush the mixture along the rib-eye steak and add inside your Instant Pot. Pour in the beef broth. Lock the lid and cook at high pressure for 25 minutes. When the cooking is done, naturally release the pressure and remove the lid. Discard the liquid.
- Press the "Sauté" function on your Instant Pot and add the olive oil.
- Add the steak and cook for 6 minutes per side or until brown. Transfer to a cutting board and slice. In a large bowl, add the steak slices and remaining salad ingredients. Serve and enjoy!Serve and enjoy!

Easy Sage Soft-Boiled Eggs
Time: 15 minutes   Servings: 4

Ingredients:

- 4 large organic eggs
- ¼ teaspoon of fine sea salt
- ¼ teaspoon of freshly cracked black pepper
- ½ teaspoon of paprika
- 1 tablespoon of sage
- 1 cup of water

Instructions:

- Add 1 cup of water and a steamer basket inside your Instant Pot. Place the eggs on the steamer basket.
- Lock the lid and cook at high pressure for 3 minutes. When done, quick release the pressure and carefully remove the lid. Transfer the eggs to an ice bath. Peel the eggs and cut in half.

- Season with sea salt, paprika, black pepper and sage. Serve and enjoy!

Asparagus and Shrimp Cauliflower Risotto
Time: 15 minutes   Servings: 4

Ingredients:

- Around 16 shrimps, peeled and deveined
- 1 pound of asparagus, trimmed and cut into bite-sized pieces
- 1 ½ cups of mushrooms, chopped
- 1 cup of cauliflower rice
- 1 cup of homemade low-sodium chicken stock
- 1 tablespoon of olive oil
- 1 cup of spinach
- ¾ cups of parmesan cheese, finely grated

Instructions:

- Press the "Sauté" function on your Instant Pot and add the olive oil.
- Once hot, add the mushrooms and asparagus. Sauté for 6 minutes or until lightly softened, stirring occasionally. Add the remaining ingredients except for the parmesan cheese
- and stir until well combined. Lock the lid and cook at high pressure for 4 minutes.
- When the cooking is done, quick release the pressure and remove the lid. Stir in the parmesan cheese. Serve and enjoy!

Jalapeno Green Sauce
Time: 10 minutes   Servings: 2

Ingredients:

- 2 medium jalapeno peppers, seeds removed and chopped
- 1 medium green bell pepper, seeds removed and chopped
- 2 medium garlic cloves, minced
- ½ cup of white vinegar
- 1 tablespoon of apple cider vinegar
- 1 teaspoon of fine sea salt
- ¼ cup of homemade low-sodium vegetable broth

Instructions:

- Add all the ingredients and stir until well combined.
- Lock the lid and cook at high pressure for 2 minutes.
- When the cooking is done, naturally release the pressure for 5 minutes, then quick release the remaining pressure. Carefully remove the lid.
- Use an immersion blender to blend the contents until smooth. Store into jars and use accordingly. Enjoy!

Fire-Roasted Tomatoes and Chorizo Soup
Time: 30 minutes   Servings: 6

Ingredients:

- 3 chorizo sausages, chopped
- 2 tablespoons of olive oil
- 2 medium shallots, finely chopped
- 3 medium garlic cloves, peeled and minced
- 2 (14.5-ounce) cans of fire-roasted tomatoes
- 1 (28-ounce) can of crushed tomatoes
- 4 cups of homemade low-sodium beef broth
- 1 teaspoon of fine sea salt
- 1 teaspoon of freshly cracked black pepper

Instructions:

- Press the "Sauté" function on your Instant Pot and add the chorizo. Sauté until crispy. Remove and transfer to a plate lined with paper towels.
- Add the shallots and garlic. Sauté for 5 minutes or until softened, stirring occasionally.
- Return the chopped chorizo sausages and remaining ingredients. Stir until well combined.
- Lock the lid and cook at high pressure for 8 minutes. When the cooking is done, naturally release the pressure and remove the lid. Serve and enjoy!

Stewed Pork and Mushroom
Time: 50 minutes   Servings: 2

Ingredients:

- 2 pork chops, cut into pieces
- 1 cup of cremini mushrooms, chopped
- 1 small onion, finely chopped
- 2 medium garlic cloves, peeled and minced
- 2 large carrots, roughly chopped
- 2 tablespoons of extra-virgin olive oil
- 1 cup of homemade low-sodium beef broth
- 1 tablespoon of apple cider vinegar
- 2 tablespoons of cornstarch
- 1 teaspoon of fine sea salt
- 1 teaspoon of freshly cracked black pepper

Instructions:

- Press the "Sauté" function on your Instant Pot and add the olive oil. Brown the pork chops on both sides. Remove and set aside.
- Add the chopped onions, mushrooms and minced garlic. Sauté for 4 minutes or until softened, stirring occasionally.
- Return the pork chops and the remaining ingredients inside your Instant Pot.
- Lock the lid and cook at high pressure for 20 minutes. When the cooking is done, quick release the pressure and remove the lid. Serve and enjoy!

Steamed Mediterranean Cod
Time: 20 minutes   Servings: 4

Ingredients:

- 1 pound of halved cherry tomatoes
- 1 bunch of fresh sprigs of thyme
- 4 medium fillets of cod
- 1 cup of Kalamata olives, pitted and sliced
- 1 tablespoon of extra-virgin olive oil
- 1 medium garlic, crushed
- 1 teaspoon of fine sea salt
- ½ teaspoon of freshly cracked black pepper
- 2 cups of water

Instructions:

- Add 2 cups of water and a trivet inside your Instant Pot.
- Lay parchment paper flat onto a flat surface. Add the cod fillets, cherry tomatoes, crushed garlic, olives, thyme, salt and black pepper. Drizzle with olive oil. Fold the parchment paper.
- Place the parchment paper on top of the trivet.
- Lock the lid and cook at low pressure for 7 minutes.
- When the cooking is done, quick release the pressure and remove the lid. Serve and enjoy!

Lemon Rotisserie Chicken
Time: 50 minutes   Servings: 6

Ingredients:

- 1 (2.5-pound) whole chicken
- 1 onion, cut into wedged
- 3 medium garlic cloves, whole
- 1 whole lemon, wedged
- 2 tablespoons of extra-virgin olive oil
- 1 teaspoon of fine sea salt
- 1 teaspoon of garlic powder
- 1 teaspoon of freshly cracked black pepper
- 1 teaspoon of smoked or regular paprika
- 1 cup of homemade low-sodium chicken broth

Instructions:

- Season the whole chicken with salt, garlic powder, black pepper and paprika.
- Stuff the chicken with onion wedges, garlic and lemon.
- Press the "Sauté" function on your Instant Pot and add the olive oil.
- Add the chicken and for 4 minutes per side or until brown. Remove the chicken from your Instant Pot.
- Add 1 cup of chicken broth and a trivet inside your Instant Pot. Place the chicken on top.
- Lock the lid and cook at high pressure for 20 minutes.
- When the cooking is done, naturally release the pressure and remove the lid. Serve and enjoy!

Greek-Style Chicken

Time: 50 minutes   Servings: 4

Ingredients:

- 2 pounds of boneless, skinless chicken breasts
- 6 medium garlic cloves, finely minced
- 1 (8-ounce) jar of marinated artichoke hearts, drained
- 1 cup of Greek salad dressing
- 1 cup of Kalamata olives, sliced
- ½ medium red onion, finely sliced
- 2 tablespoons of olive oil
- 1 teaspoon of fine sea salt
- ½ teaspoon of freshly cracked black pepper
- 1 tablespoon of arrowroot starch
- ½ cup of feta cheese, crumbled (for serving)

Instructions:

- Press the "Sauté" function on your Instant Pot and add the olive oil. Once hot, add the garlic and cook until fragrant. Remove and set aside
- Season the chicken with salt and black pepper. Sauté for 2 minutes per side or until brown. Turn off "Sauté" setting.
- Add the artichokes and olives to your Instant Pot. Top with red onions and pour in the Greek dressing.
- Lock the lid and cook at high pressure for 15 minutes.
- When the cooking is done, quick release the pressure and remove the lid. Remove and set aside the chicken.
- Sprinkle the arrowroot starch over the liquid and allow to thicken.
- Serve the chicken with the sauce and feta cheese. Serve and enjoy!

Greek-Style Blueberry Yogurt

Time: 9 hours   Servings: 12

Ingredients:

- 1 pound of blueberries
- 1 cup of erythritol or other keto-friendly sweeteners
- 3 tablespoons of gelatin
- 1 tablespoon of freshly squeezed lime juice
- 8 cups of almond milk
- ¼ cup of Greek yogurt

Instructions:

- In a large bowl, dd the blueberries and mash using a potato masher.
- Add the erythritol and continue to mash. Mix in the freshly squeezed lime juice and gelatin.
- Add the almond milk to your Instant Pot and close the lid. Press the "Yogurt" function and wait until "Boil" appears on the display screen.
- Remove the lid and allow the pot to cool.
- In a bowl, add ½ cup of the almond milk along with the Greek yogurt. Mix well and return to the Instant Pot.
- Lock the lid and press the "Yogurt" function and set the time to 8 hours.
- Once done, remove the lid and allow the yogurt to chill inside your refrigerator.
- Mix in the blueberry mixture. Serve and enjoy!

Part 11: 20-Minute Recipes

Chicken BLT Salad
Time: 20 minutes   Servings: 4

Ingredients:

- 1 pound of boneless, skinless chicken thighs
- ½ pound of bacon strips, chopped
- ½ cup of cherry tomatoes, halved
- 1 ½ cup of lettuce leaves, roughly chopped

Mayonnaise Ingredients:

- ¾ cups of mayonnaise

- ½ teaspoon of fine sea salt
- ½ teaspoon of freshly cracked black pepper
- 1 cup of homemade low-sodium chicken stock

- ½ tablespoon of garlic powder

Instructions:

- Season the chicken thighs with salt and black pepper
- Press the "Sauté" setting on your Instant Pot and add the chopped bacon. Cook until brown and crispy. Transfer the bacon to a plate lined with paper towels.
- Add the chicken thighs to the bacon grease and cook for 4 minutes per side or until brown.
- Add 1 cup of chicken stock and lock the lid. Cook at high pressure for 15 minutes. When the cooking is done, quick release the pressure and remove the lid.
- Transfer the chicken to a cutting board and shred using two forks.
- In a bowl, add the mayonnaise and garlic powder and mix well.
- In another large bowl, add the shredded chicken, chopped bacon, cherry tomatoes and lettuce. Gently toss until well combined. Drizzle with the mayonnaise and enjoy!

Cheesy Brussel Sprouts
Time: 20 minutes   Servings: 6

Ingredients:

- 2 pounds of brussel sprouts, halved or quartered
- 4 tablespoons of extra-virgin olive oil
- 4 medium slices of bacon, chopped
- 1 cup of white or yellow onion, finely chopped
- 2 cups of heavy cream
- ½ cup of sour cream

- 1 cup of smoked gouda cheese, grated
- 1 cup of mozzarella cheese, grate
- ¼ cup of crumbled feta cheese
- 1 teaspoon of fine sea salt
- ½ teaspoon of freshly cracked black pepper
- 2 cups of water

Instructions:

- Press the "Sauté" setting on your Instant Pot and add the olive oil. Once hot, add the brussel sprouts and sauté for 6 minutes, stirring occasionally. Remove the brussel sprouts and set aside.
- Add the bacon to your Instant Pot and cook until brown and crispy. Transfer to a plate lined with paper towels.
- Add the onions and sauté for another 4 minutes. or until translucent, stirring occasionally. Remove and set aside Turn off "Sauté" setting on your Instant Pot and pour in 2 cups of water. Place a trivet inside your Instant Pot.
- In a heat-safe dish, add the brussel sprouts, bacon, onions, and remaining ingredients. Stir until well combined. Cover with aluminum foil. Place the dish on top of the trivet and lock the lid.
- Cook at high pressure for 3 minutes. When the cooking is done, quick release the pressure and remove the lid. Serve and enjoy!

Zucchini Noodles with Meat Sauce
Time: 20 minutes   Servings: 6

Ingredients:

- 2 pounds of zucchini, peeled and spiralized
- 2 pounds of lean ground beef
- 2 (16-ounce) jar of marinara sauce
- 2 tablespoons of extra-virgin olive oil
- 1 onion, finely chopped

- 4 medium garlic cloves, minced
- 3 cups of baby spinach
- 1 teaspoon of fine sea salt
- 1 teaspoon of freshly cracked black pepper

Instructions:

- Press the "Sauté" function on your Instant Pot and add the ground beef, onion, garlic cloves and celery. Cook until the meat is browned and vegetables have softened
- Add the remaining ingredients except for the spiralized zucchini and spinach. Stir well and lock the lid. Cook at high pressure for 12 minutes. When the cooking is done, quick release the pressure and remove the lid. Gently stir in the zoodles until well coated with the meat sauce. Serve and enjoy!

Chicken and Cauliflower Rice

Time: 20 minutes　　　　　Servings: 4

Ingredients:

- 1 cup of cauliflower rice
- 2 tablespoons of olive oil
- 1 pound of boneless, skinless chicken breasts, cut into bite-sized pieces
- 1 medium white or yellow onion, finely chopped
- 2 medium carrots, cut into ½-inch pieces
- 3 medium garlic cloves, peeled and crushed
- ¼ cup of coconut aminos
- 1 tablespoon of white vinegar
- 1 teaspoon of fine sea salt
- 1 teaspoon of freshly cracked black pepper

Instructions:

- Press the "Sauté" function on your Instant Pot and add the olive oil. Once hot, add the chicken pieces and cook for 5 minutes or until brown.
- Add the onions, garlic and carrots and cook until the vegetables have softened, stirring occasionally.
- Add the cauliflower rice, coconut aminos, white vinegar, salt and black pepper. Cook until the chicken is cooked through, stirring occasionally. Serve and enjoy!

Butternut and Cauliflower Soup

Time: 20 minutes　　　　　Servings: 6

Ingredients:

- 1 large white or yellow onion, finely chopped
- 2 tablespoons of extra-virgin olive oil
- 3 medium garlic cloves, peeled and crushed
- 1 pound of cauliflower florets
- 1 pound of butternut squash cubes
- 2 cups of homemade low-sodium vegetable stock
- 1 teaspoon of paprika
- 1 teaspoon of dried thyme
- ½ teaspoon of crushed red pepper flakes
- ½ teaspoon of fine sea salt
- ½ cup of heavy cream

Instructions:

- Press the "Sauté" function on your Instant Pot and add the olive oil.
- Once hot, add the chopped onions and minced garlic. Sauté for 4 minutes or until softened, stirring occasionally.
- Add the remaining ingredients except for the heavy cream. Lock the lid and cook at high pressure for 5 minutes. When the cooking is done, naturally release the pressure and remove the lid.
- Use an immersion blender to blend the contents until smooth. Gently stir in the heavy cream and adjust the seasoning if necessary. Serve and enjoy!

Quick Steak Tacos

Time: 10 minutes　　　　　Servings: 6

Ingredients:

- 1 (8-ounce package of sirloin steak, sliced into thin strips
- ½ cup of red onions, finely chopped
- ¼ cup of roma tomatoes, roughly chopped
- ¾ cups of shredded Mexican cheese
- 2 tablespoons of sour cream
- 6 tablespoons of mild Mexican salsa
- 1 tablespoon of extra-virgin olive oil
- 2 tablespoons of fresh cilantro, chopped

Instructions:

- Press the "Sauté" function on your Instant Pot and add the olive oil. Once the oil is hot, add the steak strips and cook for 3 minutes or until brown. Remove and set aside.
- Assemble the tacos with the chopped red onions, chopped tomatoes, Mexican cheese, mild salsa, and fresh cilantro. Serve and enjoy!

Pork and Green Pepper Stir-Fry
Time: 10 minutes   Servings: 2

Ingredients:

- 1 (10-ounce) pork shoulder, sliced
- 2 green bell peppers, seeds removed and sliced
- 2 scallions, chopped
- 4-ounces of butter
- 2 tablespoons of almonds
- 1 teaspoon of chili paste
- Fine sea salt and freshly cracked black pepper (to taste)

Instructions:

- Press the "Sauté" function on your Instant Pot and add the butter. Once melted, add the pork slices and cook until brown.
- Add the sliced green bell peppers and scallions. sauté until softened, stirring occasionally.
- Add the almonds, chili paste, sea salt and black pepper. Turn off "Sauté" setting. Serve!

Faux Cauliflower Mashed Potatoes
Time: 15 minutes   Servings: 4

Ingredients:

- 1 large head of cauliflower, cut into large florets
- 1 cup of homemade low-sodium vegetable stock
- 2 tablespoons of butter
- ¼ cup of heavy whipping cream
- ½ teaspoon of freshly cracked black pepper
- ½ teaspoon of fine sea salt
- 1 handful of fresh chives, chopped

Instructions:

- Add 1 cup of vegetable stock and a steamer basket inside your Instant Pot. Place the cauliflower florets on the steamer basket.
- Lock the lid and cook at high pressure for 4 minutes. When the cooking is done, quick release the pressure and remove the lid.
- Transfer the cauliflower florets to a food processor along with the heavy whipping cream, butter, black pepper, salt and fresh chives. Pulse until smooth. Serve and enjoy!

Garden Salsa
Time: 15 minutes   Servings: 6

Ingredients:

- 4 cups of finely diced tomatoes
- 1 medium yellow or white onion, finely chopped
- 4 tablespoons of coconut oil, melted
- 2 large green bell peppers, seeds removed and chopped
- 2 jalapeno pepper, seeded and chopped (optional)
- 4 medium garlic cloves, crushed
- 1 tablespoon of cumin
- 1 tablespoon of fine sea salt
- 1 tablespoon of cayenne pepper sauce (optional)
- ½ cup of apple cider vinegar
- 1 (15-ounce) can of crushed tomatoes
- 1 (6-ounce) can of tomato paste
- ½ cup of homemade low-sodium vegetable stock

Instructions:

- Press the "Sauté" setting on your Instant Pot and add the coconut oil. Once hot, add the chopped onions and garlic cloves. Sauté for 4 minutes or until translucent, stirring occasionally.
- Add all the remaining ingredients inside your Instant Pot and stir until well combined.
- Lock the lid and cook at high pressure for 10 minutes. When the cooking is done, naturally release the pressure and remove the lid.

- Transfer the salsa to mason jars and refrigerate. Serve and enjoy!

Chili Con Carne
Time: 15 minutes Servings: 6

Ingredients:

- 1 ½ pound of lean ground beef
- 1 (28-ounce) can of whole peeled tomatoes
- 1 large onion, finely chopped
- 6 medium garlic cloves, minced
- 1 large red bell pepper, seeds removed and chopped
- 1 (6-ounce) can of tomato paste
- 2 tablespoons of chili powder
- 1 tablespoon of cumin
- 2 tablespoons of smoked paprika
- 1 ½ cup of homemade low-sodium beef broth
- 2 teaspoons of fine sea salt
- 2 teaspoons of freshly cracked black pepper

Instructions:

- Press the "Sauté" function on your Instant Pot and add the ground beef. Cook for 5 minutes or until brown, breaking up the meat with a wooden spoon.
- Add the onions, bell pepper and garlic cloves. Sauté for another 2 to 4 minutes, stirring occasionally.
- Add the tomato paste and beef broth. Give a good stir.
- Add the remaining ingredients and stir until well combined.
- Lock the lid and cook at high pressure for 5 minutes. When the cooking is done, naturally release the pressure for 10 minutes, then quick release the remaining pressure.
- Press the "Sauté" function and cook until most of the liquid evaporates. Adjust the seasoning if necessary. Serve and enjoy!

Part 12: 5-Ingredient or Less Recipes

5-Ingredient Pulled Pork
Time: 1 hour and 40 minutes   Servings: 8

Ingredients:

- 4 pounds of pork shoulder roast, cut into chunks
- 2 cups of homemade low-sodium chicken broth
- 1 teaspoon of fine sea salt
- 1 teaspoon of freshly cracked black pepper
- 2 tablespoons of smoked paprika

Instructions:

- Season the pork shoulder roast with sea salt, black pepper and smoked paprika.
- Add the pork pieces to your Instant Pot along with the chicken broth.
- Lock the lid and cook at high pressure for 65 minutes. When the cooking is done, naturally release the pressure and carefully remove the lid.
- Transfer the pork pieces to a serving platter and use forks to shred. Serve and enjoy!

Paprika Chicken with Rutabaga
Time: 20 minutes   Servings: 4

Ingredients:

- 1 pound of chicken thighs
- 1 pound of rutabaga, peeled and cut into bite-sized pieces
- 4 tablespoons of olive oil
- 1 tablespoon of paprika
- 1 cup of homemade low-sodium chicken stock

Instructions:

- Season the chicken thighs with paprika.
- Press the "Sauté" function on your Instant Pot and add the chicken thighs. Cook for 4 minutes per side or until brown.
- Add the chicken stock and rutabaga pieces.
- Lock the lid and cook at high pressure for 15 minutes.
- When the cooking is done, quick release the pressure and remove the lid. Serve and enjoy!

Easiest Sloppy Joes Ever
Time: 30 minutes   Servings: 4

Ingredients:

- 1 pound of ground beef
- 1 (15-ounce) can of sloppy joe sauce
- 1 medium onion, finely chopped

Instructions:

- Press the "Sauté" function on your Instant Pot and add the ground beef and onions. Cook until brown and breaking up the meat with a wooden spoon.
- Add the sloppy joe sauce and lock the lid. Cook at high pressure for 5 minutes. When done, naturally release the pressure and remove the lid. Serve and enjoy!

3-Ingredient Cauliflower and Cheese
Time: 5 minutes   Servings: 4

Ingredients:

- 1 cup of cauliflower florets
- ½ cup of cheddar cheese, shredded
- 1 tablespoon of heavy whipping cream

Instructions:

- Add 1 cup of water and a steamer basket inside your Instant Pot. Place the cauliflower on the steamer basket.

- Lock the lid and cook at high pressure for 3 minutes. When the cooking is done, quick release the pressure and remove the lid.
- In a bowl, add the cauliflower, cheese and cream. Allow the cheese to melt. Serve.

Easy Cranberry Meatballs

Time: 10 minutes   Servings: 10

Ingredients:

- 2 pounds of ground beef
- 1 tablespoon of extra-virgin olive oil
- 1 (15-ounce) can of jellied cranberry sauce
- ½ cup of homemade low-sodium beef broth

Instructions:

- Form 1-inch meatballs with the ground beef and set aside.
- Press the "Sauté" function on your Instant Pot and add the olive oil.
- Working in batches, add the meatballs and cook until slightly brown.
- Add the beef broth and cranberry sauce to your Instant Pot.
- Lock the lid and cook at high pressure for 5 minutes. When the cooking is done, naturally release the pressure and remove the lid. Serve and enjoy!

Chicken Sausage and Green Beans

Time: 6 minutes   Servings: 4

Ingredients:

- 2 cups of homemade low-sodium chicken stock
- 2 (16-ounces) of frozen green beans
- 1 (16-ounce) of chicken sausage, slice
- ½ medium onion, finely chopped

Instructions:

- Add all the ingredients to your Instant Pot and lock the lid. Cook at high pressure for 6 minutes.
- When the cooking is done, quick release the pressure and carefully remove the lid.Serve!

Spanish Cauliflower Rice

Time: 35 minutes   Servings: 12

Ingredients:

- 4 cups of cauliflower rice
- 2 tablespoons of extra-virgin olive oil
- 4 ½ cups of homemade low-sodium vegetable broth
- 1 yellow onion, finely chopped
- 1 (28-ounce) can of diced tomatoes and green chilies

Instructions:

- Press the "Sauté" function on your Instant Pot and add the olive oil.
- Once hot, add the onions and cook until lightly brown, stirring occasionally.
- Add the remaining ingredients and lock the lid. Cook at high pressure for 3 minutes.
- When the cooking is done, quick release the pressure and carefully remove the lid. Stir everything. Serve and enjoy!

Simple Spaghetti Squash

Time: 25 minutes   Servings: 4

Ingredients:

- 2 pounds of spaghetti squash
- 1 cup of water

Instructions:

- Use a fork to poke holes over the spaghetti squash.

- Add 1 cup of water and a steamer basket to your Instant Pot. Place the spaghetti squash on top.
- Lock the lid and cook at high pressure for 15 minutes.
- When the cooking is done, naturally release the pressure and carefully remove the lid. Remove the spaghetti squash to a cutting board and shred using forks. Serve and enjoy!

5-Ingredient Broccoli and Cheddar Cheese Soup

Time: 15 minutes   Servings: 8

Ingredients:

- 2 cups of broccoli, roughly chopped
- 1 yellow onion, finely chopped
- 4 cups of homemade low-sodium chicken stock
- 1 cup of cheddar cheese, shredded
- 1 (12-ounce) can of evaporated milk

Instructions:

- Add the broccoli and chicken stock to your Instant Pot.
- Lock the lid and cook at high pressure for 5 minutes.
- When the cooking is done, quick release the pressure and remove the lid.
- Press the "Sauté" function on your Instant Pot and stir in the evaporated milk and cheddar cheese. Cook until the cheese has melted, stirring frequently. Serve and enjoy!

Sautéed Shredded Zucchini and Feta

Time: 20 minutes   Servings: 8

Ingredients:

- 4 medium zucchinis, finely shredded
- 1 cup of feta cheese
- 4 medium garlic cloves, peeled and crushed
- 1 tablespoon of extra-virgin olive oil
- 1 tablespoon of fresh dill

Instructions:

- Press the "Sauté" function on your Instant Pot and set to the lowest setting.
- Add the extra-virgin olive oil and garlic. Sauté for 1 minute.
- Add the shredded zucchini and sauté for around 8 minutes, stirring occasionally.
- Add the feta cheese. Continue to cook until the cheese has melted, stirring occasionally. Discard any excess liquid. Serve and enjoy!

Part 13: Wicked Recipes

Fabulous Goose Meat
Time: 30 minutes   Servings: 4

Ingredients:

- 4 goose breasts, boneless, skinless (or any other goose meat)
- 1 (12-ounce) can cream of mushroom soup
- 2 Tablespoons coconut oil
- 1 teaspoon garlic powder

- 1 teaspoon onion powder
- 1 teaspoon paprika
- 2 teaspoons salt
- 2 teaspoons fresh ground black pepper

Instructions:

1. Press Sauté button on Instant Pot. Heat the coconut oil.
2. Sauté goose meat until golden brown crust per side.
3. Press Keep Warm/Cancel button to end Sauté mode.
4. In a small bowl, combine the spices. Sprinkle the seasoning over the goose.
5. Pour cream of mushroom soup over meat.
6. Close and seal lid. Press Manual button. Cook at High Pressure for 10 minutes.
7. When the timer beeps, naturally release pressure. Open the lid with care.
8. Allow dish to rest 5 minutes before removing from Instant Pot. Serve.

Nourishing Jambalaya
Time: 15 minutes   Servings: 4

Ingredients:

- 1 pound chicken breasts, boneless, skinless
- 1 pound Italian sausage
- 2 Tablespoons coconut oil
- 1 red onion, chopped
- 2 garlic cloves, minced
- 2 cups cauliflower rice

- 2 bell peppers, chopped
- 2 cups crushed tomatoes
- 1 Tablespoon Worcestershire sauce
- 3 cups chicken broth
- 1 teaspoon salt (to taste)
- 1 teaspoon fresh ground black pepper (to taste)

Instructions:

1. Rinse the chicken, pat dry. Chop into bite-size pieces. Slice Italian sausage into circles, ¼ inch thick. Press Sauté button on Instant Pot. Heat the coconut oil,
2. Sauté red onion and garlic for 2 minutes. Add chicken and Italian sausage. Sauté until meat is brown. Press Keep Warm/Cancel to end Sauté mode.
3. Add cauliflower rice, bell peppers, crushed tomatoes. Stir well.
4. Stir in chicken broth, Worcestershire sauce, salt and pepper.
5. Close and seal lid. Press Manual button. Cook at High Pressure for 10 minutes.
6. Quick-Release the pressure when done. Open the lid with care. Serve.

Party Octopus
Time: 20 minutes   Servings: 4

Ingredients:

- 1 octopus, cleaned
- 2 Tablespoons ghee, melted
- Juice from ½ lemon
- 1 Tablespoon fresh rosemary, chopped
- 1 Tablespoon fresh oregano, chopped
- 1 Tablespoon of fresh thyme, chopped

- 1 teaspoon garlic powder
- 1 teaspoon onion powder
- 1 teaspoon salt
- 1 teaspoon fresh ground black pepper
- 2 cups of water

Instructions:

1. Place octopus in Instant Pot.

2. Add melted ghee, water, lemon juice, herbs, and seasonings. Stir well.
3. Close and seal lid. Pres Manual button. Cook at High Pressure for 15 minutes.
4. When the timer beeps, naturally release pressure. Open the lid with care. Serve.

Thankful Thanksgiving Whole Turkey
Time: 45 minutes   Servings: 6

Ingredients:

- 1 whole turkey (large enough for your Instant Pot)
- 1 Tablespoon fresh rosemary, chopped
- 1 Tablespoon fresh thyme, chopped
- 1 Tablespoon fresh sage, chopped
- 2 Tablespoons coconut oil
- 1 cup white wine vinegar

- 2 cups turkey or chicken broth
- 2 teaspoons onion powder
- 2 teaspoons garlic powder
- 2 teaspoons paprika
- 2 teaspoons salt
- 2 teaspoons fresh ground black pepper

Instructions:

1. Remove all parts in turkey cavity. Wash and pat dry.
2. Drizzle coconut oil over the turkey.
3. Combine seasoning and herbs. Rub all over surface of turkey.
4. Press Sauté button on Instant Pot.
5. Place turkey in Instant Pot. Sauté for 3 minutes; flip cook another 3 minutes. (Don't worry if parts of turkey are not golden brown.)
6. Press Keep Warm/Cancel setting to stop Sauté mode.
7. Pour white vinegar and broth over your turkey.
8. Close and seal lid. Press Manual switch. Cook at High Pressure for 30 minutes.
9. When the timer beeps, naturally release pressure. Open the lid with care.
10. Allow the turkey to rest for 5 minutes before removing. Set turkey on a platter. Rest 20 minutes before slicing. Serve.

Luscious Broccoli and Asparagus with Roasted Almonds
Time: 20 minutes   Servings: 4

Ingredients:

- 1 head broccoli, chopped into florets
- 1 pound asparagus, stemmed and chopped
- 4 garlic cloves, minced
- 1 cup almonds, chopped
- 2 Tablespoons coconut oil

- 1 shallot, thinly sliced
- 1 cup vegetable broth
- ¼ cup fresh parsley, chopped
- 1 teaspoon salt (to taste)
- 1 teaspoon fresh ground black pepper (to taste)

Instructions:

1. Press Sauté mode on Instant Pot. Heat the coconut oil.
2. Sauté shallots and garlic for 2 minutes. Add broccoli florets and asparagus. Cook until vegetables soften. Add remaining ingredients. Stir well.
3. Close and seal lid. Press Manual button. Cook on high pressure for 15 minutes.
4. Quick-Release the pressure when done. Open the lid with care. Stir well. Serve.

Yummy Mango Puree
Time: 20 minutes   Servings: 4

Ingredients:

- 2 mangos, chopped
- ¼ cup plump golden raisins
- 1 shallot, chopped
- 1 Tablespoon coconut oil
- 1 apple, cored and chopped

- 1 teaspoon cinnamon
- 2 Tablespoons fresh ginger, minced
- 1 cup granulated Splenda
- 1 Tablespoon apple cider vinegar
- 2 cups of water

Instructions:

1. Press Sauté button on Instant Pot. Heat the coconut oil.
2. Sauté shallot and ginger until translucent. Press Keep Warm/Cancel button to cancel Sauté mode. Add remaining ingredients. Stir well.
3. Close and seal lid. Press Manual button. Cook at High Pressure for 7 minutes.
4. When the timer beeps, quick-release pressure. Open the lid with care. Stir ingredients.
5. Use immersion blender to blend ingredients until smooth. Allow to cool in refrigerator.

Crunchy Pumpkin Pie
Time: 30 minutes   Servings: 6

Filling Ingredients:

- 3 cups pumpkin puree
- ½ cup granulated Splenda
- ½ cup coconut milk

- 2 teaspoons pumpkin pie spice
- 1 large egg

Crust Ingredients:

- 1 cup pecan cookies, crushed
- 1 cup toasted pecans, roughly chopped

- 2 Tablespoons ghee, melted

Instructions:

1. In a large bowl, combine pecan cookies and ghee.
2. In a separate bowl, combine filling ingredients.
3. Grease pie pan, suitable for Instant Pot, with non-stick cooking spray.
4. Firmly press crust mixture into bottom of pan.
5. Pour filling into crust. Top with toasted pecans. Cover with aluminum foil.
6. Pour 2 cups of water in Instant Pot. Place trivet in Pot. Place pie pan on the trivet.
7. Close and seal lid. Press Manual button. Cook at High Pressure for 15 minutes.
8. When the timer beeps, naturally release pressure. Open the lid with care.
9. Cool for 30 minutes on counter. Refrigerate remaining portion.

Thai Green Curry with Special Broccoli Rabe
Time: 30 minutes   Servings: 4

Ingredients:

- 1 bunch of broccolis rabe, ends trimmed
- 2 boneless, skinless chicken breasts, cut into 1-inch pieces
- ½ cup of chicken stock
- 3 tablespoons of green curry paste
- 1 (8-ounce) can of full-fat coconut milk
- 2 tablespoons of coconut aminos

- 1 fennel bulb, sliced into 2-inch pieces
- 1 tablespoon of extra-virgin olive oil
- 2 medium garlic cloves, peeled and minced
- 1 tablespoon of fresh ginger, minced
- 2 cups of cauliflower rice
- ½ cup of fresh cilantro, chopped (optional)

Instructions:

- Press the "Sauté" function on your Instant Pot and add the olive oil.
- Once the Instant Pot is hot, add the chicken pieces and cook until brown. Turn off "Sauté" function.
- Add the chicken stock and lock the lid. Cook at high pressure for 8 minutes. When the cooking is done, quick release the pressure and remove the lid.
- Add the remaining ingredients except for the broccoli rabe and cilantro to your Instant Pot.
- Lock the lid and cook at high pressure for 2 minutes. When the cooking is done, quick release the pressure.
- Stir in the broccoli rabe and put back the lid. Allow to sit for a couple of minutes. Serve !

Moroccan Lemon Chicken with Olives
Time: 50 minutes   Servings: 4

Ingredients:

- 2 pounds of boneless, skinless chicken thighs or chicken breasts

- 2 large yellow onions, finely sliced

- 2 tablespoons of extra-virgin olive oil or other cooking fat
- 4 medium garlic cloves, peeled and minced
- ½ cup of homemade low-sodium chicken broth or stock
- 2 medium lemons, cut into quarters and seeds removed
- ½ cup of whole green olives, sliced in half and pits removed
- 1 teaspoon of smoked paprika
- 1 teaspoon of ground cumin
- 1 teaspoon of ground ginger
- 1 teaspoon of ground coriander
- 1 teaspoon of turmeric powder
- 1 cinnamon stick
- A fine pinch of sea salt and freshly cracked black pepper

Instructions:

- In a large bowl, add all the ingredients and stir until well combined. Cover with plastic wrap and marinate overnight.
- Add all the ingredients to your Instant Pot and lock the lid. Cook at high pressure for 15 minutes. When the cooking is done, naturally release the pressure for 10 minutes. Then quick release the remaining pressure. Carefully remove the lid.
- Remove and set the chicken aside. Press the "Sauté" function on your Instant Pot and continue to cook for 5 minutes or until the onions become mushy, stirring occasionally.
- Return the chicken to your Instant Pot and cover with the sauce. Serve and enjoy!

North African Beef Stew
Time: 1 hour and 30 minutes   Servings: 6

Ingredients:

- 2 pounds of beef stew meat, cut into bite-sized pieces
- 2 to 3 cups of homemade low-sodium beef stock or water
- 4 tablespoons of extra-virgin olive oil, more or less
- 1 medium yellow onion, finely chopped
- 4 Roma tomatoes, chopped
- 4 medium garlic cloves, peeled and minced
- 1 celery stalk with leaves
- 2 basil leaves
- 1 teaspoon of fresh thyme
- 1 (14-ounce) can of tomato sauce
- ½ teaspoon of curry powder
- 1 teaspoon of fine sea salt
- 1 teaspoon of white pepper
- 2 teaspoons of smoked paprika

Instructions:

- Press the "Sauté" function on your Instant Pot and add 2 tablespoons of olive oil.
- Working in batches, add the beef pieces and cook until brown.
- Add the beef stock and lock the lid. Cook at high pressure for 35 minutes. When the cooking is done, naturally release the pressure and carefully remove the lid. Discard the liquid.
- In a blender, add the onions, tomatoes, tomato sauce, celery, basil leaves, fresh thyme, curry powder, sea salt, white pepper and smoked paprika. Blend until smooth.
- Add the mixture to the beef pieces. Lock the lid and cook at high pressure for another 10 minutes. When the cooking is done, naturally release the pressure and carefully remove the lid. Check if the meat is tender. Serve and enjoy!

Jollof Cauliflower Rice
Time: 12 minutes   Servings: 6

Ingredients:

- 2 cups of vegetable stock
- 2 ½ cups of cauliflower rice
- 2 tablespoons of extra-virgin olive oil
- 1 medium white onion, finely sliced
- 2 medium garlic cloves, minced
- 4 tablespoons of tomato puree
- 1 teaspoon of ground coriander
- ½ teaspoon of ground ginger
- ½ teaspoon of ground nutmeg
- ½ teaspoon of ground cinnamon

Instructions:

- Press the "Sauté" function on your Instant Pot and add the extra-virgin olive oil.
- Once hot, add the onions and garlic. Sauté for 5 minutes, stirring occasionally.

- Add the remaining ingredients and stir until well combined.
- Lock the lid and cook at high pressure for 2 minutes.
- When the cooking is done, naturally release the pressure and remove the lid. Serve!

Crustless Crab Quiche

Time: 1 hour   Servings: 4

Ingredients:

- 4 organic large eggs
- 1 cup of half and half
- 1 cup of parmesan or swiss cheese, shredded
- 1 cup of green onions, chopped
- 2 cups of crab meat
- 1 teaspoon of smoked paprika
- 1 teaspoon of herbes de provence
- 1 teaspoon of fine sea salt
- 1 teaspoon of freshly cracked black pepper

Instructions:

- In a large bowl, add the eggs and beat.
- Add the sea salt, black pepper, herbes de provence and smoked paprika. Stir until well combined.
- Stir in the green onions, crab meat and shredded cheese.
- Add the egg mixture into a spring form pan that fits inside your Instant Pot. Cover with foil.
- Add 2 cups of water and a trivet to your Instant Pot. Place the spring form pan on top of the trivet and lock the lid.
- Cook at high pressure for 40 minutes. When the cooking is done, naturally release the pressure for 10 minutes and then quick release the remaining pressure. Carefully remove the lid. Serve and enjoy!

Pot Roast with Mocha Rub

Time: 1 hour and 10 minutes   Servings: 4

Mocha Ingredients:

- 2 tablespoons of ground coffee or decaffeinated coffee
- 2 tablespoons of smoked paprika
- 1 tablespoon of unsweetened cocoa powder
- 1 tablespoon of freshly cracked black pepper
- 1 teaspoon of fine sea salt
- 1 teaspoon of cayenne pepper
- 1 teaspoon of chili powder
- 1 teaspoon of organic ground ginger

Pot Roast Ingredients:

- 2 pounds of beef chuck roast, cut into bite-sized pieces
- 1 cup of brewed coffee or decaffeinated coffee
- 1 cup of homemade low-sodium beef broth
- 1 small yellow or white onion, finely chopped
- 3 tablespoons of balsamic vinegar
- 2 tablespoons of extra-virgin olive oil

Instructions:

1. In a small bowl, add all the seasoning ingredients and mix until well combined. Rub 3 to 4 tablespoons of the seasoning mixture onto the beef pieces. You can save the extra seasoning for future use.
2. In a blender, add the coffee, beef broth, onions, and balsamic vinegar. Blend until well combined.
3. Press the "Sauté" function on your Instant Pot and add the olive oil.
4. Working in batches, add the beef pieces and cook until brown. Add the liquid.
5. Lock the lid and cook at high pressure for 35 minutes. When the cooking is done, naturally release the pressure and remove the lid. Check if the meat is tender.
6. Transfer the beef pieces to a cutting board and shred using two forks. Serve and enjoy!

Perfect Baba Ghanoush Eggplant Dip

Time: 30 minutes   Servings: 10

Ingredients:

- 1 eggplant, skin removed, halved and sliced
- 1/3 cups of olive oil or cooking oil
- 5 medium garlic cloves, minced
- ½ teaspoon of fine sea salt

213

- ¼ cup of homemade low-sodium vegetable stock
- 2 tablespoons of tahini
- 2 tablespoons of fresh parsley, finely chopped

Instructions:

- Press the "Sauté" function on your Instant Pot and add a few tablespoons of olive oil.
- Once hot and working in batches, sauté the eggplant slices until slightly charred on each side.
- Add the minced garlic, sea salt and vegetable stock. Lock the lid and cook at high pressure for 3 minutes.
- When the cooking is done, quick release the pressure and carefully remove the lid.
- If there is still excess liquid inside your Instant Pot, press the "Sauté" function on your Instant Pot and cook until most of the liquid evaporates.
- Stir in the tahini and fresh parsley and transfer to a bowl. Serve as a dip!

Swedish Meatballs
Time: 45 minutes   Servings: 8

Ingredients:

- 1 pound of ground beef
- 1 pound of ground pork
- 2 large egg yolks
- 1 medium shallot, finely chopped
- 2 medium garlic cloves, minced
- 3 tablespoons of coconut flour
- 1/3 cup of unsweetened coconut milk
- ½ teaspoon of dried thyme
- ½ teaspoon of fine sea salt
- ½ teaspoon of freshly cracked black pepper
- 2 tablespoons of extra-virgin olive oil
- 2 cups of homemade low-sodium beef broth
- ½ cup of sour cream
- 2 tablespoons of fresh dill, chopped
- 2 tablespoons of fresh parsley, chopped

Instructions:

- In a large bowl, add the ground beef, ground pork, egg, chopped shallot, minced garlic, coconut flour, coconut milk, dried thyme, sea salt, and black pepper. Stir until well combined and form 1-inch meatballs.
- Press the "Sauté" function on your Instant Pot and add the olive oil.
- Working in batches, add the meatballs and cook for 1 minute or until lightly browned.
- Return all the meatballs to your Instant Pot along with the beef broth. Lock the lid and cook at high pressure for 8 minutes.
- When the cooking is done, quick release the pressure and carefully remove the lid. Remove the meatballs and set aside.
- Press the "Sauté" function on your Instant Pot and cook the liquid until most of it evaporates. Stir in the sour cream.
- Return the meatballs and spoon the sauce over. Serve and enjoy!

Mumbai Pav Bhaji
Time: 30 minutes   Servings: 6

Ingredients:

- 2 tablespoons of olive oil or ghee
- 2 medium onions, finely chopped
- 5 medium tomatoes, chopped
- 1-inch fresh ginger, minced
- 8 medium garlic cloves
- 3 dried red chilis, minced
- 1 red bell pepper, chopped
- 3 carrots, cut into bite-sized pieces
- 2 cups of cauliflower, finely chopped
- ½ cup of homemade low-sodium vegetable broth or vegetable stock
- 2 tablespoons of garam masala
- 2 teaspoons of fine sea salt
- 1 tablespoon of freshly squeezed lemon juice

Instructions:

- Press the "Sauté" function on your Instant Pot and add the 2 tablespoons of olive oil.
- Once hot, add the onions and sauté for 3 minutes.
- Add the other chopped vegetables and sauté for 4 to 6 minutes, stirring occasionally. Pour in the vegetable broth. Lock the lid and cook at high pressure for 8 minutes.
- When the cooking is done, naturally release the pressure and carefully remove the lid. Use a potato masher to mash the vegetables until it reached your desired consistency.

- Press the "Sauté" function on your Instant Pot and allow the vegetables to cook for a little longer. Stir in the seasoning and lemon juice. Serve and enjoy!

Hollandaise Sauce
Time: 20 minutes   Servings: Almost 1 cup

Ingredients:

- 2 cups of cauliflower
- 2 large egg yolks
- 4 teaspoons of freshly squeezed lemon juice

- ¼ teaspoon of white pepper
- ¼ teaspoon of fine sea salt
- 2 tablespoons of unsalted butter, melted

Instructions:

- Add 1 ½ cup of water and a steamer basket to your Instant Pot. Place the cauliflower in the steamer basket.
- Lock the lid and cook at high pressure for 2 minutes. When the timer beeps, quick release the pressure and remove the lid. Add all the ingredients to a food processor or blender and blend until extremely smooth and creamy. Serve and enjoy!

Baingan Bharta
Time: 25 minutes   Servings: 4

Ingredients:

- 2 tablespoons of coconut oil
- ½ teaspoon of cumin seeds
- 1 small onion, finely chopped
- 1-inch fresh ginger, finely chopped
- 5 medium garlic cloves, minced
- 1 hot green chili, finely chopped
- 1 large tomato, finely chopped
- 1 large eggplant, peeled and cut into cubes

- ½ cup of homemade low-sodium vegetable stock
- ¼ cup of fresh cilantro, chopped
- ½ teaspoon of fine sea salt
- 1 teaspoon of turmeric
- 1 teaspoon of ground coriander
- ½ teaspoon of smoked paprika
- ½ teaspoon of garam masala

Instructions:

- Press the "Sauté" function on your Instant Pot and add the coconut oil.
- Once hot, add chopped onions, ginger, garlic and chili. Sauté for 3 minutes or until fragrant, stirring occasionally. Add the diced tomatoes and all seasonings. Sauté for another minute, stirring occasionally.
- Add the remaining ingredients and lock the lid. Cook at high pressure for 10 minutes.
- When the cooking is done, naturally release the pressure and carefully remove the lid.
- Use a potato masher to mash the contents until it reached your desired consistency. Adjust the seasoning if necessary. Serve and enjoy!

Sicilian Meat Sauce
Time: 40 minutes   Servings: 12

Ingredients:

- 2 pounds of boneless pork ribs
- 3 tablespoons of extra-virgin olive oil
- 1 medium onion, finely chopped
- 4 medium garlic cloves, minced
- 2 (28-ounce) cans of crushed tomatoes
- 1 (6-ounce) can of Italian tomato paste
- 3 bay leaves
- 1 cup of homemade low-sodium beef stock

- ½ cup of low-sugar keto-friendly red wine or more beef stock
- 2 tablespoons of fresh parsley, chopped
- 2 tablespoons of capers, chopped and drained
- ½ teaspoon of dried basil
- ½ teaspoon of crushed dried rosemary
- ½ teaspoon of dried thyme
- ½ teaspoon of crushed red pepper flakes
- ½ teaspoon of fine sea salt

Instructions:

- Press the "Sauté" function on your Instant Pot and add 2 tablespoons of olive oil.
- Working in batches, add the pork ribs and cook for 2 to 4 minutes per side or until brown. Set aside.

215

- Add the onions and garlic and sauté until fragrant, stirring occasionally.
- Add the remaining ingredients and return the pork ribs to your Instant Pot.
- Lock the lid and cook at high pressure for 35 minutes.
- When the cooking is done, naturally release the pressure for 10 minutes before quick releasing the remaining pressure.
- Remove the bay leaves and transfer the pork ribs to a serving platter. Use two forks to shred the meat and return to the sauce. Adjust the seasoning if necessary. Serve and enjoy!

Vegetables En Papillote
Time: 20 minutes   Servings: 3

Ingredients:

- 4-ounces of fresh green beans, trimmed
- 4 small carrots, peeled and sliced into strips
- ¼ teaspoon of fine sea salt
- ¼ teaspoon of freshly cracked black pepper
- 1 large garlic clove, peeled and minced
- 1 tablespoon of olive oil
- 1 tablespoon of freshly squeezed lemon juice
- 1 tablespoon of herbs of choice, chopped
- 1 (15-inch) sheet of parchment paper

Instructions:

- Add 1 cup of water and a trivet to your Instant Pot.
- Lay the sheet of parchment paper on your kitchen counter and add the vegetables. Season with salt, pepper and herbs. Add the garlic and drizzle with olive oil and lemon juice. Carefully fold the parchment paper and place on top of the trivet. Lock the lid and cook at high pressure for 2 minutes.
- When the timer beeps, naturally release the pressure for 3 minutes before quick releasing the remaining pressure. Carefully remove the lid. Serve and enjoy!

Jamaican Curry Chicken
Time: 30 minutes   Servings: 6

Ingredients:

- 2 pounds of chicken legs
- 1 tablespoon of fine sea salt
- 2 tablespoons of Jamaican curry powder
- 1 small white onion, chopped
- 1 sprig of fresh thyme
- 1 tablespoon of coconut oil

Instructions:

- Press the "Sauté" function on your Instant Pot and add the coconut oil.
- Once hot, add the chopped onions and sauté until translucent, stirring occasionally.
- Season the chicken legs with the sea salt and Jamaican curry powder.
- Add 1 cup of water and thyme. Lock the lid and cook at high pressure for 15 minutes.
- When the cooking is done, naturally release the pressure and carefully remove the lid. Serve and enjoy!

Cranberry Chutney
Time: 30 minutes   Servings: 6

Ingredients:

- 1 ½ cup of fresh cranberries
- 1 cup of sweet onion, finely chopped
- ¼ cup of fresh ginger, finely grated
- ½ cup of dried cranberries or dried blueberries
- 1 teaspoon of garam masala
- ½ teaspoon of organic cayenne pepper
- ¼ cup of truvia low-carb brown sugar
- 1 teaspoon of fin sea salt
- 1 teaspoon of organic turmeric
- ½ teaspoon of organic apple pie spice
- ¼ cup of filtered water

Instructions:

- Add all the ingredients to your Instant Pot and stir until well combined.
- Lock the lid and cook at high pressure for 4 minutes.

216

- When the cooking is done, naturally release the pressure for 10 minutes. Then quick release the remaining pressure.
- Use an immersion blender to blend the contents until smooth or reach your desired consistency.
- Serve and enjoy!

Part 14: Holiday Recipes

Creamed Kale
Time: 15 minutes   Servings: 6

Ingredients:

- 2 cups of kale, stemmed and roughly chopped
- 3 tablespoons of unsalted butter
- 1 tablespoons of extra-virgin olive oil
- 2 small shallots, finely chopped
- 1 medium garlic clove, minced
- 6-ounces of cream cheese, softened
- ½ cup of homemade low-sodium chicken broth
- ½ cup of heavy whipping cream
- 2 tablespoons of almond flour
- ¼ cup of parmesan cheese, grated
- Fin sea salt and freshly cracked black pepper (to taste)

Instructions:

- Press the "Sauté" function on your Instant Pot and add the olive oil.
- Once the oil is hot, add the shallots and garlic. Sauté until translucent, stirring occasionally.
- Add the remaining ingredients except for the almond flour and parmesan cheese to your Instant Pot. Stir until well combined.
- Lock the lid and cook at high pressure for 5 minutes.
- When the cooking is done, quick release the pressure and remove the lid.
- Sprinkle the almond flour and parmesan cheese. Stir the contents. Serve and enjoy!

Superbowl Spinach Artichoke Dip
Time: 8 minutes   Servings: 10

Ingredients:

- 1 (15-ounce) jar of artichoke hearts, drained
- 1 small white or yellow onions, finely chopped
- ½ cup of homemade low-sodium chicken stock
- 3 medium garlic cloves, peeled and minced
- 1 (10-ounce) bag of frozen spinach
- 8-ounces of cream cheese, softened
- ½ cup of sour cream
- ½ cup of low-carb mayonnaise
- 1 cup of parmesan cheese, shredded
- 1 cup of mozzarella or Monterey jack cheese, shredded
- A pinch of fine sea salt and freshly cracked black pepper

Instructions:

- In your Instant Pot, add the artichoke hearts, chopped onions, chicken stock, and minced garlic.
- Add the frozen spinach, mayonnaise, sour cream and mayonnaise. It's important not to stir the contents. Just place it on top.
- Lock the lid and cook at high pressure for 4 minutes. When the cooking is done, quick release the pressure and carefully remove the lid.
- Stir in the shredded parmesan cheese, shredded mozzarella cheese, salt and freshly cracked black pepper. Serve and enjoy!

Caramelized Bacon Green Beans
Time: 30 minutes   Servings: 6

Ingredients:

- 1 ½ pound of fresh green beans, trimmed and cut into 2-inch pieces
- 1 tablespoon of fresh ginger, finely grated
- 1 pound of bacon, finely chopped
- 1 red onion, finely chopped
- 2 medium garlic cloves, peeled and minced
- ¼ cup of water
- ¼ cup of coconut aminos
- 1 teaspoon of fine sea salt
- ½ teaspoon of freshly cracked black pepper

Instructions:

- Press the "Sauté" function on your Instant Pot and add the bacon. Cook until brown and crispy, stirring occasionally. Transfer to a plate lined with paper towels.
- Add the onions and sauté for 4 minutes or until translucent, stirring occasionally.
- Deglaze with ¼ cup of water and add the green beans. Lock the lid and cook at high pressure for 5 minutes.
- When the cooking is done, quick release the pressure and carefully remove the lid.
- Press the "Sauté" function on your instant pot and stir in the coconut aminos, sea salt and freshly cracked black pepper. Sauté for minutes or until caramelized. Stir in the chopped bacon. Serve and enjoy!

Bacon Wrapped Asparagus
Time: 12 minutes   Servings: 3

Ingredients:

- 12 asparagus spears, cleaned
- 3 medium slices of bacon
- 1 cup of water

- ½ cup of heavy cream
- ½ teaspoon of fine sea salt
- ½ teaspoon of freshly cracked black pepper

Instructions:

- Add water and a trivet to your Instant Pot.
- In a bowl, add the asparagus along with the heavy cream. Remove and season with salt and pepper.
- For each four asparagus spears, wrap with bacon slices and place on top of your trivet. Lock the lid. Cook at high pressure for 3 minutes. When the cooking is done, naturally release the pressure. Serve and enjoy!

Pumpkin Pie Pudding
Time: 40 minutes   Servings: 6

Ingredients:

- 2 large organic eggs
- ½ cup of heavy whipping cream
- ¾ cups of erythritol, swerve, or Splenda

- 1 (15-ounce) can of pureed pumpkin
- 1 teaspoon of pumpkin pie spice
- 1 teaspoon of pure vanilla extract

Instructions:

- In a bowl, add and stir the eggs, heavy whipping cream, erythritol, pureed pumpkin, pumpkin pie spice and pure vanilla extract.
- Grease a pan that fits inside your Instant Pot with nonstick cooking spray and pour in the mixture.
- Add 1 cup of water and a trivet to your Instant Pot. Place the pan on top of the trivet and cover with foil.
- Lock the lid and cook at high pressure for 20 minutes.
- When the cooking is done, naturally release the pressure for 10 minutes. Then quick release the remaining pressure. Carefully remove the lid.
- Transfer the pumpkin pie spice pudding inside your refrigerator and allow to chill.Serve and enjoy!

Eggnog
Time: 15 minutes   Servings: 8

Ingredients:

- 6 egg
- 2/3 cups of granulated Splenda or keto-friendly sweeteners
- 2 cups of whole unsweetened milk
- 1 cup of heavy cream

- ½ teaspoon of pure vanilla extract
- ½ teaspoon of nutmeg
- ¼ teaspoon of fine sea salt
- 5 cups of water

Instructions:

- Add a trivet and 5 cups of water. Press the "Sauté" function to get the water to boil.
- In a blender, add the eggs and blend for 15 minutes or until fully broken up.
- Add the granulated Splenda, unsweetened milk, heavy cream, pure vanilla extract, nutmeg, and sea salt. Blend for another 30 seconds or until well combined.

- Pour the eggnog into a dish that fits the liquid. Place on top of the trivet and whisk the eggnog while the water is boiling.
- Once the eggnog is at 150 degrees Fahrenheit, turn off your Instant Pot and continue to mix until your eggnog is at 160 degrees Fahrenheit. Transfer the eggnog to a container and refrigerate. Serve and enjoy!

Mashed Garlic Cauliflower

Time: 35 minutes   Servings: 6

Ingredients:

- 1 large cauliflower head, chopped
- 1 cup of homemade low-sodium chicken stock
- 1 head of garlic
- ¼ cup of unsweetened almond milk
- 1 tablespoon of ghee
- 1 teaspoon of fine sea salt
- 1 teaspoon of freshly cracked black pepper

Instructions:

- Add the chicken stock, garlic and a trivet to your Instant Pot. Place the cauliflower on the trivet and lock the lid. Cook at high pressure for 15 minutes. When the cooking is done, quick release the pressure and carefully remove the lid. Discard the liquid. In a food processor, add the cauliflower and garlic. Process until smooth.
- Stir in the ghee, unsweetened almond milk, sea salt and freshly cracked black pepper.Serve!

Holiday Deviled Eggs

Time: 30 minutes   Servings: 12

Ingredients:

- 6 organic large eggs
- 2 tablespoons of low-carb, sugar-free mayonnaise
- 1 tablespoon of unsweetened milk
- 1 teaspoon of dill pickle juice
- A pinch of fine sea salt and freshly cracked black pepper
- 1 cup of water
- Paprika (for garnish)
- Fresh dill (for garnish)

Instructions:

- Add 1 cup of water and a rack to your Instant Pot.
- Place the eggs on top of the track and lock the lid. Cook at high pressure for 5 minutes and naturally release the pressure for 5 minutes before quick release the remaining pressure.
- Transfer the large eggs to an ice bath and remove the shells.Slice the eggs in half and transfer the yolks to a bowl. Mash with a fork and stir in the mayonnaise, unsweetened milk, dill pickle juice, salt and freshly cracked black pepper. Spoon the yolk mixture onto each egg half. Sprinkle with paprika and fresh dill. Serve and enjoy!

Christmas Whole Turkey

Time: 1 hour and 10 minutes   Servings: 12

Ingredients:

- 1 whole (8 pound) turkey, fresh
- 1 medium yellow or white onion, quartered
- 1 celery stalk, quartered
- 1 medium carrot, quartered
- 2 whole garlic cloves, halved
- 1 dried bay leaf
- 1 cup of water
- 2 tablespoons of butter
- 1 teaspoon of fine sea salt
- 1 teaspoon of freshly cracked black pepper
- ½ teaspoon of paprika

Instructions:

- Season the turkey with sea salt, freshly cracked black pepper and paprika.
- Rub and gently spread the butter on the turkey. Get inside the turkey as well.
- Add some onions and garlic inside the turkey and add the remaining vegetables to your Instant Pot. Pour in the cup of water and add a trivet. Place the turkey on top of the trivet and lock the lid.
- Cook at high pressure for 50 minutes and naturally release the pressure. Carefully remove the lid. Allow the turkey to cool before serving. Enjoy!

Thanksgiving Ham
Time: 30 minutes   Servings: 24

Ingredients:

- 4 pounds of boneless ham
- 1 cup of apple cider vinegar
- 1 tablespoon of Worcestershire sauce
- 1 whole cinnamon stick
- 1 bay leaf
- 1 tablespoon of rosemary, chopped

- 2 tablespoons of fresh lemon juice
- 1 teaspoon of fine sea salt
- 1 teaspoon of freshly cracked black pepper
- ¼ cup of Splenda sweetener or other keto-friendly sweeteners
- 1 cup of water

Instructions:

- Add a trivet and all the ingredients to your Instant Pot except for ham.
- Place the ham on the trivet and lock the lid. Cook at high pressure for 10 minutes.
- When the cooking is done, naturally release the pressure and carefully remove the lid.
- Pour the liquid on top of the ham and allow to cool. Serve and enjoy!

Healthy Cranberry Sauce
Time: 10 minutes   Servings: 6

Ingredients:

- 1 ½ cup of cranberries
- ¾ cups of water
- 1 teaspoon of fresh orange zest

- ½ teaspoon of pure vanilla extract
- 1 cup of powdered erythritol

Instructions:

- Add all the ingredients to your Instant Pot and lock the lid. Cook at high pressure for 2 minutes.
- When the cooking is done, naturally release the pressure and remove the lid.
- Press the "Sauté" function and use a wooden spoon to break the cranberries. Stir until reach your desired cranberry sauce consistency. Serve and enjoy!

Thanksgiving Turkey Legs
Time: 40 minutes   Servings: 6

Ingredients:

- 4 turkey legs
- 2 tablespoons of extra-virgin olive oil
- 1 teaspoon of onion powder
- 1 teaspoon of garlic powder
- 1 teaspoon of fine sea salt

- 1 teaspoon of freshly cracked black pepper
- 1 teaspoon of dried oregano
- ½ teaspoon of smoked paprika
- 1 cup of homemade low-sodium chicken broth

Instructions:

- Season the turkey legs with onion powder, garlic powder, dried oregano, sea salt and freshly cracked black pepper. Press the "Sauté" function on your Instant Pot and add the olive oil.
- Once the oil is hot, add the turkey legs and cook on both sides for 2 to 4 minutes or until brown.
- Add the chicken broth to your Instant Pot and lock the lid. Press the "Manual" button and cook at high pressure for 20 minutes. When the cooking is done, naturally release the pressure for 10 minutes and quick release the remaining pressure. Carefully remove the lid. Serve and enjoy!

Green Bean Casserole with Cheese and Bacon
Time: 25 minutes   Servings: 8

Ingredients:

- 6 cups of green beans, fresh and stems removed

- 4 medium slices of bacon, chopped

- 3 medium garlic cloves, peeled and minced
- 2 small shallots, finely chopped
- 1 (10.5-ounce) can of cream of mushroom soup
- ½ cup of mozzarella cheese, shredded
- 1 cup of mozzarella cheese, cubed
- 1 cup of cheddar cheese, shredded
- ½ teaspoon of fine sea salt
- ½ teaspoon of freshly cracked black pepper
- 1 tablespoon of almond flour
- 2 tablespoons of water

Instructions:

- Press the "Sauté" function on your Instant Pot and add the chopped bacon. Cook until brown and crispy, stirring occasionally. Transfer the bacon to a plate lined with paper towels.
- In a small bowl, add the almond flour and water. Stir until well combined.
- Add the garlic and shallots to your Instant Pot and sauté for 2 minutes, stirring occasionally/
- Stir in the green beans and cream of mushroom soup. Season with salt and freshly cracked black pepper. Lock the lid and cook at high pressure for 12 minutes. When the cooking is done, quick release the pressure and carefully remove the lid. Press the "Sauté" function again and stir in ½ cup of the shredded cheddar cheese and ¼ cup of the shredded mozzarella cheese. Stir and allow the cheese to melt.
- Preheat your oven to 425 degrees Fahrenheit and grease a casserole dish with nonstick cooking spray.
- Transfer the green bean contents to the baking dish and top with the bacon and remaining cheese.
- Place inside your oven and bake for 5 to 8 minutes or until golden on top. Serve and enjoy!

Cauliflower and Spicy Sausage Stuffing
Time: 20 minutes　　　　　　　Servings: 12

Ingredients:

- 1 pound of mild Italian sausage
- 2 pounds of cauliflower florets
- 6 tablespoons of unsalted butter
- 1 large onion, finely chopped
- 4 medium celery stalks, chopped
- ½ cup of fresh parsley, finely chopped
- 1 teaspoon of fine sea salt
- ½ teaspoon of freshly cracked black pepper
- ½ teaspoon of dried thyme
- ½ teaspoon of dried sage
- ½ teaspoon of freshly cracked black pepper
- 2 cups of homemade low-sodium chicken or turkey stock
- 2 tablespoons of olive oil

Instructions:

- Press the "Sauté" Function on your Instant Pot and add the olive oil.
- Add the Italian sausage and cook for 10 minutes. Use a wooden spoon to break it up.
- Transfer the sausage to a large bowl.
- Add the cauliflower florets and cook for 2 minutes, stirring occasionally. Transfer to a bowl.
- Add the butter to the Instant Pot, once melted, add the chopped onions and chopped celery. Sauté for 5 minutes, stirring occasionally. Add the seasonings and fresh parsley. Return the sausage and cauliflower to the Instant Pot, stir until well combined. Add the chicken stock and lock the lid. Cook at high pressure for 20 minutes.
- When the cooking is done, quick release the and carefully remove the lid. Adjust the seasoning if necessary. Serve and enjoy!

Special Turkey Gravy
Time: 30 minutes　　　　　　Servings: 4 cups

Ingredients:

- Turkey pan drippings
- Turkey neck, giblets and backbone
- 1 teaspoon of xanthan gum
- 1 teaspoon of fresh thyme
- 4 cups of homemade low-sodium chicken broth or turkey broth
- A pinch of fine sea salt and freshly cracked black pepper

Instructions:

- Add parts of the turkey along with the broth to your Instant Pot.
- Lock the lid and cook at high pressure for 15 minutes. When done, naturally release the pressure and remove the lid. Transfer the turkey pan drippings to the Instant Pot along with the fresh thyme, sea salt and black pepper. Press the "Sauté" function and stir in the xanthan gum. Allow to cook until thickened, stirring occasionally. Serve and enjoy!

Part 15: Weekend Recipes

Authentic Indian Butter Chicken
Time: 25 minutes   Servings: 4

Ingredients:

- 4 chicken breasts, boneless, skinless
- 2 jalapeno peppers, chopped (remove seeds)
- 1 onion, chopped
- 4 garlic cloves, minced
- 1 cup heavy cream
- 2 teaspoons garam masala
- 1 cup Greek yogurt
- 2 Tablespoons cornstarch
- 2 Tablespoons chicken stock

- ¼ cup of fresh cilantro, chopped
- 2 (14-ounce) cans diced tomatoes
- 2 Tablespoons fresh ginger, grated
- ½ cup ghee, melted
- 2 Tablespoons coconut oil
- 2 teaspoons ground cumin
- 1 teaspoon cayenne pepper
- 1 teaspoon salt (to taste)
- 1 teaspoon fresh ground black pepper (to taste)

Instructions:

1. Rinse chicken, pat dry. Cut into chunks.
2. In a food processor, add canned tomatoes, ginger, jalapenos. Pulse until blended.
3. Press Sauté button on Instant Pot. Heat the coconut oil.
4. Sauté onion and garlic for 2 minutes, Add chicken breasts. Brown on all sides.
5. Press Keep Warm/Cancel button to stop Sauté mode.
6. Add rest of ingredients, including pureed tomato mixture. Stir well.
7. Close and seal lid. Press Manual button. Cook at High Pressure for 10 minutes.
8. When the timer beeps, quick-release pressure. Open the lid with care. Stir well. Serve.

Rockstar Chicken Wings
Time: 20 minutes   Servings: 4

Ingredients:

- 1 pound chicken wings
- 6 garlic cloves, minced
- 1 Tablespoon fresh ginger, grated
- 2 Tablespoons coconut oil
- 1 Tablespoon fresh rosemary, chopped

- 1 Tablespoon fresh thyme, chopped
- 1 teaspoon salt
- 1 teaspoon fresh ground black pepper
- 2 cups chicken broth

Instructions:

1. Drizzle coconut oil over chicken wings, turning so they are coated.
2. Season with ginger, rosemary, thyme, salt, and black pepper.
3. Press Sauté button on Instant Pot.
4. Sauté chicken wings until golden brown. Add garlic while cooking.
5. Press Keep Warm/cancel setting to end Sauté mode. Add chicken broth.
6. Close and seal lid. Press Manual button. Cook at High Pressure for 8 minutes.
7. When the timer beeps, naturally release pressure. Open the lid with care. Serve.

Festive Okra Pilaf
Time: 25 minutes   Servings: 4

Ingredients:

- 1 pound okra, sliced
- 8 bacon slices, minced
- 2 cups cauliflower rice
- 1 cup tomatoes, minced
- 2 cups of water

- 1 Tablespoon ghee, melted
- 2 teaspoons paprika
- ¼ cup fresh cilantro, chopped
- 1 teaspoon salt
- 1 teaspoon fresh ground black pepper

Instructions:

1. Press Sauté button on Instant Pot. Cook bacon until brown.
2. Sauté okra and cauliflower rice until softened. Add remaining ingredients. Stir well.
3. Close and seal lid. Press Manual button. Cook at High Pressure for 10 minutes.
4. Quick-Release the pressure when done. Open the lid with care. Serve.

Beef Bulgogi
Time: 30 minutes   Servings: 5

Ingredients:

- 1 pound of flank steak, sliced into strips
- 3 tablespoons of extra-virgin olive oil
- 2 tablespoons of low-sodium coconut aminos
- 1 tablespoon of apple cider vinegar
- 1 teaspoon of onion powder

- 1 teaspoon of ground ginger
- 1 teaspoon of garlic powder
- 1 teaspoon of fine sea salt
- 1 teaspoon of coconut flour or other keto-friendly thickeners
- ¼ cup of homemade low-sodium beef broth

Instructions:

- In a bowl, add the flank steak strips, apple cider vinegar and coconut aminos. Allow to marinate for 15 minutes or overnight.
- Press the "Sauté" function on your Instant Pot and working in batches, add the flank strip pieces. Cook until brown and pour in ¼ cup of beef broth
- Close and seal the lid. Cook at high pressure for 10 minutes. When done, quick release the pressure and remove the lid.
- Sprinkle with the coconut flour and stir in the marinade. Press the "Sauté" function on your Instant Pot and allow to thicken. Serve and enjoy!

Barbecue Pot Roast
Time: 1 hour and 30 minutes   Servings: 12

Ingredients:

- 1 (6 pound) beef shoulder roast
- 1 large onion, finely chopped
- 4 medium garlic cloves, peeled and minced
- 3 tablespoons of butter, unsalted
- 4 tablespoons of apple cider vinegar
- 1 tablespoon of organic Dijon mustard
- 2 tablespoons of Worcestershire sauce

- 4 tablespoons of Splenda or other keto-friendly sweeteners
- 1 teaspoon of liquid smoke
- 1 teaspoon of fine sea salt
- 1 teaspoon of freshly cracked black pepper
- 2 tablespoons of olive oil
- 3 cups of homemade low-sodium beef broth

Instructions:

- Press the "Sauté" function on your Instant Pot and add the olive oil.
- Once hot, add the beef shoulder roast and sear for 3 to 4 minutes on each side or until brown. Remove and set aside.
- Add the onions and garlic cloves. Sauté until translucent, stirring occasionally.
- Return the beef shoulder roast and add the remaining ingredients. Close and seal the lid. Cook at high pressure for 35 minutes.
- When the cooking is done, naturally release the pressure and remove the lid. Adjust the seasoning if necessary. Serve and enjoy!

Delicious Porter-house Steak with a Special Parsley Shallot-Garlic Butter Sauce
Time: 1 hour and 30 minutes   Servings: 6

Ingredients:

- 2 (1 pound) porterhouse steaks
- 2 tablespoons of olive oil or other cooking fat
- 1 teaspoon of fine sea salt
- 1 teaspoon of freshly ground white pepper

- ½ medium-sized lemon, juice
- 2 tablespoons of fresh parsley, finely chopped
- 2 medium garlic cloves, peeled and minced
- ½ of a small shallot, finely chopped

- 1 stick of unsalted butter, softened
- 1 cup of homemade low-sodium beef broth

Instructions:

- Season the porterhouse steaks with sea salt and ground white pepper
- Press the "Sauté" function on your Instant Pot and add 2 tablespoons of olive oil.
- Once hot, add the steaks and sear for 4 minutes on each side or until brown.
- Pour in 1 cup of beef broth and close the lid. Cook at high pressure for 35 minutes.
- When done, naturally release the pressure and carefully remove the lid.
- Remove the steak from your Instant Pot and allow to cool. Discard the liquid.
- Meanwhile, press the "Sauté" function on your Instant Pot and add the butter.
- Once melted, add the minced garlic and minced shallot. Cook until translucent, stirring occasionally. Add the fresh parsley and lemon juice.
- Return the steak to your Instant Pot and spoon the butter sauce over the porterhouse steaks. Turn off "Sauté" function. Serve and enjoy!

Texas Brisket
Time: 2 hours and 35 minutes   Servings: 16

Ingredients:

- 4 pounds of beef brisket
- 1 tablespoon of smoked paprika
- ½ teaspoon of organic ground coriander
- 1 teaspoon of dried oregano or Italian herbs
- 3 teaspoons of fine sea salt
- ½ teaspoon of freshly cracked black pepper
- 2 teaspoons of ground cumin
- 2 teaspoons of garlic powder
- 2 teaspoons of onion powder
- 2 tablespoons of olive oil or other cooking fat
- ¼ cup of homemade low-sodium beef stock

Instructions:

- In a small bowl, mix the paprika, ground coriander, dried oregano, sea salt, black pepper, ground cumin, garlic powder, and onion powder.
- Rub the seasoning mixture over the beef brisket.
- Press the "Sauté" function on your Instant Pot and add the olive oil.
- Once hot, add the brisket and cook for 4 minutes on each side or until brown.
- Pour in the beef stock. Cover and seal the lid; cook at high pressure for 1 hour.
- When the cooking is done, naturally release the pressure and remove the lid. Serve!

Jerk-Spiced Duck
Time: 25 minutes   Servings: 4

Ingredients:

- 4 duck legs
- 1 habanero pepper, chopped
- 1 tablespoon of coconut aminos
- 1 medium-sized lime, freshly squeezed and zested
- 1 teaspoon of fresh ginger, finely minced
- ½ teaspoon of nutmeg
- 1 teaspoon of ground allspice
- 3 medium-sized garlic cloves, peeled and minced
- 1 tablespoon of extra-virgin olive oil
- 2 teaspoons of creole seasoning
- ½ teaspoon of sea salt
- ½ teaspoon of freshly cracked black pepper

Instructions:

- In a blender, add all the ingredients except for the duck legs and extra-virgin olive oil. Blend until smooth.
- In a large Ziploc bag, add the duck legs with half of the marinade.
- Refrigerate and allow to marinate for 2 hours or overnight.
- Press "Sauté" function on your Instant Pot and add the olive oil.
- Add the duck legs and cook for 2 to 3 minutes on each side or until brown.
- Close and seal the lid; cook at high pressure for 15 minutes.
- When the timer beeps, quick release the pressure and allow to cool. Serve and enjoy!

Oxtail and Red Wine Stew
Time: 1 hour and 20 minutes   Servings: 8

Ingredients:

- 4 pounds of oxtails, cut into 2-inch pieces
- 3 tablespoons of extra-virgin olive oil
- 2 large leeks, sliced into ½-inch pieces
- 4 celery stalks, sliced
- 1 medium yellow onion, finely chopped
- 4 medium garlic cloves, minced
- ¼ cup of organic tomato paste
- 2 cups of keto-friendly low-carb red wine
- 2 cups of homemade low-sodium beef broth
- 1 teaspoon of fine sea salt
- 1 teaspoon of freshly cracked black pepper

Instructions:

- Press the "Sauté" function on your Instant Pot and add the extra-virgin olive oil.
- Working in batches, add the oxtail pieces and cook until brown. Remove and set aside.
- Add the onions and garlic cloves. Sauté for 4 to 6 minutes or until translucent.
- Add the sliced celery stalks and leeks and sauté for another minute or two, stirring occasionally.
- Stir in the beef broth and red wine. Lock the lid and cook at high pressure for 45 minutes.
- When the cooking is done, naturally release the pressure and remove the lid.
- Season with sea salt and black pepper. Serve and enjoy!

Coq au Vin
Time: 45 minutes   Servings: 4

Ingredients:

- 4 chicken legs or chicken drumsticks
- 2 tablespoons of extra-virgin olive oil
- 1 teaspoon of fine sea salt
- 1 teaspoon of freshly cracked black pepper
- 2 cups of keto-friendly dry white wine
- 1 bunch of fresh thyme
- 2 to 4 medium slices of bacon, thickly-cut into pieces
- 1 cup of shiitake mushrooms, chopped
- 4 tablespoons of butter, unsalted and melted
- 1 cup of carrots, peeled and cut into bite-sized pieces
- 4 medium shallots, peeled and finely chopped
- 2 medium garlic cloves, peeled and minced
- 1 tablespoon of xanthan gum or almond flour (for thickening)
- 1 tablespoon of fresh parsley

Instructions:

- In a large resalable bag, add the chicken, white wine and fresh thyme. Chill for up to 2 days.
- Press the "Sauté" function on your Instant Pot, add and cook the bacon until brown and crispy, stirring occasionally. Transfer the bacon to a plate lined with paper towels.
- Add the mushrooms and cook for 6 minutes or until golden brown, stirring occasionally.
- Remove the mushrooms and bacon bits. Add the chicken and olive oil if needed.
- Add the chicken and cook for 4 minutes per side or until brown. Remove and set aside.
- Add the remaining tablespoon of along with the chopped carrots, chopped shallots and minced garlic. Sauté for 4 minutes or until golden brown, stirring occasionally.
- Return the chicken, bacon and mushrooms to the Instant Pot along with the dry white wine and thyme.
- Lock the lid and cook at high pressure for 15 minutes.
- When the cooking is done, naturally release the pressure and carefully remove the lid.
- In a small bowl, add the melted butter and xanthan gum. Mix until well combined. Pour over the contents and stir until well combined.
- Press "Sauté" function and allow to cook until thickened. Adjust the seasoning if necessary.
- Serve and enjoy!

Keto-Friendly Pot Roast
Time: 50 minutes   Servings: 8

Ingredients:

- 4 pounds of beef roast, cut into 4 to 6 pieces
- 1 medium yellow or white onion, finely chopped
- 2 garlic cloves, peeled and minced
- 2 large celery stalks, chopped

- 2 tablespoons of organic tomato paste
- 3 tablespoons of olive oil or coconut oil
- ½ cup of mild pepperoncini peppers
- 2 cups of low-sodium beef broth or bouillon cube
- 1 teaspoon of sea salt
- 1 teaspoon of freshly cracked black pepper

Instructions:

- Press the "sauté" function and add 2 tablespoons of olive oil or coconut oil.
- Working in batches, add the beef pieces and sear for 2 to 3 minutes on each side, or until brown. Remove the beef pieces and set aside.
- Add the remaining tablespoon of olive oil. Add the chopped onions and minced garlic. Sauté for 3 to 4 minutes or until translucent, stirring occasionally.
- Add the chopped celery and cook for 1 minute, stirring occasionally.
- Stir in the red wine and beef broth. Return the beef roast along with the pepperoncini peppers.
- Close and seal the lid. Cook at high pressure for 35 minutes.
- Once the timer beeps, perform a natural release method and remove the lid.
- Press the "sauté" function and season with salt and black pepper. Serve and enjoy!

Conclusion

Thank you again for reading and finishing this book! I hope you enjoy all these recipes for today and for tomorrow.

The goal of this book is to provide you with a wide variety of Instant Pot recipes. With these 1000 Instant Pot recipes, you will live healthier and happier!

Made in the USA
San Bernardino, CA
03 May 2020